BELIEFS
ABOUT
INEQUALITY

*Americans'
Views of
What Is and
What Ought to Be*

SOCIAL INSTITUTIONS AND SOCIAL CHANGE

EDITED BY

Peter H. Rossi
Michael Useem
James D. Wright

Bernard C. Rosen, **The Industrial Connection: Achievement and the Family in Developing Societies.** 1982.

Paul Diesing, **Science and Ideology in the Policy Sciences.** 1982.

James D. Wright, Peter H. Rossi, and Kathleen Daly, **Under the Gun: Weapons, Crime, and Violence in America.** 1983.

Walter L. Wallace, **Principles of Scientific Sociology.** 1983.

Robert C. Liebman and Robert Wuthnow (eds.), **The New Christian Right: Mobilization and Legitimation.** 1983.

Paula S. England and George Farkas, **Households, Employment, and Gender: A Social, Economic, and Demographic View.** 1986.

Richard F. Hamilton and James D. Wright, **The State of the Masses.** 1986.

James R. Kluegel and Eliot R. Smith, **Beliefs About Inequality: Americans' Views of What is and What Ought to Be.** 1986.

James D. Wright and Peter H. Rossi, **Armed and Considered Dangerous: A Survey of Felons and Their Firearms.** 1986.

Roberta G. Simmons and Dale A. Blyth, **Moving into Adolescence: The Impact of Pubertal Change and School Context.** 1987.

BELIEFS
ABOUT
INEQUALITY

Americans'
Views of
What Is and
What Ought to Be

James R. Kluegel
and
Eliot R. Smith

ALDINE DE GRUYTER

New York

ABOUT
THE
AUTHORS

James R. Kluegel is Chairman of the Department of Sociology at the University of Illinois at Urbana-Champaign. He is a major contributor to many professional journals and is the author of *Evaluating Contemporary Juvenile Justice.*

Eliot R. Smith is Associate Professor of Psychological Sciences at Purdue University. He has published research in the area of social cognition and political attitudes.

ALDINE DE GRUYTER
Division of Walter de Gruyter, Inc.
200 Saw Mill River Road
Hawthorne, New York 10532

Library of Congress Cataloging-in-Publication Data

Kluegel, James R.
    Beliefs about inequality.

    Bibliography: p.
    Includes index.
    1. Equality—Public opinion.   2. Equality—United
States—Public opinion.   3. Public opinion—United
States.   I. Smith, Eliot R.   II. Title.
JC575.K58   1986   320'.01'1   86-4476
ISBN 0-202-30326-8 (lib. bdg.)
ISBN 0-202-30327-6 (pbk.)

Printed in the United States of America
10 9 8 7 6 5 4 3 2

CONTENTS

Acknowledgments ix

1 INTRODUCTION

A Description of Americans' Beliefs and Attitudes 2
A Theoretical Perspective 5
Plan of the Book 8

2 THINKING ABOUT INEQUALITY

Basic Social-Psychological Processes 12
Consequences of These Processes for Reactions to
Inequality 21
Alternative Theories of Reactions to Inequality 33
Summary of Our Perspective 35

I DOMINANT-IDEOLOGY BELIEFS

Distributions 37
Time Trends 37
Potential Challenges 38
Group Differences 39

3 OPPORTUNITY

Distributions and Time Trends in Perceived Opportunity 43
Potential Challenges to the Perceived Prevalence of
Opportunity 52
Group Differences in Perceived Opportunity 62
Conclusions 70

4 EXPLANATIONS FOR ECONOMIC OUTCOMES

Distribution and Time Trends in Explanations for
Inequality 76

Potential Challenges to Individualism 83
Group Differences in Explanations for Economic Position 89
Group Differences by Sex, Race, and Status 94
Conclusions 100

5 DISTRIBUTIVE JUSTICE

Distributions and Time Trends 104
Potential Challenges to the Perceived Justice of Inequality 125
Group Differences in Beliefs about Distributive Justice 129
Conclusions 141

II POLICY ATTITUDES

Outline of Chapters 143
Causal Assumptions 147
Summary 148

6 REDISTRIBUTIVE POLICY

Redistribution Toward the Poor 152
Redistribution Away from the Rich 164
Discussion 169
Summary 175

7 OPPORTUNITY FOR BLACKS

Sources of Opposition 182
Beliefs about Blacks' Opportunity 185
Affirmative-Action Attitudes 201
Conclusions 211

8 OPPORTUNITY FOR WOMEN

Description of Beliefs on Women's Opportunity 215
Determinants of Beliefs Concerning Women's Opportunity 219
Determinants of Policy Attitudes 229
Summary: The Public View of Women's Opportunity 232
Comparison with Views on Blacks 235
Summary 242

III CONSEQUENCES OF BELIEFS ABOUT INEQUALITY

Text   245

9 THE POLITICAL SIGNIFICANCE OF STRATIFICATION BELIEFS

Beliefs and Attitudes of Politically Important Subgroups   247
Voting   259
Conclusions   272

10 PERSONAL CONSEQUENCES OF BELIEFS ABOUT INEQUALITY

Distribution of Emotions   276
Relations of Emotions to Sociodemographic Factors and
Beliefs   278
Summary   283
Conclusions   286

11 CONCLUSIONS

Summary of Findings   287
Ultimate Determinants   295
Prospects for Effective Policy   301

APPENDIX: Data Sources

Beliefs about Social Stratification Survey   309

BIBLIOGRAPHY   315

INDEX   325

ACKNOWLEDGMENTS

The effort and support of many people have enabled us to write this book. The National Institute of Mental Health and the National Science Foundation provided funding for the collection and analysis of the principal survey data employed in our research. We appreciate their faith in our ability to produce results of potential use to the social science community. Other institutions provided support as well: the University of California, Riverside, with which we were both affiliated at the beginning of this project, and our current institutions, the University of Illinois at Urbana-Champaign and Purdue University. The principal survey was designed with the assistance of the Survey Research Laboratory at the University of Illinois, and carried out ably and expeditiously by its staff. Special thanks are owed its director, Richard Warnecke, for providing one of the authors with time to write, freed from the normal academic responsibilities that often slow the process of moving from ideas to the printed word.

Jan Hart, Peggy Henson, Janet Lauritsen, Miriam Lerner, and William Rudman provided very capable work as research assistants on this project. We are especially indebted to friends and colleagues who read drafts of chapters or sections of this book, and provided comments and suggestions: Kay Deaux, Joe R. Feagin, Myra Marx Ferree, James M. Jones, James H. Kuklinski, John Mirowsky, Thomas F. Pettigrew, Catherine Ross, and Bernard Weiner. We believe that the book is better for their help. Other colleagues too numerous to mention, including some anonymous reviewers, commented on earlier papers and presentations from this project and helped to shape and direct our research. In the most literal sense, this research would not have been possible without the cooperation of 2212 of our fellow American citizens who gave about an hour of their time to answering all the questions we could think of asking them. We thank them for their trust and patience.

Few experiences provide the same kind of ride on an emotional rollercoaster as writing a book. Our families—Kathleen, Alan and Leah Kluegel, and Pamela, Miranda, and Thomas Smith—by their understanding and support, and by simply being there have kept us "on track." Finally, we wish to note that the order of authorship is simply an accident of the alphabet. This book is the result of fully equal contributions. That we share credit equally, also means that we equally share responsibility for any errors.

James R. Kluegel

Eliot R. Smith

1

INTRODUCTION

Why are some Americans richer than I am? Do they work harder to succeed, or are they more talented than I am? Why are others poor: Are laziness and bad moral character primarily responsible for poverty or are lack of education and social and economic discrimination? Are the situations of the rich and the poor fair or unfair? And how am I to understand my own position in society? Perhaps my degree of economic well-being reflects my basic worth as a person, or perhaps I have experienced unusual barriers that have unfairly held me back from greater achievements. In the long run, do welfare programs or affirmative-action policies aid the disadvantaged, or do they undermine motivation and weaken the basis of the economic system? How much discrimination do racial minorities or working women experience today—isn't discrimination largely a thing of the past?

Americans of all political views and economic levels frequently consider these and similar questions about the current structure and implications of economic inequality in our society. Some of these issues seem to be important aspects of understanding the world in general; children often ask basic questions about wealth, poverty, and fairness, for example (Leahy, 1983). Others become important in the political process, as governmental policies aimed at one or another aspect of inequality are proposed and debated. All the questions together, and the tentative, incomplete answers that people construct, form the roots of the American consciousness of inequality, the subject of our investigation in this book.

It has often been remarked that Americans' attitudes about social welfare and other inequality-related policies have an inconsistent and sometimes seemingly contradictory quality. The most recent example is, of course, the sharp change in direction of federal policy associated with the Reagan administration's goals of curtailing many of the redistributive programs developed since the New Deal. There are other examples as well. Americans generally accept the idea that blacks and other minorities have suffered from discrimination and maintain an abstract commitment to equal opportunity—coexisting with widespread white opposition to specific policies to implement equal opportunity (e.g., busing to desegregate schools, affirmative-action programs). Al-though Americans highly value equal citizenship rights and democratic politics in the abstract, in practice the right of the wealthy to wield disproportionate economic and political power is unchallenged. Finally, in the face of a general commitment to ameliorative measures for the very poor and to the right to be paid a basic living wage (floor limits on earnings), there is a widespread unwillingness to place an upper limit on incomes or inheritances. These aspects of contradiction and compromise in Americans' beliefs and attitudes about inequality have stood as puzzles since at least the time of Alexis de Toqueville, drawing opinions from a variety of analysts and commentators.

Motivated by the desire to explain how Americans perceive and evaluate inequality and related programs and policies, we conducted a national survey of beliefs about social and economic inequality. Here we present the results of our research on the structure, determinants, and certain political and personal consequences of these beliefs. Our presentations in this book serve two major goals: to *describe* and *explain* the central features of Americans' images of inequality.

A DESCRIPTION OF AMERICANS' BELIEFS AND ATTITUDES

Our first goal is to provide a current, comprehensive description of Americans' beliefs and attitudes about inequality, including evidence concerning stability and change in such beliefs. The data collection for our survey, which was funded by the National Science Foundation and the National Institutes of Mental Health, took place in the summer and fall of 1980, mainly during the campaign that ended with the initial elec-tion of Ronald Reagan to the presidency. Telephone interviews aver-aging over 45 minutes long were conducted with a total of 2212 Amer-icans, scientifically selected to represent the entire United States population aged 18 and over.

A comprehensive description of what Americans believe, based on this survey, and of recent changes in beliefs may help explain some apparent inconsistencies and contradictions. Some inconsistency may simply be illusory: This is a danger to the degree that our current knowledge about Americans' beliefs is based on data from restricted or otherwise unrepresentative samples. Further, the seeming incon-sistency and contradiction may be the product of a period of transition in beliefs about inequality. Recent events—the shift from the steady economic growth of the 1960s to the stagflation of the 1970s, agitation by the civil rights and women's movements, debates about the suc-cesses or failures of antipoverty and other Great Society programs—may have substantially changed the ways Americans view aspects of inequality. The need to assess the impact of these events, many of which are unprecedented in American history, underlines the value of a current portrayal of public views. Another possibility is that younger people may adhere to substantially more liberal beliefs and attitudes than older ones. Age-group and over-time comparisons will allow us to test such hypotheses.

On many aspects of inequality, even the most rudimentary descriptions of public beliefs and attitudes are currently lacking, though other areas, such as "class consciousness" and some aspects of economic policy preferences, have been the subject of some research. There are several reasons for the failures of existing research to fill the gaps in description. The focus of research is fragmented among individual studies, as each investigator tends to study a single aspect of beliefs about inequality (opportunity alone, or social class alone, or income inequality alone). Data are available only sporadically, and often only on topical issues, as survey researchers ask questions related to current political issues or events. Samples tend to be small and unrepresentative, often restricted to specific cities or states, and sometimes questionably representative even of such limited areas. Finally, and perhaps most important, sociologically based research on beliefs and attitudes concerning inequality (e.g., Jackman & Jackman, 1983) often narrowly has focused on the single area of class perceptions as the central element of popular views on inequality, and often on a single question (Centers, 1949) as the measure of that construct (Kluegel & Smith, 1981). Identification with a social class (whether "middle" or "working") is one facet of an individual's views on the American economic system and his or her location in it, but exclusive attention to this construct has been harmful to a general breadth of focus in theoretical and empirical work.

Our survey of Americans' beliefs and attitudes about inequality permits a more comprehensive description than does past research, for two reasons. First, our data are drawn from a representative sample of the population in general, unlike most existing studies such as Verba and Oren's (1984) recent examination of beliefs about inequality in a small sample of "leaders." We also collected additional data to permit more adequate descriptions of two theoretically important subgroups: blacks and the affluent. Demands for civil rights and equal opportunity by blacks and other racial minorities have been among the most important forces toward change in the American consciousness of inequality, so black–white comparisons on various beliefs and attitudes are of great interest. Also, the power held by the affluent in many institutions of politics, the professions, communication, and other areas makes their views on inequality of special concern.

The second major characteristic of our study is its description of public beliefs and attitudes on a wide range of inequality-related issues and policies, rather than just a few topical issues. Objective, comprehensive survey data can give a broader and more reliable picture of Americans' beliefs and attitudes about inequality than other sources of information, such as inferences from election results. Different analysts tend to read different implications in election results, and it is clear that a voter's choice in an election reflects many complex and interacting factors about the voter, the candidates, and the current political situation. From an election outcome, it is difficult at best to infer reliably the particular views on economic inequality that might have contributed to voters' decisions.

There are many reasons for interest in the ways people think about inequality. Though public opinion obviously is not the sole determinant of public policy on such matters as the level of welfare spending or the nature of affirmative-action programs, shifts in public opinion are temporally related to the passage of relevant legislation (Burstein, 1979; Page & Shapiro, 1982; Monroe, 1983). In addition, appeals to public opinion are a potentially powerful resource for groups working for social change (civil rights or women's rights groups, for example), and for presidents seeking to apply pressure to Congress. Popular views on inequality and related issues also shape perceptions of the fairness of policies, which can help or hinder the implementation of policy. Consider, for example, the widespread public views of busing for school desegregation as unfair and illegitimate and the resulting turmoil and difficulty in implementing that policy in some cities; or the public dislike for welfare programs, which often diminishes their effectiveness (Wilensky, 1975).

Beyond the scope of public policy per se, individuals' views on inequality, opportunity, and related issues shape their private actions in important ways. An example is a small employer who is faced with a request from female employees for more equitable salaries in relationship to those of male employees. Such individual decisions, multiplied by thousands daily, are important in maintaining or reversing sex differences in economic outcomes. A different sort of example concerns individuals' efforts toward economic advancement. Views of the relative effectiveness of various routes to mobility (education, joining a union, starting one's own small business) will affect the specific direction of the ambitious individual's efforts.

In sum, one central aim of this book is to present a current and comprehensive description of Americans' views on social and economic inequality and related policies, including information about the extent, distribution, structure, and determinants of particular beliefs and attitudes.

A THEORETICAL PERSPECTIVE

The second major goal of this book is to present a general theoretical perspective on beliefs and attitudes about inequality, along with empirical evidence for many aspects of the theory. Our perspective provides, we believe, a viable explanation for many characteristics of public opinion on issues related to inequality, including the fluctuating, inconsistent, and seemingly contradictory quality of public attitudes toward inequality and related programs. In Chapter 2 we will present our perspective in detail. Here we summarize its major features to provide an overview of the issues we will be addressing in subsequent chapters.

We propose that attitudes toward economic inequality and related policy are influenced by three major aspects of the current American social, economic, and political environment: *(a)* a stable "dominant ideology" about economic inequality; *(b)* individuals' social and economic status; and *(c)* specific beliefs and attitudes, often reflecting "social liberalism," shaped by recent political debates and events. First, beliefs and attitudes concerning inequality reflect the stable influence of general explanations of the workings of the American stratification system, widely held by the public, which others have labeled the "dominant stratification ideology" (Huber & Form, 1973). It might also be called the "logic of opportunity syllogism," for it provides a deductive argument that justifies inequality of economic outcomes. The major premise in the argument is that opportunity for economic advancement based on hard work is plentiful. From this premise two deductions follow. Individuals are personally responsible for their own economic fate: Where one ends up in the distribution of economic rewards depends upon the effort one puts into acquiring and applying the necessary skills and attitudes and upon the native talent with which one begins. As a consequence, since individual outcomes are proportional to individual inputs (talent and effort), the resulting unequal distribution of economic rewards is, in the aggregate, equitable and fair.

Second, attitudes toward inequality are shaped by a person's objective position in the stratification system. We will examine the influence of such factors as income differences, class differences in the conditions of work (in terms of autonomy, power, etc.), sex, race, age, and education. Social and economic status, of course, provide one basis for assessing an individual's self-interest in supporting or opposing particular inequality-related policies. One's social status also influences personal experiences of various kinds, such as the experience of poverty or affluence, fair or unfair treatment on the job, and so on, which may lead to generalizations about inequality and its bases and effects.

Third, attitudes toward inequality are shaped by "social liberalism," an acceptance of social and political equality with groups such as blacks and women, without the bases of economic inequality being called into question. These attitudes have arisen in large part from recent political and economic changes, including the massive movement of women into the labor force, the social and political changes arising from the dismantling of legalized racial segregation, and an awakening to the presence of poverty in the midst of affluence, particularly in the 1960s. The impact of these events on contemporary attitudes is of two principal kinds. First, by many indications, beliefs and attitudes in several specific areas related to inequality have changed substantially in a liberal direction. The right to an old age with a decent standard of living and basic medical care through Social Security and Medicare has become so widely accepted that even the mention of benefit reductions elicits strong public protests—as in the early days of the Reagan administration. Survey data demonstrate marked reductions in traditional racial prejudice: overt racial bigotry and support for the denial of equal rights to blacks (Taylor, Sheatsley, & Greeley, 1978). And there is survey evidence for a similar trend of diminished support for sex-role traditionalism: belief in the appropriateness of a priori limits to women's social and economic opportunity (Miller, Miller, & Schneider, 1980, pp. 177–178).

However, effects of recent political trends are often multiple, not limited to increases in social liberalism. The recent history of intergroup conflict over social and economic inequality, even as it has won increasing general acceptance of minority rights, has produced negative emotional responses, based on race, that color contemporary evaluations of inequality-related policy. Whites' attitudes toward policies and programs that benefit black Americans may be the area where such negative intergroup emotions have been the most consequential. We will comment on the influence of this factor throughout the analyses presented in this book.

One proposition is a key element of our perspective. *The prevalence and stability of belief in the dominant ideology, in the face of enduring objective features of the stratification system and changing beliefs and attitudes in some areas related to inequality, produces the inconsistency, fluctuation, and seeming contradiction in the attitudes toward inequality and related policy found in the American public.* On balance, the dominant ideology disposes people to a conservative evaluation of welfare and other redistributive programs. Such programs are perceived as unnecessary because the stratification system currently presents ample opportunity to better oneself by individual efforts. Even if the necessity of such programs is admitted, their acceptance still depends on their conformity to the dominant ideology's emphasis on individual responsibility and on the necessity of economic inequality to motivate people to achieve. On the other hand, many enduring objective features of social inequality, and changing beliefs and attitudes in some specific areas such as racial equality of opportunity, dispose people to what is conventionally labeled a liberal orientation. To achieve public acceptance, inequality-related policy must accommodate both the liberal orientation that provides the impetus for their existence and the conservative implications of the dominant ideology.

The need for accommodation is particularly strong because the conservative and liberal beliefs and attitudes are often found within the same person. Indeed, one aspect of the prevalence of the dominant ideology is that *most people adhere to it to a greater or lesser extent.* If the American population were composed of consistently liberal and conservative individuals, then fashioning inequality-related policy would be much simpler. Consistent policies could be designed, and their adoption would depend in part on the political balance between liberals and conservatives in the population. The absence of individual-level consistency, however, means that most policies and programs must accommodate both liberal and conservative beliefs, often a difficult matter. Welfare payments for support of dependent children provide a telling example. Our liberal sympathies urge us to support children in poverty because they are not responsible for the circumstances in which they were born. The dominant ideology, on the other hand, leads to such distrust of the personal character of parents receiving welfare that the restrictions and stigma attached to its allocation may act, according to some analysts (e.g., Feagin, 1975; Williamson, 1974a), to perpetuate a life in poverty for the children we intend to help.

Another important element of our perspective is the proposition that *the ambivalent orientation to inequality and related policy, produced by the coexistence of liberal and conservative beliefs and attitudes within the same person, does not necessarily require resolution toward consistency.* Put another way, one of the serious flaws of attempts to read general liberal or conservative trends into the outcomes of elections or changes in single beliefs over time is the implicit assumption of a drive toward cognitive consistency among all a person's beliefs, attitudes, and values. Recent research in social psychology suggests that rather than being invariably a consistency seeker, a more appropriate model of the person is as a "cognitive miser" (Taylor, 1981). People may allow their beliefs to remain inconsistent to reduce cognitive effort, as long as important goals are not threatened by inconsistency. This and other reasons for an ambivalent orientation toward inequality and related programs in recent American history will be discussed in Chapter 2.

A final element of our perspective concerns the implications of Americans' beliefs and attitudes about inequality for their evaluations of policies and political candidates. We stress two major implications here. First, our perspective makes specific predictions about the relative public acceptance of different types of inequality-related programs and the social distribution of their support and opposition. The general public acceptance of some equal-opportunity policies and equally general opposition to others (such as busing and racial quotas for job promotion) may be understood in terms of the policies' relationships both to specific inequality-related beliefs and to the dominant ideology. The theory also predicts that views on inequality and related issues will contribute, along with such political orientations as liberalism–conservatism and political party identification, to the evaluation of political candidates. In our data, we will examine in particular the preference for Reagan versus Carter in the 1980 presidential election.

Second, on a more speculative level, our theory has implications both for understanding the past and current political environment and for predicting the likely course of inequality-related policy in the future. The theory emphasizes widespread public ambivalence and inconsistency in views on inequality, which may be partially responsible for the marked changes over time in the electoral fortunes of liberal and conservative candidates in the recent past. The politics of the 1980s and 1990s increasingly may come to be shaped by inequality-related issues, as a growing proportion of the population see inequality as a zero-sum contest, believing that they can gain economically only by forcing corresponding losses on others (Thurow, 1980). This belief, and others identified by our survey, lead to tentative predictions about the general course of inequality-related policy in the near future.

The second goal of the book, then, is to present the outlines of, and some evidence for, a theoretical perspective on the structure, distribution, determinants, and political implications of Americans' views on inequality. The perspective is rooted in general social–psychological principles of belief and attitude formation and change, and it offers what we believe to be a compelling interpretation of many characteristics of public opinion concerning inequality that can be observed both in our data and in other sources.

PLAN OF THE BOOK

The book is organized as two introductory chapters, then three major parts, followed by a concluding chapter. In Chapter 2, we discuss our theoretical perspective in detail and present the social–psychological principles on which it rests.

In Part I, we examine the most basic beliefs about inequality held by Americans, the "dominant ideology." These chapters (3, 4, and 5) describe both the current distribution and structure of these beliefs and their stability—principally via analyses of age-group differences, but to the extent possible with data from different time periods supplementing our own. Chapter 3 examines opportunity: views of how much opportunity is perceived in general, how it is distributed (equality of opportunity), the effectiveness of different routes to advancement (particularly education), and recent and future changes in opportunity. Chapter 4 deals with the second major aspect of the general American orientation toward inequality, explanations for achievement or its absence. We examine beliefs about the reasons for poverty and wealth, showing the relative prevalence of explanations that emphasize individual characteristics (such as unusual ability or effort or their lack). Links between such explanations and the perceptions of opportunity dealt with in Chapter 3 are emphasized. Finally, Chapter 5 focuses on the third major aspect of the dominant ideology, beliefs about distributive justice, including evaluations of the equity and fairness of the ways economic rewards are distributed in our society.

Part II deals with popular beliefs and attitudes directly related to public policy on inequality. Chapter 6 examines views on redistributive policies: welfare, ceilings and floors on income, and government-guaranteed jobs. Chapter 7 deals with views of minorities and discrimination, attitudes toward affirmative action, and the legacy of white racism and its attitudinal effects. Chapter 8 examines beliefs about women's opportunity, discrimination against women, and views on the place of women in society, including attitudes toward the Equal Rights Amendment. This chapter emphasizes the factors that create similarities and differences in responses to women's and blacks' opportunity.

In Part III, two chapters deal with linkages between beliefs and attitudes about inequality and broader aspects of both political and personal life. Chapter 9 considers linkages to political opinions and behaviors, particularly the presidential vote in 1980. How did beliefs about inequality and various specific policy issues contribute to the vote? How much do such beliefs and attitudes overlap with such traditional distinctions as liberal/conservative or Democrat/Republican? In this chapter, we give special attention to the beliefs and attitudes of the affluent— a group who may exert disproportionate political influence because of their economic power, education, and other attributes. Chapter 10 examines more personal consequences of beliefs about inequality. Beliefs about the causes of one's economic position affect the degree of happiness, satisfaction, frustration, or anger felt in response to good or bad economic outcomes. Beliefs about inequality thus profoundly influence feelings of life satisfaction and general psychological well-being.

Finally, Chapter 11 summarizes the general themes of the book and brings together a discussion of the underlying commonalities that appear in the analyses of the various chapters. We will speculate, in light of our findings, on the future prospects for current social movements (such as the civil rights and women's movements) and on the possibilities of shaping popularly accepted, stable, and effective social policy on inequality-related issues.

2

THINKING ABOUT INEQUALITY

Our perspective on Americans' views of inequality emphasizes three aspects of the current political and economic environment as major influences on beliefs and attitudes. First, American culture contains a stable, widely held set of beliefs involving the availability of opportunity, individualistic explanations for achievement, and acceptance of unequal distributions of rewards. These beliefs have been labeled the "dominant ideology" (Huber & Form, 1973), and they generally dispose people toward conservative attitudes toward inequality-related public policy.

Second, forces deriving from a person's own position in the hierarchy of inequality shape beliefs and attitudes about inequality by processes involving differential experience and self-interest. People in different positions (defined by status, race, gender, or other social distinctions) will be expected to react differently to social inequalities that affect them.

Third, "social liberalism" has grown in response to the social and political struggles and events of the past 25 years. As we shall see in Chapters 7 and 8, Americans' beliefs and attitudes on some aspects of poverty, race relations, and women's role in society have become markedly more liberal. However, the growth of social liberalism has not been uniform; some groups (the young and college-educated, in particular) are more socially liberal than others. Thus, the impact of both socioeconomic status and social liberalism on policy attitudes, while generally pushing people in a liberal direction, is more variable than the impact of the dominant ideology.

Perhaps the key assumption of our perspective is that social liberalism, for most people, is not logically integrated and organized with the dominant ideology. Instead, it has been "layered on," available to shape attitudes and behaviors in particular situations in ways that are potentially inconsistent with the consequences of the dominant ideology beliefs. This assumption fits with the picture drawn by modern social–psychological research of the human as a seeker of cognitive *efficiency* rather than complete *consistency* (Taylor, 1981). Research shows, for example, that people frequently use "heuristics"—shortcut methods that efficiently produce reasonably good solutions to problems—instead of rationally considering *all* relevant evidence to achieve complete consistency in their opinions and judgments (Nisbett & Ross, 1980; Sherman & Corty, 1984; Wyer & Srull, 1980). These points will be treated in more detail as part of the description of our theory in the remainder of this chapter.

BASIC SOCIAL–PSYCHOLOGICAL PROCESSES

As people seek to comprehend inequality and their position in society, a number of basic processes are intrinsically involved. The current understanding of these processes owes much to social–psychological research, often in laboratory settings. Our own perspective is perhaps unique in emphasizing the consequences of these processes for public reactions to inequality, which have not often been investigated. This is due partly to the data limitations discussed in Chapter 1, but also to the usual barriers to communications between different disciplines. Sociological research on responses to inequality has tended to start with the specific question of why the working class (or other disadvantaged groups) accept inequality, a question that leads to certain emphases and certain blind spots in research. We take, instead, the more general question of how people comprehend and react to their social context as a starting point. From this perspective, the relevance of basic social–psychological processes is clear, as they filter and shape the individual's interpretation of other sources of information and influence related to evaluations of inequality.[1]

In this section, we discuss several social–psychological processes that may shape reactions to inequality, along with a sketch of the research evidence for each. In the next section, we draw out some of their implications for specific reactions to inequality.

[1]A limited amount of social–psychological research has addressed the important issue of the cross-cultural generalizability of these "basic" processes (cf. Triandis, 1980). Conclusions are weakened by common, often severe methodological difficulties in cross-cultural research and by the concentration of cross-cultural studies on a limited number of topics to the exclusion of others. (For example, cross-cultural investigation of the "fundamental attribution error" and "just-world" beliefs is almost nonexistent.) However, though the issues remain open, our tentative conclusion is that the social–psychological processes discussed in this section are likely to have some degree of cross-cultural generalizability. Of course, even if they were strictly limited to the North American social and economic context it would be appropriate to treat them as explanatory principles within the scope of this book. But such a limitation would be theoretically unsatisfying, as the possibility would then become salient that these attributional tendencies and other processes simply reflect the overall societal economic arrangements, socialization by elites in their own interests, etc.

Psychological Processes

We present, first, four principles that describe aspects of individual-level psychological functioning. Of course, we omit a whole list of assumed principles of perception, cognition, and behavior that are generally accepted and understood. We cite here only principles that in our view are particularly crucial in determining reactions to inequality. Most of these assumptions are widely shared by social and cognitive psychologists (including Anderson, 1983; Wyer & Srull, 1980; Smith, 1984).

1. The Principle of Cognitive Mastery. People actively seek to understand the social environmental and their own place in it—that is, to construct mental representations [knowledge structures or "mental models"; (Johnson-Laird, 1983)] that they can use to guide their actions. This assumption has been central in modern cognitive psychology (e.g., Anderson, 1983) since the overthrow of behaviorism. Heider (1958), a seminal figure in the modern era in social psychology, wrote that people "grasp reality, and can predict and control it, by referring transient and variable behavior and events to relatively unchanging underlying conditions, the so-called dispositional properties of [their] world" (1958, p. 79). This type of causal analysis (attribution) is central to the ways people make sense of, and are enabled to act effectively on, their environment. Only by understanding causal relationships can reasoned action be planned and successfully carried out. People are particularly likely to seek explanations for unexpected events and for events that are likely to affect them personally (Kelley & Michela, 1980; Hastie, 1984). Since economic inequality is such a salient feature of society and possesses great personal relevance to each individual's life experiences, this principle suggests that people will attempt to understand the system of inequality and their own positions within it.

a. Corollary: The benefits of psychological control. Believing that a particular situation can be influenced by one's own actions can serve to motivate such action, bringing potential benefits if the belief is correct. Trying to act effectively in situations that are actually uncontrollable often carries little cost, compared to failing to act when it would be helpful. Thus, it seems that overall effectiveness in dealing with the environment would be maximized by a tendency to overestimate one's ability to control or influence events. Consistent with this assumption, observation of "superstitious" behavior patterns even in lower animals such as pigeons (Skinner, 1948) seems to indicate that overestimation of the effects of one's own actions on the environment is built in evolutionarily beyond the human species.

The belief that one has control of the environment, independent of the true extent of such control, has important benefits for mental and physical health. Again, the principle holds for infrahuman species as well. The ability to terminate electric shocks by pressing a lever reduces their harmful motivational, behavioral, and emotional consequences for rats compared to identical but uncontrollable shocks (Maier & Seligman, 1976). Similar effects hold for people, with controllable stressors having less deleterious consequences than uncontrollable ones (Pennebaker, Burnam, Shaeffer, & Harper, 1977; Weidner & Matthews, 1978). One prominent theory of depression (Seligman, 1975) holds that it derives from the perception of inability to control negative events. Other studies show, for example, that nursing-home patients permitted to control even minor aspects of their environments (such as when they would participate in certain activities) function better psychologically and physically than their counterparts who were assigned to activity times (Rodin & Langer, 1977; cf. Langer, 1983). As Lefcourt (1976, p. 424) summarized, "the sense of control, the illusion that one can exercise personal choice, has a definite and positive role in sustaining life."

   b. *Corollary: The belief in the "just world"—or at least the meaningful world.* Lerner and Miller (1978) postulated that a belief in the "just world," that people generally receive the outcomes that they deserve by their actions or moral quality, can serve to maintain perceived control. The belief makes disasters or accidents affecting oneself seem unlikely, since such outcomes only befall people who deserve them in some way. By behaving properly, one can reduce the subjective likelihood of negative events. A consequence of such just-world beliefs is the perception of people in unfortunate circumstances, such as poor people, in negative terms and as personally responsible for their state.

   2. *The Principle of Cognitive Efficiency.* The perceiver interacting with the social and physical world has two general goals: to act effectively on the environment and to do so with some measure of cognitive efficiency (Taylor, 1981). A very large number of facts might be relevant to any particular judgment or decision, so considering them all in order to make the best possible decision risks complete paralysis and inaction. Instead, people consider only a limited number of facts relevant to any judgment and make decisions without an exhaustive search of memory, unless extraordinary circumstances prevail (Smith, 1984; Wyer & Srull, 1980; Chaiken, 1980; Sherman & Corty, 1984). The crucial issue is, of course, which facts or aspects of the object in question are considered. The general answer given by research in social cognition is that a discrete package of beliefs or "schema" (Brewer & Nakamura, 1984; Sears, Huddy, & Schaffer, 1986) is retrieved from memory and guides inferences and judgments. A schema is cued by specific aspects of the situation or object under consideration.

The theory outlined here implies that people may often simultaneously maintain beliefs that are potentially inconsistent, because those beliefs are never considered together. The possibility that inconsistency may be accepted by an individual contradicts some traditional lines of theory about belief systems. Cognitive consistency theories (Abelson, Aronson, McGuire, Newcomb, Rosenberg, & Tannenbaum, 1968) assumed that inconsistency is aversive, creating a motivational drive toward increased consistency of beliefs and attitudes. Related assumptions are found in some theories that presume all beliefs can be scaled along a single dimension (such as liberal–conservative) and in certain Marxist theories that assume working-class people will come to recognize the contradictions between their self-interests and their system-justifying beliefs. However, as we stressed earlier, and as others have argued (Mann, 1973; Huber & Form, 1973; Free & Cantril, 1968; Lane, 1962; Parkin, 1971), inconsistencies are not invariably or even ordinarily resolved by the perceiver. The seeker of cognitive efficiency depicted by contemporary social–psychological theory will often remain unaware of potential inconsistencies between views on different topics and, even if aware, may not proceed to reshape beliefs toward greater consistency.

a. *Corollary: Salient or available factors influence judgments.* Salient objects or attributes are those that perceptually stand out or attract attention (Taylor & Fiske, 1978), and available factors are those that can be quickly and easily retrieved from memory. The term *salience* is often used in a broad sense to refer to either of these processes. To make a judgment about an object or event (e.g., evaluate it on a good–bad dimension or find an explanation for it) people do not, as noted above, undertake a search of all possibly relevant factors. Instead, they identify a few of the most salient attributes of the object and consider them to arrive at an overall evaluation of the object (Fishbein & Ajzen, 1975). Or they simply pick the most obvious—the most immediately salient—causal possibility, and select it as "the cause" of the event (Taylor & Fiske, 1978). This principle holds across a broad range of judgments and problem-solving tasks, not only the formation of attitudes and explanations (Smith, 1984) and is ultimately related to the workings of the cognitive system as it seeks efficient functioning (Anderson, 1983; Pollard, 1982).

There are three conceptually distinct ways in which a particular concept can become salient. One is perceptual: According to this principle, perceptually salient attributes (such as, perhaps, skin color) may have disproportionate impact on social judgments and social behavior. A number of factors are known to contribute to perceptual salience (McArthur, 1981); the most important for our purposes is the distinctiveness or rarity of an attribute. A lone black in a group of whites (a lone man in a group of women, etc.) will tend to stand out perceptually and will be perceived in systematically biased ways as a result (Taylor & Fiske, 1978).

Another factor is the long-term availability of a particular concept in a person's memory. For example, authoritarians (Adorno, Frenkel Brunswik, Levinson, & Sanford, 1950) are sensitive to the dimension of leadership or power in a wide range of situations and disproportionately weight that dimension in making judgments or evaluations. In terms of the principles of social cognition, authoritarians have power-related concepts highly available in memory as a chronic state, whereas other people would be likely to use such concepts only when specific situational cues activate them.

As a third factor, associative links between concepts in memory can influence availability and hence explanations and judgments. As just mentioned, situational cues may make available particular schemas with which they are associated. Besides cues intrinsic to everyday situations of social perception and judgment, such cues abound in the research context as well, including question wording and the content of preceding questions in an interview schedule (Bishop, Oldendick, & Tuchfarber, 1982). So the wealthy might be judged more favorably if the situation (or recent media reports or previous questions) cued concepts related to their (presumed) hard work and individual merits instead of concepts involving the (presumed) greedy nature of landlords and managers of big corporations. Influences of media content on political judgment have been demonstrated and interpreted in these terms by Iyengar, Kinder, Peters, and Krosnick (1984).

Alternatively, a perceiver may have a stereotype—a link in memory between a person or group and a particular trait [e.g., a link between the poor and the concept of laziness (cf. Hamilton, 1981)]. This does not imply that the perceiver will *always* consciously view the poor as lazy. But when an explanation for poverty is called for, the concept of *laziness* will become available in memory due to its associative link to the concept of *poverty*. Laziness will then likely be chosen as an explanation, based on the availability principle. Smith (1984) describes the workings of this mechanism in detail.

In summary, because perceivers generally do not examine exhaustively the implications or properties of an object when making a judgment, they are subject to short- or long-term influences that affect what they consider and therefore the outcome of the judgment process. These influences range from the situational context (e.g., the content of previous questions in a questionnaire or imagery from a recent political campaign or media reports) to stable individual differences (e.g., authoritarianism).

b. Corollary: Persons are seen as the causes of behaviors. One process known to influence causal explanations is the so-called "fundamental attribution error" described by Ross (1977). This is an observed bias toward individual (dispositional) explanations for behavior and away from situational explanations. The bias can be considered as an instance of a salience effect, for persons who perform behaviors are often highly salient as possible causes (Jones & Nisbett, 1972). For example, a person who complies with authoritative instructions to write an essay advocating an unpopular position often is thought by observers to favor personally that position—even if the observers are aware that virtually everyone in fact complies with the instructions (Jones & Harris, 1967). The bias is so extreme and pervasive that the term *error* seems clearly deserved. It has been replicated in a multitude of studies (cf. Ross, 1977; Nisbett & Ross, 1980) and may well contribute to the predominance of individualistic explanations for achievement, an element of the dominant ideology. Pettigrew (1979) has suggested that the fundamental attribution error is exaggerated in intergroup settings, leading observers to make personal (or even genetic) attributions for negative behaviors performed by members of outgroups. For example, criminality or welfare dependence may be perceived as typical of racial outgroups and attributed to internal or genetic factors. Pettigrew (1979) labels this tendency the "ultimate attribution error."

c. Corollary: Personal experiences often may be seen as uniquely caused and not generalized. When one is personally involved in an event, unique factors of one's own personality or situation are often salient as possible causes. For example, losing one's job may be explained in terms of the individual faults or prejudices of one's boss. Explanations based on such local and immediate factors can limit the perception of generalizability, compared with explanations based on the overall state of the economy or other causes that are more global, but less salient and visible.

d. Corollary: Individual and structural explanations are not alternatives. It might be thought that explaining an event by a characteristic of the actor or by an aspect of the situation constitute alternatives, as would explaining poverty by individual characteristics of the poor or by structural characteristics of the society. However, in line with the general ability of social perceivers to maintain inconsistent views simultaneously, research has generally shown that people do not respond as though such explanations are true alternatives psychologically. That is, individual and structural (or person and situation) explanations are roughly independent of each other, rather than being strongly negatively correlated (Taylor & Koivumaki, 1976; Miller, Smith, & Uleman, 1981; cf. Chapter 4). A situation or a survey question that makes certain aspects of poverty salient (such as laziness or lack of thrift on the part of the poor) may lead a perceiver to judge that individual characteristics are important. In different circumstances different aspects may be salient (such as the lack of job opportunities in the ghetto), eliciting the judgment that structural factors are important. The perceiver may give these responses without any sense of being inconsistent because they are based on the application of different schemas or judgmental principles, cued by different aspects of the stimulus being considered (such as poverty).

   3. *The Hedonic Principle*. This principle hardly requires elaboration: People seek to obtain rewards of many types, including social approval, money, and self-esteem, and to avoid punishments. Many theories (but not ours) hold that self-interest is the basic force motivating most political attitudes and behaviors.

   a. *Corollary: The principle of self-esteem maintenance*. People typically seek to maintain high levels of self-esteem by means of "defensive" biases in attribution and other cognitive processes. Defensive attribution can result in a person overattributing success or positive outcomes to himself or herself personally, while attributing failures or negative outcomes to external, situational factors (relative to the explanations that would be given by a detached observer; Miller & Ross, 1975; Snyder, Stephan, & Rosenfield, 1978; Greenwald, 1980). In this form, the explanations obviously serve to maintain or increase the individual's self-esteem.

   4. *Principles Regarding Affect and Cognition*. The relationships among affect (emotion) and cognition are currently the subject of intense research interest in social psychology (e.g., Clark & Fiske, 1982). Of course, beliefs can shape affect—as when the perception that one is failing to obtain valued rewards causes frustration and anger. However, affect may be partially independent of cognitions such as beliefs and attitudes (cf. Zajonc, 1980; Abelson, Kinder, Peters, & Fiske, 1982). For example, perceptions and beliefs can be biased by preexisting emotional responses to a person or group (as when stereotypes of enemy nations become extremely negative during wartime). A classic experiment by Rosenberg (1960) demonstrated a biasing impact of affect on cognitions. Rosenberg manipulated people's affective responses to the idea of racial integration by hypnotic means, finding that subjects then adopted beliefs and attitudes that were consistent with and supportive of the induced affect. For example, subjects who were hypnotically induced to feel warm and favorable about the idea of interracial social contacts proceeded to give all kinds of sensible reasons that rationally supported their experimentally induced emotional reaction. Thus, affect can causally precede, as well as be dependent on, beliefs.

The Individual in Social Context

An individual's beliefs, attitudes, and behaviors are shaped not only by individual-level processes like those described above. The influences of the individual's culture, society, and particular socioeconomic position are pervasive and are the particular interest of social (as opposed to cognitive) psychologists. Several aspects of the "social embeddedness" of the individual are particularly important for our purposes.

5. *The Socialization Principle*. People come to believe, often unquestioningly, what their society teaches concerning the nature of physical and social reality. For an individual raised in twentieth-century America, reality is composed of atoms and molecules, interacting by means of physical laws including gravitation, electromagnetism, and the like. For an Azande (Evans-Pritchard, 1937), reality involves the everyday experience of witchcraft, and routine steps are taken to avoid being bewitched by one's enemies. As another example, many societies (including our own in earlier times) teach their members that racial minorities are not fully human, not entitled to full social and political recognition. In cognitive terms, beliefs that are socialized early and consistently enough form a basic framework of knowledge that is difficult for an individual even to recognize, let alone overturn.

6. *The Social Identity Principle*. People have social identities, which extend beyond their individual, biological identity to include their group memberships and affiliations as well. A person may identify herself as a particular, named individual but also as a lawyer, a Methodist, a midwesterner, a mother, an American, and so on. Such aspects of social identity can influence the individual's perceptions and behaviors in social situations (Tajfel, 1982).

a. *Corollary: People may seek group interests as well as individual ones*. The hedonic principle mentioned above extends to individuals' social identities as well as their individual ones. People can seek to further the interests of the social groups with which they identify as well as (or even in opposition to) their own individual interests (cf. Bobo, 1983). This principle is related to the distinction between egoistic (individual) and fraternal (group-based) relative deprivation (Runciman, 1966). Feeling that one's group—not only oneself individually—is overlooked and unfairly deprived is a consistent predictor of political behaviors such as voting (Vanneman & Pettigrew, 1972).

7. *Group Influences on Attitudes and Beliefs*. Social–psychological research demonstrates that socialization or group identification can shape beliefs and attitudes. Negative affect such as fear and resentment directed at racial minorities or other groups, based in early socialization, may shape attitudes and beliefs concerning such groups (McConahay

& Hough, 1976). Also, emotions such as frustration or dissatisfaction may generate motivational forces that are expressed in attitudes related to outgroups or to inequality in general; this is the classic scapegoating or relative deprivation analysis of prejudice. Affective factors ultimately based in group identification or intergroup hostility can have a powerful impact on attitudes and beliefs.

Beliefs and attitudes also may be based normatively in group membership and identifications, as well as in purely cognitive processes. The influence of reference groups (groups to which an individual turns for validation and reality-testing of beliefs or attitudes) is well known in sociology and social psychology (e.g., Newcomb, 1963; Merton, 1957; Asch, 1951). The result is a tendency toward uniformity of attitudes and beliefs within groups, at least on issues that are significant to the group.

8. *Distributive Justice Principles.* Groups seek to mute intragroup conflicts over rewards, often by establishing abstract principles for the division of rewards. Such principles can limit conflicts due to the operation of self-interest (the hedonic principle) when the total sum of rewards is limited (Walster, Walster, & Berscheid, 1978). Several different distributive principles are available, and their use depends on the salience of different aspects of the situation (as discussed under Corollary; Salient or available factors influence judgments, p. 15; Deutsch, 1975). *(a)* Equality is preferred for distribution when people's sharing of the basic human condition is salient, as with food supplies in an emergency. *(b)* Equity (distribution proportional to individual inputs) can be used when people's differential inputs to an enterprise are salient—particularly when the inputs jointly determine the size of the resource to be distributed. Corporate law, in which profits are divided according to the relative size of owners' investments, is an example. *(c)* Need-based distributions are sometimes used when unequal needs for the resource are salient.

Summary: Multiple Functions of Attitudes and Beliefs

This body of principles implies that a particular belief or attitude may serve a number of possible functions for an individual, a theoretical insight that was expressed by Katz (1960), among others. A belief may be approximately *veridical,* describing the world (or the individual's experience of it) in a way that facilitates reasoned action and goal attainment. A belief may serve *social adjustment* functions, as when the individual adopts a belief to conform to a reference group. A belief or attitude may serve *individual or group interests,* such as an attitude favoring a policy that will bring concrete benefits to the individual. *Psychological defense* functions may also be important, for beliefs that bolster the individual's sense of control or mastery over the world.

The multiple functions of beliefs and attitudes constitute a potential motivational basis for inconsistency within an individual's belief structures. That is, believing one thing (say, that the poor are generally the helpless victims of unfortunate circumstances) may be functional in some ways—it may be roughly veridical or agree with the opinions favored by the perceiver's reference groups. At the same time, believing something different or even directly contradictory (that the poor could lift themselves from poverty if they tried hard enough) might be functional for different reasons, such as psychological defense or group self-interest. The individual might have substantial motivation to maintain each of these beliefs and would probably find it both difficult and psychologically costly to bring them into confrontation and resolve the potential contradiction. Research shows that, in general, people do not take this course, preferring to reap the psychological benefits of maintaining both beliefs simultaneously. The potential contradiction carries few if any costs in everyday life, because the different beliefs, being part of different schemas, will be made consciously available by different cues. Thoughts about the helpless poor might be triggered by images of racial minorities facing job discrimination and thoughts about the lazy, undeserving poor by images of welfare Cadillacs. The structures and processes of social cognition thus provide definite bases for potential inconsistency and ambivalence in people's reactions to complex, multifaceted realities such as inequality in society.

CONSEQUENCES OF THESE PROCESSES FOR REACTIONS TO INEQUALITY

The first question concerning reactions to inequality is, logically, are people at all aware of social inequality? Our perspective gives a clear answer: Because social inequality is such a salient feature of the social world and a critically important influence on individuals' lives, we assume it to be a frequent target of individual attention and thought. As the cognitive mastery principle emphasizes, people seek to understand the general causes of inequality and structure their attitudes and actions according to the causal understanding they achieve. This assumption distinguishes our theory of responses to societal inequality from the suggestion that acceptance of social inequality (particularly by the disadvantaged) results from a lack of awareness of inequality.

The essential argument in the thesis of unawareness is that people implicitly accept aspects of social reality that are so far removed from their immediate experience as to lack much substance for them. We do not claim that Americans have a detailed awareness of all aspects of social inequality. Indeed, we shall argue that in some areas (such as aspects of racial inequality) limited awareness has an important impact on policy attitudes. However, many reasons convince us that Americans have a broad sense of the social inequalities that characterize our society. We are a literate, media-oriented people with ample opportunity to receive information about the status and political power of the rich and the circumstances and demographic characteristics of the poor. Examination of even a small sampling of the content of popular media supports this assertion. Another argument is to be found in the writings of contemporary apologists for capitalism and attendant inequalities (e.g., Gilder, 1981), who do not attempt to deny the existence of marked inequalities of income or wealth or the existence of past racial injustices. Instead, they generally characterize such injustices as things of the past and offer justifications for current economic inequalities. The assumption is implicit that inequality is generally acknowledged and that it is salient enough for most people to require justification. In addition, survey data (e.g., studies of class perceptions) suggest that people are broadly aware of the marked inequalities of income, wealth, and power that exist in our society. Finally, the limited amount of work on the development of awareness of inequality in childhood (e.g., Simmons & Rosenberg, 1971; Leahy, 1983) seems to show that awareness develops in the teen years, at about the same time as other aspects of political consciousness.

If we reject the model of unawareness, then, and accept the notion that people seek to understand their environment causally in order to make predictions and act effectively on it, it follows that people are likely to ask questions about social inequality. The questions take two basic forms: How *should* the stratification system work, and how *does* it actually work? Questions of the first type concern what gives rise to economic rewards, whether or not inequality is an inevitable feature of society, what costs and benefits result from inequality, and related questions about the sources and consequences of inequality. Questions of the second type concern whether or not the stratification system is currently functioning as it should. Is there truly equality of opportunity for all groups? Are the typical incomes of different occupations proportional to their contributions to society? Is my personal position fair? Our society provides readily available answers to these questions in the form of the "dominant ideology" identified by Huber and Form (1973) and others, and we proceed next to a discussion of the roots of adherence to the dominant ideology in the social–psychological principles listed above.

Processes Supporting the Dominant Ideology

Our theory emphasizes the role of certain processes in directly supporting belief in the dominant ideology and therefore the acceptance of existing inequalities. The dominant ideology involves three beliefs: First, that opportunity for economic advancement is widespread in America today; second, that individuals are personally responsible for their positions; and third, that the overall system of inequality is, therefore, equitable and fair.

Socialization. Every member of society is exposed to multiple messages, in childhood socialization and in the mass media throughout life, which have implications for responses to inequality. Marxist and neo-Marxist theories have particularly emphasized the role of socialization in bringing about mass acceptance of economic inequality. From Marx's early writings on "false consciousness" (Marx, 1845/1956) to contemporary writings on "ideological hegemony" (Gramsci, 1971; Cheal, 1979), several themes have been consistent. Elites are said to promote beliefs that support and justify inequality (and therefore their privileged position) through their control over educational, religious, and cultural institutions. General acceptance of these beliefs is said to be important in producing popular support for inequality and other existing societal arrangements.

There is ample evidence that elites do attempt to influence the content of common sources of socialization (e.g., Domhoff, 1978). The dominant ideology itself and the general individualistic bias in American culture that has been noted by many observers (e.g., Weber, 1959; Sampson, 1977) are consistent with the predictions of Marxist theories about the contents of socialization. The predominant beliefs of the American public about the workings of the stratification system have been (Huber & Form, 1973; Feagin, 1975) and continue to be (Kluegel & Smith, 1983; see Chapter 4) predominantly individualistic in character. Wealth is seen as the product of superior individual effort and talent and poverty as the result of deficits in these factors. Consistent with an assumption of early socialization, Ross, Turiel, Josephson, and Lepper (1978, cited in Nisbett & Ross, 1980) found that American children use increasingly dispositional (individual) explanations for behavior as they grow up. Common socialization processes are thus one major potential influence on popular beliefs about inequality, though the available evidence cannot prove the case for intentional elite domination and manipulation. In addition, cross-national evidence finds individualism and other elements of the dominant ideology to be prevalent in several Western societies (Lopreato & Hazelrigg, 1972; Coughlin, 1980). If socialization is the entire explanation, it must involve beliefs that are basic in Western culture rather than beliefs that are specific to American society.

Generalization of Experiences. Quite apart from socialization and mass communication, widespread individual experiences of certain concrete aspects of recent American history appear to confirm parts of the dominant ideology. Research on occupational mobility (Featherman & Hauser, 1978) shows that while the most common pattern is stability of class position from one generation to the next, upward mobility has also been common and outweighs downward mobility by roughly two to one. The majority of Americans perceive themselves as having experienced improvements upon their parents' standard of living (Kluegel & Smith, 1982; see also Chapter 3). Most Americans thus have evidence for the possibility of upward mobility either in their own experience or in that of family members, friends, or acquaintances. Even those who have not been mobile have benefited, on the whole, from the aggregate improvement in living standards that has taken place since World War II. Lane (1962) held that people generalize relatively benign personal economic experiences to conclude that mobility is possible for anyone who works hard. The ways in which personal experiences dispose people to accept societal inequalities have been emphasized by proponents of such theses as the demise of working-class consciousness, the "embourgeoisement" of the working class, and the "end of ideology" (for reviews, see Blumberg, 1980; Kluegel & Smith, 1981).

Explanations for Economic Outcomes. Those who experience upward mobility or improvements in living standards will tend to attribute responsibility for their gains to their own personal efforts and abilities (as shown by studies of typical explanations for successful outcomes). Their experiences will thus appear to confirm the second aspect of the dominant ideology, that individuals are responsible for their own societal positions. Several reasons support this attributional tendency, including self-esteem maintenance motives or defensive attribution. The "fundamental attribution error" (Ross, 1977) also will contribute to this pattern, leading to individual explanations for observed instances of poverty as well as economic achievement.

When perceivers attempt to explain poverty, there will be a general tendency to attribute it to personal characteristics of the poor and thus to uphold the tenets of the dominant ideology. Lane (1962) emphasized a "fear of equality," particularly among the working class. Living close to the poor (both in the sense of average income and in the likelihood of falling into poverty due to unemployment or disability), working-class people need to distance themselves psychologically from the poor in order to maintain a favorable social identity and self-esteem, according to Lane. One way to do this is to emphasize the lack of moral character, effort, or talent on the part of the poor, in contrast to the more favorably viewed characteristics of the working class. Beliefs in the "just world" (Lerner & Miller, 1978) have the same effect: One who is motivated, by a need to perceive an orderly universe, to see people's outcomes as related to their deservingness will tend to see the poor as personally responsible for their plight. Finally, the benefits of psychological control (Principle 1) motivate seeing oneself in control of important outcomes and thereby motivate perceptions of individual causation in general. Thus, a number of processes at the social–psychological level operate directly to bring about or strengthen support for the dominant ideology, a conclusion supported by the cross-national predominance of the dominant ideology [at least in the industrial West (Lopreato & Hazelrigg, 1972; Coughlin, 1980)]. It may not be necessary to postulate its dissemination, in their own interests, by elites who dominate important societal institutions.

Self-Interest. Given an unequal distribution of economic rewards, simple self-interest inevitably produces potentially conflicting beliefs and attitudes. One would expect the privileged to hold beliefs that support and legitimate the stratification system that benefits them and the less privileged to adopt challenging beliefs, which would provide grounds for changes that might bring increased benefits (Chesler, 1976; Huber & Form, 1973). Members of middle-income groups face a somewhat more complex situation, as they simultaneously see the potential for economic improvements and for economic losses from changes in the stratification system. On this analysis, middle-income groups might be expected to hold certain beliefs that support the existing system and others that challenge it. Overall, we can expect the more privileged in society to believe in the dominant ideology based on their own self-interest.

Group Identification. People can come to see aspects of their social identity as being tied up in their group memberships (including social class, racial or ethnic group identification, regional pride, etc.; cf. Tajfel, 1982). Group identification can lead to two types of affective response which under certain conditions can influence responses to inequality: *identification* or *solidarity* with an in-group and *hostility* to an out-group. Group identification is prominent in Marxist theories of response to inequality. The sense of sharing a common fate and interests with others is accorded a key role in generating class consciousness and action for social change among the working class. Class identification among the privileged, on the other hand, would be important in producing organized action in support of the status quo. Group identification can also focus at more inclusive levels, such as the nation. Hostility to powerful foreign nations such as the Soviet Union might serve, therefore, to motivate opposition to salient features of the Soviet social and political system, such as communism and related concepts, based on the perceiver's identification with America.

Sources of Potentially Challenging Beliefs

The discussion above describes some bases of support for the dominant ideology among our theory's social–psychological principles. But people also may encounter experiences or adopt beliefs that potentially challenge the dominant ideology. The second major focus of our theory concerns both the typical sources of such potentially challenging experiences or beliefs and the ways people respond to them. Under what conditions are the challenges deflected so that the perceiver can maintain an acceptance of inequality, and under what conditions will challenges reshape the overall pattern of beliefs and attitudes?

Potentially challenging experiences are not limited to the conditions of working-class life, as some theorists have seemed to imply. Though relatively low incomes, insecure jobs, and limited chances for advancement may be important as sources of potentially challenging beliefs, some members of the working class have not experienced such negative economic outcomes in the recent past. Skilled workers and those in large firms with powerful unions have realized greater improvements in their standards of living than many white-collar workers (Blumberg, 1980), and their offspring have a much better chance of moving into middle-class occupations than do those of unskilled or semiskilled workers (Featherman & Hauser, 1978). Thus, groups within the working class vary in the extent to which their experiences and self-interest present them with challenges to the dominant ideology.

There also may be important and widespread sources of challenges within the middle class. Of course, in general the middle class has relatively high incomes and often favorable mobility experiences as well. But not all factors dispose the middle class toward acceptance of inequality. Besides the static or declining relative incomes of many middle-class groups (clerical workers, schoolteachers), we can point to the effects of education and of relative deprivation. Higher education, a necessity for entry into many middle-class occupations, may provide information that is potentially inconsistent with the dominant ideology, and it increases media use throughout life, with similar effects. College-educated people are less likely to express racial prejudice and sex-role traditionalism (Taylor et al., 1978; Miller et al., 1980, p. 227) and are more likely to acknowledge that opportunity for minorities and women is limited by discrimination (Kluegel & Smith, 1982; Smith & Kluegel, 1984). Such beliefs challenge the dominant ideology, which asserts that opportunity is open to all. Besides the effects of education, middle-class people are likely to be more exposed to specific information about the wealthy (perhaps by personal acquaintance) and may be more likely to use them as salient personal reference points. The result may be feelings of relative deprivation, as middle-class individuals see little chance of ever attaining wealth, or more than a modest or comfortable standard of living.

Socialization. Elites evidently do not achieve total domination of institutions of socialization and mass communication; such institutions may serve as sources of potentially challenging beliefs as well. Examples are manifold. Both black and white churches were instrumental in organizing and supporting the early civil rights movement. College campuses have been focal points for many movements for social change. The mass media devote at least some coverage to many areas of social problems and have been criticized by some conservatives (including recent presidents) for having a "liberal" bias.

Experiences. Concrete aspects of personal experiences could lead to challenges to inequality, as well as to its acceptance. A person (e.g., a black) who experiences discrimination or other barriers to opportunity may also generalize, becoming more willing to see limits to opportunity in general or for other specific groups (such as women). In contrast to the widespread improvement in standards of living that has taken place since World War II, relative differences in income and differences in chances for advancement, power, and autonomy between middle- and working-class jobs have persisted or increased. Such differences may generate feelings of relative deprivation in working-class observers and dispose many to beliefs that challenge the legitimacy of the stratification system.

Reactions to Potentially Challenging Beliefs

For any of the above reasons, people may adopt beliefs that challenge some of the tenets of widespread opportunity or individualism. However, our theory holds that such beliefs will not inevitably lead to overturning their adherence to the dominant ideology. Social–psychological research within the "symbolic politics" tradition has obtained relevant findings. People's beliefs about broad aspects of social reality and public policy (in such areas as the causes of crime, Vietnam War policy, and interracial relations) are essentially *independent* of reported personal experiences and personal fears for the future. Moreover, voting and other political behaviors tend to be influenced more strongly by the general beliefs than by the specific aspects of personal experiences and interests, except on narrow policy issues such as the level of a specific type of tax that the individual finds personally burdensome (Lau & Sears, 1981; Kinder & Sears, 1981). The key message is people's ability to maintain a psychological separation of general from specific, personally based beliefs, as summarized in our cognitive efficiency principle.

Limits to Generalization. A number of psychological mechanisms can deflect challenges arising from personal experiences or considerations of self-interest, preventing their expression in resistance to the overall stratification system. First, the dominant ideology explains how the stratification system does and should work *in general*. Thus, it has some elasticity in the face of apparent exceptions. Specific instances of the system's failure can be readily viewed as exceptions that do not threaten the generalizations that opportunity is available and individuals are responsible for their own positions. Racial barriers to opportunity provide an example of such thinking: Even if one recognizes that race discrimination exists, the potential challenge to the perception of generally available opportunity can be discounted, since blacks are only a numerical minority.

Second, explanations can limit generalizations of particular beliefs, if the perceived challenging experience is attributed to limited, specific causes rather than to features of the system. For example, consistent with the "fundamental attribution error," many people blame race discrimination on individuals rather than on general features of the stratification system. A few racially prejudiced whites are seen as unfortunately blocking blacks from realizing the benefits of a system that works well for others. Consistent with this thinking, it has been proposed that the decline of racial prejudice among Americans will suffice to produce equal opportunity for blacks, with no structural changes being required (Gilder, 1981). Our research suggests that these views are widespread among whites (Kluegel & Smith, 1982; cf. Chapter 7).

Nonintegration of Beliefs. As discussed earlier, basic psychological mechanisms permit some inconsistency in beliefs in the service of overall cognitive efficiency. This has been referred to as the "compartmentalization" of beliefs (Lane, 1962). Political psychologists have proposed that individuals can be classified as "morselizers" versus "contextualizers," people who respond piecemeal (using specific, concrete schemas) to information about political and social events versus those who put new information in a context of larger forces and trends, embodied in more abstract, interconnected schemas. For the former, "a union demand is a single incident, not part of a more general labor–management conflict" (Lane, 1962, p. 353). Beliefs and attitudes on different topics will rarely if ever even be brought into contact with each other so that inconsistencies could be noticed. Similar points are made by other theorists; for example, Sennett and Cobb (1972) speak of the creation of a "divided self" to deal with potentially inconsistent aspects of experience, and Sears et al. (1986) discuss some aspects of the use of schemas that vary in levels of abstractness. This point fits well with the emphasis by Lane and a number of Marxist theorists on the importance of a broad counterideology that can demonstrate to an individual how experiences fit together, what implications a specific belief has for the general workings of society and for the dominant ideology. Without such a counterideology, people often simply do not make such connections. Many illustrations are possible; as Chapter 7 will show, many Americans respond (to different questions) that at least some discrimination against blacks and other minorities persists *and* that minorities have a chance equal to whites to advance economically.

Motivational Reasons. Finally, there may be motivational reasons for refusing to acknowledge inconsistencies. In everyday life people have many other concerns besides those that stem from economic injustice. They may enjoy their work, must care for their families, often worry about threats to their safety from hostile foreign powers or from criminals. To entertain the thought that one is the victim of an unjust social order or that the social order victimizes others (with oneself in some degree responsible for the injustice) is profoundly distressing. Anger, frustration, shame, and other emotions may lead one to seek social change, but they may also lead to avoiding the issues. Working for social change raises doubts and fears about maintaining our other goals, such as preserving a comfortable family life, defending the nation from those perceived as hostile, and preserving the noneconomic rewards (such as satisfying work and friendships) that one currently enjoys. For these reasons, it may become easier to write off instances of injustice as aberrations than to respond seriously to them by questioning the dominant ideology.

Effective Challenges. The above discussion of the ways in which challenges to the dominant ideology can be deflected carries obvious implications about the conditions under which they will *not* be deflected but will diminish or overturn adherence to the dominant ideology. Challenges may be deflected by treating them as exceptions, but it may become impossible to maintain a belief in the dominant ideology if exceptions are seen as widespread or systematic. Causal explanations will be important: If race discrimination (for example) is attributed to a few prejudiced individuals, then no change to the overall stratification system is necessary. But if it is attributed to the system itself (as in the Marxist view that discrimination preserves capitalism by keeping workers' wages low), then the dominant ideology cannot be maintained.

Challenges may be deflected by processes of compartmentalization, but an explicit counterideology (presented by a union, political party, or other group) may show individuals how to relate their experiences and interests into an overall critique of the stratification system. And finally, we described above the motivation, created by the desire to preserve a comfortable life, to leave certain questions unasked. This motivation may be irrelevant for one whose life experiences are limited to poverty and deprivation, surrounded by crime and the other phenomena of the inner city, and may be less relevant to the unattached young than to their elders with families and mortgages. Our perspective thus allows the possibility that certain individuals may respond to challenging experiences or beliefs, showing only weak adherence to the dominant ideology or rejecting it altogether. The considerations discussed in this section can be formulated as specific predictions concerning who will be most likely to take these steps.

Adding Specific Beliefs to the Dominant Ideology

Despite the strong forces leading to accommodation of potentially challenging beliefs in ways that do not affect a basic allegiance to the dominant ideology, our perspective predicts that such challenges may have a more limited impact. While the basic elements of the dominant ideology have remained quite stable over the last several decades, there have been marked changes in other areas of beliefs relevant to social inequality and social policy. Segregationist sentiment and other measures of traditional racial prejudice have decreased very significantly over the last three decades (Taylor *et al.*, 1978). Similarly, many people have moved away from traditional views of sex roles that stressed the home as women's place (Ferree, 1974; Smith & Kluegel, 1984). Our perspective accounts for such changes by a process of adding other beliefs and attitudes to the general substrate formed by the dominant ideology, without bringing them into complete consistency.

Some of the sources of these added beliefs, over the last three decades, may be briefly mentioned. Some beliefs may be directly learned from media coverage of political movements or events. The antipoverty efforts of the 1960s carried strong messages about the causes of poverty, stressing environmental and situational explanations. The civil rights and women's movements underscored the existence of discrimination and other structural causes of economic disadvantages. Other beliefs may be based on individuals' self-interest or personal experiences. The prolonged economic stagnation, high unemployment, and inflation of the late 1970s and early 1980s have caused real economic and psychological hardships, leading many people to accept governmental programs to alleviate them. Claims for equal opportunity advanced by racial minorities and women have been perceived to threaten the self-interest of many whites and males, leading in some cases to opposition to structural changes. Finally, racial turmoil and the militant positions advanced by some civil rights activists may have created negative intergroup affect in some whites, leading them to reject blacks' demands as unjustified. The results of the social and political changes in recent decades have been variable, but the net result has been a growth in "socially liberal" beliefs in many individuals' consciousness of inequality. These beliefs (along with the dominant ideology) may influence preferences for policies or political candidates.

Policy Implications

One policy-related consequence of the addition of beliefs based on the political events of the recent past is the current widespread acceptance of some governmental support for the disadvantaged. Unemployment compensation and other programs for job-related economic problems and the rectification of outright racial and sexual discrimination and injustice are all generally accepted. Even the provision of job-related training to minorities to help them advance economically is accepted by almost three-quarters of the public (see Chapter 7); corresponding attitudes on policies aimed at women may now be developing, as Chapter 8 will discuss. So programmatic remedies for at least some of the problems faced by the disadvantaged have become broadly accepted by the public, as a result of self-interest or ideological factors.

While the growth of social liberalism has increased perceptions of the need for governmental programs in general, the dominant ideology shapes the specific type of program that will be acceptable to the public. Policies that can be easily seen as consistent with the dominant ideology often have met with popular acceptance; examples are a floor on income for the very poor (e.g., Social Security benefits for the aged) and civil rights (equal political rights, access to public accommodations and schools) for racial minorities. Such rights are entirely consistent with an ideology of individualism and can be seen as offering individuals an equal starting point in the meritocratic competition for economic success. In fact, the dominant ideology almost requires the elimination of discrimination and other such barriers to opportunity, for concrete reasons of self-interest. If major groups in our society lack opportunity to advance, what will motivate them to work hard? If they do not work hard, how can we all expect long-run improvements in economic performance?

On the other hand, policies that challenge aspects of the dominant ideology have generally met with less popular acceptance. Social welfare programs must not weaken the motivation for hard work that inequality is perceived to provide. Thus, welfare programs for the poor must not offer "handouts" and must not discourage hard work by people with low-paying jobs. Affirmative-action programs (as opposed to simple equal opportunity) have been widely viewed as calling for equal outcomes and hence as violating the necessary relationship between inputs (hard work and talents) and outcomes (e.g., Glazer, 1975). Policies that call for ceilings on incomes or inheritances are also generally unpopular, because of widespread beliefs that the desire for wealth motivates hard work and brings overall economic benefits.

The individualistic beliefs that are a part of the dominant ideology also shape policy preferences (Wilensky, 1975; Coughlin, 1980). Individualistic solutions to social problems, those aimed at changing characteristics of the persons blamed for the problem, will be more acceptable than structural solutions, involving changes to societal or institutional arrangements. Individualistic solutions to racial inequalities include providing training programs to blacks to teach them job-related skills and attitudes and have been much more popular than structural solutions such as changing the distribution of authority in the workplace, reducing income differentials between occupations, or promoting more equality of ownership or control over wealth. The dominant ideology leads to opposition to structural solutions because they challenge the ultimate inevitability and desirability of economic inequality.

The above examples illustrate the influence of the dominant ideology on policy views among the public and (indirectly) on legislation. But policy views are also affected by a number of other short- and long-term forces, some of which tend to generate support for redistributive policies and others opposition. Taking equal opportunity policy for racial minorities as an example, our research demonstrates the influence of several factors, aside from beliefs in the dominant ideology itself (see Chapter 7). Though the growing recognition of racial discrimination (and its inconsistency with individualism) disposes people to support equal opportunity policies, several factors counter this tendency. Lingering traditional racial prejudice is still to be found (particularly among the old and the southern-born), and it has effects on views of equal opportunity policy. "Symbolic racism" (Kinder & Sears, 1981), thought to be based in early-socialized negative racial affect, and negative attitudes about racial minorities based on the recent history of racial conflict may have similar effects. Aside from these factors, people who perceive themselves as members of groups that have been overlooked by the government in its attention to the problems of minorities may be led to oppose equal opportunity policy by such a sense of relative deprivation.

Finally, perceived self-interest among white workers may have multiple and complex effects. Some white workers may fear the economic threat represented by previously excluded qualified blacks under conditions of equal opportunity and so oppose such programs. But overall, since blacks constitute only about 10% of the workforce, the probability of a typical white worker's suffering significantly from black gains in opportunity is low (though it varies by occupation, firm, and industry). Considerations of long-run self-interest actually may lead to white support for equal opportunity programs, as solutions to the problems raised by racial conflicts. Women may see benefits in supporting affirmative action for blacks, on the grounds that similar programs for women may become effective. In general, the effect of self-interest on policy issues cannot be assumed to be singular. Nor can individuals easily assess their own overall interest in supporting or opposing a policy, because of incomplete information about the policy's effects, and because trade-offs between short- and long-run costs and benefits are difficult to compute. Thus, many forces besides self-interest, including views on the dominant ideology, intergroup affect, and specific political opinions, may well influence policy attitudes.

Our perspective has several long-range implications for the nature of political debate and policy outcomes. The point of departure is the observation that the dominant ideology is stable and widespread in its influence; more specific beliefs that challenge the dominant ideology, derived from recent social movements and some enduring aspects of inequality, are less stable and subject to more disagreement. As a result, inequality-related policy is characteristically a compromise, whose exact nature tends to vary as the political winds shift.

The changing salience of inequality-related issues in political dialogue (e.g., shifts in emphasis from helping the deserving poor to uprooting welfare fraud) provides conditions for major short-term changes in the positions of victorious politicians and in public attitudes themselves. Such shifts are, of course, quite evident in the history of inequality-related social policy (particularly on welfare and racial equal opportunity) over the last several decades. Since policy often represents a compromise between the stable dominant ideology and specific beliefs with more liberal implications, the shifts are contained within a limited range of the potential political spectrum, near the moderate midpoint. The egalitarian (i.e., socialist) end of the spectrum has rarely produced successful candidates. And the recent success of the conservative, pure "dominant ideology" segment of the spectrum under Ronald Reagan bears out the predictions of our perspective, in that the successes are essentially confined to economic issues (reduction in federal taxation and in spending on programs for the poor). Other elements of the conservative program (such as returning prayer to public schools and banning abortions), which are inconsistent with Americans' increased social liberalism, have not been successfully implemented to date.

ALTERNATIVE THEORIES OF REACTIONS TO INEQUALITY

Several theories stand as alternatives to our own, social–psychologically based perspective. Some will be mentioned briefly to suggest the range of existing viewpoints on the issues of public attitudes and beliefs about inequality. A simple self-interest or "economic person" theory of beliefs and attitudes would hold that individuals support the economic arrangements of society because they benefit from those arrangements. If the less advantaged in society seem to have a hard life in the short run, then their support must be based on their perception of long-run advantages from existing inequalities, or at least the superiority of the existing system to possible alternatives. Many writers in the "embourgeoisement" and "end of ideology" traditions (Blumberg, 1980) have at least a flavor of this view in their thinking, emphasizing the increasing affluence enjoyed even by working-class people in capitalist societies in the postwar era and its consequence for acceptance of inequality.

However, many theories have viewed the perception of long-run benefits by the disadvantaged as inadequate to explain their acquiescence in inequalities that seem to harm them quite directly. Marxist and neo-Marxist theories, to summarize a diverse set of writings in an oversimple way, assume that workers' self-interest would be served by changing the system. The acquiescence of the working class is explained by "false consciousness"—elite-controlled socialization that leads to the adoption of system-supporting beliefs, such as the dominant ideology or the belief in the long-run benefits of inequality (Gramsci, 1971). In fact, existing research suggests that adherence to the dominant ideology is as widespread among the working class as among the middle class (Mann, 1970; Huber & Form, 1973; Lane, 1962; Sennett & Cobb, 1972). However, the existing research is largely based on small samples of questionable representativeness, and our own data will provide more confident answers to this question (see Chapters 3–5).

However, in Marxist-influenced theory workers can overcome false consciousness under certain conditions. Three factors are generally emphasized as necessary and jointly sufficient for this to occur (different versions of this general perspective are found in Lane, 1962; Mann, 1970, 1973; Parkin, 1971; Sennett & Cobb, 1972; Moore, 1978; Vanneman, 1980). One factor is personal experiences, particularly in the workplace, that demonstrate the effectiveness of collective action. A second is socialization, by a labor union or socialist party, that counteracts the elite-dominated content of the mass media. The party must present a counterideology that articulates the challenge to the dominant ideology that is implicit in workers' job-related experiences and other sources (Mann, 1973): that translates "private troubles" into "public issues" (Mills, 1959). The third factor is group-based affect: solidarity within the working class (based on shared experiences and common interests) and hostility to the class enemy, the economic elite. The process of developing beliefs and attitudes that challenge the dominant ideology can be blocked, in these theories, by a lack of any of the three necessary factors. Writings have generally emphasized the absence of an explicit counterideology because of the lack of a true working-class political party in the United States (e.g., Vanneman, 1980). These emphases are compatible with our own theory, particularly with regard to the potential effects of group-based affect and of an ideology that provides generalizable explanations for particular experiences.

Another theory of the formation of political beliefs and attitudes, possessing a strong social–psychological base, is "symbolic politics" theory (Kinder & Sears, 1981; Lau & Sears, 1981). This theory emphasizes the potent nature of political symbols, such as the flag or references to the "American way" or democracy. Based on early socialization, people have strong responses to such symbols and use them to define and decide their positions on various issues. People respond to an issue based on their association of the issue with particular symbols or groups; for example, favoring affirmative action because "providing equal opportunity is the American way" or opposing it because racial minorities are seen as threatening central American values (such as achievement by hard work). Besides the influence of political symbolism, the theory has also emphasized group-based affect, particularly deep-seated hostility toward racial out-groups, and its consequences for race-related issues. A recent paper (Sears et al., 1986) has added more sophisticated cognitive assumptions including the concept of schemas to help account for certain findings (such as differences between people with different amounts of political knowledge) in reactions to political symbols and issues.

Symbolic politics theory characteristically denies the political force of two other types of process: self-interest and personal experiences. Repeated analyses of opinions on different issues have demonstrated weak or nonexistent effects of these classes of variables (e.g., Lau, Brown, & Sears, 1978; Kinder, 1981). Our own perspective agrees on the powerful potential effects of ideology and affectively laden symbols in shaping beliefs and attitudes but disagrees with the claim that self-interest can never be influential. Most studies in the symbolic-politics tradition have used objective self-interest measures, while subjective measures are arguably more appropriate for testing the theory. In addition, Bobo (1983) has provided a detailed empirical and conceptual critique of the use of the term symbolic in the theory, arguing that group self-interest is responsible for most of the observed effects (but see Sears & Kinder, 1985). With these caveats, our theory is quite compatible with the overall emphases of the symbolic-politics perspective, particularly the newer, cognitively sophisticated version of Sears et al. (1986).

SUMMARY OF OUR PERSPECTIVE

The following propositions or hypotheses summarize the main points of our perspective.

1. Americans are broadly aware of and responsive to patterns of economic and social inequality; they attempt to understand them by explaining them causally and to evaluate them by forming attitudes.
2. Their understandings are heavily influenced by the dominant ideology, which is a pattern of beliefs and attitudes that upholds existing inequality, is widespread among the public, and has been quite stable over the last several decades.
3. Individuals may encounter personal experiences, aspects of their self-interest, or views derived from their groups, that potentially challenge the dominant ideology.
4. The fate of such challenging beliefs may differ depending on specific conditions:
   a. The challenge is ordinarily deflected, without much consequence for the individual's overall belief pattern.
   b. The challenge may have an impact on the individual's beliefs or attitudes, but in a narrow way: shaping evaluations of affirmative-action policy, say, rather than evaluations of inequality or belief in the dominant ideology in general.
   c. Finally, particularly under circumstances where the individual is exposed to a comprehensive counterideology that can show the implications of the challenging beliefs and their inconsistency with the dominant ideology, adherence to the latter would be theoretically expected to weaken or disappear.
5. Policy views often arise as a compromise between the stably held elements of the dominant ideology and other beliefs and attitudes that generally have more liberal implications. Hence views on particular inequality-related policy issues will often be held with some ambivalence and may be subject to shifts over time as different bases for evaluating policy are made more salient by environmental forces or the changing concepts invoked in political rhetoric.

The subsequent chapters of this book will apply this theoretical perspective to a number of different issue domains. However, as these propositions do not summarize everything that might be learned from analyses of our data, we will also explore several ancillary issues concerning Americans' beliefs about the stratification system and their related policy attitudes. These exploratory analyses, as well as the tests of theoretical predictions, constitute our contribution to the overall description and explanation of the current structure and determinants of Americans' consciousness of inequality.

I

DOMINANT-IDEOLOGY BELIEFS

In Chapters 3, 4, and 5 we empirically examine features of the inter-related beliefs that form what we and others have labeled the dominant ideology. These chapters follow the order of the "logic of opportunity" syllogism"—from beliefs about opportunity for economic advancement (Chapter 3) to explanations for economic success or failure for oneself and others (Chapter 4) to beliefs about the justice of economic in-equality (Chapter 5). In each of these chapters we present analyses that explore aspects of the dominant ideology that we underscored in Chapters 1 and 2.

DISTRIBUTIONS

We begin each chapter with a review of percentage distributions for the responses to questions from our own and other surveys about sev-eral aspects of each of these three belief areas. We and others have proposed that the American public broadly adheres to a set of inter-related beliefs that serve to explain the workings of the stratification system. Specifically, most Americans believe that opportunity for eco-nomic advancement is widely available, that economic outcomes are determined by individual efforts and talents (or their lack), and that in general economic inequality is fair. As a starting point in each chapter, we examine the proportions of Americans who endorse these beliefs.

TIME TRENDS

We have also argued that widespread adherence to dominant ide-ology beliefs has been a stable feature of Americans' thinking about social stratification in recent history. To test this claim fully we should have data collected at many time points, from large representative samples, employing identically worded questions (Duncan, 1969). At present we lack such data. Instead, the direct evidence we are able to offer primarily consists of: (1) comparisons between measures of a few beliefs available for scattered points in time prior to 1980 and comparable measures in our survey and (2) comparisons of beliefs among age-groups.

Since available data do not approximate well the requirements for making strong inferences about change, some caution must be exercised in drawing conclusions about the stability of dominant ideology beliefs. The best evidence that can currently be offered about the stability of dominant-ideology beliefs permits tentative conclusions, with proper consideration of alternative explanations for our results. Because we must rely heavily on age-group comparisons, the potential for confusing effects of aging per se or life cycle effects with true change deserves special consideration as an alternative explanation for our findings (Glenn, 1977). That is, we need to keep in mind the fact that observed age-group differences in beliefs may simply stem from the association of age with certain other attributes, such as employment status, income, and so on.

POTENTIAL CHALLENGES

Our theoretical perspective also directs attention to the relationships among beliefs about economic inequality. We proposed in Chapter 2 that certain factors promote continued adherence to the dominant ideology in the face of personal experiences and beliefs about social inequality that logically seem to challenge the validity of dominant-ideology beliefs. As we discussed in Chapter 2, one reason for questioning the validity of these beliefs is generalization from unfavorable personal inequality-related experience, such as race or sex discrimination involving opportunity. A second major source of potential doubt stems from the increased attention during the last two decades given to inequality-related social problems, most notably to poverty and to racial and sexual inequality of opportunity. Blacks, women, and the poor taken together form a majority of the American population. Perhaps the American public in recent years has come to believe that these groups suffer from externally imposed barriers to economic opportunity and therefore are not individually responsible for their economic status. To the extent that they have, we might expect diminished adherence to the beliefs that opportunity is widely available in American society and that individuals are responsible for their own economic fates.

We have argued (Chapter 2) that although many Americans hold beliefs about their personal inequality-related experiences or those of specific groups that provide reasons for potentially questioning dominant-ideology beliefs, they also have several reasons for maintaining belief in them. This argument implies that there should be only weak relationships between and among beliefs about personal inequality-related experience, the experiences of one's own or other groups, and adherence to dominant-ideology beliefs. In each of the three chapters we will examine evidence concerning these relationships.

GROUP DIFFERENCES

Finally, we present analyses of our data that concern the degree of consensus in Americans' beliefs about opportunity, about the causes of economic outcomes, and about the justice of economic inequality in general. While we expect to find that endorsement of dominant ideology beliefs is widespread, we do not propose that the American public is unanimous in its perspective on how the stratification order does and should work. As discussed in Chapter 2, there are circumstances when the factors operating to deflect challenges to dominant-ideology beliefs are absent, and denial or weakened adherence to dominant ideology beliefs results from unfavorable personal inequality-related experience or beliefs about the disadvantages suffered by one's own or other groups. On balance, however, the circumstances of most Americans' lives dispose people who hold beliefs that potentially challenge the dominant ideology to try to accommodate such challenge, rather than to deny the validity of the dominant ideology.

Thus we expect to find that a substantial minority of the American public denies or weakly adheres to dominant-ideology beliefs. Furthermore, we propose that larger proportions of the American population have one or more beliefs that potentially challenge aspects of the dominant ideology. We argued in Chapter 2 that these beliefs are more directly determined than those at the core of the dominant ideology by individual self-interest, actual stratification-related experience, group-based affect, basic social–psychological processes, level of education, and other sources of information about the experiences of one's own or other groups.

If substantial minorities of Americans deny or weakly adhere to dominant ideology beliefs and hold potentially challenging beliefs, then consensus in the sense of unanimity of belief is, of course, lacking. However, another aspect of consensus becomes an important concern: To what degree is dissensus of belief structured by major group divisions in American society?

If disagreements about how the American stratification system does and should work are structured by major group divisions, the potential for group-based action involving issues of economic inequality is present. At one extreme, if there were large differences in beliefs on the average between groups and homogeneity of belief within groups, then the potential for group-based action is most strongly present. At the

other extreme (assuming some dissensus), if there were only small differences in beliefs between groups and marked heterogeneity within
groups, then the potential for group-based conflict is weakest. The latter
case involves what is often termed *cross-cutting cleavages*, factors that
divide people who otherwise may share the same group membership,
and thereby weaken the potential for concerted group effort. To assess
the extent to which dissensus of belief is structured by major group
divisions, in Chapters 3, 4, and 5 we analyze the effects of socioeconomic status (indexed by family income and education), region of the
country, religious affiliation, age, race, and sex on beliefs about how
the American stratification system does and should work.

These factors might form potential bases for divisions among groups
in their adherence to dominant-ideology beliefs for many reasons,
which there is no need to review here. There are also, of course, potential bases for group divisions other than these. In Chapter 9 we will
look at some such additional potential bases of group division in connection with our analysis of the political significance of dominant-ideology beliefs.

In this section we give special attention to race and sex differences
in beliefs about inequality. Because blacks and women experience the
problems of poverty and barriers to equal opportunity much more often
than white males, differences between these groups and others and
the homogeneity of beliefs about economic inequality within these
groups take on special significance. These differences indicate the potential for concerted and effective group action by blacks and women
toward ameliorating poverty and unequal opportunity. In Chapters 3,
4, and 5 we will examine black–white and male–female differences in
beliefs about how the stratification order does and should work.

In each of these three chapters we will also examine regressions of
dominant-ideology beliefs on age, sex, race, socioeconomic status, region, and religious groups. Given the overlap in membership among
these groups, if we were to analyze bivariate differences only, we would
be at risk of spuriously attributing an observed difference to a given
factor (e.g., race) when it may simply reflect the association between
this factor and another determinant of beliefs (e.g., socioeconomic status).

We conducted these regressions using data from all representative
sample respondents to the beliefs about social stratification survey and
in separate subsamples of white men, white women, and blacks from
this study. The separate analyses within subsamples speak to the issue
of the homogeneity/heterogeneity of beliefs within subgroups. Although in Chapters 3–5 we report regression results for the analyses
conducted in the representative sample only, we will discuss the results

of the analyses conducted within the separate subsamples in the text of these chapters and comment on the similarities and differences of effects between subgroups as appropriate. In each chapter we will present summary comparisons of percentage distributions of adherence to dominant ideology and other beliefs that show the amount of consensus or dissensus of belief within and among groups.

3

OPPORTUNITY

That America offers its citizens abundant opportunity for economic advancement has long been part of the set of beliefs that define Americans' national identity. Certain events of the last two decades, however, have offered potential challenges to the prevalent sense of plentiful opportunity. The civil rights movement and subsequently the women's movement brought discrimination to public attention, with the message that opportunity for minorities and women may be limited systematically. Although the rapid growth in average standards of living during the 1960s may have encouraged the belief that opportunity is plentiful, the rapid inflation and high unemployment of the 1970s may have raised doubt about it. Have these events diminished the traditional American optimism about the chances for the average person to get ahead? To answer this and other questions we asked our survey respondents questions concerning several aspects of opportunity in America.

DISTRIBUTIONS AND TIME TRENDS IN PERCEIVED OPPORTUNITY

Summary Assessments

Table 3.1 arrays the questions and the distribution of responses concerning three aspects of the availability of opportunity in America in general. Research on questionnaire construction (Schuman and Presser, 1981) testifies to the potential for some biasing of response due to question wording. The use of multiple, differently worded questions provides some safeguard against this possibility. The distributions of responses to each question agree in supporting the general conclusion that Americans on the whole see opportunity for economic advancement as plentiful.

A question concerning general opportunity was asked in identical form in the 1952 National Election Survey and in a 1966 survey of Muskegon, Michigan (Huber & Form, 1973). Judged by the percentage who endorse the statement that "there's plenty of opportunity, and anyone

TABLE 3.1. Summary Assessments of the Availability of Opportunity in
        America

How good a chance do you think a person has to get ahead today, if the
    person works hard?

	Percentage	(f)
A very good chance	25	(371)
A good chance	38	(574)
Some chance	26	(387)
Little chance	9	(130)
No chance at all	2	(33)

Do you think most Americans have a fair opportunity to make the most of
    themselves in life, or does something usually hold them back?

	Percentage	(f)
Fair opportunity	70	(1030)
Held back	30	(453)

America is the land of opportunity where everyone who works hard can get
    ahead

	Percentage	(f)
Strongly agree	14	(90)
Agree	56	(368)
Disagree	27	(175)
Strongly disagree	4	(25)

Some people say that there's not much opportunity in America today—that
    the average man doesn't have much chance to really get ahead. Others
    say there's plenty of opportunity, and anyone who works hard can go as
    far as he wants. How do you feel?

	1952[a]		1966[b]	
	Percentage	(N)[c]	Percentage	(N)
Plenty of opportunity	88	(1730)	78	(342)

[a]Source: 1952 National Election Survey.
[b]Source: Huber and Form (1973); see text.
[c]Total sample size.

who works hard can go as far as he wants," there is some indication
that from 1952 to 1966 the strength of belief in the prevalence of opportunity did decline. In 1952 roughly 88% of the American population
agreed with this statement. If we assume that the Muskegon sample
closely reflects national opinion in 1966, then we would conclude that
there was approximately a 10% decline in endorsement of this statement
between 1952 and 1966.

Respondents in our survey were asked a question that closely parallels that asked in 1952 and 1966 (see Table 3.1), in its incorporation
of the statement that "everyone who works hard can get ahead." Judged
by the percentage who agree with this statement, approximately 70%,

the strength of belief in the prevalence of opportunity in general has continued to decline.

Routes to Economic Advancement

As is evident from the great amount of attention paid to it, education as a route to economic advancement has great significance for the American public (Berg, 1970; Jencks, 1972, 1979; Collins, 1979). The percentage distributions of responses to questions concerning the efficacy of various routes to upward mobility, given in Table 3.2, show that Americans do attach special significance to education as a route to economic advancement. By a substantial margin our respondents see getting more education as the most effective means to economic advancement.

In recent years there have been some indications that Americans' unquestioning faith in the value of higher education, both as a route to economic gain and as a means to other ends, has declined. The phenomena of "overeducation"—an assumed decline in the labor market value of a college education, in part due to steadily increasing proportions of people in younger age cohorts who earn a college degree—has received much scholarly (Blumberg and Murtha, 1977; Burris, 1983; Freeman, 1976; Rumberger, 1981) and media attention. A more skeptical outlook on education seems to prevail today as the certainty of obtaining a high-paying job with increased levels of education has diminished.

To gauge the extent of skepticism about education as a route to advancement, we asked a series of questions. These questions and the percentage distributions for the responses to them are also given in Table 3.2. The results in this table confirm that skepticism is widespread. While, on the average, most Americans (71%) believe that people with a college education will earn substantially more money than those without one, a majority of the American public: (1) perceive that the value of a college education had declined; (2) do not agree that every young person in America has an equal opportunity to get a college education; and (3) do not agree that generally speaking a person with a college education will lead a fuller life than a person without it.

Personal Opportunity

While Americans assess favorably the opportunity for advancement in our society in general, they view their personal opportunity even more positively. Roughly 90% of the survey respondents judged their own opportunity as equal to or better than that for the average American

TABLE 3.2. Perceived Efficacy of Routes of Economic Opportunity and Beliefs
         about Educational Opportunity

Routes
  There are a number of different things a person can do to try to get
  ahead. How much chance does the average person who is willing to
  work hard have to get ahead by . . .

	A very good chance	Just some chance	Little chance	No chance at all	(N)
Getting more education	62%	35	3	0	(1496)
Starting their own business	29	51	19	2	(1468)
Seeking promotions in their present line of work	43	48	7	1	(1404)
Joining a union or other association to improve the situation of workers like themselves	32	46	17	6	(1411)

Educational opportunity

	Strongly agree	Agree	Disagree	Strongly disagree	(N)
Generally speaking, a person with a college education will earn a lot more money than a person without one	21	50	26	3	(1492)
Generally speaking, a person with a college degree will lead a fuller life than a person without one	11	39	46	5	(1476)
With more and more people going to college, the value of a college education is declining	7	53	36	4	(1458)
Every young person in America today has an equal opportunity to get a college education	7	38	46	9	(1494)

(Table 3.3). The extent of personal optimism about chances to get ahead
is demonstrated most forcefully in the pattern of joint responses to
questions concerning opportunity in society in general and personal
opportunity (Table 3.5). Of the American public, 56% see their personal
opportunity as equal to or better than opportunity that is judged as
very good or good for Americans in general—a very optimistic assess-

TABLE 3.3. Beliefs about Personal Opportunity

Compared to the average person in America, do you think the chance of getting ahead for . . . you yourself is?

	Percentage	(f)
Much better than average	5	(76)
Better than average	33	(478)
Average	54	(789)
Worse than average	7	(106)
Much worse than average	2	(24)

Do you think you have had a fair opportunity to make the most of yourself in life or has anything ever held you back?[a]

	1972		1980	
	Percentage	(f)	Percentage	(f)
Fair	73	(1934)	72	(1079)
Held back	27	(723)	28	(425)

In general, compared to your parents at the time you were growing up, do you think that the standard of living you now have is . . .

	Percentage	(f)
Much better than your parents	49	(735)
Somewhat better	30	(443)
About the same	14	(207)
Worse	6	(92)
Much worse	2	(25)

Since your first full-time job have you (did you) . . .[b]

	Percentage	(f)
Advanced (advance) rapidly in rank and status	10	(142)
Made (make) steady advances	60	(840)
Stayed (stay) at about the same	25	(356)
Lost (lose) some ground	4	(61)

Thinking about your future work career, do you expect that over the next 5–10 years you will . . .[b,c]

	Percentage	(f)
Advance rapidly	31	(280)
Make steady advances in rank and status	52	(481)
Stay at about the same level	13	(121)
Lose some ground	4	(36)

	Expected future advancement				
Past advancement	Rapid	Steady	Same	Lose	(N)
Rapid	32	50	18	1	(101)
Steady	10	57	30	3	(586)
Stayed the same	11	41	39	9	(186)
Lost ground	18	46	28	8	(39)

[a]The 1972 question is worded as follows: "Do you think you have had a fair opportunity to make the most of yourself in life or have you been held back in some ways?"
[b]Asked only of respondents currently employed in the labor force.
[c]Excludes persons who respond that they plan to retire.

ment indeed. An additional question on personal opportunity in retrospect also shows the favorable light in which the public sees personal
opportunity. Of our respondents, 72% see themselves as having had
a fair opportunity to make the most of themselves in their lives. Together the responses to these two questions suggest that most Americans believe that nothing has in the past or will in the future prevent
them personally from getting ahead. A question asked in the 1972 National Election Survey closely parallels one question concerning personal opportunity asked in our survey. A comparison of these two
questions shows that there has been virtually no change over this 8–
year period in the percentage who perceive that they have not had a
fair opportunity to make the most of themselves.

Americans also see themselves as a nation of upwardly mobile people, both intergenerationally, in comparison to their parents, and in-
tragenerationally, in terms of their work careers. Responses to a question concerning perceived improvement in one's standard of living
relative to one's parents, given in Table 3.3, indicate that roughly one-
half of the American public evaluates their current standard of living
as much better than their parents', and another 30% see it as better.
To assess public perceptions of career mobility we asked two questions:
concerning perceptions of the rate of advancement in one's work career
since the first fulltime job, and expectations for one's future career.
Individually and jointly the responses to these questions indicate that
American workers in general see their careers as characterized by steady
advancement. Judged by the cross-tabulation of responses to these two
questions (Table 3.3) few people (approximately 12%) perceive that they
have had or will have work careers that do not involve some upward
mobility.

Equal Opportunity

Issues involving equality of opportunity for various groups in American society have, of course, been the subject of much public attention
during the last three decades. Survey respondents were asked to rate
the chance to get ahead compared to the average person in America
for several different socioeconomic groups—the rich, the poor, the
working class, blacks, and women. The percentage distributions for
these ratings are given in Table 3.4.

First, the American public has little illusion that the rich share the
same opportunity for economic advancement as the rest of society.
Eighty-three percent of the public believe that the children of the rich
have a much better or better chance to get ahead than the average
person. Second, while social scientists may speak of middle-class biases
in the schools (Sennett and Cobb, 1972; Bowles and Gintis, 1976) and

TABLE 3.4. Perceived Equality of Opportunity for Rich, Poor, Working Class, Blacks, and Women

Compared to the average person in America, do you think the chance of getting ahead for . . .

	Much better	Better	Average	Much worse	Worse	*(N)*
People who grew up in rich families	35	48	14	3	0	(1468)
People who grew up in poor families	2	17	47	29	5	(1476)
People who grew up in working-class families	3	20	69	8	0	(1480)
Blacks	6	22	45	25	3	(1466)
A woman working full-time compared to a man at the same job	2	12	46	37	2	(1488)

other class-biased barriers to opportunity that diminish chances for the working class to attain high socioeconomic status, the American public seems to express little belief in the presence of such barriers. Most survey respondents rate opportunity for children of working-class parents as equal to that for the average person. Only 8% rate opportunity for this group as worse than average, and approximately three times as many people rate opportunity for the working class as better than average. Third, although there has been much discussion of barriers to equal opportunity for the poor, blacks, and women, most Americans perceive that these groups have opportunity that is equal to or better than the average.

Age-Group Comparisons

Conclusions about change based on age-group comparisons rest on the assumption of significant stability of beliefs over the life cycle. Put another way, a danger faced with the analysis of age-group differences is confusing permanent change with a pattern of life cycle differences that may be repeated anew with succeeding generations. There are clear reasons to expect lifestage differences in beliefs about personal opportunity. It seems reasonable to expect that optimism about one's personal opportunity declines as people age, as they acquire job experience, and especially as they approach retirement age. Expectations concerning life stage differences in beliefs about the prevalence of opportunity in American society are less clear. On the one hand, to the extent that generalization from personal experience affects one's belief in the prevalence of opportunity in general, we might expect people to see it as less prevalent as they get older, since optimism about per-

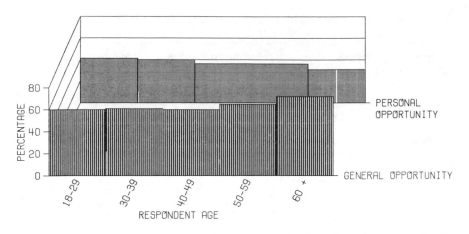

FIGURE 3.1. Beliefs about aspects of opportunity, broken down by respondent's age.

sonal opportunity declines. On the other hand, the proposition that aging leads to more conservative beliefs leads to an expected increase in the perceived prevalence of opportunity in general as people age.

Figures 3.1, 3.2, and 3.3 graph the statistically significant age-group differences in opportunity beliefs. An examination of these figures leads us to offer three main conclusions. First, age-group differences in beliefs about general opportunity, the efficacy of education as a route to advancement, and personal opportunity are consistent with the differences demonstrated in over-time comparisons. Younger people see

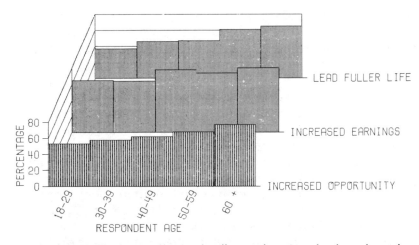

FIGURE 3.2. Beliefs about effects of college education, broken down by respondent's age.

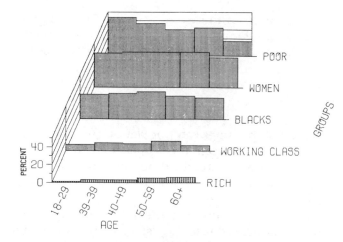

FIGURE 3.3. Percentage perceiving below-average opportunity for members of different groups, broken down by respondent's age.

opportunity in general as less prevalent than older people. Younger people are also, on the whole, less optimistic about the chances for the average person to get ahead by obtaining more education. Both of these findings are consistent with the hypothesis of a declining belief in the prevalence of opportunity. As in the comparison of 1972 to 1980 data, age-group comparisons show no significant differences in the perception of being held back from making the most of oneself in life. There are small differences in the perception of personal opportunity relative to the average, and they are in accord with a life cycle explanation of declining optimism with increasing age.

Second, younger age-groups show substantially more skepticism about the value of higher education than do older ones. The contrasts between the oldest and youngest age-groups in their responses to questions concerning the value of education as a route to economic advancement and its life-enhancing value in general are marked. Younger respondents also are more skeptical about the monetary value of a college education than older ones. Whereas a clear majority of the oldest age-group agrees with the statement that education allows one to lead a fuller life, the youngest age-group *disagrees* with it by the same majority percentage.

Third, the only statistically significant differences among age-groups in beliefs about equality of opportunity for different groups involve the rich and the poor. We will examine aspects of change and stability in beliefs about opportunity for blacks and women more extensively in Chapters 7 and 8; but these initial findings show no age-group differences concerning perceived equality of opportunity for these two groups and for children of the working class. The young more than the old rate opportunity for the children of the rich as better than average and rate opportunity for the children of the poor as worse than average.

Summary

A clear majority of the American population subscribes, largely unreservedly, to the characterization of America as the "land of opportunity." Adherence is widespread to the initial premise of the "logic of opportunity" syllogism that opportunity for economic advancement is widely available.

On the one hand, Americans do express some doubts about equality of opportunity. Although education is seen as the principal means to economic advancement, the majority of Americans do not believe that everyone has an equal chance to obtain a higher education. The American public is in virtual agreement that the rich are better off than the rest of society. Significant minorities of the public doubt that the poor, blacks, and women have equal opportunity for two reasons. Some believe that these groups have better than average opportunity, and others perceive opportunity for these groups to be worse than average.

On the other hand, Americans express little doubt about their chances as individuals to make economic advancement. On the whole they believe that no limits have or will impede their opportunity to make the most of themselves. The American public expects to have work careers characterized by steady advancement. The average American considers him or herself "better than average" in terms of his or her prospects to get ahead.

Although the majority of Americans continue to see opportunity for economic advancement as widespread, data available for over-time comparisons imply that the strength of this belief among the American public has significantly lessened during the last three decades. Despite this decline, there is no evidence for a lessening of the American public's optimism about their personal opportunity for economic advancement. Minorities of our sample respondents perceive that they have experienced blocked opportunity and rate their personal opportunity as worse than the average, but there is no indication in our data that the percentages of Americans in these minority categories are increasing in keeping with a declining belief in the prevalence of opportunity in America in general.

These findings concerning changing about opportunity provide some basis for speculation about the sources of the decline in perceived prevalence of opportunity. In part it may be attributed to the decline in the perceived efficacy of higher education as a route to economic advancement. Also, in part it may reflect a seeming increase in perceived inequality of opportunity involving the chances for economic advancement of the rich and the poor. Some evidence concerning these speculations is offered in the following section, which examines the degree to which certain beliefs about opportunity affect the assessment of the prevalence of opportunity in America.

POTENTIAL CHALLENGES TO THE PERCEIVED PREVALENCE OF OPPORTUNITY

The American public on the whole believes in the widespread availability of opportunity for economic advancement. However, we have seen that sizable minorities of Americans hold beliefs that on face value seem to challenge substantially the claim that opportunity is widespread. For example, approximately 40% of respondents perceive that opportunity for women workers is worse than that for men. Since women comprise more than one-half of the population, recognition of restricted opportunity for this group would seem to offer a significant challenge to the assertion that everyone in America has plentiful opportunity.

Viewed in their totality, the sum of the challenging beliefs we have examined would seem to imply more doubt about the prevalence of opportunity for economic advancement than we have found. For example, given that 55% of sample respondents believe that every young person in America does not have an equal opportunity to obtain a college education, and that 40% believe that women's opportunity is worse than men's, one might well expect most of the American public to disagree with the statement that "everyone who works hard can get ahead." But only 30% in fact do disagree. Clearly something acts to weaken the potential challenge to the perceived prevalence of opportunity in general presented by certain beliefs.

In Chapter 2 we discussed several forces that may mute the effect of potentially challenging beliefs on dominant ideology beliefs. Special emphasis was given to the roles played by beliefs about personal opportunity experiences and by the tendency to treat challenges as exceptions—especially those challenges stemming from perceived disadvantages suffered by other groups. We now examine the impact of beliefs about personal opportunity and of the tendency to view potential challenges as exceptional by exploring the relationships among beliefs about opportunity.

Personal and General Opportunity

The opportunity experience for many Americans, as we noted in Chapter 2, has been favorable during the last three decades. The recent history of actual improvements in the average standard of living and prevalent upward occupational mobility is reflected in our respondents' subjective assessments of improvement in their standard of living relative to their parents and in their perceptions of career mobility. It is not surprising, then, that most Americans perceive that they have had a fair chance to make the most of themselves in life and are very optimistic about their current and future personal chance to get ahead.

Table 3.5 gives cross-tabulations of two measures of perceived personal opportunity with the perceived prevalence of opportunity. The association between favorably perceived personal opportunity and perceived prevalence of opportunity for the average person in American society is quite strong. Of those who perceive their personal opportunity as much better than average, 92% rate opportunity for the average American as very good or good. In contrast, only 41% of those who view their own opportunity as worse than average rate opportunity for the average person so positively.

On first inspection the association between the perception of being held back and perceived general opportunity appears to be weaker than that between respondents' current rating of their opportunity and opportunity in general. However, there is a strong relationship if one considers what specific factors are perceived to have blocked opportunity. Table 3.6 gives the cross-tabulation of categories of the main reason given for being held back with perceived general opportunity.[1] We will focus more extensively on popular explanations of economic success and failure in Chapter 4. Here, however, two general points are in order. First, only a minority who see themselves as having been held back attribute it to unambiguously supraindividual, or structural, causes—race, sex, and job market factors. Second, when the attribution is made to these causes the correspondence between perceiving

---

[1]Respondents who replied that something had held them back to the question concerning having had a fair chance to make the most of oneself (Table 3.3) were asked "What is the one main thing that held you back?" Their responses to these questions were recorded verbatim. Our examination of these responses led us to construct nine categories of reasons in which we readily could place nearly all of the responses. For a variety of considerations, however, we readily could not place about 6% of the respondents' answers (the "other" category). The criteria defining these nine categories are on the whole evident in the labels for them. However, a few words to clarify the meaning of some of the categories are in order. "Motivation" includes responses claiming that personal values, personality traits, lack of desire, and so on held one back. "Marital status" refers to reasons citing aspects of one's marriage, such as the need to move to or otherwise accommodate spouses' employment, and to factors associated with child care. "Job market" includes perceived reasons for being held back, such as an oversupply of workers in a particular occupation, aggregate conditions of the American economy, etc. "Family background" refers to reasons citing the socioeconomic status or other such characteristics of ones parents.

TABLE 3.5. Cross-Tabulations of Perceived Availability of Opportunity in General with Aspects of Perceived Personal Opportunity

	General opportunity				
Opportunity	Very good	Good	Some	Little or none	(N)
Personal[a] (contemporary and future)					
Much better	57%	36	8	0	(76)
Better	30	42	22	6	(476)
Average	21	38	30	12	(783)
Worse	13	28	31	28	(129)
Retrospective[b]					
Fair	27	40	25	8	(1075)
Held back	18	35	28	18	(419)

[a]$\chi^2 = 128.5; p < .01.$
[b]$\chi^2 = 38.6; p < .01.$

blocked personal opportunity and limited opportunity in society in general is stronger than when attributions are made involving more limited or personal causes. For example, whereas 57% of those who give market factors as the main reason for being held back respond that there is "some," "little," or "no" chance for the average person to get ahead, only 37% of those who cite marital status as the main reason for their lack of success give such responses.

The association between beliefs about personal opportunity and opportunity in general cannot be completely attributed to generalization from perceived personal opportunity. In part, beliefs about personal opportunity may be shaped by the perceived general availability of op-

TABLE 3.6. Cross-Tabulations of Perceived Availability of Opportunity with the Main Reason for Being Held Back[a]

	General opportunity				Category	
Reason	Very good	Good	Some	Little or none	Percent	(N)
Lack of education	21%	46	18	16	19	(7)
Race	19	6	25	50	8	(32)
Sex	10	35	40	15	5	(22)
Income	20	25	41	14	12	(49)
Motivation	32	36	20	12	6	(25)
Marital status	14	49	22	15	21	(87)
Illness	21	36	31	2	10	(42)
Family background	22	22	44	11	2	(9)
Job market	13	30	36	21	11	(47)
Other	17	35	30	17	6	(24)

[a]$\chi^2 = 54.0; p < .01.$

portunity in society. On the other hand—if only because personal experience is much more salient than acquired beliefs about something as large and abstract as American society—it is implausible that a person will form beliefs about personal opportunity strictly on the basis of beliefs about opportunity in general acquired from common sources of socialization such as mass formal education, the media, or religion. Nor is it plausible that many people completely discount personal opportunity experience in forming a belief about the prevalence of opportunity in society in general. Indeed, given the greater salience of personal experience it seems reasonable to assume that the strongest causal influence is from beliefs about personal opportunity to the belief in the prevalence of opportunity in general.

Given the above assumption, our findings to this point argue that *the prevailing optimism about personal opportunity among the American public strongly limits the potential impact of challenges to the belief in widespread opportunity in American society.* The belief that one's own plentiful opportunity implies that opportunity is also plentiful for others limits potential challenges in two ways. First, claims that others in society experience limits to their opportunity are received with some skepticism by most Americans. Second, if claims of blocked opportunity are accepted, people who favorably assess their personal opportunity for economic advancement will tend to view the circumstances of others as exceptional. That is, they will tend to believe that American society presents themselves and similar others with a favorable chance for opportunity, even while presenting dissimilar others with less favorable opportunity.

Doubts about Education

Since the public traditionally has placed much faith in the role of formal education as a means to upward mobility, we well might expect that the doubts about its value discussed earlier in this chapter may lead Americans to question the assumed widespread prevalence of opportunity. Cross-tabulations of beliefs about the role of education as a means to economic advancement and the perceived prevalence of opportunity are presented in Table 3.7. There are statistically significant tendencies not only for people who doubt the efficacy of education as a route to getting ahead but also for those who perceive inequality of educational opportunity to have a less favorable assessment of opportunity in general. Again, we cannot ascribe the association between these measures totally to the effect of beliefs about education as a route to upward mobility on the assessment of the general availability of opportunity. Some people may infer that the opportunity to advance by means of acquiring more education is widely available from their belief that opportunity in general is plentiful. However, as in the case of per-

TABLE 3.7. Cross-Tabulations of Perceived Availability of Opportunity with Beliefs about Educational Opportunity

	General opportunity				
	Very good	Good	Some	Little or none	(N)
Efficacy of Education[a]					
Very good chance	32	41	19	8	(927)
Some chance	14	34	39	13	(513)
Little or no change	6	25	27	42	(48)
Equality of Educational Opportunity[b]					
Strongly agree	35	41	16	9	(101)
Agree	26	42	23	10	(564)
Disagree	24	37	28	11	(681)
Strongly disagree	18	29	38	15	(137)

[a]$\chi^2 = 157.5$; $p < .01$.
[b]$\chi^2 = 30.2$; $p < .01$.

sonal opportunity it seems reasonable to assume that beliefs about education have some basis in experience, and that people generalize from their experience in forming beliefs about society. Indeed, it is increasingly the case that we are becoming a nation of people with some college education. Ironically, it seems that an increase in the percentage of Americans realizing one aspect of the American dream—getting a college education—has resulted in a decrease in Americans' faith in another key aspect of it, that the opportunity to get ahead is prevalent for the average person.

Equality of Opportunity

During the last three decades social scientists, and more visibly, representatives of the civil rights and women's movements have asserted that opportunity for economic advancement is systematically limited for several groups—the poor, blacks, women, and the working class— that together make up roughly 80% of the American population. Even if we do not consider the working class (because as we have seen, few Americans perceive unequal opportunity for this group) claims of limited opportunity have been made concerning approximately two-thirds of the American public. In either case, the potential challenge posed by these assertions to the belief in plentiful opportunity for all Americans seems to be substantial on numerical grounds alone.

Table 3.8 gives the cross-tabulations of perceived equality of opportunity for each group individually with the assessment of the general availability of opportunity in American society. In general people who perceive that a given group has worse than average opportunity assess overall opportunity less optimistically than do those who believe that this group has average or better opportunity. However, the cross-tab-

TABLE 3.8. Cross-Tabulations of Perceived General Availabililty of
Opportunity with Perceived Equality of Opportunity for Rich,
Poor, Working Class, Blacks, and Women

	General opportunity				
	Very good	Good	Some	Little or none	(N)
Rich[a]					
Better than average	24	38	27	11	(1210)
Average	29	39	22	10	(204)
Worse than average	41	39	13	7	(44)
Poor[b]					
Better than average	36	40	17	8	(281)
Average	26	40	27	8	(692)
Worse than average	17	36	31	17	(495)
Working class[c]					
Better than average	34	42	16	8	(334)
Average	23	38	28	11	(1022)
Worse than average	19	32	33	16	(117)
Blacks[d]					
Better than average	30	36	23	11	(398)
Average	25	41	25	10	(651)
Worse than average	20	37	36	11	(409)
Women[e]					
Better than average	34	35	24	8	(212)
Average	24	41	24	11	(672)
Worse than average	22	36	30	11	(566)

[a]$\chi^2 = 13.6$; $p < .05$.
[b]$\chi^2 = 65.2$; $p < .01$.
[c]$\chi^2 = 42.8$; $p < .01$.
[d]$\chi^2 = 16.2$; $p < .05$.
[e]$\chi^2 = 18.7$; $p < .01$.

ulations in Table 3.8 also show that perceptions of unequal opportunity
offer only a limited challenge to the belief in widely prevalent opportunity. In each case, the majority of those who perceive worse than
average opportunity for specific groups rate opportunity for the average
American as very good or good. When viewed independently, of
course, one might expect the challenge of perceiving unequal opportunity for different groups to be limited. With the exception of women,
no single one of these groups constitutes a majority of the population.[2]
A much greater challenge might be expected from perceptions of limited opportunity for combinations of groups.

[2]The percentage of the population that may be placed in the working class
may differ according to one's criteria for "objective" class placement. We are
concerned here with the perceived size of the working class (i.e., with "subjective" class placement). Research on the criteria Americans use for determining someone's class membership (Jackman & Jackman, 1983) suggests that
the public on average perceives that the working class comprises less than a
majority of the population.

Because it is not possible to examine the effect of combinations of perceptions of opportunity for these five groups in their full detail, we employ two simplifications. First, because perceptions of equal opportunity for the rich and unequal opportunity for the working class are so rare we consider only combinations involving blacks, women, and the poor. Second, we categorize perceptions of equal opportunity as either (1) equal or better than average, or (2) worse than average. These simplifications produce an eight-category variable of combined perceptions involving equality of opportunity for blacks, women, and the poor. The cross-tabulation of this variable with the assessment of opportunity in general is given in Table 3.9.

There are three major observations that may be drawn from this table. The first is that there is no simple pattern of an all or nothing split in the perception of limited opportunity for different groups. Respondents who perceive average or better than average opportunity for all three groups constitute the largest single group (37%), but the percentage who perceive that all three groups have worse than average opportunity is much smaller (10%). In contrast, people who perceive that only one of the three groups has worse than average opportunity (33%) outnumber those seeing all three groups in these terms by a ratio of roughly three to one. And, those people who perceive that women have worse than average opportunity, but the poor and blacks do not, constitute the second most prevalent combination (17%).

Second, the challenge to perceiving widely available opportunity posed by certain of these combinations differs from that expected on the basis of the proportion of the population that is composed of the involved groups. On the one hand, the challenge of seeing women as the only group experiencing worse than average opportunity is weaker than expected. In fact, there is essentially no difference between this group and those who perceive that all three groups have average or better than average opportunity. On the other hand, the challenge of

TABLE 3.9. Cross-Tabulation of Combined Beliefs about Equality of Opportunity for Blacks, Women, and the Poor with Perceived General Availability of Opportunity

Combination	Percentage	(f)	General opportunity (percentage very good or good)
All three worse than average	10	(142)	50
Blacks and women only	6	(85)	57
Blacks and poor only	6	(91)	59
Women and poor only	7	(97)	46
Blacks only	6	(84)	66
Poor only	11	(153)	56
Women only	17	(234)	69
None	37	(525)	70

perceiving the poor alone as having limited opportunity is stronger than expected strictly on the basis of the proportion of the population composed of the poor.

The weak challenge of perceiving that blacks alone or women alone have worse than average opportunity may result from the ease with which unequal opportunity in these cases may be attributed to the actions of racially prejudiced or sexist individuals, rather than to supraindividual or structural factors that may limit opportunity in general. It is more difficult for Americans to attribute worse than average opportunity for poor children to individualistic causes that parallel racial prejudice or sexist attitudes than to attribute race and sex differences to these sources. Stated another way, the perception that the poor alone have limited opportunity implies stronger structural limitation of opportunity than for either blacks or women alone.

Finally, even in the cases offering the strongest seeming challenge, belief in the prevalence of opportunity in general persists. Even among those who perceive that all three groups have worse than average opportunity about one-half characterize opportunity for the average American as very good or good.

Perceived Personal Opportunity and the Limitation of Challenge

As a final aspect of our analysis of beliefs about opportunity that potentially challenge adherence to a belief in the widespread availability of opportunity in America, we examine the joint (combined) effects of perceived personal opportunity with the perceived value of education and with perceived inequality of opportunity on the general assessment of opportunity. These analyses provide information about the degree to which the prevailing optimism about personal opportunity lessens the impact of potentially challenging beliefs.

To simplify the presentation of results we (1) employ only one measure of perceived personal opportunity—the perception of being held back or having a fair chance to make the most of oneself; (2) employ one measure of the value of education—the perceived efficacy of education as a route to economic advancement; and (3) use collapsed categories of combined beliefs about inequality of opportunity.[3] Table 3.10 presents the relevant three-way cross-tabulations involving per-

[3]The categories are formed as follows: (1) "all women and poor" includes people who perceive that the poor, women, and blacks all have worse than average opportunity to get ahead, and people who believe that women and the poor only lack equality of opportunity; (2) "blacks and poor, or women and poor" includes those who indicate they believe that both groups in either of these two combinations of two groups have worse than average opportunity to get ahead; (3) "blacks and women alone" includes people who believe that either one of the groups of blacks or women (but not the other or different groups) lacks equal opportunity; and (4) "none" is as defined in Table 3.9.

TABLE 3.10. Cross-Tabulations of Perceived General Opportunity by the Perceived Efficacy of Education and by Combined Categories of Perceived Equality of Opportunity Within Categories of Held Back

	General opportunity									
	Held back					Fair				
	Very good	Good	Some	Little or none	(N)	Very good	Good	Some	Little or none	(N)
Efficacy of education										
Very good	26	40	23	12	(239)	34	42	17	7	(687)
Some to none	9	29	37	26	(175)	16	36	39	10	(386)
	(χ^2 = 37.9; p < .01)					(χ^2 = 81.6; p < .01)				
Equality of opportunity combinations										
All, women, and poor	7	26	43	25	(77)	20	36	34	10	(160)
Blacks and poor, or women and poor	14	25	36	24	(91)	23	41	25	11	(236)
Blacks or women alone	24	43	24	10	(89)	31	37	24	8	(227)
None	27	41	20	13	(128)	30	42	23	6	(393)
	(χ^2 = 40.5; p < .01)					(χ^2 = 19.2; p < .05)				

ceived personal opportunity, the perceived value of education, combined beliefs about inequality of opportunity, and the assessment of the prevalence of opportunity in general.

Results given in this table show that the prevalent optimism about personal opportunity does lessen the potential challenge of doubts about the value of education as a means to upward mobility and of perceived inequality of opportunity. Among people who do not rate the chances for the average American to get ahead through education as very good and who perceive that they have been held back, only 37% rate opportunity for the average American as very good or good. For people who share the same belief about the value of education, but who see themselves as having had a fair chance to make the most of themselves, the equivalent of very good and good ratings is 52%.

Results given in this table also show that optimism about personal opportunity lessens the potential challenge of perceiving that blacks, women, and the poor experience unequal opportunity. Interestingly, the data show an interaction effect of perceived personal opportunity with beliefs about equal opportunity on the perceived general availability of opportunity. Beliefs about opportunity for specific groups have a larger impact on general opportunity perceptions for respondents who report that they have been held back than for those who report they have had a fair chance to make the most of themselves.

People who believe that they have had a fair chance to achieve do not react strongly to restrictions on the opportunity for other groups, because they do not perceive that the same forces shape their opportunity and that for other groups. However, for those who perceive that they have been held back, perceived restrictions on the opportunity for other groups seem to carry a quite different message. Such individuals may conclude that they and others like them are affected by the same forces that govern the opportunity for groups different from themselves. They tend to see the circumstances of other groups as less exceptional than their own, in comparison to people who assess their own opportunity experience favorably and perceive that inequality of opportunity exists.

GROUP DIFFERENCES IN PERCEIVED OPPORTUNITY

Race and Sex Mean Comparisons

Women and blacks on the average are less economically privileged than white men in several respects. Blacks, and increasingly so, women (especially women who are the sole earner for a family) disproportionately make up the population of poor people in America. The average earnings for blacks and women full-time workers are substantially

TABLE 3.11. Means and Standard Deviations (in Parentheses) for Beliefs about Opportunity by Race and Sex

Item	Whites	Blacks	Men	Women
Prevalence of opportunity	3.80	3.51*	3.87	3.65*
	(.96)	(1.06)	(.98)	(1.00)
Efficacy of education	3.59	3.59	3.62	3.56
	(.55)	(.59)	(.55)	(.56)
Equality of educational	2.43	2.52*	2.42	2.43
opportunity	(.75)	(.79)	(.77)	(.74)
Personal opportunity	3.36	3.13*	3.42	3.24*
	(.73)	(.80)	(.76)	(.73)
Held back	.26	.50*	.25	.31*
	(.43)	(.50)	(.44)	(.46)
Equal opportunity				
Rich	4.12	4.33*	4.15	4.14
	(.79)	(.76)	(.82)	(.80)
Poor	2.85	2.79	2.83	2.84
	(.83)	(.94)	(.85)	(.83)
Working class	3.16	3.29*	3.17	3.17
	(.61)	(.69)	(.63)	(.59)
Blacks	3.05	2.85*	3.00	3.05
	(.89)	(.92)	(.94)	(.87)
Women	2.89	2.75*	2.80	2.73
	(.77)	(.80)	(.80)	(.76)
(N)	(1374)	(535)	(678)	(829)

* = $p < .05$.

lower than that of white males. Blacks and women workers are disproportionately found in low-paying and low-prestige jobs relative to white men.[4] Judged on the basis of objective inequality, race and gender would seem to be especially important potential bases for group divisions in beliefs about opportunity.

Table 3.11 gives means (and standard deviations) for beliefs about aspects of opportunity in general, personal opportunity, and equality of opportunity by race and by sex and the results of t tests for the statistical significance of differences between these means. These comparisons show some similarity between blacks and women in their

[4]Since 1970 roughly about 33% of blacks and about 10% of whites on average had incomes below the poverty level. In 1981 approximately 35% of all families with a female householder and no husband present had incomes below the poverty level, and these families made up about 49% of all poor families. In 1982 women full-time workers had average weekly earnings equal to 60% of that received by men. In 1982 black full-time workers had average weekly earnings equal to roughly 78% of that received by whites (U. S. Bureau of the Census, 1983: Tables 777, 779, and 716).

beliefs about opportunity in general and personal opportunity. Blacks have a less favorable assessment of opportunity in general and of their personal opportunity than do whites, and women's beliefs about these aspects of opportunity differ from men in the same direction. In Chapters 7 and 8 we will explore race and sex differences in beliefs about equality of opportunity in detail. Comparisons of beliefs about equal opportunity shown here presage results of more detailed analyses that show that whereas blacks on the average see more inequality of opportunity than do whites, women do not differ from men in this regard.

Regression Results: General and Personal Opportunity

Partial regression coefficients for the effects of income, education, age, sex, race, and region on beliefs about opportunity estimated with data from the total representative survey are arrayed in Table 3.12. Since we have found no statistically significant effect of religious affiliation on beliefs about opportunity, we do not present the partial regression coefficients for categories of affiliation.

From Table 3.12 we see that beliefs in opportunity for the average American and for oneself personally both increase with increasing socioeconomic status. Age also has significant effects on the perceived prevalence of opportunity in general and the perceived effectiveness of education as a route to economic advancement. Since the tendency of younger people to believe that opportunity is less prevalent and to have a less optimistic assessment of the efficacy of education than older people persists when the effect of socioeconomic status—one major aspect of life cycle differences—is controlled, our earlier inference about trends concerning these beliefs is strengthened.

Sex-Specific Effects. The effects of education on beliefs about opportunity in general, on the efficacy of education, and on personal opportunity differ by sex.[5] Education significantly effects perceptions of general opportunity and the efficacy of education among white men but not among white women. Education has a stronger effect on perceived personal opportunity among women than it does among men.

Race-Specific Effects. There are similar effects of socioeconomic status among blacks and whites on beliefs about one's contemporary and future chances to get ahead. However, the perception of having been held back is determined differently in these two groups. For blacks

---

[5]Tests of the statistical significance of the difference between regression coefficients have been performed, but we omit their presentation to avoid burdening the reader with statistical detail. Throughout this book, it may be assumed that a referenced difference between two regression coefficients is statistically significant at the .05 level.

TABLE 3.12. Partial Regression Coefficients for the Effects of Income, Education, Age, Sex, Race, and Region on Beliefs about Opportunity (All Respondents, $N = 1507$)

	Opportunity in[a] general	Efficacy of education	Equality of educational opportunity	Personal opportunity	Held back
Age (10 years)	.06 (.10)*	.06 (.18)*	−.02 (−.05)	−.01 (−.03)	.00 (.00)
Income (log)	.11 (.09)*	.05 (.07)*	−.04 (−.04)	.15 (.15)*	−.06 (−.10)*
Education	.04 (.11)*	.05 (.03)	−.01 (−.05)	.06 (.21)*	−.02 (−.10)*
Race (1=white)	.30 (.10)*	.00 (.00)	.00 (.00)	.15 (.07)*	−.21 (−.16)*
Sex (1=male)	.17 (.09)*	.05 (.05)	.00 (.00)	.12 (.08)*	−.02 (−.03)
Midwest[b]	.09 (−.04)	.02 (.02)	−.03 (−.02)	−.01 (−.01)	.00 (.00)
South	−.01 (−.00)	.07 (.06)	−.03 (−.02)	−.00 (.00)	.01 (.01)
West	−.08 (−.03)	.04 (.03)	−.01 (−.01)	.08 (.04)	.02 (.02)
R^2	.06	.04	.01	.12	.06

	Rich	Poor	Working	Blacks	Women
Age (10 years)	−.05 (−.11)*	.10 (.20)*	.02 (.06)*	.01 (.02)	.00 (.00)
Income (log)	−.04 (−.04)	.03 (.02)	−.01 (−.01)	.01 (.01)	−.06 (−.06)*
Education	.12 (.04)	−.02 (−.08)*	−.02 (−.10)*	−.02 (−.07)*	−.02 (−.06)*
Race (1=white)	−.27 (−.11)*	.06 (.03)	−.04 (−.02)	.25 (.09)*	−.13 (−.05)*
Sex (1=male)	.00 (.00)	.00 (.00)	.15 (.01)	−.05 (−.03)	.10 (.06)*
Midwest	−.09 (−.05)	.02 (.01)	.00 (.00)	−.04 (−.02)	.03 (.02)
South	−.10 (−.06)	.06 (.03)	.13 (.10)	.11 (.06)	.10 (.06)
West	−.14 (−.07)*	.06 (.03)	.08 (.05)	.00 (.00)	.03 (.01)
R^2	.03	.06	.03	.02	.02

[a]Values in parentheses are standardized regression coefficients.
[b]The reference category (excluded group) is Northeast.
$* = p < .05$.

65

education has no statistically significant effect, and income has a stronger effect than for whites. While age has no significant effect on the perception of being held back among whites, it does among blacks. Older blacks more often than younger ones report that they have been held back from making the most of themselves.

Among blacks, but not among whites, there are significant effects of all variables on the perceived equality of educational opportunity. The belief that every young person in America has an equal opportunity to get a college education *decreases* with increasing socioeconomic status. Younger blacks and black males see less equality of educational opportunity than older ones and black females. Blacks who live in the northeastern region of the United States perceive less equality of educational opportunity than blacks living in other regions.[6]

Education has the same effect on adherences to the belief in widespread availability of opportunity among whites and blacks, but income and age do not. In opposition to the effects of these variables among whites, among blacks the perceived availability of opportunity decreases with increasing income, and younger blacks see more opportunity than do older ones.

Regression Results: Equality of Opportunity

The most notable group differences in perceived equality of opportunity (Table 3.12), other than the sizable age-group differences in assessed equality of opportunity for poor children (see also Figure 3.3), involve the effects of education and sex. Among blacks and white women, *but not among white men,* increasing education is associated with an increasing tendency to see opportunity for the poor, blacks, and women as worse than that for the average American. White women from the South consistently see more equality of opportunity than do women from other regions. And, black women rate opportunity for poor children and blacks as more equal than do black men.

Summary

While the comparisons of means by race and sex given in Table 3.11 give direct information about the magnitude of average differences between groups, regression coefficients are not so easily interpretable. Thus, in Figure 3.4 and Table 3.13 we give selected percentage com-

---

[6]One plausible reason for this regional difference is the greater access to state-supported, lower cost higher education in regions other than the northeast. Many blacks may find prohibitive the cost of attending the privately supported colleges or universities prevalent in the northeast.

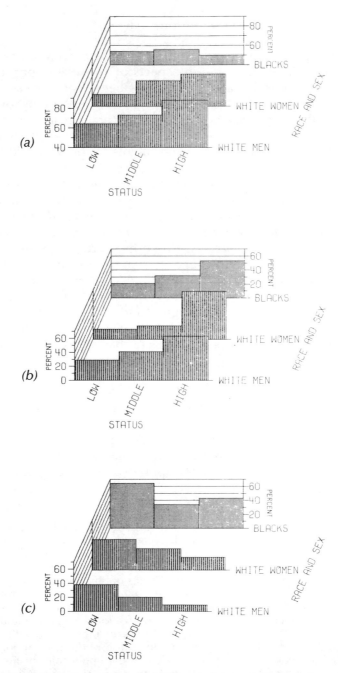

FIGURE 3.4. Beliefs about aspects of opportunity, broken down by status, sex, and race. (a) Prevalence of opportunity in general; (b) perception of personal opportunity as "good" or "very good"; (c) perception of self as having been held back.

parisons for beliefs about opportunity that build on the regression results.

The most substantial group differences in the perceived prevalence
of opportunity in general and in aspects of personal opportunity indicated by the regression analysis are those between people at different
levels of socioeconomic status. Figure 3.4 arrays, separately for whites
and blacks, the percentage of people giving certain responses to questions about these beliefs at levels defined by combinations of income
and education, selected to represent points in the low, middle, and
upper ranges of the socioeconomic status continuum.[7]

High-status whites differ substantially from others in their perspective
on opportunity in America. Few white men, especially, show any doubt
about the prevalence of opportunity for economic advancement for
the average American, and they have a very favorable assessment of
their opportunity as individuals. While the percentage of low-status
whites who express doubts about opportunity is much higher than that
for high-status whites, low-status "doubters" form a minority of their
own group. The majority of low-status whites rate opportunity for the
average American as good or very good and believe that they have had
a fair chance to make the most of themselves. Despite the fact that
objectively someone who is earning less than $12,000 and who does
not have a high school degree has quite poor chances for economic
advancement, only about one-fifth of low-status people (men and
women together) express the belief that they have a worse than average
chance to get ahead. A roughly equal fraction rate their personal
chances as better than average.

Women have a consistently less optimistic assessment of opportunity
in general and personal opportunity than men at each status level, except for perceived personal contemporary and future opportunity. In
this case high-status women are slightly more optimistic than their male

[7]The status levels were chosen to reflect qualitatively significant points along
the income and education continua. The years of education chosen are points
that correspond to the attainment of important educational credentials, usually
indicating the lack of a high school degree (11 or fewer years), having a high
school degree (12 years), and having a bachelor's or postgraduate college degree
(16 years or more). The incomes chosen are points along the income distribution
that define subjectively important qualitative economic statuses. People with
$12,000 or less income earned in 1979, of course, form the poor and the near-
poor by the federal government-specified poverty line. People with incomes
from $16,000 to $24,000 comprise the middle third of the distribution. Those
with family incomes of $25,000 or more are in the upper third of the income
distribution. The categories resulting from these combinations of points along
the income and education distributions might be labeled the "true poor" (people lacking both income and educational credentials), the "middle mass," and
the "upper-middle class."

counterparts. Moreover, the gap between middle- and high-status women in the percentage rating personal opportunity as better than average is especially large. In part this finding may be due to perceived (and arguably real) poorer career prospects among women with only a high school education than among men with the same educational level.

Among blacks, there are also substantial differences in the perceived favorability of personal chances for economic advancement among people at different status levels. While on the whole blacks are slightly less optimistic about their contemporary and future chances to get ahead as individuals, higher status blacks, like whites, are very optimistic, and only a minority of lower status blacks, like whites, see their personal contemporary and future chances to advance as worse than average. On the other hand, blacks at all status levels have a much less favorable assessment of their personal-opportunity history than do whites. A substantial majority of low-status blacks believe that they have not had a fair chance to make the most of themselves as individuals. Even among high-status blacks, who in colloquial terms have "made it," approximately 40% perceive that they have been unfairly held back.

Unlike whites, blacks at different status levels differ little in the perceived prevalence of opportunity in general. At all levels roughly one-half of our black respondents rate opportunity for the average American as very good or good. This lack of status differences reflects not only the absence of a statistically significant effect of income among blacks but also the weaker effect of education on the perceived prevalence of opportunity among blacks than among whites.

Results of regression analyses within the black sample suggest that changes in race relations and the growth of the black middle class in recent years have had some effect on the way black Americans view opportunity. Younger blacks see opportunity as more prevalent in general than do older ones—in contrast to the opposite pattern for whites. In addition, younger blacks are more likely to see themselves as having had a fair chance to make the most of themselves in life. Among blacks 18–29 years of age, 61% respond that opportunity for the average American is very good or good, and 63% respond that they have had a fair chance. In contrast, among blacks 50 years or older 55% view opportunity in general as very good or good, and only 36% report that they have had a fair chance to achieve.

The most substantial group differences in beliefs about equality of opportunity involve race, sex, and education level. Men and women do not differ significantly on the average in perceived equality of educational opportunity. Nor are there substantial differences in their perception by age, socioeconomic status, or region for men or women. In contrast, there are significant between- and within-group differences involving race. On the whole blacks see educational opportunity as slightly more equal than whites (54 of blacks versus 44% of whites agree that every young person has an equal opportunity to get a college education). Among blacks, there are marked differences in perceived equality of educational opportunity by age, socioeconomic status level, sex, and region.

Consistent with other indications of growing optimism about opportunity among blacks, younger blacks see more equality of educational opportunity than older ones. Among blacks 18–29 years of age approximately 63% agree that every young person has an equal chance to obtain a college education, and roughly 50% of blacks 30 or older do so.

Higher status, and especially more educated blacks, and black males perceive less equal opportunity for obtaining a college education than do lower status blacks and black females. The differences among educational levels, arrayed in Table 3.13, are striking. Roughly three-quarters of black college graduates deny that there is equality of educational opportunity. Perhaps blacks who have not attended college are unaware of the economic and other advantages that students from higher socioeconomic status families have for obtaining higher education. Stated differently, blacks who have attended college may be more aware than other blacks of how predominantly "white" and "middle class" college populations are.

Among white women and blacks, but not among white men, there are substantial differences in the perceived equality of opportunity for the poor, blacks, and women. As evident in Table 3.13, college-educated white women and blacks see less equal opportunity for these groups compared to white men at all levels of education and compared to white women or blacks with less education. Furthermore, women with 11 or fewer years of education rate opportunity for all three groups as more equal than men with the same level of education, and lesser educated blacks perceive opportunity for women as more equal than lesser educated whites.

In addition to the differences by education, there are also sex differences among blacks involving perceived opportunity for the poor and for blacks. Black men more often than black women rate opportunity for the poor (47 versus 30%) and for blacks (41 versus 31%) as worse than average. Viewed in conjunction with the other above noted sex differences among blacks, it is clear that black men on the whole have a less optimistic view of opportunity than black women.

CONCLUSIONS

In Chapter 2 we presented several summary hypotheses about dominant-ideology beliefs in general. Our findings in this chapter on the

TABLE 3.13. Percentage Comparisons of Beliefs about Equality of Educational Opportunity (for Blacks Only), Equality of Opportunity for the Poor, Blacks, and Women (Percentage Worse Than Average) by Education, Sex, and Race

	Poor	Blacks	Women	Equality of Educational Opportunity (percentage agree)
White men (N = 593)				
11 or fewer years	29 (109)[a]	23 (108)	37 (105)	
12 years	32 (216)	28 (216)	40 (215)	
Some college	35 (102)	27 (100)	33 (101)	
College graduate	39 (157)	36 (156)	42 (156)	
White women (N = 716)				
11 or fewer years	21 (123)	14 (125)	28 (125)	
12 years	28 (320)	23 (316)	39 (322)	
Some college	37 (132)	26 (132)	48 (133)	
College graduate	51 (127)	42 (123)	53 (125)	
Blacks (N = 535)				
11 or fewer years	32 (168)	31 (170)	21 (167)	62 (177)
12 years	32 (183)	26 (180)	31 (181)	57 (182)
Some college	46 (102)	40 (103)	36 (103)	44 (103)
College graduate	54 (67)	58 (66)	48 (67)	28 (67)

[a]Category N.

71

whole support these hypotheses for one key aspect of the dominant ideology: beliefs about opportunity. The belief is widespread that opportunity for economic advancement is present for all who work hard. However, counter to our expectation, there has been some decline in the strength of adherence to this belief among the American public over the last three decades.

In part this decline is due to growing skepticism about the value of education as a means to economic advancement. It also stems in part from perceptions that certain groups of Americans lack equal opportunity. Yet, consistent with our hypothesis, the challenge of these beliefs to the belief that opportunity is prevalent for the average American is limited by the widespread and seemingly stable optimism that Americans have about their personal chance to get ahead and by the tendency to view limited opportunity for certain groups as exceptional.

Finally, our analysis of group differences suggests that no single group of Americans is *both* markedly different on the average from others in its adherence to the dominant-ideology belief of prevalent opportunity or in its profession of beliefs about opportunity that potentially challenge it *and* strongly homogeneous in its members' perspective on opportunity. Lower status people do less often endorse the dominant-ideology belief that opportunity is prevalent, are less optimistic about their contemporary and future chances for economic advancement, and tend to see themselves as victims of barriers to opportunity more often than higher status people. However, even among low-status people the majority express a belief in the prevalence of opportunity in general and see their personal contemporary, future, and opportunity history in a favorable light.

Sex and race differences in objectively assessed opportunity for economic advancement imply that sex and race are the strongest bases for potential group differences in beliefs about opportunity. While blacks and women do express on the average a less favorable assessment of aspects of opportunity than do white men, neither group is homogeneous in this assessment.

Parallel to the case for white men, white women of higher socioeconomic status, compared to those of lower status, more strongly adhere to the dominant-ideology belief of prevalent opportunity, and they more favorably assess aspects of their personal opportunity. Women's perspectives on equality of opportunity differ substantially by their educational level, in a manner opposite to educational effects on perceived general and personal opportunity. College-educated women have a considerably more optimistic assessment of opportunity for themselves personally and for the average American than others *and* a substantially more pessimistic view of opportunity for women in general, for the poor, and for blacks.

In one respect blacks have a homogeneous perspective on opportunity. At each status level about one-half of the black population denies the prevalence of opportunity in America in general, and substantial percentages perceive that they have experienced barriers to their personal opportunity. In other respects, however, groups of blacks differ substantially from one another in their perspective on opportunity. Perhaps in response to recent gains for at least some segments of the American black population, younger blacks have a more optimistic assessment of some aspects of opportunity than do older blacks. Black males express more pessimism than black females. And, like white women, college-educated blacks see less equality of opportunity for their own group, the poor, and women than do less-educated blacks.

On the whole, then, the analyses presented in this chapter show that the traditional American optimism about opportunity for economic advancement is alive and quite well. There is some sign that the forces noted at the beginning of this chapter have somewhat lessened adherence to the key dominant ideology precept that opportunity is prevalent and equally available to all, but no signs that the average American's faith in his or her chances as an individual have at all diminished.

4

EXPLANATIONS FOR ECONOMIC OUTCOMES

The second major element of the dominant ideology, following from perceived economic opportunity, is the perception that individuals are causally responsible for their own positions in society. Observers have frequently cited individualistic beliefs as characteristic of American culture (Lewis, 1978; Sampson, 1977) and other cultures (Lopreato & Hazelrigg, 1972; Coughlin, 1980), and such beliefs have been specifically noted as part of the dominant ideology by Huber and Form (1973) and others (e.g., Abercrombie, Hill, & Turner, 1980). These beliefs locate the causes of achievement within the individual person, in ability, efforts, or other characteristics such as personality traits and educational achievement. The major alternative beliefs about the causes of achievement place them in the structure of society, in such factors as the lack or abundance of available jobs, society's provision of adequate or inadequate schools, racial or sexual discrimination, and inherited wealth or its lack. Other types of beliefs about the causes of achievement, such as its explanation by luck, fate, or God's will, are also possible.

To investigate the role of such beliefs in current American views of inequality, we will address several questions in this chapter. Poverty has been a persistent and troubling reality in our society, and the subject of much policy and public attention in the last two decades. Does the American public generally look on the poor as victims of environmental limitations or as personally responsible for their own condition?

We will also consider views on the causes of wealth, since many potential consequences flow from the perception of wealth as due to individual effort and ability (and therefore potentially available to anyone) or as limited to a privileged few by structural barriers. Individuals' own strivings for economic advancement as well as aspects of their views on public policy may be influenced by beliefs about the causes and potential availability of wealth. We will also look at views of the causes of the economic position of Americans in general, neither the poor nor the rich specifically, and at each respondent's views of the causes of his or her own personal position. Within each of these topic areas, we will describe the current distribution of public beliefs and (where possible) their changes over the last 10–20 years. We will evaluate the effects of potential challenges to individualism, derived from other explanations for economic position and beliefs about opportunity. Finally, we will examine group differences in beliefs in individualism and other perceptions of the causes of achievement.

DISTRIBUTION AND TIME TRENDS IN EXPLANATIONS FOR INEQUALITY

Explanations for Wealth and Poverty

Our most elaborate measures concern popular explanations for wealth and poverty. In each of these domains, we sought to respect the diversity of existing views of causal factors by asking about many possible causes, rather than restricting respondents a priori to just two or three possible causes such as personal ability versus luck. We used factor analyses to determine whether the large and diverse set of causal factors actually reflects a small number of underlying dimensions, which can serve as the primary measures for theoretical interpretation and further analysis. In the case of explanations for poverty, we also replicated a measure of the perceived causes of poverty used by Feagin (1975) in a national survey conducted in 1969. No comparable measure of the causes of wealth has been used, so we developed our own in a similar format.

Wealth. Respondents rated the importance of each of the factors listed in Table 4.1 as a reason why "there are rich people in the U.S." The specific causes included in the questionnaire were chosen to reflect several theoretical dimensions. One is exceptional personal characteristics of the rich themselves (effort, ability, willingness to take risks), as emphasized by current defenses of capitalism (e.g., Gilder, 1981). Another dimension is structural characteristics of society (the connection between political power and wealth, the ability of the rich to exploit the poor, or the acceptance of large inheritances), emphasized by populist and neo-Marxist attacks on the legitimacy of wealth. Finally, we included one negatively evaluated personal characteristic, dishonesty, because it is occasionally part of popular beliefs about the wealthy as portrayed in the media.

Examining the rated importance of each specific cause, we find that those consistently seen as most important are "personal drive and willingness to take risks," inheritance of wealth, and hard work and initiative. Two of these three are obviously focused at the individual level; structural explanations for wealth (such as political influence or the

TABLE 4.1. Reasons for Wealth: Marginals and Factor Analysis

	Percentage saying			Factor loadings[a]	
Reason	Very important	Somewhat important	Not important	Structural	Individual
Personal drive, willingness to take risks	64	31	5	−.03	.64
Money inherited from families	64	29	7	.44	.01
Hard work and initiative	60	32	9	−.12	.48
Political influence or "pull"	47	41	12	.46	−.02
Great ability or talent	46	42	11	.08	.77
The American economic system allows them to take unfair advantage of the poor	29	39	33	.53	−.12
Dishonesty and willingness to take what they can get	27	40	33	.53	−.07
Good luck, being in the right place	26	43	31	.30	.19

[a]Underlined factor loadings indicate factor in which each item is included.
$N = 1507$.

ability to take unfair advantage of the poor) are generally less popular than individual reasons. On average, the three individual reasons are rated as "very important" by 57% of the respondents, the four structural reasons by only 42%. Luck is also quite unpopular as an explanation for wealth. The general public picture seems to be that the wealthy attain their position (if not through inheritance) by their hard work and willingness to take risks.

We turn next to factor analysis to clarify the interrelationships of the causes of wealth in respondents' minds.[1] The results (in the form of the factor loadings) are shown in Table 4.1. The loadings essentially divide the items into a group of four structural items (including dishonesty) and a group of three individual items, defining two factors. Scales measuring the two factors are correlated in this solution, with the correlation between them being − .16. The value of this correlation is itself an interesting result whose interpretation will be discussed below, following the presentation of our data on the perceived causes of poverty.

Since we do not have data from a different time period available to

[1]The factor analysis used an iterated principal-components solution with oblique rotation. The scales formed from the variables are in all cases simple standardized sums of the variables indicated, rather than factor scores.

compare to our own measures of explanations for wealth, we must examine age-group differences to gain insights into over-time trends. The old view individualistic reasons for wealth as significantly more important than the young, while there is no age trend for structural reasons. We thus tentatively conclude that views of the causes of wealth may be becoming somewhat less individualistic over time, consistent with the results in Chapter 3 showing that the young express more doubts than the old about the widespread availability of opportunity.

Poverty. A similar analysis was performed on a series of possible causes for poverty. In this case we have available responses to the same items asked in a national survey in 1969 by Feagin (1975). Table 4.2 presents the items and the mean responses in 1969 and in 1980. The items again represent several theoretical dimensions, including individual characteristics of the poor (lack of effort or ability, poor morals, poor work skills). Other items represent a "liberal" viewpoint attributing poverty to structural characteristics of society (failure to provide adequate schooling, low wages in some industries), and one item, a "radical" viewpoint, that the poor are exploited by the rich.

On the average, individual factors are considered much more important than structural factors in accounting for poverty; this tendency is even stronger than for the causes of wealth. The most popular five items are (in order) lack of thrift and proper money management skills; lack of effort; lack of ability and talent; attitudes that prevent advancement; and failure of society to provide good schools for many Americans. Four of these five items are clearly individualistic in focus. The average proportion responding "very important" across the six clearly individualistic reasons (omitting "just bad luck") is 50%, while for the five structural reasons it is only 34%. Among the structural reasons, the "liberal" ones focusing on schools, wages, and jobs are considerably more popular than the "radical" view that poverty is the result of exploitation by the rich. Only pure luck is a less popular explanation than the latter. Individual explanations for poverty clearly dominate American thought about the issue today.

Since we retained essentially the same wording for this question that Feagin used in a national survey in 1969, we are able to make detailed over-time comparisons.[2] The ranking of the reasons for poverty

---

[2]Our wordings differed from Feagin's in several cases, mostly in minor ways (e.g., substitution of "blacks" for "Negroes" in item 10). Our item number 4 was newly constructed. In addition, for a randomly assigned one-half of the respondents, the response scale included four categories rather than Feagins' three ("very important," "somewhat important," and "not important"). The first two categories were the same, followed by "not too important" and "not at all important." The different response formats did not produce interpretable differences, and the items were standardized separately in the two halves of the sample to form scales.

TABLE 4.2. Reasons for Poverty: Marginals in 1969 and 1980 and Factor Analysis[a]

Reason	1969 Data (in percentage)			1980 Data (in percentage)			Factor loadings	
	Very important	Important	Not important	Very important	Important	Not important	Structural	Individual
Lack of thrift and proper money-management skills	59	31	11	64	30	6	.02	.37
Lack of effort by the poor themselves	57	34	9	53	39	8	-.14	.65
Lack of ability and talent	54	34	12	53	35	11	.11	.34
Their background gives them attitudes that keep them from improving their condition	(not asked)			46	42	11	.04	.35
Failure of society to provide good schools for many Americans	38	26	36	46	29	26	.65	-.16
Loose morals and drunkenness	50	32	18	44	30	27	-.01	.57
Sickness and physical handicaps	46	39	14	43	41	15	.30	.27
Low wages in some businesses and industries	43	36	21	40	47	14	.59	.05
Failure of private industry to provide enough jobs	29	38	33	35	39	28	.56	.09
Prejudice and discrimination against blacks	34	39	27	31	44	25	.46	.05
Being taken advantage of by rich people	19	32	48	20	35	45	.52	-.06
Just bad luck	8	28	63	12	32	56	.33	.13

[a]Note.: 1969 data restated to exclude "uncertain" responses. Underlined factor loadings indicate factor in which each item is included. N = 1507 (for 1980 data).

79

in order of importance is virtually identical over the decade-plus time span. The first three items in our list are also the first three in Feagin's list, in the same order. Our fourth item, poor attitudes, was not included by Feagin; we added it because of its prominence in media accounts of the "culture of poverty." Only 1 item among the other 11 differed by two ranks or more between Feagin's data and our own: failure of society to provide good schools ranked seventh in 1969 and fifth in 1980. Perhaps an increased emphasis on education, and on structural failures that deny universal access to quality education, is one significant change over the decade of the 1970s. Otherwise, the American view of the causes of poverty has been remarkably stable since the late 1960s. Results from a 1972 survey that used differently worded questions also show similar views on the causes of poverty (Nilson, 1981), and Gallup poll findings on the same issue are almost identical from the mid 1960s to 1985 (Gallup, 1985). These results show that the stability of perceptions of the causes of poverty is not an artifact of the question wording employed by Feagin and us.

The stability of opinions on the causes of poverty is surprising given the moderate decline in perceived general opportunity (Chapter 3) and the very prominent public policy focus and widespread media attention to the issue of poverty in the intervening years. It strongly suggests, as our theory implies, the central role of public explanations for economic position in organizing beliefs and attitudes about inequality in general. That is, explanations for poverty that focus on individual attributes of the poor serve many functions for the perceiver: They free him or her from feelings of guilt or indirect responsibility for the plight of the poor in society (Ryan, 1971), and they convey a feeling of control over one's own outcomes which is psychologically beneficial, as Chapter 10 will make clear. These consequences of individual explanations may support them and keep them at a fairly constant and high level despite some changes in the other elements of the dominant ideology over time.

When the responses to the reasons for poverty are submitted to a factor analysis, two factors emerge as in the case of wealth, paralleling the individual versus structural distinction. Four items each form clear scales of individual and structural explanations. They are lack of thrift, lack of ability, lack of effort, and poor morals (individual), being taken advantage of by the rich, poor schools, low wages, and lack of jobs (structural). The other items either fail to reflect strongly the factors (such as "just bad luck," which is relatively independent of both individualistic and structural explanations) or are omitted for theoretical reasons (prejudice and discrimination against blacks, omitted to avoid mixing racial issues with this measure of beliefs about poverty in general). As in the case of the two-factor solution of reasons for wealth, scales measuring the two factors are only slightly correlated with each other: $r = +.16$. Similar low to moderate correlations between individual and structural explanations for poverty were obtained by Feagin (1975) and Nilson (1981).

As in the case of reasons for wealth, age-group trends show that the old are significantly higher on individualism than the young, while structuralism has little relationship to age. However, in this case age-group trends should probably not be interpreted as indicating time trends; our data and Feagin's show remarkably similar distributions on both the individual and structural reasons. The age effect is probably a life cycle rather than a cohort effect, since otherwise cohort replacement would have resulted in some overall change since 1969.

Summary. As the analyses of reasons for both wealth and poverty show, people distinguish between classes of individual and structural reasons for economic position, and the individual reasons are viewed as much more important, particularly in the case of poverty. Explanations for wealth are more mixed, suggesting some degree of inconsistency in popular views of the wealthy. Chapter 3 showed, along similar lines, that the wealthy are widely acknowledged to have better economic opportunity than others, despite a general endorsement of the ideal of equal opportunity. The theme of inconsistency in popular views of the rich will be taken up again in Chapter 5. Age-group differences on the causal factors suggest a moderate increase with age in individual reasons. Over-time data on reasons for poverty, however, show virtually no changes over a period of more than a decade.

Explanations for Individuals' Own Positions

Ability versus Luck. One measure of explanations for economic standing was asked with exactly parallel wording about the respondent personally and about "Americans in general," permitting precise comparisons. The question, modeled after one that has been used in other surveys, asks:

> A person's standard of living can be influenced by characteristics of the *person,* such as education, ability, and effort. It can also be influenced by *other* things, such as good or bad luck, being helped or held back by other people, or the circumstances of the job a person holds. Is your *own* standard of living these days [the standard of living of most Americans] due primarily to your [their] *own* ability, education, or effort; is it due primarily to *other* factors; or is it due to both equally?

The item concerning Americans in general shows a majority (51%) responding that both individual characteristics and external factors are important causes of economic position. Pure internal characteristics are named by 39%, far more than the 10% who cite external factors alone. Other surveys have used similar but differently worded quesions, generally naming only "hard work" and "luck" as the two possible factors. Time trends in the results are shown in Figure 4.1. It appears that perceptions of the causes of most Americans' achievements, like the causes of poverty mentioned above, have been quite stable recently: The General Social Survey results show virtually no time trend over the 9-year period they cover (the difference between the General Social Survey results and ours is probably due to wording differences). Examining age-group differences for indications of time trends, explanations for Americans in general are unrelated to age. Both over-time and age-group analyses thus suggest substantial stability of explanations for most Americans' economic position, as measured by this simple item.

The similarly worded item concerning one's personal position shows similar results, with some tendency toward greater perception of personal causation for one's own position (47% cite pure internal factors and 43% both internal and external). This measure is also virtually unrelated to the respondent's age, with a slight tendency for middle-aged people to use ability explanations more than the young or the old.

Specific Barriers to Achievement. Another item involving explanations for one's personal position has already been mentioned in the previous chapter on opportunity: It asks whether one has had a fair opportunity to achieve or has been held back for some reason. Respondents were also asked about the specific reasons that they felt had held them back. In order, the most common reasons mentioned are: lack of education;

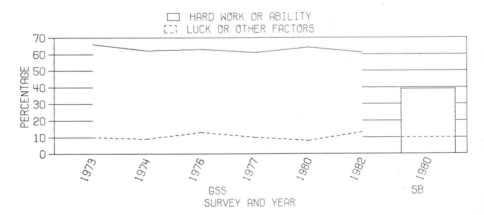

FIGURE 4.1. Time trends in views on causes of economic position for "most Americans." (Data sources: GSS is General Social Survey; SB is our Stratification Beliefs survey. Question wording differs between these sources).

lack of income; having children or having to support them; illness or disability; lack of motivation or ambition; getting married; my sex; the job market or availability of jobs. Many of these common reasons refer to family status and are given much more often by women than men (getting married and having children, as well as the specific mentions—all by women—of sex as a barrier to achievement). Otherwise the list of common barriers is not surprising (no money, no education, no jobs) except for the relatively frequent mention of the internal factor of lack of motivation. Perhaps many individuals now, looking back at their early adult years, feel that they did not work hard enough then at self-improvement or at acquiring education.

The most significant aspect of these explanations is their narrowness and specificity. People tend to refer to their own personal attributes or to aspects of their individual situation (such as their family status or geographic location) to explain a lack of achievement, rather than pointing to general or structural trends. Though there are a few mentions of sex or race discrimination, such explanations are unusual. Even when people mention supraindividual factors, they stop short of making a structural critique of society in general. As we shall see shortly, the specificity of individuals' thinking about barriers they experience in their personal lives may be important in limiting challenges to the dominant ideology that arise from personal experience, as people fail to see the barriers that they experience as related to general, society-wide structures. This attributional pattern supports perceptions of individual responsibility for economic outcomes, to the extent that even some of the "barriers" to achievement that people perceive as having held them back are internal factors like a lack of motivation.

POTENTIAL CHALLENGES TO INDIVIDUALISM

Challenges to individualism, as part of the dominant ideology, may arise from any of three general sources. One is external or structural explanations adopted by a person for his or her own situation and generalized to apply to other people as well. A person who experiences poor economic outcomes may give external explanations for them, perhaps to avoid the psychological costs of perceiving his or her own characteristics as inadequate (ego-defensive attribution). These external explanations then may be generalized, resulting in a perception of widespread structural barriers to achievement.

However, our theoretical perspective predicts that the generalization of explanations from one's personal situation to others will usually be quite limited. The amount of salient, specific knowledge every person has about his or her own history may tend to block generalization. One's poor economic outcomes may be attributed to the personality of one's boss, one's own individual characteristics, or other specific features of the situation (as noted above in the analysis of factors named by respondents as having held them back). Such specific causal factors would not be assumed to influence most others, so generalization may be minimal.

The second source of challenge to individualism is the recent perceived decline in general opportunity in society that was discussed in Chapter 3. If opportunity to advance is seen as less widespread, then perceived individual responsibility for economic outcomes also may be lessened. People whose opportunity is limited cannot reasonably be assigned full individual responsibility for the position in which they find themselves.

Finally, challenges to individualism may arise from directly learned alternative structural explanations, for poverty in particular, that form part of "social liberalism." Social and political discourse since the early 1960s often has pointed out structural causes of poverty (such as racial discrimination, low-quality schools in poor neighborhoods, a "culture of poverty," etc.), and it would be surprising if at least some individuals did not learn and accept the validity of these explanations. For some, learning structural explanations may lessen the belief in individualism, though our theoretical perspective holds that individual and structural explanations are not necessarily psychological opposites. Mixed and compromise views (such as beliefs that *both* individual and structural causes are important) may be more common outcomes of the learning process than the absolute rejection of individualism. In this section we will analyze the impact of these three types of challenges on individualism.

Generalization of Personal Explanations

To begin with, we examine the degree of correspondence between explanations that people give for their own situation, for most Americans, and for the rich and the poor. The data show, as noted above, that people believe in the importance of personal characteristics in causing their personal situation even more strongly than they do for Americans in general. Though most people (about 64%), of course, give similar responses to these two similarly worded questions, 22% attribute their own position more to personal factors than the position of most Americans, and only 15% differ in the opposite direction. Because of the strong tendency to explain one's own position by personal characteristics, the effect of generalization from one's personal experience is likely to *increase* beliefs in individualism rather than challenge them. The relationship between perceived personal opportunity and general opportunity is analogous, as Chapter 3 showed. Personal opportunity is widely viewed as extremely positive, and this perception functions to block challenges to the perception of opportunity in general.

The degree of correspondence between explanations for one's own position and explanations for the rich and poor can be assessed using the individual and structural items discussed above. These analyses reveal only low to moderate levels of association, suggesting low levels of generalization from views of one's personal situation to the rich and the poor. For example, the individual factor of risk-taking is rated a very important cause of wealth by 67% of those who attribute their own position to their own efforts and abilities, but also by 60% of those who attribute their own position purely externally, a difference of only 7%. In fact, most of the reasons for wealth and poverty show percentage differences in such analyses that are even smaller than this. The exceptions are three structural reasons for poverty, where low wages, lack of jobs, and exploitation by the rich are cited by 10–12% more of those with external personal explanations than internal, still not impressively strong relationships. (The percentages are 40 and 52%, 31 and 41%, and 17 and 28%, respectively.) The weakness of these relationships indicates that potential challenges arising from external explanations for one's personal situation do not generally lead to an overthrow of beliefs in individualism or the dominant ideology as a whole, though they may moderately increase beliefs in structural reasons for poverty.

Finally, we can examine the nature of the specific factors that individuals cite as having held them back to determine whether they influence the extent of generalization from personal experiences to the causes of achievement in general. On the scale measuring belief in structural reasons for poverty, for instance, those who feel that they personally have not been held back are somewhat below the overall mean, averaging −.10 ($N = 1074$). Those who report being held back average +.25, but there is great variation depending on the nature of the reason that they see as having held them back. Those held back by race or religion, for example, average +.95, those citing the job market +.77, family problems (such as having to support sick parents or too large a family) +.63, financial problems +.37, "personal problems" −.32, and those specifically mentioning their spouse −.49. Similar patterns hold across the other scales measuring explanations: The degree of perceived structural or individual causation of wealth or poverty varies widely among people who see themselves as having been held back by different factors. Our categorization of the free-response reasons given by our respondents is too coarse to draw precise conclusions, but the general pattern is as predicted. Those who see themselves as having been held back by such structurally linked factors as the job market, race, or race discrimination are the most likely to generalize their own experiences to high levels of structural and low levels of individual causation for Americans in general. Narrowly focused individual reasons such as personal problems or one's spouse lead to little generalization from personally experienced barriers to achievement.[3]

Overall, then, challenges to the dominant ideology arising from one's personal situation are limited in several ways: *(a)* Most people give strongly internal explanations for their own situation, even more so than they do for Americans in general; *(b)* the correspondence between explanations for one's own situation and explanations for the rich and the poor is quite weak, except for a moderate relationship to structural reasons for poverty; *(c)* generalization of personally experienced barriers to achievement depends on the perceived nature of the barrier. The factors that respondents most often cite as having held them back are fairly narrow and specific, applying only to the individual, and are associated with little generalization.

Declining General Opportunity

The dominant ideology is assumed to constitute a connected set of beliefs resembling a logical syllogism (Huber & Form, 1973). Individual explanations for economic position (whether one's own or others') are said to follow from the perception of widely available opportunity. Since Chapter 3 demonstrated that perceptions of the general level of opportunity in society have declined in recent years from the levels of the 1950s and 1960s, we would expect individual explanations to decline as well.

The correlations between perceptions of opportunity (the overall availability of opportunity and one's personal opportunity) and explanations are generally weak (in the .10—.20 range). The data show that the "logic of opportunity syllogism" operates here, though weakly: The acceptance of one key belief in the dominant ideology (opportunity) implies others (regarding the causes of achievement).

To what extent do these correlations show effects of challenges to individualism posed by perceptions of limited opportunity? The relationship between opportunity perceptions and individual explanations for wealth is weak, accounting for only 4% of the variance in explanations. And individual explanations for poverty are almost unrelated to perceptions of general opportunity. So the decline in opportunity

---

[3]The causal order is somewhat ambiguous here. People sometimes may learn general explanations first and then apply them to their own situation.

perceptions analyzed in the previous chapter may not be great enough in magnitude to pose a great challenge to individualism, overall. Lane (1962) argued that perceptions of widespread opportunity, or even of equal opportunity, are not necessary to support individual explanations for economic position. All that is required is the belief in *some* opportunity, however limited, to advance one step above one's current position. Our data are consistent with Lane's conclusion on this issue. In particular, increasing perceived opportunity above the threshold value would be expected to have little impact on explanations, accounting for the lack of a strong linear correlation.

The Impact of Structural Explanations

If people learn structural explanations for wealth or poverty from early socialization in the family or subculture (as might be the case among blacks or Jews, for example) or from media reports of governmental programs and the social movements of the 1960s and 1970s, those structural explanations themselves directly may challenge individualism. We therefore examine the relationships between structural and individual explanations. First, across the two domains of wealth and poverty, there is a good correspondence between structural explanations for wealth and poverty ($r = .42$, $p < .001$) and a slightly lower value for individual explanations for wealth and poverty ($r = .28$, $p < .001$). People thus seem to have a relatively consistent "explanatory style," emphasizing structuralism or individualism, which they apply to both the poor and the rich.

However, as our theoretical perspective predicts, individual and structural explanations are not opposed to each other in the sense that more of one implies less of the other type. A strong negative correlation between endorsement of individual and structural reasons is *not* found in the data. The correlations are $-.16$ for wealth and $+.16$ for poverty. True, some perceivers rate individual reasons as important and structural reasons as unimportant; others do the reverse, showing relatively pure structural explanations. But about as many respondents fall into two other groups. Some see both classes of reasons as relatively important, a view of the world that might be expressed as "Structural barriers to achievement do exist, but individual efforts can often overcome them." Other people see both individual and structural reasons as relatively unimportant, perhaps seeing economic position as due to such other factors as luck, fate, or God's will (see Chapter 7). Because of the existence of these latter two groups of respondents, the individual and structural explanation measures are almost statistically independent of each other, sometimes have different determinants, and (as we shall see) they may have similar or different effects on other variables.[4]

These findings have implications for understanding how people respond to beliefs that pose challenges to the dominant ideology. Recognizing structural barriers to economic advancement would seem to call into question the dominant ideology of individualism. How can individuals be held totally responsible for their positions if the race for economic advancement does not offer everybody an equal starting point? However, people do not often seem to draw that conclusion and follow through by reorganizing the entire complex of their beliefs about achievement. Instead, compromise views that deflect the potential challenge seem to be chosen, such as the idea that barriers exist but can be overcome by individual efforts. The popularity of this sort of compromise is suggested by fragmentary evidence beyond our own data. In the 1972 National Election Survey (Inter-University Consortium for Political and Social Research, 1972), 73% of the sample agreed that people with ability and talent can get ahead, even if they were born poor. However, 64% of the *same population* agreed that poor people did not have a chance to get a good education. At a minimum, 37% of the population must have agreed with both statements, based on the marginals. Similarly, Nilson (1981) reported analyses of 1972 data that she interpreted as showing the popularity of compromises between individual and structural explanations for poverty.

Such responses upholding the importance of both structural and individual causes of poverty may represent latent inconsistency in people's belief structures. Inconsistencies of this sort, as well as other types of inconsistencies (between beliefs and self-interest, for example) may contribute to the popularity of public policies that attempt to strike a compromise position, neither completely accepting nor rejecting the tenets of individualism on which the dominant ideology rests. While other analysts (Mann, 1973; Hochschild, 1981; Free & Cantril, 1968) have arrived at similar conclusions, our viewpoint differs from theirs in stressing the social–psychological bases of inconsistency outlined in Chapter 2.

Summary

Our examination so far leads us to emphasize the weakness of each of the three potential sources of challenge to individualism: general-

---

[4]These considerations appear to rule out a simple "response-set" interpretation for the existence of two factors rather than one. The response-set explanation would not account for meaningful empirical associations of both factors with other variables in different analyses (i.e., for the existence of two factors with good construct validity).

ization of explanations for one's own situation, declines in perceived general opportunity, and learned structural explanations. Since explanations for people's personal situations are strongly internal, their generalization to other people would result in *increased* levels of individualism, if anything. Where individuals do see limitations on their own opportunity to advance, they tend to attribute them quite narrowly and specifically, resulting in no general challenge to individual explanations for society as a whole.

Declining perceptions of general opportunity—at the level present in our data, at least—may also pose little challenge to individualism, for the relationship between such perceptions and individual explanations for wealth and poverty are weak. And, finally, holding structural explanations does not invariably result in a rejection of individual explanations, indicating that the potential challenge logically posed by structural explanations is not carried through into a full reorganization of beliefs by many individuals. We emphasize the construction of compromise images of achievement (such as the idea of barriers that strenuous efforts can overcome) in the deflection of these challenges to pure individualism.

GROUP DIFFERENCES IN EXPLANATIONS FOR ECONOMIC POSITION

We turn to analyses of the social distribution of explanations for economic position. As the introduction to this section noted, we seek insights into the sources of adherence to the dominant ideology and the processes that can result in its rejection. We particularly emphasize potential race and sex differences in explanations for economic position, because of the prominence of these group divisions in recent American political debate concerning discrimination and the causes of achievement in general.

There are several previous analyses of public perceptions of the reasons for poverty (though little data exist on perceptions of the causes of wealth). In general, the findings are that those with higher status (including people with higher incomes, whites, and older people) favor individualistic explanations for poverty (e.g., Centers, 1949; Kornhauser, 1939; Huber & Form, 1973; Feagin, 1975; Nilson, 1981). Lower status often is found to be associated with increased adherence to structural explanations, but not necessarily with greatly diminished support for individualism. Ordinarily, race has stronger effects than income or other status variables. Different studies obtain conflicting findings about the effects of education, perhaps because it both increases status and increases people's contact with liberal and humane values, with potentially opposite effects on explanations. The general pattern found in the literature, then, is of pervasive status effects on explanations for poverty, with race the most important influence.

Wealth and Poverty

The scales measuring structural and individual explanations for wealth and poverty were entered in regression analyses to determine their relationships to sociodemographic variables, and Table 4.3 presents the results. The independent variables used are those discussed in Chapter 3. The effects of religion are of particular interest because analysts since Weber (1959) and Durkheim (1951) have hypothesized connections between religious affiliation and beliefs in individualism.

Wealth. Structural causes for wealth are more often cited by females, the young, nonwhites, those with lower incomes, lower education, and Northeasterners. Structural causes are thus perceived by people who are themselves likely to be distant from the wealthy and perhaps from

TABLE 4.3. Regressions of Attributions for Wealth and Poverty on Sociodemographic Variables[a]

Independent variable	Structural wealth	Individual wealth	Structural poverty	Individual poverty
Sex (female)	.15*	−.11*	.20*	.02
	(.08)	(−.05)	(.10)	(.01)
Age (10 yr)	−.04*	.06*	−.04*	.08*
	(−.07)	(.10)	(−.06)	(.14)
Race (nonwhite)	.35*	−.25*	.70*	−.02
	(.12)	(−.09)	(.24)	(−.01)
Education (years)	−.06*	−.01	−.06*	−.06*
	(−.17)	(−.04)	(−.17)	(−.17)
Income (log)	−.22*	.30*	−.27*	.10
	(−.07)	(.10)	(−.09)	(.03)
West	−.19*	.25*	−.15*	.02
	(−.08)	(.10)	(−.06)	(.01)
Midwest	−.09	.02	−.11	−.08
	(−.04)	(.01)	(−.05)	(−.03)
South	−.12	.12	−.11	.01
	(−.05)	(.05)	(−.05)	(.00)
Religion	—	[b]	—	[c]
R^2	.08	.05	.14	.07

[a]Note: $N = 1438$.

[b]Compared to no religion (lowest mean): No religion .00, other religion .04, conservative Protestant .20, Catholic .23, Jewish .28, other Protestant .33.

[c]Compared to no religion (lowest mean): No religion .00, Jewish .04, other religion .07, Catholic .25, conservative Protestant .31, other Protestant .33.

*p < .05.

chances to personally obtain wealth. Those for whom wealth is unlikely personally seem to see the wealthy in negative terms and see wealth itself as the result of structural factors—one might call them biases in this context—rather than individual efforts and abilities.

Individual causes of wealth portray the wealthy in a more positive light. Males, the old, whites, those with high incomes, and Westerners are more inclined to see individual causes of wealth. Catholics, Protestants, and Jews are all higher on this variable than adherents of other religions or no religion. Except for the absence of an education effect, this regression looks like the reverse of that for structural causes of wealth: The advantaged see wealth as achievable by individual talents and efforts and thus as potentially attainable by themselves. The unusual responses of Westerners may reflect regional cultural differences, such as the star-discovered-in-Hollywood-drugstore or Gold Rush myths of wealth potentially available to anyone who has the right individual attributes or efforts.

Poverty. Structural explanations for poverty constitute the view that the poor suffer from circumstances largely beyond their control. Such explanations are more widespread among females, the young, non-whites, those with low income and education, and residents of the Northeast region. The picture is nearly identical to that of structural explanations for wealth, with which (as noted above) this variable has about a .40 correlation.

Finally, individual explanations for poverty hold the poor to be personally responsible for their plight, through their lack of ability, efforts, or morals. The old and less educated tend to use these explanations, as do Catholics and Protestants (compared to Jews and adherents of other religions or no religion).

In this case the picture is *not* very much like individual explanations for wealth. The general commitment of high-income people, males, whites, and Westerners to individualist and nonstructuralist views does not extend to endorsing individual reasons for poverty. On the other hand, education decreases individual explanations for poverty while having no effect on individual explanations for wealth.

Summary: Status Effects. Several important points emerge from the analyses of the determinants of structural and individual explanations for wealth and poverty. First, across three of the four analyses (all but individual explanations for poverty), there is a general tendency for overall status (measured by income, race, and sex) to influence individualism and structuralism in opposite directions. The picture of the prototypical believer in the dominant ideology emerges quite clearly and, perhaps not coincidentally, resembles Ronald Reagan: an older, white, male, Westerner with a relatively high income. Our earlier analyses demonstrated that perceptions of a high level of economic opportunity have similar effects, increasing individualist and decreasing structuralist explanations for wealth and poverty. Similar effects of economic status have been found in other studies as well, including Centers (1949), Huber and Form (1973), Feagin (1975), and Nilson (1981) in the United States, and British and Australian studies by Furnham (1982) and Feather (1974), respectively.

Education effects are quite interesting, with the more educated being lower on both measures of structuralism and also on individual explanations for poverty. Education acts like an indicator of status (similarly to income) in its effects on the two structural explanation measures, but *not* on the two measures of individualism. It may be that socially liberalizing effects of education counteract the status effects in these two instances, as those with more education are more likely to see the flaws of the purely individualistic view of economic achievement (Robinson & Bell, 1978). On individual explanations for wealth, the liberalizing effect would counterbalance the status effect and result in a net effect near zero. In the case of individual explanations for poverty, where status effects are small (e.g., income has no effect), only the liberalizing effect would show up, resulting in a net negative effect of education.

Group differences in explanations by race, sex, and socioeconomic status will be considered in more detail later in this chapter, following analyses of two more explanation measures.

Summary: Other Effects. Age effects on explanations for wealth and poverty are also of interest. As in other similar analyses (e.g., Nilson, 1981), here the old tend to be higher than the young on individualism and lower on structural views of poverty. Chapter 3 also noted parallel age differences on perceptions of equal opportunity for the poor. In recent years, emphasis on potential structural causes of poverty and a corresponding denial of pure individualism has been widespread in American culture. The civil rights movement of the 1950s and 1960s, the antipoverty programs of the 1960s and 1970s, and the women's movement of the same period have all carried messages about potential structural causes of economic position and denied that individuals are invariably personally responsible for their situations. We would expect the young to be more influenced by such socially liberalizing trends than their elders, on the basis of findings that political socialization is most effective in the young and then endures throughout a lifetime in most cases (Sears, 1975). However, recall that in the available over-time data (on explanations for poverty since 1969) almost no change is visible.

A final notable aspect of the above analyses is the differences in R^2 levels. Structural explanations are in both cases more predictable from individuals' background and social position than are individual explanations. Along with the greater popularity of individual explanations, this pattern is consistent with our overall interpretation (cf. Nilson, 1981). Individualism is a central aspect of the American cultural pattern (the dominant ideology) and is held to a major extent across social strata. There is not much variation, even along such powerful structural divisions as race or status, in perceptions of the importance of individual causes of achievement. Structural explanations, however, are adopted by some and not by others, depending on their status, life experiences, and cultural exposures, resulting in somewhat greater predictability from sociodemographic variables. When adopted the structural explanations tend to be added to, rather than replace, the preexisting individualist ideology; otherwise we would observe a strong negative correlation between individual and structural explanations. This theme will recur in our later analyses: The elements of the dominant ideology are broadly distributed across social groups with relatively little systematic variation, while the prevalence of beliefs that potentially challenge the dominant ideology is much more variable, depending on individuals' objective status and life experiences.

Personal Position and Americans in General

We turn in Table 4.4 to examining the single-item measures explaining economic position by effort and ability versus other factors, for both the individual's own position and the situation of Americans in general. The item measuring explanations for one's personal standard of living shows significant effects of two variables. Men and those with high incomes tend to see their standard of living as due to personal rather than external factors. In the case of most Americans, explanations in terms of internal factors are given more often by whites, those with high incomes, and Catholics and Protestants relative to Jews. With these single-item measures producing less power than the scales analyzed in Table 4.3, it is to be expected that these effects should be a subset of those found in most of the prior analyses.

People's perceptions of the causes of their own achievements are thus shaped by some of the same factors that influence their perceptions of the causes of achievement in general. Status effects and racial and sexual group divisions continue to be prominent, as those with higher status use internal explanations. The effect of sex is larger on personal explanations and that of race on explanations for Americans in general. Perhaps this is because race is a more salient dividing line for society-wide political conflict than is sex; nonwhites may be more ready to generalize their personal attitudes to responses about society as a whole.

TABLE 4.4. Regressions of Ability versus Luck Variables on Sociodemographic Variables[a]

Independent variable	Personal position	Most Americans
Sex (female)	−.08*	−.02
	(−.10)	(−.03)
Age (10 years)	.01	.00
	(.03)	(.01)
Race (nonwhite)	−.05	−.06*
	(−.05)	(−.05)
Education (years)	.01	−.01
	(.04)	(−.05)
Income (log)	.08*	.08*
	(.07)	(.06)
West	.04	.03
	(.05)	(.03)
Midwest	.04	.05
	(.04)	(.05)
South	.01	.06
	(.01)	(.06)
Religion	—	[b]
R^2	.03	.02

[a]Note: $N = 1438$.
[b]Compared to Jewish (lowest mean): Jewish .00, other religion .10, no religion .16, other Protestant .19, Catholic .20, conservative Protestant .20.
*$p < .05$.

GROUP DIFFERENCES BY SEX, RACE, AND STATUS

Differences in people's explanations for wealth and poverty are more likely to be politically consequential if they are structured along the lines of major group divisions in society, such as race, sex, or socioeconomic status. The alternative possibility is that most people are cross-pressured, having reasons to maintain both structural and individual explanations by reason of their diverse group memberships. To examine these possibilities, Table 4.5 presents means and standard deviations for the explanation measures in the sex and race subgroups, and Figure 4.2 presents selected explanation items broken down by race, gender, and a composite status measure (the same measure used in Chapter 3).

In Table 4.5, blacks differ on the average from whites on five of the six measures, with whites being higher on individual explanations and lower on structural explanation measures. The exception is individual explanations for poverty, which as noted above has a distinctly different pattern of determinants, with small or no status effects. The race effects are generally quite large (in the metric of the mean difference in stan-

TABLE 4.5. Attribution Items: Means and Standard Deviations by Sex and Race

Variable	Males	Females	Whites	Blacks
Structural wealth	−.03 (1.04)	.12 (0.97)*	−.06 (0.99)	.32 (0.98)*
Individual wealth	−.01 (1.05)	−.07 (1.02)	.04 (0.97)	−.23 (1.13)*
Structural poverty	.02 (1.04)	.26 (0.97)*	−.10 (0.98)	.71 (0.81)*
Individual poverty	−.06 (1.04)	.03 (1.01)*	.00 (0.99)	−.04 (1.09)
Americans ability/luck	1.71 (0.33)	1.62 (0.42)*	1.68 (0.40)	1.62 (0.34)*
Personal ability/luck	1.63 (0.39)	1.60 (0.38)	1.63 (0.39)	1.57 (0.36)*

*$p < .05$ for comparison of men versus women or blacks versus whites.

dard deviation units), reaching almost 1 SD in the case of structural explanations for poverty.

Sex differences in the expected direction (females higher on structural and lower on individual explanations) are also evident in four of the six analyses. Only on individual explanations for wealth and explanations for the respondent's personal situation do sex differences fail to attain significance. The sex effects are generally smaller than the race effects.

Socioeconomic status also has important effects on explanations, as the regression analyses presented earlier suggest. Figure 4.2 presents selected results by sex, race, and a composite status variable made up of education and income. The general pattern is for increasing status to lead to lower levels of structural explanations and higher levels of individual explanations for wealth. Again, individual explanations for poverty are an exception, as those with higher status are somewhat less likely to cite such personal factors as lack of thrift and proper money management or effort on the part of the poor. (This status effect is essentially due to education rather than income, as the regression analyses in Table 4.3 showed.) Status effects are often attenuated among blacks and white women as compared with white men, and occasionally even reverse, as with the importance of inheritance and hard work for wealth. This difference in status (or education) effects between white males and others has been noted in Chapter 3 and will recur in later chapters as well.

To further explore possible differences in the distribution of explanations for economic position among white men, white women, and blacks, analyses of the four explanation scales and two single-item measures were performed separately for these three subgroups. As in Chapter 3, data from the special sample of blacks were added to the representative sample data to obtain higher numbers of blacks.

The effects of independent variables on explanations differ significantly between the different subgrups in only a few instances. The effects of education in decreasing structural explanations for wealth and

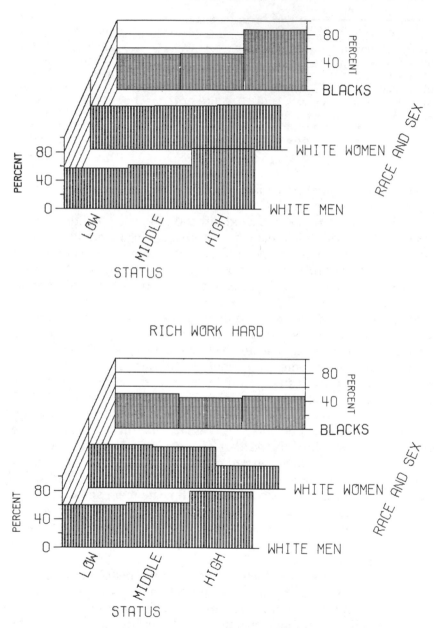

FIGURE 4.2. Selected explanations for wealth and poverty—percentage saying "important" or "very important" broken down by status, sex, and race.

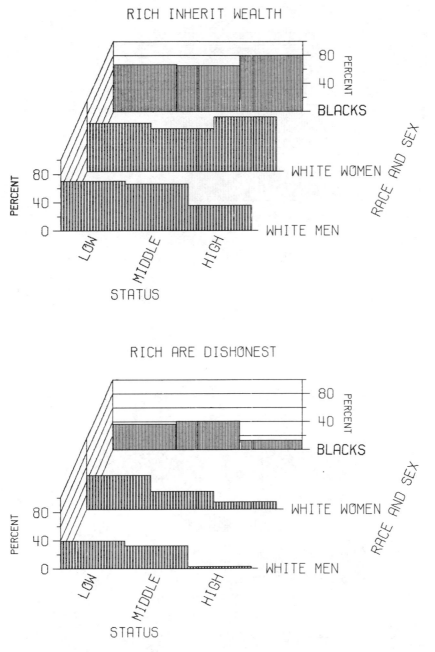

FIGURE 4.2. *Continued.*

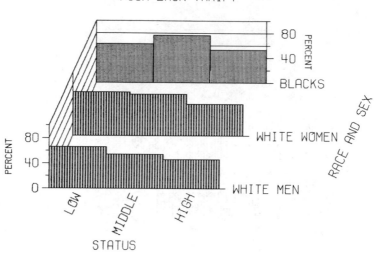

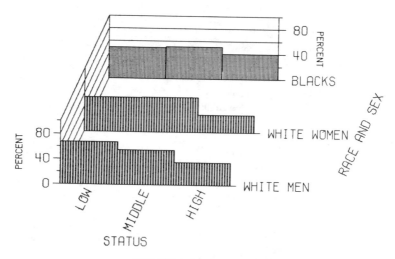

FIGURE 4.2. *Continued.*

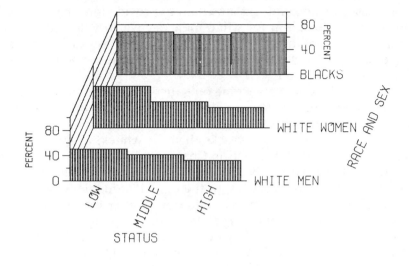

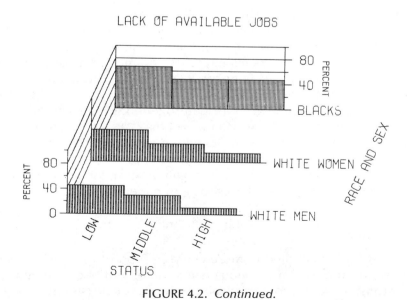

FIGURE 4.2. *Continued.*

individual explanations for poverty are strongest for white men, weaker for white women, and nonsignificant for blacks. Perhaps education has a different balance of functions for the different groups, serving more to increase socioeconomic status than to provide information and increase social liberalism for white men relative to white women and blacks. Recall that in Chapter 3 a similar pattern appeared: Education led to perceptions of unequal opportunity for white women and blacks, but not for white men.

Similarly, the effect of income on structural explanations for wealth is strong and negative among whites and nonsignificant among blacks. Status differences (effects of education and income on explanations), then, seem weaker among blacks than for whites, as in comparable analyses of opportunity beliefs in Chapter 3. Blacks thus may view the world as if they have a fairly uniform status. Middle- and upper-middle-class blacks may doubt aspects of the dominant ideology on the basis of an identification with their racial group, rather than responding in terms of their personal status. High levels of group identification among blacks have been identified by other researchers as well (e.g., Gurin, Miller, & Gurin, 1980). Other recent analyses (Nilson, 1981; National Urban League, 1983, cited in Rule, 1983) have obtained similar results, questioning claims that the relatively educated and affluent black middle class has come to differ dramatically from more disadvantaged blacks in their politically relevant attitudes (Wilson, 1978).

This pattern of group-based responses and a corresponding weakness of individual-level effects is not at all visible among white women. White males and females share generally similar distributions of beliefs about the causes of economic achievement, as of beliefs about opportunity (Chapter 3). Group identification centering on explanations for economic inequality seems much less prominent among women than among blacks, an issue to be expanded upon in Chapter 8. Possible reasons for this difference are unclear (cf. Gurin et al., 1980) but may involve not only the much more heterogeneous status position of women relative to blacks but also the fact that status for many women (e.g., housewives) is essentially derived from the household's overall status rather than personally achieved. Both of these factors should operate psychologically to block recognition of a common fate with common causes, important bases for group identification.

CONCLUSIONS

The main points noted in these analyses support our general perspective on the role of individualism as an essential component of Americans' thinking about inequality. Americans consistently strongly endorse individual reasons for economic position, particularly for poverty, and reject liberal and (especially) radical explanations emphasizing structural causes. Individualistic responses are also preponderant in explanations for one's own situation and for that of Americans in general, though feelings about the wealthy are a bit more mixed. Comparisons with other available data show remarkable over-time stability on all measures where data exist since at least the late 1960s, and cross-national data (e.g., Coughlin, 1980; Lopreato & Hazelrigg, 1972) show a similar prevalence of individualistic explanations in other societies. The stability of these beliefs in a period of extensive political debate and action concerning poverty points to the function of the beliefs in supporting a more general belief system, the dominant ideology, for many people.

The data also reveal the effects of potential challenges to individualism from different sources (perceptions of one's own case, of opportunity, and of structural causes for wealth and poverty). The results suggest the following. *(a)* Individuals generally perceive their own economic position as caused by internal factors, so that generalization from one's individual circumstances to those of most Americans potentially would support rather than challenge the dominant ideology. *(b)* The links from perceptions of opportunity to individualist beliefs are weak, suggesting that the moderate recent decline in the perceived availability of opportunity has posed little concrete challenge to individualism. *(c)* People may respond to political debate by adopting beliefs in structural causes of achievement, but the effect of structural beliefs is usually *not* to overthrow the belief in individual causation but to produce compromise images (e.g., the idea that barriers to opportunity exist but can be overcome by strenuous individual efforts).

The relationships of explanations to respondents' sociodemographic characteristics were also analyzed. Explanations are related in systematic ways to status (measured by education and income, sex, or race), with higher status increasing individual and decreasing structural explanations almost across the board. Several exceptions and complications qualify this basic pattern, however. *(a)* Individual explanations for poverty display a different pattern of determinants from other explanations, showing few status effects. *(b)* The relationship of structural explanations to sociodemographic variables is more systematic than that of individual explanations, supporting the notion that individualism is culturally based and structuralism more often a product of individual life experiences and conditions. *(c)* Education functions partly as an indicator of social status (i.e., similarly to income)—particularly for white men—but also produces socially liberal beliefs, which seem to decrease individual explanations for both wealth and poverty. *(d)* Explanations of all kinds show fewer status effects among blacks than among whites, meaning perhaps that blacks view the world in terms of racial group identification; in effect, as if they possessed a uniform status. *(e)* Finally, sex differences in the determinants of these explanations are both few and small. Despite these details, the general picture is of broad agreement on individual causes of achievement in American society, agreement which is held only somewhat less firmly among the disadvantaged than among the privileged—with blacks furnishing the only major exception to this statement.

5

DISTRIBUTIVE JUSTICE

Does the American public believe that economic inequality is just? The results of our analyses in Chapter 4 argue that in one sense the answer is "yes." In general the American public believes that unequal economic status is primarily earned by the efforts and talents of individuals: that economic outcomes on the whole are equitable relative to individual merit. Equity relative to individual merit, however, is but one aspect of economic justice. Justice also involves the evaluation of equity relative to the collectivity (i.e., the fairness of the average incomes earned by incumbents of different social positions relative to the differential worth of their contribution to society).

Several questions may be asked about the beliefs about societal equity held by the American public. First, does the American public believe that economic inequality is just in principle? Several more specific questions are implied by this broad question. What factors produce economic inequality? What ends (if any) does it serve for society? That is, what are the perceived benefits (and costs) of economic inequality for people in general?

Second, if the justice of inequality in principle is accepted, questions about how unequal rewards should be distributed become relevant. *How much inequality is just?* Should there be a minimum or maximum income paid to various jobs? Or is any degree of inequality fair if it results "naturally"? *What are just criteria for the differential allocation of incomes to jobs?* Should jobs be paid according to how much education they require? Does ownership of property or of businesses entitle people to more income than nonowners or employees?

The above questions concern beliefs about what is fair in theory or in the ideal. A third area concerns the actual distribution of income. *Is the current distribution of income fair?*

To examine the American public's beliefs about these aspects of distributive justice, in the national survey we asked many questions concerning beliefs about income inequality. We also make use of data from a survey of Illinois residents conducted in 1979 to examine beliefs about certain aspects of income inequality not directly covered in the national survey.[1] As in Chapters 3 and 4 we begin our analysis of beliefs about income inequality with a descriptive profile and an examination of available information on their stability and change.

DISTRIBUTIONS AND TIME TRENDS

Perceived Sources and Consequences of Income Inequality

Since scholars first began to analyze critically the workings of society, theories have been proposed of why economic inequality exists as a pervasive feature of society. While there are many such scholarly theories (for a review see Kriesberg, 1979), they share two major elements. First, they offer explanations of how economic inequality has come to be (i.e., of its sources). Second, they propose reasons for why economic inequality should or should not exist. In general they either seek to defend its legitimacy by arguing for the beneficial consequences of economic inequality for society or attack its legitimacy by arguing for its harmful consequences (or the benefits or equality). Here we examine theories held by the American public of why inequality exists. What do they believe are the sources and consequences of income inequality?

To answer this question we presented to our survey respondents a series of statements that incorporate proposed sources of income inequality and proposed consequences of equality or inequality and asked them to indicate agreement–disagreement with these statements on a 4-point response scale. To provide a context for respondents' evaluations of these statements they were introduced as reasons that people have given for why incomes should or should not be more equal than at present. Question wordings and the frequency distribution for responses to each of the statements are given in Table 5.1.

The statements were constructed to incorporate proposed sources and consequences of income inequality found in scholarly theories of why inequality exists and identified in previous research on citizens' beliefs (Lane, 1962; Rainwater, 1974). Previous research, of course, provides some insight into public beliefs about the sources and consequences of economic inequality. However, since prior research on these beliefs (cf. Hochschild, 1981) has employed open-ended or unstructured interviewing with very small samples of unknown representativeness, it does not provide a strong basis for generalization about Americans' beliefs, or does it permit analysis of their determinants.

[1]This survey of English-speaking adult residents of the state of Illinois was carried-out by telephone with the assistance of the Survey Research Laboratory at the University of Illinois. Respondents were selected by means of random-digit dialing procedures.

The list we presented to our respondents includes seven statements that provide reasons for maintaining current income inequality and four statements that provide reasons for making the distribution of incomes more equal. The larger number of the former reasons reflect both the fact that there are more scholarly theories that offer reasons to justify inequality than equality and the fact that in open-ended questioning about these reasons people give a larger number of reasons justifying economic inequality than reasons supporting equality. In part this imbalance in favor of justifying reasons may be due to the interest elites have in promoting theories that justify economic inequality. It should also be noted that the size of imbalance is in part overstated, since some theories that offer justifications for equality implicitly or explicitly incorporate negations of statements we have worded in a manner that justifies income inequality. For example, denial of the proposition that it is human nature to always want more than others have, forms part of certain major theories—such as that of Karl Marx—that argue that human wants in large part are the product of socialization rather than innately given.

Popular Theories of Inequality

The statements presented to our respondents relate to major elements of three influential theoretical perspectives on the sources and consequences of economic inequality. In the Marxist or *conflict perspective*, wealth derives from the division of labor in society to which all contribute equally. Consequently, the justice of income *equality* is underscored, and need is advocated as the criterion for a just allocation of income. Current economic inequality is seen as the product of historical and contemporary exploitation of others by people who own or control wealth. *Structural–functionalism* proposes that positional inequality stems from the differential importance of the contributions made by different positions in society to the collective well-being. Inequalities of ability, motivation, and training among people are assumed. In this perspective, income inequality serves to motivate the most able people to take on and to perform effectively the most important positions. *Classical economic theory,* as found in the writings of Adam Smith and contemporary apologists for capitalism (e.g., Gilder, 1980) proposes that wealth derives from the actions of those who own or control wealth (i.e., of capitalists). People are assumed to be self-interested by nature, and a capitalistic market economy (and by implication the economic inequality associated with private ownership of capital) is thought to channel the pursuit of individual self-interest such that collective benefit for society results.

The percentage distributions of agreement–disagreement with the

TABLE 5.1. Beliefs about the Sources and Consequences of Income Inequality

Belief items	Strongly agree	Agree	Disagree	Strongly disagree	Loadings[a] I	Loadings[a] II
More equality of incomes would allow my family to live better *(family)*	3	39	55	3[b]	-.11	.67
More equality of incomes would avoid conflicts between people at different levels *(conflict)*	10	52	32	6[c]	-.01	.56
	5	50	38	7		
Incomes *should* be more equal, because every family's needs for food, housing, and so on, are the same *(need)*	3	36	56	6	-.04	.61
Incomes *should* be more equal, because everybody's contribution to society is equally important *(equal contribution)*	3	36	53	8	-.05	.63
If incomes were more equal, nothing would motivate people to work hard *(motivation)*	7	56	25	2	.47	-.17
Incomes cannot be made more equal since people's abilities and talents are unequal *(unequal ability)*	13	72	14	1	.39	-.23

Item					
Incomes should *not* be more equal since the rich invest in the economy, creating jobs and benefits for everyone *(trickle down)*	4	51	41	4	.36	.00
If incomes were more equal, life would be boring because people would all live in the same way *(boring)*	8	53	34	5	.63	–.04
Incomes *cannot* be made more equal since it's human nature to always want more than others have *(human nature)*	9	73	17	1	.55	–.18
Incomes should *not* be made more equal since that would keep people from dreaming of someday becoming a real success *(dream success)*	6	64	28	2	.70	.00
Making incomes more equal means socialism, and that deprives people of individual freedoms *(socialism)*	14	60	24	2	.61	–.15

[a] Factor analysis loadings.
[b] Response percentages from Version 1, the first random subsample (*N* = 844).
[c] Response percentages from Version 2, the second random subsample (*N* = 663).

11 statements presented to our respondents (Table 5.1) show that in general the American public's view of the sources and consequences of income inequality corresponds most closely to the structural–functionalist perspective. To a somewhat lesser degree their view shares elements of classical economic theory. On the whole, the American public rejects the conflict perspective.

Support for the structural–functionalist view is seen in the prevalent disagreement with the statement that everybody's contribution to society is equally important. As is also evident in Table 5.1, substantial majorities of our respondents agree with both the proposition that incomes cannot be made more equal because of unequal ability and talent, and the proposition that inequality is needed to motivate people to work hard.

Most Americans share the assumption of classical economic theory that humans are by nature self-interested—as evidenced in the prevalent endorsement of the statement that it is human nature to always want more than others have. However, only a slight majority of our respondents agree that incomes should not be more equal because the rich invest in the economy, creating jobs and benefits for all. Fewer Americans seem to share the premise of classical economic theory that wealth is derived from the actions of the wealthy. American opinion of the merits of the "trickle-down" theory that is a key element of contemporary conservative rhetoric is clearly divided.

Rejection of the conflict perspective is implied, of course, by the prevalent endorsement of elements of the structural–functionalist and classical economic perspectives. Moreover, as we have seen in Chapter 4, on the whole the American public does not share the conflict perspective view that wealth is the product of exploitation by the wealthy. Although some of our findings in Chapter 4 and the split opinion on the merits of "trickle-down theory" suggest that the American public does not fully share the high esteem of the wealthy found in much conservative rhetoric; negative opinion of the wealthy seems to lie more in the evaluation of their personal attributes (e.g., dishonesty) than in support for the conflict perspective thesis of exploitation.

The American public sees expressive benefits to income inequality in addition to the instrumental benefits (efficient functioning of society and economic gain) stressed by the structural–functionalist and classical economic perspectives. There is majority agreement that income inequality permits expression of basic needs and desires: Americans in general see economic inequality as a source of variety, seem to derive vicarious enjoyment from it, and thus agree with the statement that more equality would make life boring. Perhaps because the public believes that people are by nature self-interested and acquisitive and therefore want to have economic inequality to allow the expression of this acquisitive nature, our respondents predominantly agree with the statement that incomes should not be more equal because it would prohibit dreaming of becoming a success.

One perceived expressive benefit of income inequality involves another aspect of the rejection of the conflict perspective. Most Americans, in the words of Lane (1962), "fear equality." The statement that equality means socialism and entails loss of individual freedom receives widespread endorsement by our survey respondents. Antisocialist rhetoric has long been a part of American politics, and it no doubt contributes to the popularity of this belief. The contrast between Americans' images of social and political conditions in the United States and in nations most strongly identified with income equality, the People's Republic of China and the Soviet Union, also seem to underlie the identity of equality of incomes with loss of freedom. The sentiment that equality means sameness of lifestyle may be due in part to the popular image of an enforced sameness of living conditions in these countries, perhaps especially the image of life in communist China. In both cases, of course, greater equality of incomes, relative to the distribution in the United States, coexists with totalitarian political regimes and denials of certain political, religious, and other freedoms. Many Americans seemingly make a causal link between income equality and the denials of individual freedom.

Although the American public widely believes that income *inequality* is beneficial, a substantial proportion also believes that *equality* has certain benefits. Slightly over one-half of our respondents agree that greater equality would reduce conflicts between different strata. Thus many Americans perceive that income inequality presents a threat to maintaining a conflict-free social order.

On the individual level, one seemingly obvious benefit from greater equality for people with incomes below the average is increased income. Given the skewed nature of the income distribution—that is, there are proportionally more Americans with family income below the arithmetic mean than above it—roughly 60% of the population would potentially benefit to some degree from greater equality in the income distribution. On this basis, one might expect to find, for the reasons of simple self-interest, that approximately 60% of survey respondents would agree with the statement, "More equality of incomes would allow my family to live better."

Table 5.1 gives two sets of percentage distributions for responses to this question—resulting from a split-ballot experiment. One randomly selected group of respondents responded to the self-interest statement *before* all other statements (Version 2). The other group responded to this statement *after* all others (Version 1). Two findings of this experiment are important to note.

First, there are substantial and statistically significant differences in response to the self-interest statement between groups. When the self-interest statement was presented first, 62% of our respondents expressed agreement. When it was presented after all other statements, 41% agreed. Second, there are no substantial or statistically significant differences between groups in the distributions of responses to any other statements.

We conducted this experiment because we conjectured that a better gauge of perceived simple self-interest—self-interest evaluated only on the basis of personal, immediate loss or gain—would be obtained when the self-interest statement is presented before the others. However, we also were concerned with the possible effects that presenting this item first might have on responses to other statements if many people were influenced by the desire to make responses seem consistent across statements (Schuman & Presser, 1981).

The results of this experiment suggest that indeed a better assessment of perceived simple self-interest is achieved when the relevant item is presented first. The percentage agreeing in this case is quite close to the expectation on objective grounds of the proportion who potentially would benefit from greater equality.

The results also argue that responses to these statements are little influenced by the desire to simply appear consistent in responses across items. Respondents in Version 2 did not endorse more often than those in Version 1 reasons supporting the justice of more equality of incomes or reject reasons supporting the justice of existing income inequality, as would be expected if they were simply seeking to give answers consistent with their greater average agreement with the self-interest item.

These results suggest that the assessment of self-interest is not unidimensional, consistent with our theory's postulates. When reminded of the potential collective benefits to economic inequality—as they were in Version 1—respondents appeared to use broader criteria than simple immediate economic loss or gain in evaluating their self-interest. Without such a reminder, however, simple economic self-interest is the primary criteria employed and, indeed, may have primacy in general. In Part II we will comment more extensively on the multidimensional nature of self-interest.

Age-Group Differences in Perceived Sources and Consequences

Because there are no over-time data on them, we must rely solely on age-group differences to make inferences about change in beliefs about the sources and consequences of income inequality. Figure 5.1

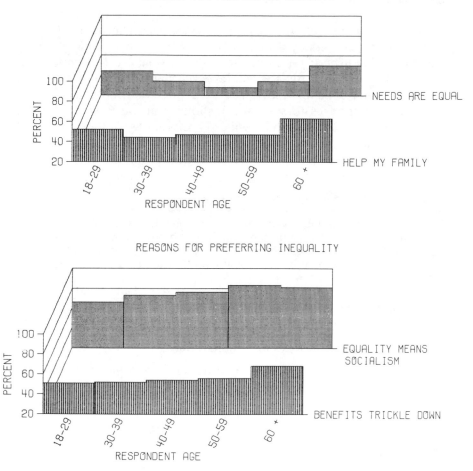

FIGURE 5.1. Percentage agreement with selected reasons for preferring income equality and reasons for preferring income inequality, broken down by respondent's age.

illustrates the percentage agreement with two representative statements supportive of income inequality and two supportive of more equality by age-group. In general age-group differences are slight. These differences are, however, somewhat larger for reasons supportive of equality than for reasons supportive of inequality. In the former case, there is a curvilinear pattern such that the old and the young more strongly agree on the average with reasons supporting equality than do other age groups. In the latter case, the percentage agreeing with statements supportive of inequality increases linearly with age.

Criteria for a Just Distribution

In general, there are three major criteria for justly allocating incomes: equality, need, and equity (Deutsch, 1975). Further, two kinds of equity may be distinguished: (1) equity at the individual level or "microjustice", and (2) equity at the societal level or "macrojustice" (Brickman, Folger, Goode, & Schol, 1981). Table 5.2 presents percentage distributions for responses to several questions from our survey and the survey of Illinois residents that concern preferences for these different justice criteria.

Two questions concern the preference for equality as a just criterion.

TABLE 5.2. Criteria for a Just Distribution of Income

Some people say that incomes should be completely equal, with every family making roughly the same amount of money; others say that things should stay about the same as they are now; and still others think incomes should be less equal than they are now. Ideally do you think there should be . . .

	Percentage	(f)
Complete equality of income	3	(35)
More equality than there is now	38	(543)
About the present level of income equality	52	(732)
Less equality of incomes than there is now	7	(105)

It would be a good thing if all people received the same amount of money no matter what jobs they do. Do you . . . (Illinois survey)

	Percentage	(f)
Strongly agree	1	(8)
Agree	6	(43)
Disagree	64	(434)
Strongly disagree	29	(99)

Do you think that the income a person receives should be based more on the person's skills and training or more on what their family needs to live decently?

	Percentage	(f)
Skills	81	(1183)
Family needs	13	(196)
Both (volunteered)	6	(89)

It would be more fair if people were paid by how much they needed to live decently rather than the kind of work they do. Do you . . . (Illinois survey)

	Percentage	(f)
Strongly agree	5	(36)
Agree	36	(239)
Disagree	45	(300)
Strongly disagree	14	(94)

Continued

Workers should receive additional wages for each additional child they have. Do you . . . (Illinois survey)

	Percentage	(f)
Strongly agree	2	(14)
Agree	31	(211)
Disagree	56	(377)
Strongly disagree	11	(75)

A company pays workers according to how much their work group produces. Some workers feel they should be paid more because they produce more. Do you . . . (Illinois survey)

	Percentage	(f)
Strongly agree	12	(79)
Agree	71	(475)
Disagree	16	(110)
Strongly disagree	1	(6)

Two people are doing the same type of work but the one with more education gets more pay. The person with more education should get more pay. Do you . . . (Illinois survey)

	Percentage	(f)
Strongly agree	3	(17)
Agree	24	(161)
Disagree	64	(426)
Strongly disagree	10	(64)

Responses to both questions show that very few Americans (approximately 3 and 7% in the national and the Illinois surveys, respectively) see strict equality as just. In contrast, need is seen as a just criterion by substantially more people.

Three questions from the two surveys concern the criterion of need. In our survey we asked respondents whether they thought income should be based more on a person's skills and training or more on what their family needs to live decently. This question involves a choice between individual equity and need as criteria for distributing income. In the Illinois survey, one question concerns one aspect of need—paying additional wages for the support of children—and the other concerns need in general. The wording of the latter question, "paid by how much they needed to live decently rather than the kind of work they do," implies a choice between societal equity (the kind of work) and need.

The relatively higher levels of support for need compared to strict equality may be due in part to a perceived conflict between equality and need. It appears that many people oppose the justice of strict equality on grounds that families do not have equal need; some have more children than others, some must cope with greater health-related problems, and so on. Also, in part, the higher level of support for need may be due to the greater logical compatibility of balancing need with equity as joint criteria for a just distribution. If one believes (as most Americans do) that individuals inherently differ in their ability and talent and that people differ in the importance of their contribution to society, then absolute equality precludes equity. On the other hand, it is possible to have a distribution that is in general equitable that also incorporates need to some degree.

A higher percentage of respondents show a relative preference for need over equity on the Illinois survey question than on the national survey question, 41 versus 20%, respectively. Perhaps residents of Illinois are more egalitarian on the average than the general population, but on its face this seems implausible. A more plausible explanation is that Americans on the whole give greater importance to individual equity than to societal equity as criteria for a just income distribution; when the decision involves opting for individual equity or individual need the choice seems clearer for more Americans than when the decision involves choosing between societal equity and individual need.

By whichever measure we choose to indicate the degree of sentiment for egalitarian criteria (equality or need), these findings indicate that the large majority of the American public prefers equity as the criterion for a just allocation of income. As the above discussion implies, the public most strongly emphasizes individual-level equity as the criterion for a just distribution.The emphasis placed on this criterion is evident in responses to two additional questions from the Illinois residents survey (Table 5.2). Of respondents, 83 and 74%, respectively, oppose using group production levels and educational credentials per se (apart from use of credentials to select people for jobs) as criteria for differential pay. Simple proportionality of income to individual productivity is what Americans seek most in a just distribution.

Why is individual-level equity the most salient criteria of distributive justice? Our data do not allow us to directly answer this question, but we suggest that in part individual-level equity is stressed because it serves the need to believe that one can control one's own outcomes by one's own efforts. The use of other criteria, such as group production levels, means that the determination of one's economic outcomes rest in factors outside of an individual's direct control. As we shall see in Chapter 10, the belief that one personally determines his or her economic fate enhances psychological well-being.

Age-Group Differences in Criteria for a Just Distribution

Figure 5.2 shows the statistically significant age-group differences in measures of preferred justice criteria. On the whole, age-group differences in these measures are 'insubstantial and not statistically sig-

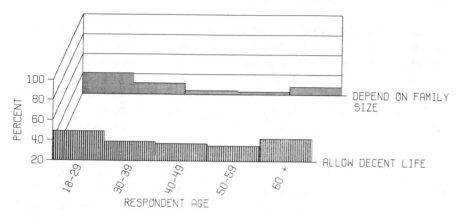

FIGURE 5.2. Preference for different criteria for fair income levels by respondent's age.

nificant. Concerning the preference for strict equality only, there is one available indicator of over-time change. In his 1969 survey Feagin (1975) asked about this preference. The percentage of survey respondents indicating a preference for a strict equality in this survey, 13%, is quite close to our findings.[2]

Significant differences exist for the Illinois survey questions concerning additional wages for child support and the preference for need in general. In both cases the pattern of age-group differences is curvilinear. The young (18–20 years), especially, and the old (over 60 years), to a lesser degree, show more support for need as a criterion than other age groups. In each case, a life cycle as opposed to a trend explanation seems more plausible. Because children place a substantial financial strain on the resources of younger parents it is more in their self-interest to favor additional wages for child support. Perhaps because as people age they acquire grandchildren, sentiment in favor of wages for child support increases with age (after 40). The difference in general preference for need may also be due to the differential burden of children and other financial strains at different points in the life cycle. In sum, available evidence argues for stability of preferred criteria for a just distribution in the last few decades.

[2]Feagin (1975, p. 137) asked respondents in his 1969 survey whether they agreed that "every family in this country should receive the same income, about $10,000 or so." Since he did not give respondents the alternative to choose more rather than strictly complete equality, some of the difference in results may be due to question wording.

Beliefs about Income Inequality in Fact

Our examination of beliefs about the sources and consequences of income inequality and of perceived just criteria for the distribution of income shows that most Americans view income inequality as just in principle. Do Americans also see the current distribution as just in fact?

The Perceived Amount of Income Inequality. To answer this question we begin with an examination of our survey respondents' beliefs about how much income inequality exists in America. Beliefs about the amount of income inequality relate to two major aspects of the evaluation of the current income distribution. First, they have implications for its perceived fairness. It seems reasonable to assume that most people would see a society characterized by prevalent poverty in the midst of plentiful material wealth as inherently unjust. The presence of widespread poverty does not fit well with an image of America as the land of opportunity, populated in the main by hard-working, earnest people. The more widespread poverty is perceived to be, especially if a high percentage of the population is also seen as well-to-do, the more this image is threatened.

Second, beliefs about the amount of inequality have implications for the perceived necessity and desirability of actions to change the income distribution, and specifically for beliefs about potential gains from such policy. Even if one questions the necessity or desirability of income inequality in principle, if he or she perceives that in fact there is little inequality, there is little reason to seek policy to promote change. The perceived amount of inequality indicates how large a potential for conflict among strata exists—a belief that society is divided between the rich and the poor, for example, implies a high potential for conflict. And it defines one aspect of self-interest in redistributive policy. If, for example, a middle-income person perceives that there are roughly equal percentages of wealthy and poor individuals in America, then redistribution may be possible without cost for this person by transfers from the wealthy to the poor. If on the other hand, this same person views the distribtuion as consisting of many more poor than wealthy, then redistribution cannot be viewed as costless.

To measure beliefs about the amount of income inequality we asked respondents to our survey to indicate what percentage of the American population they believe are poor and what percentage they believe are rich. We can infer beliefs about the size of the middle classes by subtracting these two percentage figures from 100. This procedure admittedly produces only a rough estimate of the perceived amount of inequality. However, given the complexity of the concept of inequality, direct questioning is difficult (e.g., how much inequality do you believe there is?), and given the limitations of telephone interviewing (such as the inability to use visual aids) we believe this approach is the most feasible. The questions employed and grouped frequency distributions for perceived percentage poor, rich, and in the middle classes are given in Table 5.3.

The official government poverty line provides one objective standard for determining what percentage of Americans live in poverty. Federal government reports on the prevalence of poverty in the United States use this standard, and these reports generally receive wide media attention. In 1980 approximately 12% of Americans lived in families with incomes below this line (U.S. Bureau of the Census, 1981).

The distribution of the perceived percentage poor shows quite clearly that Americans are aware of the prevalence of poverty. Since there is a tendency in response to percentage questions to round up or down to the nearest 5%, responses under 10% are a reasonable criterion for determining the percentage unaware of poverty. By this criterion only about 7% of our respondents are unaware. If we use the range 10–15% to allow for rounding up or down from 12%, we find that approximately

TABLE 5.3. Grouped Frequency Distributions for the Perceived Percentage Poor, Rich, and in the Middle Classes

Range	Percentage	(f)
Poor		
0–5	6	(86)
6–9	1	(13)
10–15	14	(201)
16–20	10	(140)
21–30	20	(285)
31–40	15	(212)
41–50	14	(194)
51+	21	(305)
Rich		
0–5	23	(332)
6–10	25	(365)
11–20	21	(302)
21–30	16	(225)
31–40	7	(98)
41–50	6	(81)
51+	3	(45)
Middle classes		
0–10	22	(307)
11–24	5	(69)
25–49	22	(322)
50–74	31	(445)
75–89	16	(221)
90–100	4	(66)

14% of our respondents may be designated as people who believe poverty to be as prevalent as indicated by government reports.

Most Americans perceive that poverty is more prevalent than the official figure—the median perceived percentage poor is approximately 31% percent. Rainwater (1974) found that his respondents (a small sample of residents of a single community) considered the official poverty line to be substantially too low relative to their personal views of what living in poverty means, and Gallup (1985) recently obtained similar results in a national sample.

There is, of course, no parallel official government "rich" line. Correspondingly there is no regular media reporting of the prevalence of "richness" in America. To provide an estimate of awareness of the prevalence of people who are rich we must rely on the public's conceptions of what income it takes to be rich. Respondents in the Illinois survey were asked for the dollar figure that in their opinion defines a person as rich. While there is considerable variation in these subjective "rich lines," most respondents (83%) gave figures of $50,000 or more. This figure may be taken as a conservative criterion for judging the awareness of how prevalent the rich are as a porportion of the population.

In 1980 about 5% of Americans had family income of $50,000 or more. Judged by prevailing views of what being rich means, about one-half of the public give percentage estimates of the prevalence of rich Americans that are reasonably close to the actual prevalence (i.e., between 0 and 10%). The remaining one-half tends to rather substantially overestimate the percentage rich. Overall, the median percentage is 15% rich.

The median percentage of the American population perceived to be in the middle classes is approximately 50%. Judged by the official poverty line and the conservative subjective "rich line," in actuality about 80% of Americans have family incomes that place them in the middle classes. If we instead define the poverty line as equal to about 60% of the median income—where most Americans place the subjective poverty line (Rainwater, 1974)—then according to 1980 income statistics approximately two-thirds of Americans have family incomes in the middle classes. By either estimate of the actual percentage in the middle classes, *Americans on the whole tend to see somewhat more inequality in the distribution of income than is actually there*. In this regard it is notable that a substantial percentage of our respondents have the most pronounced "rich man–poor man" image of society possible. Of these, 16% by implication perceive 0% in the middle classes—that is, they see America as composed completely of the rich and the poor.

The Fairness of Positional Inequality. As we have seen, the American public on the whole believes that an unequal allocation of incomes to different positions is just in principle because people in some positions make a greater contribution to the effective functioning of society than others. Accepting the justice of positional inequality in principle, however, does not imply acceptance of the justice of actual positional inequality. People may agree that positional inequality helps to produce an effectively functioning society but disagree on the goals they believe that society should realize. For example, a person may believe that the payment of higher average income to engineers than to elementary school teachers gives too much importance to the efficient production of material goods and too little importance to the training of literate, effectively functioning citizens.

People may disagree about the justice of actual positional inequality even when they agree on both means and goals. People may believe that certain occupations deserve to be more highly rewarded than others but believe that the actual discrepancy in incomes is too large or too small relative to a just rank ordering of incomes. For example, a person may believe that doctors deserve to be paid more than secretaries, but also that doctors use the broader powers inherent in their position (such as control of licensing), and lacking for secretaries, to obtain more income than they deserve relative to the differential importance of contributions by secretaries and doctors.

To assess Americans' evaluation of the justice of actual positional inequality we asked our respondents to indicate whether they felt people in various occupations in general make too little, about the right amount, or too much relative to their contribution to society. Respondents were asked to evaluate the income received by people in commonly used categories for general types of occupations. In all, we asked for evaluations of the income received by 15 types of occupation. Some were evaluated by random halves of sample respondents only, so the number of respondents differs among the occupations evaluated. The frequency distributions for these evaluations are presented in Table 5.4.

Evaluations of the average incomes of people in the occupational categories presented to our respondents, viewed in their totality, give an impression of a highly mixed assessment of the fairness of current positional income inequality. The lists we presented to respondents include some occupations that have very few incumbents, such as professional athletes or corporate executives, and therefore one may wish to give them low weights in an assessment of perceived overall fairness. However, even if we limit attention to the most representative occupations, the mixed quality of the public's overall assessment of fairness remains evident. Among the representative occupations (excluding corporate executives, stockholders, professional athletes, movie stars, and top entertainers) only middle-level managers and

TABLE 5.4. Perceived Fairness of the Income Received by Persons in
           Different Types of Occupations

I'd like you to tell me about the amount of income that different kinds of
people receive. For the contribution that they make to society do ___ receive
. . .

	Too little	About the right amount	Too much	Don't know
Government officials	4	24	67	4
Middle-level managers in business	18	58	8	16
Skilled blue-collar workers	8	47	42	3
Owners of small business	40	49	4	8
Lower level white-collar workers	62	33	2	4
Landlords	5	39	49	8
Owners and executives of large corporations	1	23	71	5
Unionized factory workers	14	53	28	5
Professional athletes	3	18	77	2
Teachers in elementary and high schools	62	31	5	2
Medical doctors	2	27	69	1
Stockholders of large corporations	4	34	47	15
Non-unionized factory workers	61	28	2	9
Movie stars and top entertainers	1	18	78	4
Teachers in colleges and universities	53	34	7	7

unionized factory workers are evaluated by a clear majority of respondents as receiving average salaries that are fair relative to the contribution
they make to society. Three occupations in this set receive split evaluations. A plurality of our respondents (47%) perceive that skilled blue-
collar workers receive income that is on the average "about right," but
a substantial proportion (42%) perceive that this group receives "too
much." Similarly, a plurality (49%) believes that small business owners
have earnings that are about right on the average, but here a substantial
proportion (40%) believes that this group receives "too little." In general
the public believes that landlords are overrewarded relative to their
contribution, but a large minority (39%) see their income as fair on the
average.[3]

Americans more uniformly see the remaining six occupations as
either under- or overrewarded. Non-unionized factory workers, lower

[3]We, of course, cannot assess from responses to these questions the accuracy
of the public's perceptions of what the average incomes are for incumbents
of the occupations rated. However, we think it reasonable to assume that for
the broad occupational categories that we presented respondents have a ranking
of average occupational incomes that is, at least monotonically, related to the
actual average incomes in these occupations.

level white-collar workers, high school and college teachers, make up the underrewarded group. Government officials and doctors make up the overrewarded group.

These evaluations show that many Americans perceive several discrepancies between average incomes for major types of occupations and what they believe they should be ideally. Some of these perceived discrepancies seem to stem from the belief that a just distribution of incomes should be based on considerations of need, at least to some degree. Two of the four occupations seen as underrewarded by substantial majorities of our respondents, non-unionized factory workers and lower level white-collar workers, have average incomes that place them near the subjectively assessed "just able to get along" standard of living. Many Americans seem to be expressing the sentiment that anyone who works for a living should receive enough income to avoid having to struggle to make ends meet.

There also seems to be a prevailing belief that there is a maximum level of income that any person, regardless of the importance of his or her contribution, is worth, indicated by high percentages who rate as "too high" the average incomes received in the most highly paid occupations in our list—doctors, corporate executives, movie stars and top entertainers, and owners and stockholders of large corporations. It is interesting to note the contrast between the attributed causes of wealth examined in Chapter 4 and the evaluated fairness of average incomes for occupations that are commonly held by the wealthy. On the one hand, most Americans believe that as individuals the wealthy have merited their positions through superior talent and effort. On the other hand, most Americans also believe that the average incomes from the occupations that the wealthy typically hold are too high in proportion to their contributions to society. In general, our findings in Chapters 3, 4, and 5 show that the average American views wealth and the wealthy critically on one level and positively on another. The average person believes that much wealth is inherited and that the wealthy receive income greatly disproportionate to their roles' contributions to society. Perhaps because he or she wishes to believe that through individual effort alone one can become wealthy, the average American *also* thinks highly of the rich as individuals—attributing wealth to superior individual talent and effort.

Taken together, the sentiment that people in occupations with incomes substantially below the median earnings for all workers should receive more than they do and the belief that those in occupations with incomes markedly above the median should receive less than they do suggest that for many Americans an ideal or just distribution judged in terms of societal equity would have a more restricted range of inequality than there is in the actual distribution of income. Prior research

(Rainwater, 1974; Jasso & Rossi, 1977; Alves & Rossi, 1978) has hypothesized that many Americans would prefer a more restricted range of incomes in the ideal than currently exists. Our research confirms this hypothesis. Furthermore, a look back at the responses to a question presented earlier in this chapter (Table 5.2) provides an estimate of how prevalent this preference is. Approximately 40% of our respondents reported that ideally there should be more equality of incomes than there is now.[4]

The Fairness of Personal Income. In addition to the list of specific occupational categories, all respondents were asked to evaluate the fairness of the income they personally receive, and employed respondents were asked to evaluate the fairness of the income others in their own line of work receive. The highly mixed assessment of the fairness of positional inequality in general indicated by evaluations of average occupational incomes is also evident in these two self-based evaluations. In both cases there is a nearly equal division among the American public between people who see themselves (53%) and others in their own line of work (48%) as fairly paid as judged by the contribution made to society, and those who see themselves (46%) and others in their own line of work (48%) as unfairly underpaid.

Age-Group Differences in Beliefs about Inequality in Fact

Insofar as age-group differences are indicative of trends in recent years, there is no evidence of change in the perceived amount of inequality. Mean percentages of perceived poor, arrayed in Table 5.5, do not differ significantly by age-group. There are statistically significant differences among age-groups in the means for the perceived percentage rich. However, these differences follow curvilinear pattern by age, with the young (18–29 years) and the old (60+ years) having slightly higher means than other groups, rather than a pattern of linear increase or decrease. The corresponding curvilinear pattern of age-group differences in perceived percentage of people in the middle classes, like the parallel pattern of differences in beliefs about the sources and consequences of income inequality and perceived just criteria, seems to be more consistent with a life cycle interpretation than an inference of consistent change.

---

[4] Also note, however, that roughly 7% of our respondents indicated a belief that the current distribution of income is *too egalitarian*. Perhaps this group believes that social programs such as aid for the poor or affirmative action have acted to inequitably compress the distribution of incomes.

TABLE 5.5. Age-Group Differences in Beliefs about Aspects of Economic Inequality in Fact

Age-group	Mean percentage poor*	Mean percentage rich[t]	Mean percentage in the middle classes[t]
18–29	36.74	19.15	44.04
30–39	34.90	16.48	48.63
40–49	37.56	16.79	45.59
50–59	38.32	16.87	44.42
60+	38.25	22.81	39.03

Age-group	Mean number of don't knows[t]	Mean proportion about right[‡]	Personal income fair[a,t]
18–29	.20	.41	45
30–39	.40	.41	50
40–49	.65	.42	57
50–59	.65	.41	57
60+	1.18	.44	62
		$(p > .25)$	

Age-group	Income others' in own line of work[a,t]
18–29	45
30–39	52
40–49	56
50–59	57
60+	65

[a]Percentage "about right" or "too much."
* $p > .3$; [t]$p < .01$; [‡]$p > .25$.

Table 5.5 also presents tests for the statistical significance of age-group differences in two summary aspects of fairness evaluations for types of occupation, the number of "don't know" and the number of "about right" responses given in evaluations of nine occupations.[5] Age-group differences in the average number of "about right" responses

[5]The aim in constructing this measure was to obtain an assessment of the fairness of positional inequality across the range of occupations. Given the very small percentage of the workforce they comprise, we excluded professional athletes and movie stars. Since questions concerning several occupations were split-balloted, we paired similar occupations from the two versions and used evaluations of all of the six occupations asked on both versions of the questionnaire. The pairs employed were: (1) owners and executives of large corporations; (2) teachers in elementary and high schools and teachers in colleges and universities; and (3) unionized factory workers and non-unionized factory workers.

provide evidence concerning trends in the overall assessment of the fairness of positional inequality.

Judged by the statistically significant and substantial age-group differences in the average number of "don't know" responses, awareness of positional inequality has been steadily growing in recent years. Although it might be argued that the tendency to avoid giving the impression of ignorance decreases with increasing age, there are reasons for believing that the pattern of linear decline in the average number of "don't know" responses indicates real change. This pattern is consistent with both increases in the average years of education and greater media attention paid to aspects of positional inequality in recent years. Younger Americans, perhaps in part because of increasing interest in high pay as a criterion for career choice, seem to know more about the relative average incomes of different occupations.

Judged by the lack of statistically significant age-group differences in the average number of "about right" responses, the overall assessment of the fairness of positional inequality has not changed in recent years. Increasing awareness of positional inequality seemingly has not led to any corresponding increase or decrease in the assessed fairness of positional inequality in general.

Finally, there are significant age-group differences in the evaluated fairness of personal income. Younger respondents, between 18 and 39 years of age, often evaluate their income and the average income for people in their own line of work as too low relative to the contribution made to society.

Summary

On the one hand, the majority of the American public agrees on what is just in principle. They believe that economic inequality in principle is necessary and desirable. They believe that equity is the fair criterion for allocating incomes—that is, people should be rewarded in proportion to effort and the differential importance of the contribtutions they make to the collectivity.

On the other hand, at the same time many Americans express doubts about the fairness of several aspects of actual economic inequality. About one-half of our respondents report that they and others in their own line of work get less income than they deserve relative to their contribution to society. Substantial majorities evaluate the average income for some (generally low-paid) occupations as unfairly low and for other occupations as unfairly high relative to the contributions made to society, implying a preference for a less unequal income distribution. And many Americans perceive that at least a substantial minority of their fellow citizens are poor.

POTENTIAL CHALLENGES TO THE PERCEIVED JUSTICE OF INEQUALITY

Challenges from Perceived Injustice in Fact

The concurrent widespread acceptance of the justice of economic inequality in principle and widespread doubt about the justice of some aspects of economic inequality in fact implies that these two kinds of beliefs are weakly related. It appears that in general people do not infer that because inequality is just in theory, therefore any unequal distribution of income is fair. Nor does it seem that doubts about the fairness of actual economic inequality lead many Americans to question the necessity and desirability of inequality in principle. To determine how strongly related are beliefs about the justice of economic inequality in principle and in fact we examine here the correlations among our measures of distributive justice beliefs.

As a preliminary step, we factor-analyzed the correlations among responses to statements incorporating proposed sources and consequences of economic inequality. Results show two correlated factors accounting for these correlations, with the factor loadings for each statement given in Table 5.1.[6] The first factor is defined by the seven statements that support current inequality, and we label it "inegalitarianism." The second factor is defined by the four statements supporting greater equality, and we label it "egalitarianism." Summated indices were formed for each factor.[7]

The finding of two factors underlying correlations among beliefs about the sources and consequences of economic inequality—rather than a single bipolar factor with preferences for equality at one end and preferences for inequality at the other—suggests that a substantial proportion of the American public sees both benefits and drawbacks to economic inequality. That is, they neither view economic inequality or equality as strictly or unequivocally just.

The correlation between the two indices formed from this factor analysis is − .34. The expected negative sign indicates that people who

[6]A principle-components factor analysis was performed, and the resulting two factors were obliquely rotated. The loadings given in Table 5.1 are from the rotated factors.

[7]Scores on items for each of the respective scales were summed and divided by the total number of items that an individual responded to. For the egalitarianism scale, if responses to more than two items were missing, a missing data code for the scale was assigned to that person. For the inegalitarianism scale, the same outcome resulted from having more than three items with missing data. For the egalitarianism scale, estimated reliability (Cronbach's alpha) equals .68. For the inegalitarianism scale it equals .76.

endorse statements supporting the justice of economic inequality do tend to reject statements supporting the justice of economic inequality. However, the correlation between inegalitarianism and egalitarianism also argues that a substantial proportion of the population has mixed beliefs—agrees with both statements that support inequality and those that support equality.[8]

This correlation coefficient does not provide an intuitively clear sense of how large this mixed population is. To get a rough estimate of its size we consider the cross-tabulation of responses to the statements that greater equality would reduce conflict and that inequality is needed to motivate people to work hard. There are 28 possible cross-tabulations involving the four statements supporting equality and the seven supporting inequality, but this one is quite representative of the pattern of proportions found in the remaining 27 tables. People indicating agreement with both statements constitute the mixed group. Those who agree that inequality is needed to motivate hard work and deny that more equality would reduce conflict among social strata seem to be indicating largely unequivocal acceptance of the necessity and desirability of inequality. Roughly equal proportions, about 37%, of the population are found in each of these two groups.

Table 5.6 arrays the correlations among beliefs about the justice of economic inequality in principle (egalitarianism and inegalitarianism scales) and beliefs about aspects of economic inequality in fact (the perceived amount of inequality, the fairness of positional inequality, and the perceived fairness of personal income). The small correlations between inegalitarianism and beliefs about aspects of economic inequality in fact are consistent with the inference that doubts about the fairness of actual economic inequality do not often lead Americans to question the necessity and desirability of inequality in principle. Note, however, that there are substantially higher values for the correlations between inegalitarianism and beliefs about aspects of economic inequality in fact.

It appears that beliefs about the fairness of existing economic inequality do provide a basis for believing that greater equality would be just and beneficial. Especially noteworthy in this regard is the substantial correlation between the perceived amount of inequality and egalitarianism. Seeing a large amount of inequality (i.e., that large percentages of the American population are poor and rich) seems to encourage beliefs that the potential for conflict between social strata over

---

[8]The lack of a stronger correlation between these two scales is not due in large part to unreliability of measurement. Corrected for attenuation due to unreliability of measurement (Nunnally, 1967), this correlation equals − .47.

TABLE 5.6. Intercorrelations of Beliefs about the Justice of Economic
Inequality in Principle and in Fact

	Egali-tarianism	Inegali-tarianism	Percentage			Pro-portion about right
			Poor	Rich	Middle	
Egali-tarianism						
Inegali-tarianism	− .34					
Percentage poor	.29	− .11				
Percentage rich	.25	− .04	.11			
Percentage middle classes	.36	− .10	.85	.61		
Proportion about right	− .14	.13	− .23	− .02	.20	
Personal income fair	− .20	.11	− .21	− .12	.23	.26

unequally distributed economic rewards is high, that greater equality
would benefit one's self-interest, and so on.

Viewed as a whole, the pattern of correlations between beliefs about
the justice of economic inequality in principle and in fact suggests that
doubt about the justice of aspects of actual economic inequality encourages people to adopt beliefs that support greater equality, rather
than to reject beliefs that advocate the necessity and desirability of
income inequality. Doubt about the justice of actual economic inequality more often results in mixed beliefs—in seeing both benefits
and drawbacks to economic inequality—than in unequivocally rejecting
the justice of inequality and advocating the justice of equality in principle.

Other Potential Challenges

The correlations in Table 5.6 address aspects of the potential challenge to the perceived justice of economic inequality stemming from
personal stratification-related experience and from increased public attention to the issue of poverty during the last two decades. We have
seen that both perceived unjust personal income and the perception
of a large amount of inequality encourage a mixed assessment of the

justice of economic inequality in principle. Do other potentially challenging beliefs concerning personal experience and relating to poverty
have the same effect?

Table 5.7 arrays the correlations among perceived contemporary (and
future) personal opportunity, the perception of being held back (or
not), structuralist attributions for poverty and wealth, and beliefs about
distributive justice. The same pattern as in the case of the correlations
between beliefs about the justice of economic inequality in principle
and in fact is found in this table. Structural attributions for poverty and
wealth and both measures of perceived personal opportunity correlate
more strongly with egalitarianism than with inegalitarianism. Also, we
see from this table that the two structuralism scales and beliefs about
the justice of aspects of actual economic inequality are substantially
interrelated.

These correlations argue that although a sizeable segment of the
American population has broad-ranging doubts about whether the
American stratification order functions as it should in the ideal, these
doubts do not lead many Americans to question the necessity of beneficial nature of economic inequality in principle. Instead doubt about
whether the stratification system functions as it should seems to result
more often in the compromise belief that there are also drawbacks to
economic inequality in addition to its benefits in principle. As we shall
see in Chapter 6, this compromise encourages a preference for policy
(e.g., a floor on income for workers) that lessens the impact of the
perceived drawbacks to economic inequality without seeming to much
reduce the benefit that many people believe derive from it.

TABLE 5.7. Correlations between: (1) Beliefs about Opportunity, Structuralist
Attributions for Poverty and Wealth, and (2) Beliefs about
Distributive Justice

	Personal opportunity	Held back	Structuralist poverty	Structuralist wealth
Egalitarianism	−.21	.13	.42	.26
Inegalitarianism	.10	−.04	−.18	−.10
Percentage poor	−.19	.21	−.33	−.29
Percentage rich	−.10	.05	.20	.08
Percentage middle classes	.20	−.20	−.37	.27
Proportion about right	.08	−.13	−.21	−.27
Personal income fair	.17	−.19	−.20	−.16

GROUP DIFFERENCES IN BELIEFS ABOUT DISTRIBUTIVE JUSTICE

Race and Sex Mean Comparisons

Black Americans, as evident in Table 5.8, markedly differ from whites in their views of the justice of economic inequality. The difference between blacks and whites in beliefs about aspects of economic inequality in fact are especially pronounced. Blacks see poverty as much more prevalent than whites do, and correspondingly on the average they place about one-fifth of the American population in the middle classes in contrast to the average of one-half for whites. Blacks see positional inequality (occupational incomes) on the average as less fair than whites. Whereas 57% of white Americans believe that the they receive income that is "about right" (or "too much") relative to the contribution made to society, only one-quarter of black respondents share this belief.

Black Americans also express more support for the justice of equality in principle than do whites, though the majority of blacks still see in-

TABLE 5.8. Means and Standard Deviations (in Parentheses) for Beliefs about the Justice of Economic Inequality by Race and Sex

Item	Whites	Blacks	Men	Women
Skills versus need[a]	.82	.62*	.82	.79
	(.39)	(.49)	(.38)	(.40)
More equality[b]	.38	.66*	.35	.46*
	(.49)	(.47)	(.48)	(.50)
Egalitarianism	2.40	2.75*	2.40	2.47*
	(.49)	(.48)	(.50)	(.50)
Inegalitarianism	2.81	2.66*	2.82	2.78
	(.40)	(.42)	(.44)	(.46)
Percentage middle classes	47.12	20.07*	51.05	38.99*
	(28.67)	(25.10)	(29.35)	(28.14)
Percentage poor	34.73	56.95*	33.91	39.46*
	(22.36)	(23.64)	(24.42)	(21.96)
Percentage rich	18.07	23.17*	14.95	21.48*
	(15.12)	(17.28)	(13.78)	(16.14)
Positional inequality fair	.42	.36*	.44	.49*
	(.21)	(.23)	(.21)	(.21)
Personal income fair[c]	.57	.27*	.61	.49*
	(.50)	(.44)	(.49)	(.50)

[a]Percentage "skills" (versus "family needs" or "both skills and family needs").
[b]Percentage responding "complete equality" or "more equal" (versus "same level" or "more inequality").
[c]Percentage "about right" or "too much" (versus "too little").
* = $p < .05$.

equality as just in principle. While 20% more blacks than whites believe that income should be distributed more on the basis of family need than on individual skills and training, 60% of our black respondents indicated that they believed income should be based more on individual skills and training than on family need. Furthermore, blacks differ less from whites in their endorsement of statements supporting the justice of equality.

A few percentage comparisons serve to illustrate the contrast between race differences in egalitarianism and inegalitarianism. Table 5.9 arrays race differences in two items from the egalitarianism scale and three items from the inegalitarianism scale. Two observations are salient. First, the average race difference in the percentage agreeing with items from the egalitarianism scale is more than double that for items from the inegalitarianism scale. Second, among both whites and blacks majorities agree with the necessity and desirability of income inequality. However, whereas the majority of blacks sees equality as just and beneficial, this is not the case for whites. They are equally split in their agreement and disagreement with the statement that more equality would reduce conflict between different strata, and the majority of whites disagree with the statement that more equality is just because everyone's contribution to society is equally important.

Sex differences parallel race differences but are smaller. Women tend to see more inequality in the distribution of income, to see positional inequality as less fair, and to believe that their personal income is less fair than do men. On the whole, white women are somewhat more egalitarian than white men, but their level of egalitarian sentiment is much closer to that among white men than among blacks. Eleven percent more women than men indicate that there should be more equality in the distribution of incomes, and slightly more women see equality as just and beneficial. However, white women do not differ significantly from white men in their average endorsements of skills and training as the bases of a just distribution and in mean levels of inegalitarianism.

Regression Results: Beliefs about Inequality in the Ideal

Partial regression coefficients for the effects of age, income, education, sex, race, and region on beliefs about how the distributive system should work in the ideal and does function in fact are given in Table 5.10. There are no significant differences in beliefs about distributive justice (in the ideal or in fact) among religious groups so, again, we do not present partial regression coefficients for religious groups.

From Table 5.10 we see that in general endorsement of the justice of income inequality in principle increases with increasing income. The higher the income level the more likely one is to prefer the current

TABLE 5.9. Race Comparisons in Selected Items from the Egalitarianism and Inegalitarianism Scales

Egalitarianism

	Conflict[a]					Equal contribution[b]				
Race	Slightly agree	Agree	Disagree	Slightly disagree	(N)	Slightly agree	Agree	Disagree	Slightly disagree	(N)
White	5%	47	41	7	(1285)	2	33	56	9	(1276)
Black	13	60	23	4	(514)	8	57	31	5	(518)

Inegalitarianism

	Motivation[c]					Socialism[d]				
Race	Slightly agree	Agree	Disagree	Slightly disagree	(N)	Slightly agree	Agree	Disagree	Slightly disagree	(N)
White	18	57	24	2	(1297)	15	61	23	1	(1270)
Black	11	53	33	3	(520)	6	57	34	3	(501)

	Human nature[e]				
Race	Slightly agree	Agree	Disagree	Slightly disagree	(N)
White	9	74	17	1	(1293)
Black	8	66	25	2	(521)

[a] X^2 = 82.79; $p < .01$.
[b] X^2 = 139.18; $p < .01$.
[c] X^2 = 26.67; $p < .01$.
[d] X^2 = 46.88; $p < .01$.
[e] X^2 = 22.33; $p < .01$.

TABLE 5.10. Partial Regression Coefficients for the Effects of Age, Education, Income, Sex, Race, and Region on Beliefs about Economic Justice (All Respondents, N = 1507)

	More equality[a]		Need		Inegalitarianism		Egalitarianism	
Age (10 years)	-.02	(-.06)*	-.01	(-.09)	.01	(.06)*	-.16	— *
Age squared (× 100)	—		—		—		.01	— *
Income (log)	-.07	(-.11)*	-.06	(-.11)*	.08	(.15)*	-.11	(-.17)*
Education	.00	(-.00)	-.01	(-.06)*	-.02	(-.13)*	-.03	(-.20)*
Race (1-white)	-.23	(-.16)*	-.10	(-.09)*	.15	(.13)*	-.25	(-.17)*
Sex (1-male)	-.09	(-.09)*	-.01	(-.01)	.03	(.03)	-.02	(-.02)*
Midwest	-.06	(-.05)	-.02	(-.03)	.03	(.03)	-.02	(-.02)
South	-.05	(-.05)	-.03	(-.03)	.06	(.07)*	-.06	(-.05)
West	-.08	(-.06)*	-.07	(-.07)*	.06	(.06)*	-.08	(-.07)
R^2	.06		.04		.05		.15	

	Percentage middle		Percentage poor		Percentage rich		Positional inequality fair		Personal income fair	
Age (10 years)	.12	(.01)	-.12	(-.01)	-.02	(-.00)	.01	(.08)*	.05	(.16)*
Income (log)	5.82	(.15)*	-3.42	(-.11)*	-2.48	(-.12)*	.02	(.06)*	.13	(.21)*
Education	2.81	(.27)*	-1.77	(-.22)*	-1.06	(-.20)*	.01	(.09)*	.02	(.01)
Race (1-white)	20.88	(.24)*	-18.60	(.27)*	-2.50	(-.05)*	.04	(.06)*	.19	(.12)*
Sex (1-male)	9.19	(.16)*	-3.72	(-.08)*	-5.47	(-.18)*	.04	(.09)*	.09	(.09)*
Midwest	5.60	(.09)*	-4.36	(-.09)*	-1.61	(-.05)	.01	(.01)	-.02	(-.02)
South	-1.37	(.02)	1.01	(.02)	-3.18	(-.08)*	-.01	(-.02)	-.05	(-.04)
West	5.50	(.07)*	-2.64	(-.04)	.06	(.00)	.00	(.00)	.10	
R^2	.26		.19		.13		.04		.10	

[a] Values in parentheses are standardized regression coefficients.
[b] The reference category (excluded group) is Northeast.
*$p = < .05$.

132

distribution of income (relative to a more equal distribution), to believe that income should be distributed on skills and training rather than need, to endorse the benefits of inequality, and to reject the proposed benefits of more equality. Adherence to the justice of income inequality in principle also increases with increasing age, with the exception of the previously noted curvilinearity in the relationship of age to egalitarianism. There are no such consistent effects of education on beliefs about the justice of economic inequality in principle, as there are for income and age. Net of other variables, the greater the years of education the more likely is one to believe that income should be distributed on the basis of skills and training, and the more likely is one to see inequality as just and desirable. Yet, net of the effects of other variables, adherence to egalitarianism also increases with increasing years of education, and education has no statistically significant partial effect on preference for more equality in the distribution of income.

Race- and Sex-Specific Effects. Region has no statistically significant effects on these beliefs among white men or blacks. Women living in the Northeast of the United States tend to favor a more equal distribution of income than do women living in other regions, and they have a higher average level of egalitarianism than others.

The curvilinear pattern, noted earlier in this chapter, for the effect of age on egalitarianism (represented here by the age and age squared terms) is present for white men and women but not blacks. Among white men only, the same curvilinear pattern of age effects is present in the preference for need as a criterion for the distribution of income. Younger blacks and younger white women—but not younger white men—indicate a preference for more equality in the income distribution than do older blacks and older women.

Income has significant effects on the preferences for more equality among whites but not blacks. Higher income and education encourage a lesser preference for need as a criterion for a just distribution among white women and blacks. For white women and blacks, but not white men, education has a statistically significant effect on inegalitarianism; such that, the higher the education the lower the level of agreement with statements supporting the necessity and desirability of income inequality. Again (as in several analyses in previous chapters), education increases social liberalism for other groups more strongly than for white men.

Regression Results: Beliefs about Inequality in Fact

Partial regression coefficients for the effects of age, income, education, sex (for blacks only), and region on beliefs about how the distributive system does work in fact—the perceived percentages poor, rich, and in the middle classes, and the fairness of positional inequality and personal income—are also given in Table 5.10.

From Table 5.10 we can see that in general the perceived amount of economic inequality decreases with increasing socioeconomic status, and perceived fairness of economic inequality increases with increasing socioeconomic status. Income has effects on beliefs about aspects of economic inequality in fact for all groups that are predictable from self-interest. Higher income, more than lower income people, see their personal income as fair and tend to see a higher percentage of people in the middle classes. Education likewise has effects on the perceived amount of inequality that are much the same for white men, white women, and blacks. In general, the higher the years of education the smaller is the perceived amount of inequality (i.e., the larger is the perceived percentage of people in the middle class and the smaller are the perceived percentages of rich and poor).

Age has a statistically significant partial effect on the perceived fairness of positional and personal inequality—as people get older, net of other factors, they increasingly tend to believe that existing economic inequality is fair.

Race- and Sex-Specific Effects. Statistically significant regional differences involving these beliefs are found among white women only. Women living in the southern and northeastern regions of the United States perceive on the average that higher percentages of the population are poor than those living in the Midwest or West, and women living in the West see a smaller proportion of rich on the average than do other women. Correspondingly, women from the South and the Northeast perceive a smaller proportion of Americans in the middle classes (i.e., more inequality of incomes than do women in the midwestern or western regions).

The previously noted finding that women from the Northeast are more egalitarian than those from other regions may have a basis in the perceived amount of inequality. They may favor greater equality of incomes, more than women from the Midwest or West, because they perceive more inequality in the income distribution than do these two groups. However, seeing more inequality is not sufficient to produce a greater preference for more equality. Women from the South, who share with women from the Northeast the perception of more extensive inequality than those from other regions, are no more egalitarian than women from the Midwest or the West.

Younger white women only see positional inequality as less fair than older white women. For blacks only, younger people see the United States as composed of a higher proportion of rich and smaller proportion of people in the middle class than do older ones.

Summary

Figures 5.3 and 5.4 give selected percentage comparisons for beliefs about economic inequality that build on the regression results. Figure 5.3 gives comparisons involving beliefs about economic inequality in the ideal by selected status levels defined by combinations of income and education. Figure 5.4 gives parallel comparisons for beliefs about aspects of actual economic inequality.

Differences in the percentage expressing a preference for more equality among people at different status levels are on the whole quite small. Sex differences in this preference are roughly the same magnitude as status differences. In contrast, the race difference in the preference for more equality is much stronger.

For women and blacks there are significant status differences in the preference for need as a fair criterion for the distribution of income. In both cases the largest difference is between those at low-status levels and all others. The size of this difference and the lack of status differences among white men may reflect qualitative differences in the circumstances of low status between white men, on the one hand, and blacks and women, on the other. Low-status blacks, of course, more often than their white counterparts live in racially segregated inner city areas, amid prevalent poverty and other social problems that are disproportionately found in American inner cities. Low-status women with children are often the sole earner for their families. In short, lower status blacks and women more so than lower status white men may live in "true poverty" circumstances—that is, currently lacking employment, having characteristics (such as young children or living in the inner city) that diminish the prospects for future work, and living among many others in the same circumstances. It appears that only in the case of living in true poverty, with the attendant sense of lack of hope for economic advancement, do people strongly come to support need as a just criterion for the distribution of income.

Figure 5.3 gives percentages agreeing with selected items from the egalitarianism and inegalitarianism scales. Examining those percentages, we note first that in general the differences among status levels in agreement with the egalitarianism items are larger than those with the inegalitarianism items. This parallels a Chapter 4 finding that individualism (part of the dominant ideology like inegalitarianism) is based less strongly in social and demographic factors than are structurally based doubts about the dominant ideology (analogous to egalitarianism). The contrast in status differences is especially marked for agreement with the statement that incomes should be more equal because every person's contribution to society is equal. On the average there

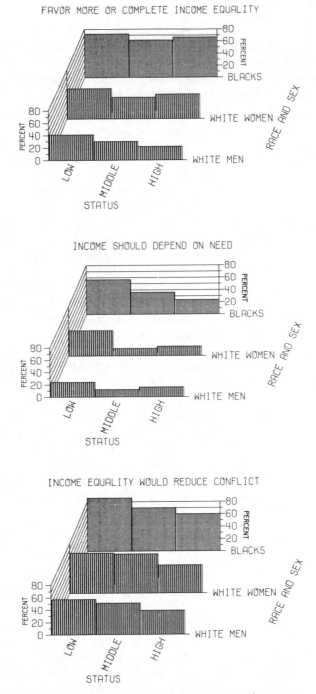

FIGURE 5.3. Selected items concerning preferences for income inequality in the ideal, broken down by status, sex, and race.

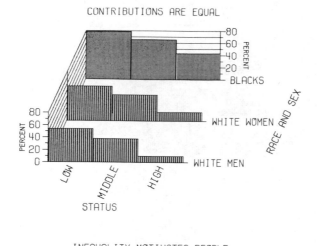

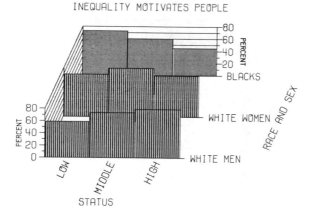

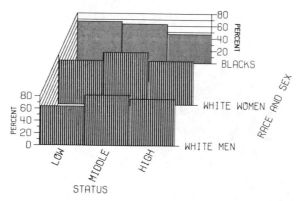

FIGURE 5.3. *Continued.*

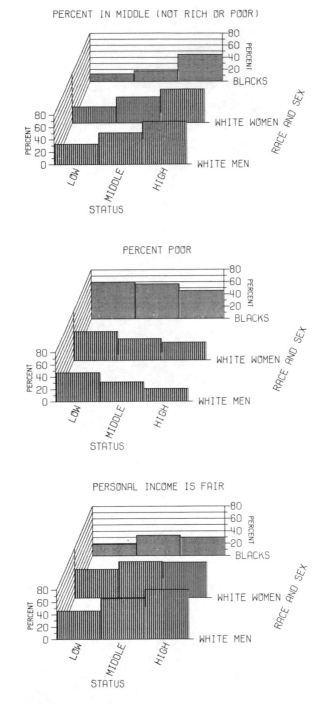

FIGURE 5.4. Selected items concerning aspects of existing income inequality, broken down by status, sex, and race.

is about a 40% difference in agreement with this item between lower and higher status individuals, and only about 11% (men and women together) of high-status whites agree with this statement.

Second, among women the percentage in agreement with the two inegalitarianism items follows a curvilinear pattern by status level, such that high- and low-status women have roughly equal percentages of agreement, and middle-status women endorse statements supporting the necessity and desirability of economic inequality more often than either high- or low-status women. Furthermore, among blacks the percentage in agreement with these statements declines as status level increases. Both patterns stem from the tendency of highly educated blacks and women to agree less with statements supporting the justice of inequality than do lesser educated blacks and women.

An explanation that we find plausible takes note of related findings in Chapters 3 and 4. On the one hand, the years of education obtained is indicative of potential exposure to ideas and information that support or challenge prevailing beliefs about how the American stratification order does and should work. It is "potential" exposure because one may attend colleges and universities that are ideologically liberal or conservative and thus not be exposed to ideas and information that challenge or that support dominant-ideology beliefs. And it is "potential" in the sense that once on a college campus no one is required to receive information that supports or challenges prevailing beliefs about social inequality, even if he or she is required to take courses where such information is offered.

As members of groups who have a less privileged status than white men, blacks and women seem to be more receptive to information that challenges dominant-ideology beliefs than are white men. This greater receptiveness is reflected in the tendencies of educated blacks and white women to see less equality of opportunity for different groups, to less often agree with statements supporting the necessity and desirability of economic inequality in principle, and (in the case of white women) to blame poverty on the failings of individuals less than their less educated counterparts. With the exception of individual attributions for poverty, among white men higher education does not produce the same consequences for the above beliefs as it does for blacks and women. College-educated white males differ little from their noncollege-educated counterparts in their adherence to dominant-ideology beliefs.

On the other hand, the years of education obtained also indicate one's social status. It is indicative of status both in terms of life style— the status level of friends, neighbors, and co-workers—and in terms of one's own and others' definition of success. Formal education in America in the past, and perhaps more so today, has a competitive character that encourages the recipients and others to view those who have achieved college degrees as winners of a contest.

Consistent with the status implications of education, among both blacks and whites and men and women, highly educated respondents more than the less educated tend to see opportunity in general as more prevalent, have a more optimistic view of their personal opportunity, less often express support for need as a fair distributive criterion, and less often endorse statements supporting the justice and desirability of greater equality of incomes. Among white men and women, the higher the years of education the less likely is one to attribute poverty or wealth to structural causes.

In Chapter 2 we argued that education is an important source of seemingly inconsistent beliefs among middle-class Americans. For women and for black middle-class Americans, but not white males, this does clearly seem to be the case. Perhaps it is because of this inconsistency that among women and especially among blacks, preference for more equality does not differ much by status level. Preference for more equality provides a useful compromise solution for the educated who desire, on the one hand, to maintain the relatively privileged status that they ascribe to their own favorable personal characteristics, and who, on the other hand, are exposed to ideas and data that potentially challenge the legitimacy of the system from which they personally benefit. A more equal distribution, as opposed to a strictly equal one, potentially can be accomplished without reducing one's own relatively privileged status. For example, transfers from the wealthy to the poor can make things more equal without leveling the relative privilege of a middle-class person in the process.

Sizable differences in the average perceived amount of inequality—percentage poor, rich, and by implication percentage in the middle classes—among those at different status levels are evident in Figure 5.4. The partial effect of income that contributes to these status-level differences is readily interpretable in terms of self-interest. The tendency of higher income people to perceive America as composed of a small percentage rich and, perhaps especially, a small percentage poor serves the desire to see one's privileged position as just and, hence, to maintain it. Seeing small percentages of poor and rich makes it easier for one to blame poverty on the failures of individuals and to attribute wealth to superior individual qualities.[9]

The partial effect of education that contributes to these status-level

_____

[9]Research in social psychology supports this inference. Kelley (1967) found that the larger the number of people that an actor believes occupies a given state the lower the likelihood of believing that occupying that state is attributable to individual rather than situational causes.

differences is in one regard a bit puzzling. One might argue that net of income, increasing education should increase the amount of inequality perceived since exposure to statistical information about the prevalence of poverty and wealth is assumed to be more readily available on college campuses than elsewhere. Apparently, the status implications of increasing education strongly outweigh the impact (if any) of its informational content. Information about the composition of the social world is in part based on generalization from the characteristics of one's personal, more immediate social environment. Since the college educated in America tend to live in the suburbs, interact with other college-educated people socially and at work, have educated parents, and in general personally inhabit a middle-class world, they tend to see America in general as more middle-class than do the lesser educated.

In general, paralleling findings from Chapter 4, we see from these analyses that group differences along lines of race, sex, and socioeconomic status in beliefs about the justice of actual economic inequality are substantially larger than corresponding group differences in beliefs about the justice of economic inequality in principle. As with the comparison between structural and individual explanations of poverty and wealth, R^2 levels for equations predicting beliefs about the justice of inequality in fact are higher than for corresponding equations for beliefs about the justice of inequality in principle, indicating the greater predictability of the former beliefs. Blacks, women, and people of low socioeconomic status view actual economic inequality as less fair on the average than do other Americans. Yet, consistent with our argument in Chapter 2, doubt about the fairness of economic inequality in fact generally does not result in rejection of the belief that economic inequality is just in principle. Instead, as we underscored earlier in this chapter, doubt stemming from race, sex, socioeconomic status, and other sources more often results in mixed views on the desirability of inequality in principle.

CONCLUSIONS

Most Americans believe that economic inequality is just in principle, and correspondingly, endorse individual and societal equity as just criteria for the distribution of income. On the whole, as we have seen in Chapter 4, respondents to our survey believe that individual equity holds in fact—that is, most Americans get what they deserve relative to their individual effort and talents. However, the majority of the public does *not* perceive that the American stratification order is currently characterized by societal equity in fact. More Americans express doubt that incomes are proportional to the contributions made to the collectivity as a whole than express doubt that people get the income they deserve relative to differences in effort and ability among individuals. As we have seen, the majority of Americans believe that several common types of occupation—especially those with average incomes marginally above the poverty line—are underrewarded and also believe that several types of occupations are overrewarded relative to the contributions made to society. And about one-half of the sample respondents perceive that they as individuals are underrewarded relative to their personal contribution to society.

Age-group comparisons involving the beliefs about distributive justice examined in this chapter are consistent with the hypothesis that Americans' view of the justice of economic inequality has been stable. Within the limitations of age-group comparisons for inferences about change, our analyses imply that over the last few decades Americans in the aggregate have maintained the same views of the justice of economic inequality both in principle and in fact.

Two aspects of the doubt respondents express about the justice of inequality in fact support the argument about Americans' consciousness of economic inequality we presented in Chapter 2. Doubt about the justice of economic inequality in fact is found more often among lower status Americans than others, but there is little difference between lower status and higher status Americans in the size of the respective majorities that perceive that economic inequality is just in principle. Doubt about the justice of economic inequality seems to add the belief that it also has drawbacks to the prevalent belief that economic inequality is necessary and beneficial, but this doubt often does not seem to result in people denying the justice of economic inequality in principle. As we have seen throughout Chapters 3, 4, and 5, adherence to the dominant ideology persists in the face of many potential challenges to it.

II

POLICY ATTITUDES

In Chapters 1 and 2 we proposed that public opinion on inequality-related policy is influenced both by the conservative beliefs of the dominant ideology and by other, more liberal, and less stable beliefs. The next three chapters test these propositions by examining the factors that influence beliefs and attitudes involving redistribution and the provision of equal opportunity. These factors include the dominant-ideology beliefs in opportunity, individualism, and the benefits of inequality, in addition to self-interest, personal experiences, and other, generally "socially liberal" beliefs that people may adopt based on political events of recent years.

In Chapter 6 we explore Americans' attitudes toward welfare spending and other redistributive policies. Redistributive programs can take several forms, including the provision of jobs by the government, a guarantee of a minimum income for those who work (i.e., a floor on wages), or direct transfer payments. Direct payments to the poor in cash or other forms (such as food stamps and subsidized housing), popularly labeled "welfare," have been the subject of continual criticism and many proposals for reform in the last two decades.

Besides direct redistribution of income, the other major arena of inequality-related policy is equality of opportunity for black Americans and for women. In Chapters 7 and 8 we examine public beliefs about aspects of opportunity for these groups and then analyze attitudes toward equal opportunity policy. For blacks, equal employment opportunity or "affirmative-action" programs, and for women, the Equal Rights Amendment, have been the focus of policy and of debate. Chapters 7 and 8 analyze the ways that racial affect, sex-role attitudes, self-interest, and the dominant ideology influence public evaluations of these policies.

OUTLINE OF CHAPTERS

Distribution and Over-Time Trends

Each of these chapters begins with an examination of current beliefs and attitudes, in the form of frequency distributions of responses to the relevant questions. Available data from other time periods are also presented to give some indications of whether public opinion has shifted or remained stable in the face of political controversies and events of recent years. Our theory predicts that public views on specific policies and programs are often a compromise between the stable influence of the dominant ideology and the less stable forces of "social liberalism" that increased in the 1960s and 1970s. Therefore, policy attitudes should also show some shifts with the times, while the influence of the dominant ideology should remain.

Self-Interest Effects on Beliefs and Attitudes

The chapters then turn to examinations of the determinants of policy-related beliefs and attitudes, drawing out our theory's implications for the ways people evaluate policies. Perhaps the most popular view of the forces underlying policy attitudes is that they reflect individuals' views of their own self-interest: How will the policy in question affect *me?* So blacks would be expected to favor, and whites to oppose, affirmative-action programs that would benefit blacks; the rich should oppose, and the poor favor, a program of increased taxation to provide more ample welfare benefits. The economic model of the person as rationally seeking individual interests was extended to politics by Downs (1957). The "pocketbook voter" is also common in everyday and journalistic discussions of election outcomes; people are said to support or oppose policies or candidates primarily on the basis of their expected consequences for the voter personally, particularly in such close-to-home domains as "paychecks, grocery bills, children's schooling, sons at war" (Neustadt, 1960, p. 97). As Chapter 2 discussed, many theories of the evaluation of inequality in general give similar prominence to the role of individual calculations of self-interest. To analyze the effects of self-interest, these chapters present regressions of public beliefs and attitudes on sociodemographic variables alone. This analysis will show any effects of sex, race, income, and other significant self-interest factors, whether they are direct or indirect (mediated through beliefs in the dominant ideology or other factors).

Other Determinants

However, our theory predicts that the effects of self-interest on policy attitudes are far from the whole story. Most obviously, self-interest can provide no guidance for sections of the public that have no direct economic stake in particular policies. For example, blacks are a minority of the workforce in most occupations and an even smaller minority of those with the training and educational credentials necessary for many skilled blue-collar and white-collar jobs. Thus, most whites face little real prospect of economic loss from the implementation of equal opportunity for blacks. People in such situations may adopt or change attitudes for transitory reasons or may choose answers randomly in order to give the appearance of interest—rather than ignorance—when polltakers ask them questions. This argument, in effect, is that on policy issues that are not of immediate relevance to self-interest, many Americans simply do not have attitudes.

We reject both the extreme claims that attitudes are purely determined by self-interest and that they are essentially randomly chosen epiphenomena. As outlined in Chapter 2, our overall theory gives several reasons for our position.

First, most people benefit from such overall public goods as the maintenance of social order. If social problems arising from inequality threaten violence, crime, or other disruptions of order, then citizens have a stake in policies that remove the threats. That is, people may judge their self-interest from the perspective of their identification with the nation as a whole [or perhaps with some smaller group such as an ethnic group, occupation, or class (Bobo, 1983)] rather than as isolated individuals. Kinder (1981) and others showed that public evaluations of policies and politicians are strongly influenced by "sociotropic" evaluations—those weighing the impact of policies on society as a whole as opposed to the impact on the individual perceiver.

Second, the extent or even direction of one's self-interest in any particular policy is often unclear. Economists and other experts often disagree about the potential long-term effects of policies such as tax cuts or increased welfare spending, so a citizen who wants to identify policies that would serve his or her self-interest is left without clear guidance. Other factors besides self-interest must be relied on in such situations.

Finally, beliefs and attitudes about the stratification order may be rooted in part in a basic need to feel that the social environment is predictable and controllable. Policies related to inequality may challenge individuals' understanding of how the stratification system does and should work, possibly conflicting with basic values of justice or equity or challenging the sense that the environment is predictable and understandable. Policies that pose such challenges may be disliked regardless of their implications for direct self-interest.

For several reasons, then, the picture of a social perceiver who simply maximizes self-interest is incomplete at best. According to our theory, people have many different principles potentially available to form attitudes toward policies. One is the self-interest principle "support what will benefit me," but there is no reason to expect it to be used in preference to all others. When the most salient factors in evaluating a policy are dislike for a group that will benefit from the policy (such as welfare recipients) or a sense that the policy will challenge one's overall values (such as equity), evaluations on the basis of these principles may well override considerations of self-interest.

Even in the calculation of self-interests, beliefs about how the social and economic order does and should work will be involved—that is, beliefs in the dominant ideology or other types of beliefs about the world will be influential. As Chapters 3–5 showed, the dominant ideology is by far the most widespread and stable version of beliefs about how the stratification system does and should work, and as such it provides individuals with a basis for calculating the effects of different policies. Its impact on policy attitudes is likely to be generally conservative. Thus a person who believes in the full form of the dominant ideology is unlikely to support redistributive policy, because he or she will see the poor as having ample opportunity to better themselves by their own efforts. Moreover, even if a need for some policy is recognized, only those programs that are consistent with individualism and inegalitarianism are likely to be at all acceptable.

The discussion to this point has outlined reasons for believing that self-interest and the dominant ideology will influence policy attitudes. Our theory suggests that other beliefs and attitudes may also have effects. Some of these factors are affective, including relative deprivation (feelings of distrust for the government) and intergroup affect (feelings of hostility toward racial or other outgroups). Public funds spent on dealing with the problems of particular groups (such as the poor) may be seen as limiting the possibilities of solving the problems of one's own group. Several analysts (Binzen, 1970; Ransford, 1972; Sennett & Cobb, 1972) have argued that in the American working class this sense of relative deprivation, of having one's own problems overlooked in favor of the problems of other groups, motivates opposition to welfare and to equal opportunity for blacks. In addition, direct racial animosity (or dislike for other groups, such as the poor or women) may motivate some people to oppose policies that benefit disliked groups. To the extent that particular policies (such as welfare) become identified as benefiting a particular racial group in the minds of some, they may be opposed because of racial hostility.

Policy attitudes also may be affected by the changing forces of current political argument and media attention. The civil rights and women's rights movements, antipoverty activists, and other recent political forces have strongly expressed certain messages about the causes of poverty, the existence and nature of racial and sexual discrimination, and the like. Some individuals may adopt these beliefs, adding them to their repertoire of schemas for explaining patterns of inequality and changing their policy attitudes accordingly.

Though such influences are clearly more transient than the enduring realities of self-interest and stable beliefs in the dominant ideology, their effects on policy attitudes may be substantial. The effects may be evident particularly in the major shifts that American public opinion has shown on several of the issues that have been at the center of recent political debate, such as the sharp decline in segregationist sentiment and expressed racial prejudice and the increase in antiwelfare sentiment. These chapters test the above notions about the effects of the dominant ideology and of other beliefs in regression analyses that include them as predictors along with the sociodemographic variables. These analyses will examine the effects of these beliefs on policy attitudes controlling for their associations with the respondent's social position and background.

CAUSAL ASSUMPTIONS

The analyses performed in the chapters in this section rest on a series of causal assumptions, which we briefly present and justify here. The general model is depicted in Diagram 1. The sociodemographic variables (sex, race, age, income, education, occupational characteristics, region, and religion) causally precede all others in the model. This assumption is routinely made, but it could be violated in cases where a person's occupational choice reflects his or her attitudes and beliefs, as women might choose traditional or nontraditional occupations based on their sex-role attitudes.

In analyses examining the effects of self-interest, the regressions of beliefs and attitudes on the sociodemographic variables alone, excluding the measures of dominant ideology and other beliefs ("reduced form" regressions), will be performed. This model will detect self-interest effects that are either direct (hold even when beliefs are con-

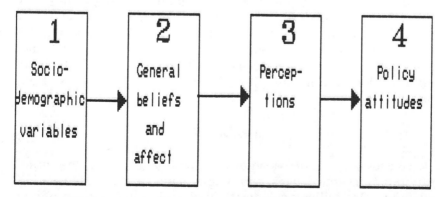

DIAGRAM 1. Assumed causal sequence for four classes of variables.

trolled) or indirect (operate by disposing individuals to particular types of beliefs which in turn cause specific policy attitudes). For example, one's sociodemographic position (such as being in a particular occupation, having a high income, or being female) might operate directly to influence a policy attitude, perhaps because of calculations of self-interest, without changing the individual's overall belief pattern in major ways. This would constitute a direct effect—one that is not based on the perceiver's beliefs. On the other hand, sociodemographic factors may predispose one to a particular pattern of beliefs (such as adherence to the dominant ideology or the adoption of nontraditional sex-role attitudes). These beliefs may in turn lead the individual to particular attitudes on concrete policy issues: an indirect effect. Effects of self-interest might operate either directly or indirectly in this sense, and our analysis will detect either form.

We also assume that the dominant-ideology beliefs and measures of intergroup affect and such related constructs as sex-role attitudes all precede measures of perceptions and policy attitudes. The rationale for this assumption is that such general beliefs and affect are generally thought to be socialized early in life (e.g., Sears, 1975; Leahy, 1983; Simmons & Rosenberg, 1971).

Finally, it is assumed that perceptions (e.g., perceptions of the extent of poverty or of antiblack discrimination) precede policy attitudes. This assumption is logical in that perceptions of the existing state of affairs serve as the justification for policies intended to change things, and it is consistent with prevailing social–psychological theories of attitude formation (Fishbein & Ajzen, 1975). However, there may be instances of rationalization: adoption, post hoc, of beliefs in order to justify an attitude that is held for some other reason (such as racial affect). We cannot disentangle analytically such possible processes with our current data. However, rationalization should be less widespread than the reverse, more logical sequence. And even if it occurs it should not distort the *sign* (only, possibly, increase the magnitude) of regression coefficients, because the directional relationship between a belief and an attitude must be the same in either case. Since sign is considerably more important than magnitude in our interpretations of our results, we accept the risk of this model misspecification as a reasonable price to pay for the powerful analytic techniques made possible by strong causal assumptions.

SUMMARY

In conclusion, our purpose in this section is to investigate the current distribution, recent changes, and determinants of attitudes toward inequality-related policies and related beliefs in the American public.

These analyses will allow us to test several ideas suggested by our theory and outlined above. *(a)* Policy-related opinions may show some over-time trend toward increased liberalism, to the extent that they are influenced by beliefs that have recently shifted toward "social liberalism" on such issues as the causes of poverty and rejection of race or sex discrimination. *(b)* However, the conservative influence of the stable dominant ideology should remain strong. *(c)* Self-interest, dividing the population along socioeconomic, racial, and sexual lines, will influence beliefs and attitudes. *(d)* The effects of social liberalism and intergroup affect (such as racial animosity), less stable and derived from recent political debate and events, will be variable but occasionally strong. *(e)* Overall, we expect that those policies that provide a compromise between the dominant ideology and social liberalism will attain the highest levels of public support.

6

REDISTRIBUTIVE POLICY

In one sense the simplest solution to many social problems, such as poverty and unequal access to quality education and medical care, is the direct redistribution of income. At the extreme, redistribution to complete equality of incomes would eliminate poverty (in the relative sense, and in the United States in the absolute sense as well). Even less extreme redistribution of income could bring all America's poor up to the subjectively defined "get along" income level.[1] Of course, most governmental activity—from taxation to defense or Medicare spending—has redistributive effects in that citizens do not share the cost and benefits equally. We are concerned here only with those policies that are explicitly aimed at helping the poor or removing resources from the rich: decreasing the variance of the distribution of income. Support for redistributive policies may potentially arise from a generalized sympathy for the helpless which Lipset (1963) characterizes as a part of traditional American culture, or from more selfish desires to avoid threats to the social order posed by crime and violence among the poor (Piven & Cloward, 1971). And, of course, in a democracy the poor may politically support redistribution by their own votes or by attracting powerful allies such as middle-class liberals or organized labor.

Research from the late 1960s and early 1970s (Feagin, 1975; Williamson, 1974a,b), however, found strong majority opposition to redistributive policies—especially to the direct transfer of income to the poor, usually labeled "welfare." Moreover, recent impressionistic evidence, including media interpretations of Ronald Reagan's election victories in 1980 and 1984, suggests that opposition to redistribution may even be increasing. In this chapter we will address two broad questions con-

[1] The median U. S. household income in 1980 was around $18,000, and the average income is slightly higher, over $20,000 (given the skewed distribution of incomes). So complete redistribution could theoretically bring every household up to this level, while Rainwater's data (1974) show that about 60% of the median level is generally perceived as that at which a family can "get along."

cerning public attitudes on redistributive policy. Has opposition to the redistribution of incomes truly increased, as impressionistic evidence suggests? What factors shape the ways in which the American public responds to redistributive programs? We answer these questions with regard to two types of redistributive policy: redistribution toward the poor and redistribution away from the rich.

REDISTRIBUTION TOWARD THE POOR

American social policies directed at redistributing income toward the poor have taken three broad forms: *(a)* direct income transfers, rent subsidies, food stamps, and so on, generally labeled as "welfare" by the public; *(b)* efforts to place a floor on earnings, such as by a minimum wage, to aid the "working poor"; and *(c)* direct efforts to create jobs. Our survey included questions concerning each of these general types of policy, without bringing in details of any specific program or implementation.

Overall public endorsement of redistributive policies aimed at the poor is shown in Table 6.1. On specific policy items, the largest number favors government-guaranteed jobs for all who are willing to work (47% agree), and guaranteed incomes for all workers (61%). Welfare is clearly the least popular class of programs; none of the four items we asked gained a majority of pro-welfare responses, and across the four an average of only about 30% are favorable.

The items fall into two different clusters, with items 1 and 3 referring to welfare *policies* and items 2 and 4 referring to characteristics of welfare *recipients*. The strongest antiwelfare sentiment is found on item 1, characterizing the total amount of welfare spending as excessive, while the most sympathy for welfare is found on item 3, which states (in somewhat contradictory fashion) that welfare does not provide an adequate level of support. This pattern of responses graphically illustrates the American ambivalence about inequality that we stress throughout the book. Characterizations of welfare recipients are more consistent, wih 70–80% of respondents endorsing the common stereotypes that they are lazy and are dishonest about their need.

The differential endorsement of welfare versus the other policies can be explained in terms of their consistency with self-interest and the dominant ideology, based on our results in Chapters 3–5. Guaranteed jobs represent a disguised form of redistribution, since it may not be clear to many people that the government would have to tax to provide such jobs. Threats to self-interest thus may not be very salient. In addition, guaranteed jobs (as well as guaranteed incomes for those who work) can be seen as allowing people the chance to work hard and achieve, so they conflict little with the dominant ideology.

Table 6.1. Redistribution Aimed at the Poor: Marginals and Over-Time
Trends (in Percentage)[a]

Question	Welfare				Pro-Welfare	
	Strongly Agree	Agree	Disagree	Strongly disagree	1969	1980
1. Generally speaking, we are spending too *much* money on welfare programs in this country.	45	36	_15_	_3_	39[b]	18
2. Most people getting welfare are *not* honest about their need.	37	40	_22_	_2_	19	23
3. One of the main troubles with welfare is that it doesn't give most people enough to get along on.	_11_	_38_	42	8	51	49
4. Most people on welfare who can work try to find jobs so they can support themselves.	_3_	_28_	50	19	47	31

Government jobs and guaranteed incomes		
Government should guarantee jobs	Agree	Disagree
The Federal government should guarantee a job to every person who wants to work.		
1980	61	39
Government should guarantee incomes		
The Federal government should guarantee an income above the poverty level to every person who works.		
1980	47	53

In general some people feel that the government in Washington should see
to it that every person has a job and a good standard of living. Others think
the government should just let each person get ahead on his own.

	Government help	Each person
1958 National Election Survey[c]	68	32
1956 National Election Survey	68	32

[a]Note: 1969 results restated to exclude "uncertain" responses. Underlined response categories are those classed as pro-welfare in last two columns.
[b]Wording in 1969 differed, asking "too little" instead of "too much."
[c]Note: National Election Survey results restated to exclude "don't know" and "depends" responses.

Direct transfer payments are less consistent with the dominant-ideology principle of equity. Since most Americans believe (as Chapter 5 showed) that inequality motivates people to work hard and brings benefits to society as a whole, transfer payments that are not connected with a work requirement may seem to undermine motivation and may be opposed for that reason.

Over-Time and Age-Group Trends

Table 6.1 presents the available over-time data on redistribution related to the poor. The four items that make up our welfare attitude scale were also asked in Feagin's 1969 survey. The data show notable shifts away from support of welfare on two of the items and only small shifts on the other two. Compared to 1969, the public is now more likely to agree that we are spending too much money on welfare and to deny that people on welfare try to find work to support themselves. These two items have a flavor implying that "welfare has failed," a frequent argument made by antiwelfare writers and politicians (e.g., Gilder, 1981). An item reflecting doubt about the honesty of welfare recipients shows little change, perhaps because of a floor effect—it was already very negative in 1969. In contrast, the item on which people show the most sympathy or support for welfare, recognizing that welfare often does not give recipients enough to get along on, has changed little since 1969. Other scattered results from the early 1970s (Williamson, 1974b; Allston & Dean, 1972) are consistent with the conclusion that attitudes toward welfare policies and welfare recipients were already quite negative at that time.

Other measures of attitudes toward welfare spending, worded differently from our items, show increasing opposition to welfare over time. One question series (Figure 6.1) shows a general conservative trend from 1961 through 1980, particularly in the increased percentage saying "too much" is being spent. Note, however, that the questions are relative to current spending levels, introducing some interpretive ambiguity: "about right" may be seen as a conservative response in 1961 but as more liberal in the 1970s. The figures then show a small reversal in 1982 as the widely publicized Reagan Administration cuts in welfare programs coincided with some increase in the percentage responding that we are spending too little.[2] The marginal shifts of 30 or more points found on this question are quite large: Page and Shapiro (1982) found that only about 4% of over 600 opinion items that they examined showed marginal shifts this large.

[2] The question wording differs slightly between the survey series shown, but since the 1973 results are nearly identical across the two wordings, combining the latter two series probably does not lead to great distortions.

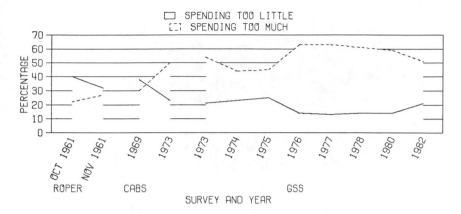

FIGURE 6.1. Time trends in views on welfare spending. Data sources: Roper is Roper Poll, CABS is Consumer Attitude and Behavior Survey, GSS is General Social Survey.

Public support for guaranteed jobs shows a much smaller decline in approval between the late 1950s and 1980. In fact, fragmentary over-time data show roughly constant levels of support for both guaranteed jobs and guaranteed incomes since the 1930s (Schlitz, 1970). In general, it seems that support for welfare has declined in the last two decades, in contrast to the stability of attitudes on other types or redistribution and the dominant ideology beliefs analyzed in earlier chapters. Some suggestions as to what makes welfare different have already been mentioned, and this issue will be considered further later in this chapter.

More indirect evidence for over-time changes is available in the examination of age-group trends presented in Figure 6.2. Many of the items considered in this chapter show no significant relationship to the respondent's age. The young are most likely to favor government-guaranteed incomes, but two of the four welfare items and support for guaranteed jobs are unrelated to age. Respondents over 50 are less likely to agree that welfare support is inadequate, while those under 30 and those between 50 and 64 are least likely to characterize welfare recipients as honest. Thus the pattern of relationships to age is mixed, suggesting that the age trends do not reflect a simple evaluation of the overall goal of redistribution of incomes.

Determinants of Attitudes on Redistribution toward the Poor

Why does the American public generally support government guaranteed jobs or guaranteed incomes and reject welfare programs? According to our theory, the answers may be found in three considera-

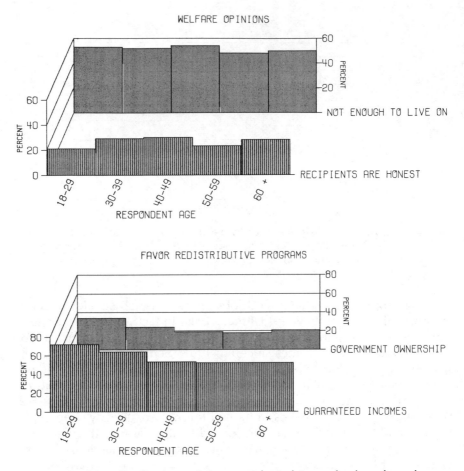

FIGURE 6.2. Proredistributive opinion on selected items, broken down by respondent's age.

tions. First and most obviously, many individuals' self-interest will lead them to oppose redistribution. Individuals who stand to lose by a proposed program's adoption will tend, of course, to oppose it; if the program is redistributive in intent then the losers are likely to be the more advantaged members of society and hence very likely the more powerful. Self-interest will also lead those who potentially stand to benefit from a program, presumably those with low incomes or insecure economic situations, to favor it. In terms of self-interest alone, welfare is likely to be less favored than the other types of program, since a smaller number of respondents will consider themselves as potential beneficiaries of welfare than of guaranteed jobs or income levels.

Second, popular adherence to the dominant ideology may lead many Americans to oppose redistributive programs, and the degree of opposition may depend on the consistency of the specific program with the dominant ideology. This argument is consistent with cross-national findings of Lopreato and Hazelrigg (1972), Coughlin (1980), and others. As Chapter 3 showed, one part of the dominant ideology is a belief in widespread opportunity for individual economic advancement. This belief implies that the poor can eventually solve their own problems by traditional upward mobility, with no need for any redistributive effort. As noted in Chapter 4, under the dominant ideology different levels of income essentially reflect differences in individual efforts and talents (i.e., individualistic explanations for wealth and poverty are widespread). Thus redistribution is often seen as taking from the more deserving to give to the less deserving. Chapter 5 showed that there is also strong and broad popular support for the existence of income inequality *in principle,* as the public accepts arguments for the functionality of income differences to motivate people and generate rewards that are shared by all.

Considering the different types of programs, support for guaranteed jobs may be greater than for welfare because it presents less of a challenge to norms of equity: no income level is guaranteed, and people may be seen as working for what they receive. By the same token, providing guaranteed incomes to those who work poses less conflict with equity than does welfare, which primarily benefits the nonworking.

Third, welfare attitudes may be more affectively based than attitudes toward other programs aimed at redistribution, for several reasons. The result may be stronger opposition to welfare than would be expected on grounds of self-interest or the dominant ideology alone. One source of negative feelings about welfare may be the common antiwelfare rhetoric of many American political figures. Politicians have often seemed to see benefits for themselves in creating a sense of relative deprivation in their audiences by attacking welfare as free handouts and contrasting it with the audience's need to work hard to earn a living. Welfare spending has become a major symbolic issue, often representing a whole cluster of conservative issue positions in political shorthand. The focus on welfare in political debate may have also created the impression that public spending on welfare is truly massive in scope, further fueling anger among the nonpoor who see themselves as struggling under heavy tax burdens.

Some antipathy toward the poor and hence toward welfare may be "natural," inherent in the dominant-ideology belief in individualism— which holds the poor responsible for their own position through their blameworthy personal characteristics—or in other psychological processes (Chapter 2). The latter may include the fundamental attribution error, the desire to create psychological distance between oneself and the poor as a defense, and the belief in a just world.

Finally, negative feelings about welfare and about racial outgroups may be coupled in American political attitudes, as demonstrated by our respondents' high average estimate, 50%, of the proportion of welfare recipients who are black. The tragic history of race conflict in America and its lingering effects both in traditional race prejudice among some whites and in "symbolic racism" may dispose some whites to oppose welfare because it disproportionately benefits blacks. For all these reasons, the greater affective loading of welfare attitudes may in part account for the lesser acceptance of welfare in comparison with other types of programs.

By the same token, however, there are individuals who have reasons to favor redistributive policies. Those who depart from the general consensus in questioning the tenets of the dominant ideology (widespread opportunity, individual explanations for position, support for inequality in principle) may join those whose self-interest would be directly served by redistribution. Some individuals may experience positive affect toward disadvantaged groups such as the poor or racial minorities, who may serve as symbols of societal compassion and generosity. The considerations discussed in the earlier chapters concerning the nature and fate of beliefs that challenge the dominant ideology suggest that the outcome of conflicts among beliefs and between beliefs and self-interest will often be compromise. Programs that offer a compromise between elements of the dominant ideology and more "liberal" impulses toward redistribution may have a broad appeal among the large group of Americans who hold mixed beliefs.

As outlined in the introduction to Part II, our efforts to test these theoretical predictions begin with an examination of the effects of sociodemographic variables on attitudes toward redistributive programs. In particular, *income* obviously indicates a respondent's direct self-interest for or against redistribution, and *race* does so indirectly. For this chapter we add several objective measures intended to indicate other aspects of respondents' self-interest in redistribution. *Wealth* is the respondent's report of his or her family's holdings of productive investments including savings, stocks, bonds, or real estate excluding an owner-occupied home. The categories are "none," under $1000, under $10,000, under $25,000, under $50,000, and $50,000 and over. Wealth should be particularly relevant to attitudes concerning redistributive policies affecting the rich. We also categorize respondents according to the nature of their work. With *nonworkers* as the reference category, others are classified as *self-employed, government employees* (federal, state, or local), and *employees of private businesses*. The potential costs of redistribution may be higher for the self-employed business owner than for private or government employees, because the income potential of the self-employed is higher. Effects of these sociodemographic and economic variables in regressions that exclude the belief measures will indicate self-interest influences on attitudes, whether direct or indirect (mediated through beliefs).

Following these analyses, we add a series of independent variables assessing belief in aspects of the dominant ideology and other potentially relevant factors, repeating the regression to determine the effects of these variables above and beyond self-interest effects. These analyses appear in Table 6.3. Besides the dominant ideology measures of individual and structural explanations for wealth and poverty, egalitarianism and inegalitarianism, we employ measures of *relative deprivation* and *racial affect*, because these factors are theoretically expected to influence attitudes on redistribution, as Chapter 2 and the above discussion indicate. Relative deprivation is a three-item index measuring the perception that one is part of a group overlooked by the government in favor of other groups. Racial affect is composed of two items tapping

TABLE 6.2. Redistribution Aimed at the Poor: Regressions on
			Sociodemographic Variables

Independent variable	Welfare support	Guaranteed jobs	Guaranteed Income
Sex (female)	−.19	.18*	.20*
	−.04	(.10)	.11
Age (10 years)	.01	−.06*	−.08*
	(.00)	(−.11)	(−.14)
Race (nonwhite)	1.21*	.55*	.36*
	(.19)	(.22)	(.13)
Education (years)	.11*	−.03*	−.02
	(.14)	(−.10)	(−.06)
Income (log)	−.93*	−.30*	−.15
	(−.14)	(−.10)	(−.06)
South	.20	.04	−.05
	(.04)	(.02)	(−.02)
Wealth	−.03	−.03	−.05[†]
	(−.02)	(−.05)	(−.08)
Self–employed	−1.07*	−.37*	−.46*
	(−.12)	(−.10)	(−.13)
Government employee	.07	−.12	−.04
	(.01)	(−.05)	(−.01)
Private employee	−.24	−.10	−.09
	(−.05)	(−.05)	(−.05)
R^2	.09	.14	.11
(N)	(1132)	(544)	(684)

*$p < .05$; [†]$p < .10$ (shown in split-sample columns only).

TABLE 6.3. Redistribution Aimed at the Poor: Regressions on
Sociodemographic Variables and Dominant Ideology

Independent variable	Welfare support	Guaranteed jobs	Guaranteed income
Sex (female)	−.32*	.11	.16*
	(−.07)	(.06)	(.09)
Age (10 years)	.04	−.05*	−.07*
	(.03)	(−.09)	(−.12)
Race (nonwhite)	.45*	.28*	.06
	(.07)	(.11)	(.02)
Education (years)	.06*	−.01	−.01
	(.07)	(−.02)	(−.02)
Income (log)	−.79*	−.14	−.06
	(−.12)	(−.05)	(−.02)
South	.33*	.06	−.03
	(.07)	(.03)	(−.02)
Wealth	.02	.00	−.01
	(.01)	(.01)	(−.03)
Self-employed	−.74*	−.20	−.32*
	(−.09)	(−.05)	(−.09)
Government employee	−.02	−.11	−.01
	(−.00)	(−.04)	(−.00)
Private employee	−.24	−.06	−.08
	(−.05)	(−.03)	(−.04)
Structural wealth	−.04	.01	.06
	(−.02)	(.01)	(.06)
Individual wealth	.05	.08*	.03
	(.02)	(.09)	(.03)
Structural poverty	.47*	.10*	.13*
	(.21)	(.11)	(.15)
Individual poverty	−.39*	−.03	−.02
	(−.18)	(−.03)	(−.02)
Egalitarianism	.08	.50*	.27*
	(.02)	(.28)	(.14)
Inegalitarianism	−.77*	−.22*	−.06
	(−.15)	(−.10)	(−.03)
Relative deprivation	−.18*	−.00	.02
	(−.13)	(−.00)	(.03)
Racial affect	−.23*	−.00	−.08*
	(−.17)	(−.01)	(−.14)
Percentage middle	−.19	−.31*	−.23†
	(−.02)	(−.10)	(−.07)
R^2	.25	.28	.21
(N)	(1131)	(543)	(683)

*$p < .05$; †$p < .10$ (shown in split-sample columns only).

the perception of blacks' demands for change as legitimate or illegitimate, and evaluations of civil rights groups.[3]

Finally, we include a measure of the respondent's perception of the *percentage of Americans classified as "middle,"* neither rich nor poor. This measure ought to reflect the perceived need for redistributive programs and therefore influence attitudes toward such programs. In our data, most forms of redistribution are supported by those who see larger proportions of Americans at the extremes of wealth or poverty. Seeing a higher percentage "in the middle" of the income distribution, neither poor nor rich, amounts to saying that the economic system works well, not creating a great deal of poverty, and no form of redistributive policy is needed. These effects are weaker for welfare support (correlation with percentage middle is $-.11$) than for other policy attitudes (correlations range from $-.19$ to $-.34$). As we shall see, welfare attitudes' links to affective and other factors make welfare a less pure reflection of beliefs about the income distribution.

Who, then, are the primary supporters and opponents of welfare? The measure of attitudes for or against welfare is a 4-item scale, as noted above, to provide high reliability of measurement. Table 6.2 shows that those particularly supporting welfare are nonwhites, those with high education or low incomes, and those who are not self-employed. These relationships are quite interesting, and some are apparently contradictory. In part, there is a straightforward effect of apparent self-interest, with the effects of race, income, and self-employment, which generally affect welfare attitudes in the same ways as they do beliefs in the dominant ideology. Whites, those with high incomes, and the self-employed are the most supportive of the dominant ideology and the most opposed to welfare, which they may not see as potentially benefiting them.

However, although education is associated strongly and positively with income, its relationship to welfare attitudes has the opposite sign.

---

[3] The reliability (alpha) of the relative deprivation scale is .64. The correlation between the two racial affect items is .35. We assume that these questions tap negative affect stemming either from traditional racial prejudice or from the factors identified in the "symbolic racism" literature (McConahay & Hough, 1976). In data from the 1976 American National Election Survey, nearly 76% of whites who support strict racial segregation saw blacks as trying to move too fast, showing that this item taps traditional prejudice. About 25% of whites who say they favor complete desegregation also think blacks have tried to move too fast, consistent with the symbolic racism idea that the perception of blacks as socially disruptive may also affect these responses, net of the influence of conventional racial prejudice. The racial-affect measure also has strong effects in theoretically expected directions in analyses presented in Chapter 7, supporting its validity. However, this measure may be relatively weak, particularly because of its use of only two items.

As education increases, there is more support for welfare at the same time as higher income leads to decreasing support. There are several possible explanations. The more educated may be less psychologically threatened by the poor, so less likely to derogate them and oppose supportive policies. In addition, the highly educated are more likely to be liberal on racial issues (showing more support for civil rights and lower levels of race prejudice, for instance). To the extent that welfare attitudes reflect racial attitudes (discussed below), this would be an additional reason for the more educated to be more liberal on welfare. Finally, as Chapter 4 showed, the educated are less likely to cite individual reasons for poverty, which are strongly associated with opposition to welfare (see below). Indeed, the analyses below (comparison of Table 6.2 with 6.3) show that approximately one-half of the education effect is indirect, mediated by the dominant ideology, racial affect, and other belief variables included in Table 6.3, so these explanations seem to have some validity. Broadly speaking, the effect of education indicates that its role in increasing income and status (and hence generally conservative attitudes) is here outweighed by a more "ideological" effect, increasing social liberalism. These data show that social liberalism influences attitudes toward welfare as well as sex and race.

We turn from the sociodemographic and self-interest factors to the role of beliefs as determinants of welfare attitudes, shown in Table 6.3. Among the dominant-ideology beliefs, structural and individual explanations for poverty are related in the obvious directions to welfare attitudes, while explanations for wealth have no effect, as might be expected. Inegalitarianism also influences attitudes, with those seeing inequality as desirable tending to oppose welfare. Thus, elements of the dominant ideology are strongly related to welfare attitudes. Those who see individuals as primarily responsible for their own poverty and inequality as generally desirable are unlikely to support welfare.

Welfare attitudes are also influenced by political and racial affect: relative deprivation and negative sentiment toward blacks. Welfare serves as a target for the displacement of some individuals' negative feelings about government unresponsiveness (relative deprivation) and of white racial prejudice and animosity toward blacks.

Attitudes toward government-guaranteed jobs are significantly influenced by a number of sociodemographic variables. More favorable attitudes are held by females, the young, nonwhites, those with lower education and income levels, and those who are not self-employed. Many of these relationships are simply interpretable in terms of self-interest since these groups are in fact likely to have relatively high unemployment rates. Comparing Tables 6.2 and 6.3 shows that most of the effects (except race) are mediated by differences in the belief variables shown in Table 6.3. Individual explanations for wealth, structural

explanations for poverty, egalitarianism, and inegalitarianism have significant effects. The strongest effect is of egalitarianism: Those who
endorse arguments for a more equal distribution of incomes particularly
favor government-guaranteed jobs. In addition, those who see a larger
percentage of the population as in the middle, neither rich nor poor,
tend to oppose guaranteed jobs. Dominant-ideology beliefs and self-
interest thus seem to constitute the major determinants of these attitudes, with relative deprivation and racial affect playing little part.

Guaranteed incomes (a floor on incomes for all who work) and guaranteed jobs have a similar pattern of determinants among the sociodemographic variables, except that the effects of income and education
are weaker for guaranteed incomes. The role of self-interest in shaping
attitudes is thus somewhat less clear in the case of the latter policy.
Turning to Table 6.3, the pattern of effects of the dominant-ideology
variables is also similar, but there is a significant effect of racial affect
on guaranteed income attitudes. Antiblack attitudes thus play some
role in generating opposition to this policy, as with welfare, but unlike
the case of guaranteed jobs. Perhaps this policy has greater resem-
blances to welfare than to guaranteed jobs, in the public mind, because
it involves "unearned" income.

Summary: Welfare Is Different

The three policies of redistribution toward the poor considered in
this chapter differ widely in popular acceptance, with welfare the least
popular. Public attitudes on welfare have been shifting in the direction
of increased opposition since the 1960s. However, available over-time
data suggest only minor changes in attitudes toward the other policies,
as in endorsement of the dominant ideology (Chapters 3–5).

In our analysis of the determinants of these attitudes, we found some
evidence of self-interest effects (e.g., effects of income and race) on
all three policies, but strongest for welfare and weakest for guaranteed
incomes. Education has strikingly different effects on the three policies,
making attitudes on welfare more favorable but diminishing support
for the other two. It appears, as discussed above, that education influences welfare attitudes primarily through ideological mediators (e.g.,
the dominant ideology and socially liberal attitudes about poverty and
perhaps race) while influencing the other policy attitudes primarily
through self-interest effects (e.g., through income).

Effects of dominant-ideology beliefs are similar on all three policies
but strongest on welfare attitudes, perhaps reflecting its greater inconsistency with the dominant-ideology elements of individual explanations for poverty and inegalitarianism (cf. Coughlin, 1980; Lopreato
& Hazelrigg, 1972 for similar findings in other western nations). Indeed,

these two beliefs are important determinants of welfare attitudes but not of attitudes toward the other policies. Antiwelfare sentiment seems to be linked to a "victim-blaming" view of the poor as lazy, lacking thrift and good morals, etc.: the items representing individual explanations for poverty. The other redistributive policies do *not* pick up the negative affect toward the poor that is tapped by welfare. In addition, welfare support—more than support for the other redistributive policies—is decreased by beliefs in the functions of unequal incomes. Welfare seems to call to the public's mind schemas involving feelings of dislike for the poor, attributions of their individual responsibility for their situations, and reflections on the benefits of inequality. The other two policies, in contrast, are supported by those who believe in the benefits of equality (the egalitarianism measure). The other policies— but not welfare—seem to be perceived more instrumentally, as a means to a redistributive end. They cue schemas involving the perceived benefits of somewhat greater equality of incomes and the existence of structural barriers, which (as Chapters 4 and 5 showed) are reasonably widely held.

Finally, welfare also attracts opposition based on affective factors: relative deprivation and negative racial affect. (Guaranteed incomes are also influenced to a lesser extent by the latter.) People often may displace resentment occasioned by government policies or by perceived racial threats onto welfare programs. This displacement may be more widespread than is the case for other redistributive policies precisely because of the inconsistency of welfare with widely accepted elements of the dominant ideology. The displacement may be encouraged by the fact that it is now generally thought to be socially undesirable to express overtly racially prejudiced attitudes but acceptable to express negative racial affect indirectly, as antiwelfare sentiment (Kinder & Sears, 1981).

REDISTRIBUTION AWAY FROM THE RICH

Redistribution involves both give and take. The rich, because of their large surplus income and small numbers, appear to be a logical group to provide the income that will be redistributed toward the poor. Especially as seen from the perspective of the middle class, if redistribution is believed to be warranted, then redistribution from the rich to the poor may appear to be the least costly kind. However, the evidence reviewed so far suggests that attitudes on such policies may be mixed and ambivalent.

On the one hand, one of our findings from Chapter 5 suggests that the American public may favor redistribution away from the rich, since most people believe that average earnings for occupations often held by the rich are too high in proportion to their contribution to society. More generally, many Americans favor a more restricted range of incomes than presently exists. This sentiment would seem to lead to support for upper limits on income and other redistributive policies.

On the other hand, several reasons may predispose the American public to oppose programs that take income from the rich. First, as Chapter 3 showed, Americans are strongly optimistic about their personal chances of economic advancement. If their optimism includes the possibility of entering the ranks of the wealthy, it may motivate opposition to redistribution away from the rich, out of anticipatory self-interest. Lipset (1963) suggests that this logic of expected mobility may account for the lack of popular support for socialism among the American working class. Second, as Chapter 4 showed, most Americans attribute wealth to superior individual characteristics of the wealthy (ability, effort, and initiative). Wealth is seen as legitimately earned and should not be arbitrarily taken away. Third, Chapter 5 showed general endorsement of the benefits of income inequality in principle, which should also lead to a reluctance to tax the rich too heavily.

How do people generally resolve these conflicting tendencies to favor and oppose redistribution away from the rich? Table 6.4 shows data from our sample on three frequently discussed policies: limiting incomes, limiting inheritances, and instituting government ownership and control of industry. All are generally unpopular policies, as the marginals make clear. They all seem to violate the dominant-ideology principles of proportionality of rewards to effort and talent by threatening to prevent people from potentially earning very high rewards. Limiting inheritances (which are less clearly deserved than incomes) is therefore slightly more acceptable than limiting incomes, based on the relatively better fit with the dominant ideology.

One interesting issue is the potential inconsistency between the general lack of enthusiasm for limiting high incomes and the widespread

TABLE 6.4. Redistribution Aimed at the Rich: Marginals

Question	Strongly agree	Agree	Disagree	Strongly disagree
There should be an upper limit on the amount of money any person can make.	3	18	65	14
Tax laws should be strengthened to limit the amount of wealth that can be inherited.	3	23	62	11
Government ownership and control of basic industries would benefit society.	2	23	53	22

feeling that members of high-paying occupations earn more than would be fair given their contributions to society (Chapter 5). Perhaps distrust of *government intervention* to limit incomes may be more salient than attitudes toward limitations in principle in determining these policy attitudes (see the related argument by Kuklinski & Parent, 1981). It is also possible that respondents may identify themselves as potential future victims of overall limitations on incomes but feel free to term specific occupations (athletes, government bureaucrats) as overpaid, since most respondents are not in these occupations. Indeed, redistributive policies in general seem to be evaluated on the basis of fairness in principle rather than on the basis of people's beliefs about the current state of inequality in fact, with the exception of beliefs in structural causes of poverty. This tendency is part of the general strength of "symbolic politics" over concrete issues in shaping political attitudes (Kinder & Sears, 1981). It may also reflect a tendency of respondents to become habituated and inured to unfair aspects of the current system but to be quite sensitive to any elements of unfairness in a new policy proposal, which will be novel and highly salient.

Attitudes on redistribution away from the rich are unrelated to age, with the exception of government ownership of industry, which has a curvilinear relationship (Figure 6.2). The middle-aged are most strongly opposed to this policy.

Determinants of Attitudes on Redistribution from the Rich

Tables 6.5 and 6.6 present regression results involving these redistributive policies. As before, the first table (6.5) presents the effects of sociodemographic variables alone to show direct or indirect self-interest effects, and Table 6.6 adds the belief and affect variables.

Income limits are favored by nonwhites, the less educated, and government employees and nonworkers (compared to private employees and the self-employed). Interestingly, the obvious self-interest prediction that income itself should be related to this attitude is not fulfilled. However, the effect of education is in the predicted self-interest direction: The more educated (who generally command higher incomes) oppose income limits.

Turning to the effects of beliefs, Table 6.6 shows that structural explanations for wealth increase and individual explanations for wealth decrease support for such a policy. Structural explanations for poverty continue (as in Table 6.3) to increase support for all forms of redistribution, and egalitarianism and inegalitarianism affect the attitude in the obvious ways. The dominant ideology thus strongly contributes to shaping attitudes on this policy, while affective reactions to the government (relative deprivation) or to racial minorities have little or no effect.

TABLE 6.5. Redistribution Aimed at the Rich: Regressions on
          Sociodemographic Variables

Independent variable	Limitation of incomes	Limitation of inheritances	Government ownership of industry
Sex (female)	.02	.01	.05
	(.01)	(.00)	(.03)
Age (10 years)	−.02	.01	−.08*
	(−.05)	(.03)	(−.17)
Race (nonwhite)	.15[+]	.25*	.34*
	(.09)	(.12)	(.16)
Education (years)	−.03*	.01	−.04*
	(−.14)	(.02)	(−.17)
Income (log)	−.11	−.24*	−.25*
	(−.05)	(−.12)	(−.11)
South	−.02	.02	.08
	(−.02)	(.01)	(.05)
Wealth	−.01	−.03[+]	−.03
	(−.03)	(−.08)	(−.06)
Self-employed	−.33*	−.02	−.24*
	(−.12)	(−.01)	(−.08)
Government employee	.01	−.07	−.06
	(.01)	(−.03)	(−.03)
Private employee	−.13[+]	−.01	−.09
	(−.10)	(−.00)	(−.06)
R^2	.07	.04	.15
(N)	(544)	(684)	(1132)

*$p < .05$.
[+]$p < .10$ (shown in split-sample columns only).

Limiting inheritances attracts particular support from nonwhites and those with low incomes and little wealth. Of the belief variables, explanations for wealth are unrelated to this policy attitude, but structural explanations for poverty, egalitarianism, and inegalitarianism continue to have effects. Again, relative deprivation and racial affect have no effects.

Government ownership and control of industry is supported particularly by the young, nonwhites, those with low incomes and low levels of education, and those who are not self-employed in their own business. Older people oppose this policy more than other means of redistribution, perhaps because they distrust the government as a tool for increasing equality. Among the dominant-ideology beliefs, this policy is influenced by structural explanations for poverty and egalitarianism. Notably, it is opposed by those who feel relatively deprived, which presumably reflects their specific distrust of the government. It does not reflect racial affect according to our measure. Finally, it is opposed by those who believe that a major proportion of the population falls in the middle between poverty and wealth and favored by those with a more dichotomous, rich and poor, vision of society.

TABLE 6.6. Redistribution Aimed at the Rich: Regressions on
Sociodemographic Variables and Dominant Ideology

Independent variable	Limitation of incomes	Limitation of inheritances	Government ownership of industry
Sex (female)	−.06	.01	.01
	(−.05)	(.01)	(.01)
Age (10 years)	−.01	.02	−.08*
	(−.02)	(.04)	(−.17)
Race (nonwhite)	−.05	.10	.15*
	(−.03)	(.05)	(.07)
Education (years)	−.01	.01	−.03*
	(−.05)	(.05)	(−.10)
Income (log)	−.02	−.11	−.14*
	(−.01)	(−.06)	(−.06)
South	−.02	.02	.07
	(−.01)	(.01)	(.04)
Wealth	.02	−.01	−.00
	(.05)	(−.01)	(−.01)
Self-employed	−.22^{+}	.10	−.09
	(−.08)	(.04)	(−.03)
Government employee	−.02	−.04	−.05
	(−.01)	(−.02)	(−.02)
Private employee	−.11^{+}	−.01	−.08
	(−.08)	(−.01)	(−.05)
Structural wealth	.05^{+}	−.00	.01
	(.08)	(−.00)	(.02)
Individual wealth	−.08*	−.01	−.00
	(−.13)	(−.02)	(−.00)
Structural poverty	.07*	.09*	.08*
	(.11)	(.13)	(.11)
Individual poverty	−.02	−.02	−.02
	(−.04)	(−.04)	(−.03)
Egalitarianism	.27*	.21*	.37*
	(.22)	(.15)	(.25)
Inegalitarianism	−.17*	−.25*	−.10
	(−.11)	(−.15)	(−.05)
Relative deprivation	−.00	.00	−.04*
	(−.01)	(.00)	(−.08)
Racial affect	.02	.00	.01
	(.05)	(.01)	(.03)
Percentage middle	−.14	−.17	−.27*
	(−.06)	(−.07)	(−.11)
R^2	.22	.14	.27
(N)	(543)	(683)	(1131)

*$p < .05$; $^{+}p < .10$ (shown in split-sample columns only).

Summary

Redistribution aimed at the upper end of the income spectrum is unpopular in any form. Though it would seem logical for lower income people to support such policies, status effects on attitudes toward such policies are relatively infrequent and weak. Aside from government ownership of industry, where age, race, and education have major effects, these policy attitudes seem to be relatively interchangeable as fairly pure indicators of an overall disposition to support or oppose redistribution. Those who see poverty as structurally caused, favor equality, and deny the benefits of inequality tend to support all three of these types of income-equalizing policies.

DISCUSSION

Self-Interest Effects

Among the social correlates of redistributive policy attitudes, whether aimed at the poor or the rich, the most frequently evident pattern is an overall status bias, with the objectively deprived favoring redistributive policies of various sorts. Race is the most frequently influential variable, with nonwhites significantly favoring all forms of redistribution toward the poor and away from the wealthy. It is clear that group identification among nonwhites centers on these issues, particularly welfare. The effects are group-based rather than simply due to differences in respondents' personal economic situations, as they appear when income, occupational, and educational differences between whites and nonwhites are controlled in the regressions. That is, they are interpretable in terms of fraternal (as opposed to individual-level) relative deprivation (Runciman, 1966) or group self-interest (Bobo, 1983).

Income also has effects, leading to decreased support for four of the six redistributive policies. Self-employment also leads to decreased support for redistribution in five of six cases. However, despite these examples of self-interest effects, there were failures of clear self-interest prediction in several cases, some noted in the text.

Age has an effect in three cases; the old tend to oppose policies that overtly mention government intervention (government ownership of industries, guaranteed jobs, and guaranteed incomes). Perhaps the old feel that the government should limit itself to distributing Social Security checks and otherwise not intervene in the distribution of incomes; other data show that Social Security itself is not widely perceived as a redistributive policy (Schlitz, 1970).

The pattern of education effects is complex. In line with self-interest and its causal relationship to income, education increases opposition to three of the six policies but, interestingly, leads to strongly increased support for welfare (though even the highly educated express majority disapproval of welfare). Possible interpretations for this effect were discussed above.

Figure 6.3 presents a summary of attitudes on selected redistributive policies, broken down by status (a composite of education and household income) and race. In most cases, as the regression analyses showed, both race and status have effects, with race being more influential. In general the pattern of status making little difference among blacks, frequently observed in Chapters 3–5, is not found here. Status effects (as judged by percentage differences) are generally about the same size among blacks as among whites and are even stronger among blacks for the item about welfare providing enough to live on. Status effects are also generally parallel in form for whites and for blacks, even where status does not have simple linear effects, as with the item on welfare spending. The middle-status group is more likely than either the low or the high group to complain that overall expenditures on welfare are excessive. In general, the effects of status hold across both racial groups and add to the effects of race. The implication of this pattern is that *(a)* there is some effect of group identification among blacks, who are more supportive of redistribution even if they are personally rather well-off and *(b)* at the same time blacks' opinions are not uniform; personal status makes a difference as well.

Links to the Dominant Ideology

Structural explanations for poverty are extremely influential, increasing support for all redistribution, across the board; the effect on welfare is the strongest. One essential basis for favoring redistribution, then, is the idea that structural barriers exist in society that disadvantage the poor and keep them from achieving to the level of their ability. Individual explanations for poverty, in sharp contrast, influence only antiwelfare attitudes. One implication is, as argued above, that antiwelfare attitudes have a strong affective component. Individual explanations refer to individual "moral" faults of the poor, and an antiwelfare stance represents an important attitudinal outlet of hostility to the poor. Individual explanations for poverty do *not* reduce support for other forms of redistribution—the effect on welfare is unparalleled (cf. Coughlin, 1980). As noted above, welfare cues different associations (including the personal responsibility of the poor and the benefits of inequality) which elicit negative policy attitudes in many people. Other policies are more likely to be evaluated in a context of thoughts concerning the benefits of reducing inequality and an acknowledgment of structural barriers to opportunity, leading to more favorable views.

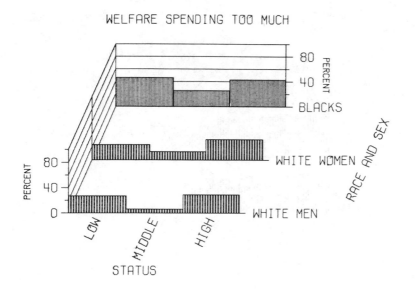

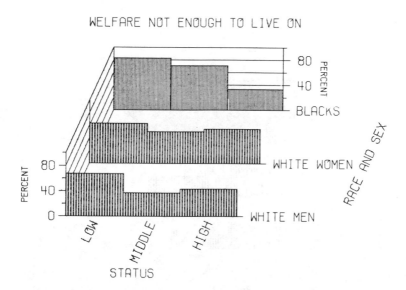

FIGURE 6.3. Proredistributive opinion on selected items, broken down by status, sex, and race.

GUARANTEED INCOME FOR THOSE WHO WORK

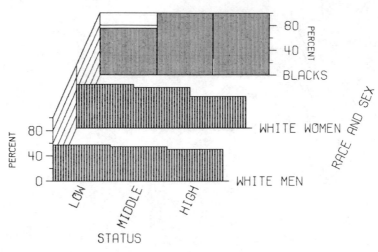

GUARANTEE JOB FOR ALL WHO WANT ONE

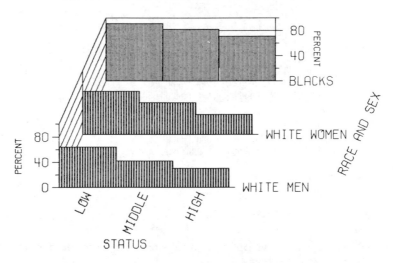

FIGURE 6.3. *Continued.*

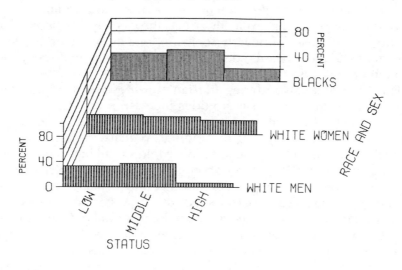

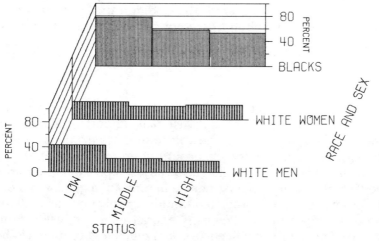

FIGURE 6.3. *Continued.*

Explanations for wealth have few significant effects, even on policies aimed at the rich. They do influence the attitude toward limitation of incomes, one policy that explicitly affects the wealthy. The individual's picture of the causes of poverty seems to be a more important determinant of attitudes toward redistribution in general than does the perception of the causes of wealth.

Finally, egalitarian and inegalitarian attitudes are also important. Across the board, egalitarian attitudes increase support for all redistributive policies except welfare, underlining once again the special, more affect-laden nature of that policy. Welfare seems to be less strongly linked than other policies in people's thinking to the goal of income equality and its potential benefits. Evaluations of welfare seem to depend more on the application of other judgmental principles, such as equity and negative affect directed toward welfare recipients.

Inegalitarianism also influences most policy views, reducing support for all forms of redistribution except government ownership and guaranteed incomes. This element of the dominant ideology, then—the belief in the benefits of inequality for all in society—does negatively affect attitudes toward most forms of redistributive policy, as is theoretically expected.

In general, the dominant-ideology beliefs add considerably to the predictability of policy attitudes over and above that based on knowledge of respondents' sociodemographic position. More than their own self-interest and personal experiences (which are reflected in objective variables such as sex, age, race, income, and occupation), people's general beliefs about the actual and desired workings of the stratification system determine their views on policies aimed at changing the distribution of income in this country. In general, the R^2 levels increase by a factor of two or more with the addition of the belief variables. Attitudes toward redistribution are *not* strongly determined by sociodemographic position, even indirectly.

Affect

Negative affect directed at either the government (relative deprivation) or at racial minorities is occasionally important in determining attitudes on redistributive policies. Both of these elements contribute in the case of welfare attitudes, again underlining its specially affect-laden nature. Relative deprivation also causes opposition to government ownership of industry, understandable in terms of a generalized distrust of government. In an unpredicted finding, racial affect also influenced attitudes on guaranteed incomes. Generally, though, aside from the case of welfare, affective influences seem much less central than beliefs in the dominant ideology in determining attitudes on policies related to redistribution.

SUMMARY

What do the results say about the relative effects of general beliefs (in the dominant ideology, for example), self-interest, and affective factors on attitudes toward redistributive policy? The relationships of dominant-ideology beliefs to policy attitudes are strong and systematic. Egalitarian and inegalitarian attitudes and structural explanations for poverty influence attitudes almost across the range of policies considered. Redistribution is opposed if it is believed to take away rewards that are earned by individual efforts and abilities or to reduce incentives that motivate people to work hard. Individual explanations for poverty, having overtones of negative affect toward the poor, influence welfare attitudes in particular.

In contrast to these pervasive effects of dominant-ideology beliefs, other variables have more specific influences. Self-interest in redistribution of income is clearly indexed by one's own income, education, occupation, and other aspects of social position. These variables do affect attitudes toward various redistributive policies but have less impact than the dominant ideology. Race (interpreted in terms of group identification by nonwhites) in particular had a broad impact, influencing all six of the attitudes considered in this chapter.

Redistributive policy attitudes are thus influenced by individuals' beliefs in the dominant ideology and their self-interest and, in the case of welfare, by affective reactions to the government and to racial outgroups. As our earlier chapters discussed, then, the general nature of accepted redistributive policy may often arise as a compromise between forces (particularly belief in the dominant ideology) that dispose people to resist redistribution and other forces that lead to acceptance of redistribution. For example, welfare programs are publicly accepted and implemented but rarely permit a decent or dignified life for most recipients. We speculate that the compromise nature of policy is often responsible for its failure to achieve the goals of either side: Welfare programs neither end poverty nor escape a political backlash of antipoor sentiment.

The data pose one major puzzle, however. If redistributive policy views are so firmly based in beliefs in the dominant ideology, which themselves have changed little in the last 10–15 years, why have attitudes toward welfare in particular shifted so strongly toward opposition over the same time period? Attitudes on other redistributive programs seem to have changed little. If anything, the small changes in beliefs over time have been *away* from the pure dominant-ideology pattern toward an increasing recognition of structural barriers in society that limit individual achievement. Why then should welfare attitudes shift in the opposite direction?

We suggest four potential explanations. First, welfare programs currently exist, in contrast to the other types of redistributive programs in our questions, which are largely hypothetical. In fact, there has been a large absolute increase in welfare spending since the early 1960s (U. S. Bureau of the Census, 1980). The increasing magnitude of the programs itself may generate increasing opposition, even among individuals who would be comfortable with small, inexpensive spending programs. In fact, Heclo (1984) and Wilensky (1975) argue that welfare programs were initially implemented largely for bureaucratic reasons, independent of public opinion (or at least without widespread public backing). As the programs' size and scope increased and they came to public awareness, opposition also increased.

Second, the belief that welfare has *failed* may have grown out of political debate over the relevant time period, again because welfare programs are in actual existence. Politicians often campaign against the "welfare mess" and suggest that welfare is ineffective even in meeting the modest goals of preserving recipients in a tolerable condition, let alone in making them productive (working) citizens. Some even argue that welfare programs create poverty by encouraging dependence (Gilder, 1981). So Americans may not have changed their underlying beliefs about the causes of poverty or the need for some ameliorative programs for the poor but have reached the conclusion that current welfare programs do not work well and therefore do not deserve political support.

Third, the affective components that are so much more prominent in the case of welfare than of the other programs may be responsible. People who feel that the government has failed to listen to their legitimate grievances (i.e., who experience relative deprivation), or those who hold negative attitudes toward racial minorities, may deflect their anger onto "undeserving" welfare recipients and the programs that support them. Distrust in government or relative deprivation has increased greatly in recent years, so this factor may partially account for increases in antiwelfare sentiment.

In addition, the "racializing" of welfare attitudes may have increased in recent years, though we know of no directly relevant data. That is, in earlier years poverty may have been thought of as largely a problem of the old, retired, or disabled, groups that are generally considered highly deserving of help (Cook, 1979). More recently, media coverage may have shaped a perception of welfare recipients as more likely to be black, young, unemployed, and perhaps unmarried and with children; these characteristics may trigger higher levels of negative affect rather than sympathetic reactions. In either case, the special affective loading of welfare attitudes may be important in explaining the rapid changes in welfare support despite relative stability of beliefs in the dominant ideology and self-interest factors.

Finally, increasing opposition to welfare may derive from hard economic times. Welfare may be singled out because most people do not see it as potentially helping them personally, while its perceived cost in taxes is seen as increasingly burdensome when unemployment or inflation hurt one's personal situation. The disentangling of these possible explanations of the special case of welfare attitudes must await further research.

7

OPPORTUNITY FOR BLACKS

In this chapter we examine beliefs about opportunity for blacks and attitudes toward equal opportunity programs. These beliefs and attitudes constitute an important element of the climate of race relations in America, which by some indicators has changed markedly in recent history. Three decades ago racial segregation in housing, schooling, public transportation, and other spheres of everyday life was strongly normative or in some areas a matter of law. Denial of equal opportunity in the workplace was not prohibited by law. Legislation of the 1960s, of course, made illegal both racial segregation practices and racial discrimination in employment. Matching these legal changes, there seems to have been substantial reduction in overt attitudes of racial prejudice and sentiment for employment discrimination over this period (Taylor, Fiske, Etcoff, & Ruderman, 1978)

Figure 7.1 illustrates the now-familiar data on change in commonly used indicators of race prejudice over the last two decades. Marked reduction in what may be termed *traditional* racial prejudice (pro-segregation sentiment) is clearly shown in this table. Moreover, over the last three decades whites have come to endorse virtually unanimously the belief that blacks should have opportunity equal to that of whites. In the late 1940s roughly one-half of the American public responded that whites should have "the first chance at any kind of job." In 1972 only 5% expressed this sentiment (Burstein, 1979).

If only because much of the change in racial prejudice indicators has been from individuals who have changed their attitudes (Condran, 1979; Smith, 1981)—as opposed to cohort replacement—Americans seemingly now recognize that widespread racial prejudice and discrimination were part of our recent history. Such recognition would logically seem to entail the belief that black Americans suffer past and current disadvantages in their chances to achieve economic parity with whites due to employment discrimination and other forms of race prejudice in practice. Further, it would seem to follow that most white Americans now believe that as a result of restricted opportunity for blacks, extensive assistance is owed blacks in the effort to achieve economic equality relative to whites.

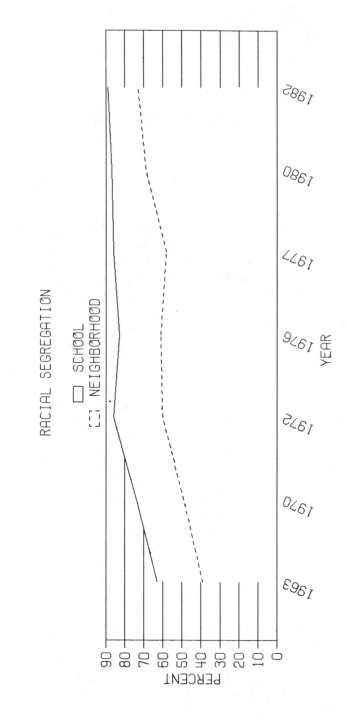

FIGURE 7.1. Time trends in "liberal" views on race relations. Data sources: 1963 and 1970 (Taylor et al., 1978); 1972–1982 (Davis, 1982). Question wordings: Do you think white students and black students should go to the same schools or to separate schools? (school segregation). White people have a right to keep blacks out of their neighborhoods if they want to, and blacks should respect that right (neighborhood segregation). How strongly would you object if a member of your family wanted to bring a black friend home to dinner? (invite to dinner). Do you think there should be laws against marriages between blacks and whites? (racial intermarriage).

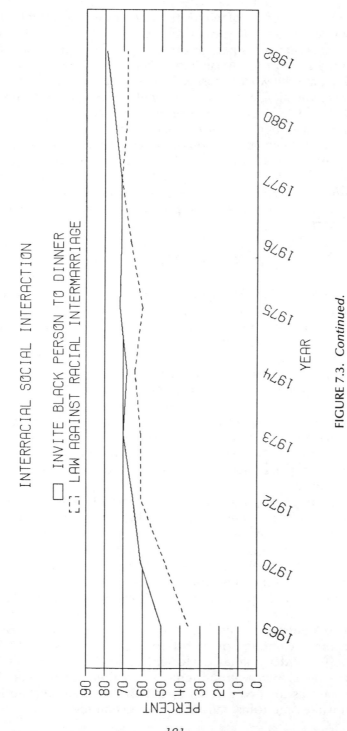

FIGURE 7.3. Continued.

Judged by the reaction of whites to programs to implement equality of educational and economic opportunity, however, recognition of extensive race prejudice as part of our recent history has *not* brought with it broad support for assistance to blacks in the effort to achieve economic parity with whites. Busing for desegregation of public schools has met overwhelming and sometimes violent opposition by the white public (Kelley, 1974). From their inception affirmative-action legislation and programs have been widely criticized. Affirmative-action programs have been the subject of numerous court challenges and characterized as promoting "reverse discrimination." Public opinion about these programs is sharply divided (Lipset, 1978; Kluegel & Smith, 1983). Funding for equal opportunity programs of all kinds has been unstable and low relative to the size of the problem they address (Benokraitis & Feagin, 1978).

SOURCES OF OPPOSITION

Why, when there is seemingly strong evidence that the racial beliefs and attitudes of white Americans have become more liberal, are equal opportunity policy and programs involving blacks so controversial and so strongly opposed in public opinion? There are several plausible answers to this question.

First, it may be argued that the change in racial prejudice indicated by responses to survey questions is simply superficial. Whites are aware that it is no longer "fashionable" or socially acceptable to express race prejudice and respond accordingly when asked about their racial beliefs and attitudes on surveys (McConahay, Hardee, & Bates, 1981). It is not socially undesirable, however, to express opposition to equal opportunity programs. Opposition to these programs may represent disguised racial prejudice.

In interpreting a response to any survey item the influence of social desirability must be considered, but other indications of change in "oldline" racism argue that the observed change in the distribution of attitudes reflects more than just social desirability. It is difficult to argue that Americans truly hold the same strength of prosegregationist sentiment and sense of the inferiority of blacks that was expressed in the violent opposition of whites to the early stages of the civil rights movement.

A related argument, and one that seems a priori more plausible, is found in the "symbolic" or "modern" racism thesis (Sears & McConahay, 1973; McConahay & Hough, 1976; Kinder & Sears, 1981; McConahay et al., 1981). Proponents of this thesis argue that change in the responses to survey items does indicate a real decline in one aspect of white Americans' racial beliefs and attitudes, in what may be

termed *traditional* or *old-fashioned* race prejudice (i.e., prosegregationist, white supremacy sentiment.) However, antiblack sentiment
stemming from other sources persists and shapes the public's evaluation of efforts to further economic parity for blacks. Specifically, white
Americans see blacks as a major disruptive force in society and as making demands for change that violate cherished values such as individualism and self-discipline. Many whites blame blacks for social problems
such as crime and the "welfare mess." As a consequence, blacks are
viewed as undeserving of government assistance, their demands for
change are viewed as illegitimate, anger results, and opposition to equal
opportunity programs for blacks follows.

Opposition to equal opportunity for blacks may also stem from anger
that is not directly racial in character. It may be based in a sense of
relative deprivation resulting from the perception that one's problems
as an individual or as a member of a group are overlooked by the government while attention is paid to problems of the poor, blacks, and
other minorities (Binzen, 1970; Ransford, 1972; Sennett & Cobb, 1972;
Vanneman & Pettigrew, 1972). Many whites may see themselves as performing "honest labor" that is underrewarded monetarily and in terms
of social esteem, while the government gives disproportionate attention
to the improvement of social and economic conditions of minorities
and the poor, often believed to be undeserving.

White opposition may also be based on economic self-interest. For
whites whose work circumstances place them in potential competition
with blacks for jobs and promotions, opposition to equal employment
opportunity programs may be due to the threat of economic loss implied by gains for blacks. Given the tendency toward racial segregation
in jobs—blacks are overrepresented in unskilled or semiskilled jobs
and underrepresented in white-collar jobs—and the simple fact that
blacks make up only 10% of the workforce, blacks objectively do not
present a direct competitive threat to most whites. Yet, self-interest in
the sense of a person's general stake in maintaining the economic status
quo may have a broader impact. Programs to realize greater economic
equality may challenge the perceived legitimacy of existing economic
inequality (Wellman, 1977).[1] Thus one might expect that whites of higher
incomes oppose equal opportunity programs—especially those that
appear to be egalitarian in character—because of their implicit challenge
to the legitimacy of the stratification order.

[1]Bobo (1983) makes a similar argument in proposing that white opposition
to busing for racial integration and other programs for racial change stems
from the group self-interest of whites in maintaining the existing stratification
order.

The Impact of Stratification Beliefs

Major aspects of the civil rights legislation have achieved broad public support. In recent times there has been little challenge to or controversy involving laws supporting the voting rights of minorities and making discrimination in housing and employment illegal.[2] Why does the American public support civil rights legislation and oppose many equal opportunity programs?

The answer may lie in the sources of opposition discussed above. Passing laws may be seen as costless, whereas programs to bring about actual economic parity between blacks and whites may be seen as costly. Opposing civil rights legislation may be seen as socially undesirable, whereas expressing opposition to equal opportunity programs may not be seen as indicative of race prejudice. However, we suggest that the answer to this question involves more than economic self-interest or disguised race prejudice. We must also consider the role played by stratification beliefs. The challenge of the civil rights movement to the white American public was to live up to the "American Creed"—that is, to abide by the central American values of equality of basic human legal, political, and economic rights (Myrdal, 1962). The challenge of equal opportunity programs is of a different sort. They challenge the validity of aspects of the American creed, of beliefs about how the American stratification order should and does work.

We propose that in part opposition to equal opportunity programs is based on prevailing beliefs about how the stratification order should work. As we have seen in Chapter 5, most Americans believe that economic inequality is functionally necessary and beneficial to society. Equity is the criterion for a just distribution of income that is most broadly supported. Whites may oppose some equal opportunity programs because they are believed to promote equality of economic outcomes at the expense of equity (Lipset & Schneider, 1978). To the extent that whites equate affirmative-action programs with policies, such as strict racial hiring quotas, that are believed to favor lesser qualified blacks over more qualified whites, opposition may be due to perceived violation of equity norms. There may be some whites who in general favor programs to help blacks acquire the training and education required to compete with whites for jobs but object to some equal opportunity programs strictly because they believe that they are unfair as judged by equity considerations.

We also propose that some whites may oppose equal opportunity

[2]The lack of public support for the recent challenge to civil rights legislation implied by efforts to block the renewal of the voting rights bill (in 1983) supports the assertion that the American public in general favors civil rights legislation.

programs because of their beliefs about how the American stratification order does work in fact. As we have seen in Chapter 4 the white American public strongly attributes economic success or failure to the presence or absence of individual ability, talent, effort, and character and sees their own opportunity as plentiful. To the extent that whites base their beliefs about opportunity for blacks on beliefs about how the stratification order works in general, they will tend to deny that blacks' opportunity is limited structurally, and consequently believe that equal opportunity programs are unneeded.

Many white Americans seem to believe that a reduction in individual prejudice against blacks is sufficient to produce opportunity for blacks equal to that of whites. Barriers to achieving economic parity between blacks and whites currently involve the class conditions of blacks as much as or more than they involve strictly racial considerations (Wilson, 1978; Pettigrew, 1981). The history of American racism and race discrimination has resulted in greatly disproportionate numbers of blacks raised in poverty and currently living in the ghettos of large American cities (Pettigrew, 1981). Furthermore, blacks much more often than whites are raised in lower income families, whose parents are employed in unskilled or semiskilled labor. Such conditions limit chances for upward socioeconomic mobility (Featherman & Hauser, 1978).

However, most Americans, as we have seen in Chapter 3, do not believe that growing up in poverty or social-class background in general places any limitation on one's chances for economic advancement. Such beliefs encourage whites to perceive the "race problem" as one of individual prejudice and acts of discrimination on the part of whites, not one of structural barriers to equal opportunity. They further encourage opposition to equal opportunity programs on the grounds that "now that individual race prejudice is on the decline such programs are unnecessary."

BELIEFS ABOUT BLACKS' OPPORTUNITY

A major implication of the above discussion of sources of opposition to equal opportunity programs is that declining traditional racial prejudice has not been accompanied by increasing recognition of structural limits to blacks' opportunity. To the contrary, the arguments advanced above suggest that the white American public in general believes that opportunity for blacks is less restricted now than it has been in the past. Tables 7.1 through 7.4 and Figures 7.2 and 7.3 present data on several aspects of Americans' beliefs about opportunity that speak to the merits of those inferences.

The questions in Table 7.1, asked in the 1972 and 1976 National Election Surveys, concern beliefs about the impact of racial discrimination

TABLE 7.1. Beliefs about Racial Discrimination and Opportunity
        (Whites Only)

	1972		1976	
	Percentage	*(f)*	Percentage	*(f)*
A1. Many black people who don't do well in life do have good training, but the opportunities just always go to whites.	11	(182)	10	(160)
A2. Black people may not have the same opportunities as whites, but many blacks haven't prepared themselves enough to make use of the opportunities that come their way.	90	(1452)	90	(1423)
B1. It's lack of skill and abilities that keep many black people from getting a job, it's not just because they're black. When a black person is trained to do something, he is able to get a job.			75	(1203)
B2. Many qualified black people can't get a good job. White people with the same skills wouldn't have any trouble.			25	(405)
C1. Blacks and other minorities no longer face unfair employment conditions. In fact they are favored in many training and job programs.	64	(1039)	71	(1035)
C2. Even with the new programs, minorities still face the same old job discrimination once the program is over.	36	(585)	29	(419)

D.   In the past few years we have heard a lot about civil rights groups
     working to improve the position of the Negro/black people in this
     country. How much real change to you think there has been in the
     position of the Negro/black people in the past few years, a lot, some or
     not much at all?

Whites	1964	1966	1968	1970	1972	1974	1976
A lot	39	41	49	55	57	58	63
Some	40	40	36	35	35	36	31
Not much at all	21	19	18	11	8	6	6
Blacks							
A lot	60	41	59	39	44	44	32
Some	31	48	32	47	47	45	50
Not much at all	9	11	8	14	9	11	18

Continued

TABLE 7.1. (Continued)

	1972		1976	
	Percentage	(f)	Percentage	(f)
E1. The attempt to fit in and do what's proper hasn't paid off for blacks. It doesn't matter how "proper" you are, you still meet serious discrimination if you're black.			24	(347)
E2. The problem for many blacks is that they aren't really acceptable by American standards. Any black who is educated and does what is considered proper will be accepted and will get ahead.			76	(1073)
F1. Discrimination affects all black people. The only way to handle it is for blacks to organize together and demand rights for all.			12	(189)
F2. Discrimination may affect all blacks, but the best way to handle it is for each individual to act like any other American.			88	(1429)

Source: American National Election Surveys as reported in Converse et al. (1980) and the 1972 and 1976 American National Election Survey codebooks.

on blacks' opportunity for economic advancement. Three conclusions seem evident in the distribution of responses to these questions. First, most Americans have come to believe that blacks no longer face strictly racial barriers to achieving economic parity with whites. This aspect of beliefs about blacks' opportunity is shown most clearly in responses to questions B and C. The majority of Americans believe that blacks who have the same skills and training as whites will receive the same treatment as whites in the workplace.

Second, there is a strong element of blaming blacks for their lower average level of socioeconomic status relative to whites. Responses to question A show a pronounced tendency to attribute racial economic inequality to a lack of "preparation" on the part of blacks. Responses to questions E and F show that much of the public attributes racial economic inequality to the failure of blacks to behave like whites. While these questions do not specifically mention morality, it is implicitly invoked in the use of the words "proper" and "act like any other American." Thus, there seems to be a strong tendency, paralleling that in

TABLE 7.2. Perceived Sources of Black–White Socioeconomic Status
           Differences

1972[a]

Now, I'd like you to tell me what you consider the most important reason,
   of all those on the card, for whites getting more or the good things in
   life than blacks.

	Percentage	(f)
1. A small group of powerful and wealthy white people control things and act to keep blacks down.	7	(64)
2. The differences are brought about by God; God made the races different as part of his divine plan.	5	(46)
3. It's really a matter of some people not trying hard enough; that if blacks would only try harder they could be just as well off as whites.	40	(352)
4. Generations of slavery and discrimination have created conditions that make it difficult for blacks to work their way out of the lower class.	38	(332)
5. Black Americans teach their children values and skills different from those required to be successful in American society.	5	(46)
6. Blacks come from a less able race, and this explains why blacks are not so well off as whites in America.	5	(42)

1977

On the average blacks have worse jobs, income, and housing than white
   people. Do you think these differences are . . .

	Percentage yes	(N)[b]
Mainly due to discrimination	41	(1297)
Because most blacks have less inborn ability	26	(1281)
Because most blacks don't have the motivation or will power to pull themselves up out of poverty	66	(1270)

Joint responses

	Percentage	(f)
Discrimination alone	20	(238)
Discrimination and motivation	13	(155)
All sources	8	(90)
Motivation alone	29	(340)
Innate differences and motivation	17	(201)
None of these sources	12	(145)
Other	2	(23)

---

[a]Source: 1972 National Election Survey (whites only).
[b]Total number of cases (excluding don't knows and missing data; nonblacks
only). Source: 1977 General Social Survey (Davis, 1982).

TABLE 7.3. Age-Group Differences in Perceived Sources of Black–White Socioeconomic Status Differences (Joint Responses; Nonblacks Only)[a]

Age-Group	Discrimination	Discrimination and motivation	All sources	Motivation	Innate and motivation	None	(Total)
18–29	31.5	15.0	4.2	29.7	6.6	12.9	(206)
30–39	25.9	13.4	4.6	35.6	8.8	11.7	(239)
40–49	13.5	14.6	5.2	32.8	21.3	12.5	(192)
50–59	15.6	12.2	4.9	29.8	22.9	14.6	(205)
60+	11.5	10.7	18.9	18.5	30.0	10.3	(243)

[a]$\chi^2 = 166.94$; $p < .001$.

189

TABLE 7.4. Beliefs about Blacks' Opportunity

	Black		White	
	Percentage	(f)	Percentage	(f)
Extent of discrimination[a]				
How much discrimination do you feel there is against blacks and other minorities in any areas of life that limits their chances to get ahead? Would you say . . .				
A lot	53	(274)	26	(333)
Some	36	(186)	48	(619)
Just a little	10	(52)	17	(211)
None at all	2	(12)	9	(115)
Extent of preferential treatment[b]				
How much preferential treatment for racial minorities is there that *improves* their chances to get ahead?				
A lot	18	(94)	31	(397)
Some	50	(257)	57	(641)
Just a little	27	(137)	16	(196)
None at all	5	(516)	3	(32)
Reverse discrimination[c,d]				
A lot	14	(66)	24	(293)
Some	25	(122)	29	(344)
Little	17	(81)	10	(115)
None	3	(14)	2	(21)
Compensatory treatment	42	(202)	36	(434)
Do you think that during the last 10–20 years the chances for blacks to get ahead have . . .[e]				
Improved greatly	31	(164)	61	(794)
Improved somewhat	60	(273)	35	(452)
Stayed about the same	11	(57)	4	(47)
Become worse	5	(25)	0	(5)
Become much worse	1	(7)	0	(1)

[a] $\chi^2 = 124.3$; $p < .001$.
[b] $\chi^2 = 56.21$; $p < .001$.
[c] Persons responding that they believe preferential treatment is unfair are categorized as holding a belief indicated by their response to the question concerning the extent of preferential treatment. Persons indicating that they believe preferential treatment is fair are placed in the "compensatory treatment" category.
[d] $\chi^2 = 40.51$; $p < .001$.
[e] $\chi^2 = 182.64$; $p < .001$.

the case of beliefs about the causes of poverty, to attribute race differences in economic status to the failings of blacks as individuals.

Third, the trend among whites is toward an increasing sense that the "race problem" insofar as it involves opportunity is diminishing. From 1972 to 1976, those believing that blacks no longer face unfair employment practices (question D) increased from 64 to 71%. Paralleling the steady decline in racial prejudice indicated in opinion surveys from the middle 1960s to the middle 1970s, there has been a steady increase in the percentage of white Americans who believe that the position of American blacks has improved "a lot in the past few years."

Table 7.2 arrays responses to questions about the sources of the black–white gap in socioeconomic status asked in the 1972 National Election Survey and in the 1977 General Social Survey.[3] Like the data presented in Table 7.1, the data in Table 7.2 show that the majority of whites believe that blacks do not face strictly racial barriers to opportunity (in 1977, 60% deny that discrimination is the main source of race differences) and attribute race differences in socioeconomic status to a lack of motivation among blacks. In 1972 approximately 47% of respondents (including nonwhites) indicated that they believed the race difference in socioeconomic status was due to structural forces (responses 1 and 4). Approximately 48% of respondents in this survey attributed this difference principally to the individual failings of blacks (responses 3, 5, and 6). Lack of motivation is the single most frequently indicated perceived cause. Consistent with its status as an aspect of traditional race prejudice, there is roughly the same level of minority endorsement of the innate inferiority of blacks (in 1977) as in the case of indicators of traditional prejudice (Figure 7.1).

Although the use of "mainly" and "most" seems to imply that discrimination and the other two sources are mutually exclusive alternatives, the pattern of joint responses to these questions (bottom panel, Table 7.2) shows that respondents to this survey did not view the questions in this way. Only one-half of the 40% who indicate that race differences in socioeconomic status are "mainly due to discrimination" deny the influence of both innate ability differences and lack of mo-

---

[3]The 1977 General Social Survey also includes an item attributing race differences to the lack of a chance for education needed to rise out of poverty. Our analysis of responses to this item suggests that they have quite ambiguous meaning. People who attribute this difference to discrimination and those who attribute it to innate ability differences both frequently agree with this question. They may believe that the chance for an education is denied by structural forces or because they believe that blacks do not have the ability to complete the education necessary to be upwardly mobile.

tivation. Respondents apparently looked at this set of questions as asking for their view of how these factors combine in determining black–white socioeconomic status differences.

Viewed in this light, perhaps the most striking feature of the distribution of joint responses is *its similarity to the mix of structuralist and individualist explanations of poverty.* In both cases individual factors—especially motivation and morals—are given more importance than structural factors. Approximately 45% of the American public indicates a belief that race differences in socioeconomic status are purely due to individual faults of blacks—either due to their lack of motivation alone or to innately inferior ability. In contrast, only 20% respond that race differences are due to discrimination alone. We cannot give a definitive assessment of the extent of purely structural attributions. Some percentage of those who deny the influence of all three sources may attribute race differences to strictly class-related disadvantages experienced by blacks, likewise a structural attribution. This group may also contain people who give a purely religious or supernatural explanation for race differences (see response 2 in Table 7.2) or other unknown types of attributions (Apostle, Glock, Piazza, & Suelzle, 1983). However even if we were to assume that all of this group was composed of people who attribute race differences to strictly class-related disadvantages, the most liberal estimate of purely structural attributions would be 32% of Americans—substantially lower than the pure individualists.

Also, as in the case of beliefs about the causes of poverty, a substantial proportion of the population attributes race differences to both structuralist and individualist factors. *Paralleling beliefs about poverty, it appears that many Americans simply have added discrimination to motivation or innate ability differences in constructing their explanations of race differences in socioeconomic status.*

Age-group differences in responses to the 1977 questions about the sources of the black–white socioeconomic status disparity, individually and jointly, are given in Figure 7.2 and Table 7.3, respectively. These data show a marked decline in the attribution of race differences to innately inferior ability of blacks that is of the same order shown in age-group differences in conventional race prejudice measures (Condran, 1979; Kluegel & Smith, 1983). They also indicate a liberal trend in whites' views of the sources of race differences. The percentage attributing race differences at least in part to discrimination is substantially higher among younger age groups, and there is a corresponding difference in the percentage who attribute race differences to discrimination alone. Individualistic explanations of race differences are prevalent, however, even among the youngest age group. Of whites aged 18–29, 36% attribute race differences to purely individualistic fac-

CAUSES OF RACE DIFFERENCES

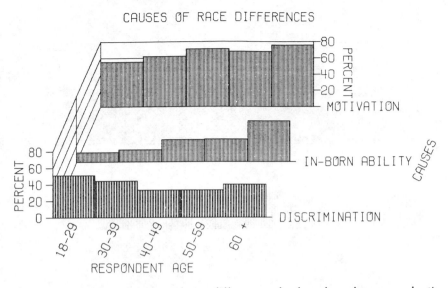

FIGURE 7.2. Perceived causes of race differences, broken down by respondent's age. Data source: 1977 General Social Survey (Davis, 1982).

tors, and roughly between 32% and, the most liberal estimate, 45% attribute race differences to purely structuralist factors.[4]

We complete our descriptive profile of beliefs about blacks' opportunity with an examination of responses to questions from the stratification beliefs survey concerning aspects of blacks' opportunity and age-group differences in them. These data are given in Table 7.4 and Figure 7.3, respectively.

It is quite clear that black Americans and white Americans differ in their views of opportunity for blacks. Blacks see discrimination as more extensive and preferential treatment as less extensive than do whites. Furthermore, consistent with the data presented in Table 7.1, blacks give a much less optimistic assessment of improvement in the opportunity chances of blacks over the last 10–20 years.

In the last several years the charge that affirmative-action programs promote "reverse discrimination" has frequently been made. To what extent does the American public believe that blacks benefit from reverse discrimination? The popular definition of "reverse discrimination" embodies the idea that blacks are unfairly given preference over more

[4]These same patterns of age-group differences in explanations for the black–white gap in socioeconomic status present in the 1977 General Social Survey data are also present in the responses to questions concerning this gap asked in the 1972 National Election Surveys (Kluegel, 1985).

Opportunity for Blacks

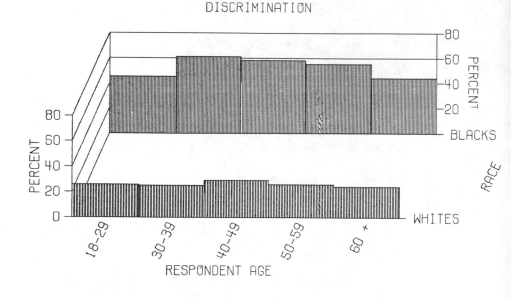

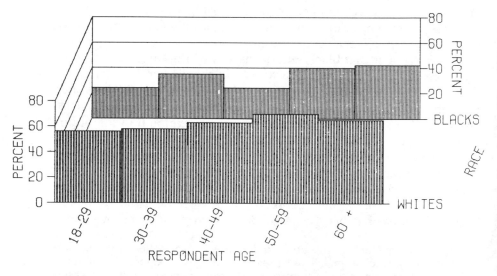

FIGURE 7.3. Perceptions of aspects of blacks' opportunity, broken down by
age and race.

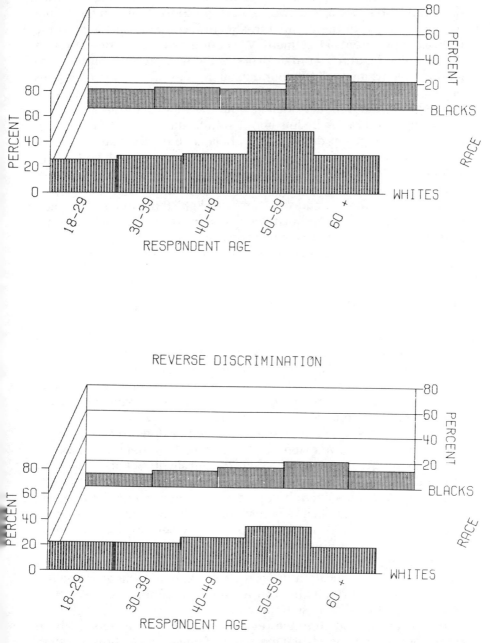

FIGURE 7.3. *Continued.*

qualified whites simply because they are black. To obtain a rough sense of how pervasive the belief in reverse discrimination is among the white American public we asked two related questions concerning (1) the perceived extent of preferential treatment favoring blacks and (2) the fairness of preferential treatment. We define reverse discrimination as the perceived extent of unfair preferential treatment. Roughly one-fourth of the white public, by our definition, sees blacks as beneficiaries of "a lot" and another one-fourth of "some" reverse discrimination.

Age-group differences in beliefs abut the aspects of blacks' opportunity measured in the beliefs about stratification survey (Figure 7.3), contrary to age-group differences in beliefs about the sources of the black–white difference in socioeconomic status, are small and inconsistent. The data suggest that the cohort of ages 50–59 see preferential treatment, and correspondingly reverse discrimination, as more pervasive than do others, and they show a slight tendency for younger people to have a less optimistic assessment of improvement in opportunity for blacks. There are no statistically significant age-group differences among blacks in any of these aspects of beliefs about blacks' opportunity.

Determinants of Beliefs about Blacks' Opportunity

Whites may deny that blacks experience discrimination that limits their opportunity for reasons of economic self-interest and antiblack affect, along the lines discussed earlier in this chapter. For the same reasons, and perhaps especially as an expression of antiblack sentiment, whites may embrace the belief that blacks benefit extensively from preferential treatment and reverse discrimination. We argue, however, that the tendency of white Americans to deny extensive race discrimination and to perceive extensive preferential treatment is *also* based in aspects of the dominant ideology, specifically in beliefs about how the stratification order works in fact. We propose that even as overt racial bigotry has declined, and as direct economic conflict between blacks and whites has diminished (Wilson, 1978), the tendency of whites to deny structural limits to blacks' opportunity persists because Americans' adherence to dominant-ideology beliefs has remained widespread during recent decades. Thus our argument implies that beliefs about how the stratification order does work in fact will affect beliefs about blacks' opportunity net of the influence of antiblack sentiment and aspects of economic self-interest.

To test this proposition we regressed measures of beliefs about blacks' opportunity on several measures of beliefs about how the stratification order works in fact; specifically, on individual and structural explanations for wealth and poverty and the assessment of one's personal opportunity for economic advancement. To control for the effects of aspects of self-interest, we included measures of sociodemographic characteristics and indicators of competitive economic threat (industry and occupational segregation) in the regression equations. Affective influences are measured by perceived relative deprivation and racial affect (as employed in Chapter 6).

Results of these regressions among white respondents are given in Tables 7.5 and 7.6. Table 7.5 gives results for all whites from the representative sample, while results in Table 7.6 pertain to full-time white workers only and include measures of work characteristics that concern the competitive threat blacks may pose to white workers. Industry segregation is the percentage blacks in a worker's industry of employment.[5] Occupational segregation refers to the percentage black in a worker's main occupation.[6] Four categories of occupation are employed: (1) middle to upper level white-collar occupations (Upper Middle); (2) lower level white-collar occupations (Lower Middle); (3) skilled blue-collar workers (Upper Working); and (4) semi- and unskilled blue-collar workers (Lower Working).[7]

The higher the value of the measures of discrimination and preferential treatment the more extensive is each one perceived to be. The measure of reverse discrimination employed here is a one/zero variable indicating whether (1) or not (0) a respondent sees "a lot" of unfair preferential tretment. The measure of the perceived trend in black opportunity is also a zero-one variable indicating whether (1) or not (0) a respondent believes that opportunity for blacks has "improved greatly" in the last 10–20 years.

From Tables 7.5 and 7.6 we see that, as we proposed—net of the impact of racial affect, relative deprivation, indicators of competitive threat, and sociodemographic factors—aspects of beliefs about how the American stratification order works in fact do have statistically significant effects on each aspect of whites' beliefs about blacks' oppor-

---

[5]The percentage black in each detailed occupation and industry code was taken from current population surveys and available census data. For ease of interpretation three categories of occupational segregation were formed: *(a)* a score of 3 indicates 0–4% black (most segregated); *(b)* a score of 2 indicates 5–9% black, and *(c)* a score of 1 indicates 10% or more black (least segregated).

[6]Three categories of industry segregation also were formed: *(a)* a score of 3 indicates 0–5% black; *(b)* a score of 2 indicates 6–10% black; and *(c)* a score of 1 indicates over 10% black.

[7]Occupations were categorized according to census detailed occupation groups: (1) "Upper Middle" white-collar jobs in general include those in the technical and professional groupings; (2) "Lower Middle" white-collar jobs in general include those in the clerical and sales groupings; (3) "Upper Working" generally includes jobs in the crafts grouping and farm owners; (4) overall the remainder of jobs form the "Lower Working" category.

TABLE 7.5. Partial Regression Coefficients for the Effects of Sociodemographic Characteristics, Stratification Beliefs, and Racial Affect on Whites' Beliefs about Blacks' Opportunity

	Discrimination	Preferential	Reverse discrimination	Opportunity trend
Age (10 years)	-.02 (-.04)[a]	.00 (.00)	.01 (.05)	.01 (.04)
Region (1 = South)	-.19 (-.10)*	.01 (.00)	.01 (.01)	.11 (.08)*
Sex (1 = male)	-.13 (-.07)*	.03 (.02)	.04 (.04)	.02 (.02)
Income (log)	-.03 (-.02)	.06 (.06)*	.03 (.05)	.01 (.01)
Education	.03 (.11)*	.02 (.08)	.00 (.00)	-.00 (-.01)
R^2	.03	.01	.01	.02
Relative deprivation	.00 (.00)	.02 (.05)	.03 (.10)	.01 (.03)
Personal opportunity	.06 (.05)	.03 (.03)	.04 (.06)	.03 (.03)
Individualist wealth	.02 (.02)	.03 (.04)	-.01 (-.02)	.02 (.03)
Structuralist wealth	.05 (.05)	.06 (.08)*	.03 (.07)*	.02 (.04)
Individualist poverty	-.10 (-.12)*	.09 (.11)*	.03 (.07)*	.07 (.11)*
Structuralist poverty	-.14 (-.16)*	-.08 (-.11)*	-.07 (-.17)*	-.10 (-.16)*
Racial affect (× 10)	-.10 (-.19)*	.07 (.15)*	.06 (.22)*	.07 (.18)*
R^2	.11	.07	.11	.10

[a] Values in parentheses are standardized regression coefficients.

* = $p < .05$.

TABLE 7.6. Partial Regression Coefficients for the Effects of Sociodemographic Characteristics, Stratification Beliefs, and Racial Affect on Whites' Beliefs about Blacks' Opportunity—Full-Time Workers Only (N = 703)

	Discrimination		Preferential		Reverse discrimination		Opportunity trend	
Age (10 years)	−.08 (−.11)*	−.05 (−.07)*	.06 (.11)*	.06 (.10)*	.04 (.10)*	.03 (.08)*	.06 (.13)*	.05 (.10)*
Region (1 = South)	−.20 (−.10)*	−.13 (−.07)*	.00 (.00)	−.02 (−.01)	.00 (.00)	−.02 (−.02)	.18 (.14)*	.14 (.11)*
Sex (1-male)	−.04 (−.02)	.00 (.00)	.03 (.02)	.01 (.01)	−.01 (−.01)	−.03 (−.03)	−.02 (−.01)	−.03 (−.03)
Income (log)	.05 (.04)	.07 (.05)	.04 (.04)	.03 (.03)	.04 (.06)	.04 (.05)	−.04 (−.05)	−.05 (−.06)
Education	.01 (.03)	.00 (.00)	.01 (.03)	.03 (.10)	−.01 (−.03)	.00 (.02)	−.00 (−.01)	−.01 (−.06)
Upper middle class	.03 (.01)	.10 (.06)	.23 (.15)*	.20 (.13)*	.20 (.22)*	.16 (.18)*	.01 (.01)	.04 (−.03)
Lower middle class	.09 (.04)	.16 (.07)	.19 (.10)*	.17 (.09)*	.10 (.09)*	.08 (.07)	.00 (.00)	−.02 (−.01)
Upper blue collar[a]	−.10 (−.05)	−.03 (−.01)	.22 (.11)*	.20 (.10)*	.24 (.21)*	.16 (.18)*	.05 (.03)	−.00 (−.00)
Occupational segregation	.02 (.02)	.00 (.00)	−.08 (−.10)*	−.07 (−.09)	−.05 (−.10)*	−.04 (−.08)	.03 (.05)	.04 (.06)
Industrial segregation	.09 (.06)	.13 (.07)	−.06 (−.04)	−.06 (−.04)	−.02 (−.03)	−.02 (−.03)	−.04 (−.04)	.05 (−.04)
Relative deprivation		−.02 (−.03)		.03 (.06)		.03 (.09)*		−.01 (−.01)
Personal opportunity		−.02 (.01)		.04 (.04)		.03 (.04)		.03 (.04)
Individualist wealth		.02 (.08)		.02 (.03)		−.02 (−.05)		−.01 (−.01)
Structuralist wealth		.07 (.08)*		.03 (.04)		.01 (.03)		.02 (.03)
Individualist poverty		−.13 (−.14)*		.10 (.14)*		.05 (.10)*		.09 (.15)*
Structuralist poverty		.14 (.16)*		−.05 (−.06)		−.08 (−.18)*		−.08 (−.14)*
Racial affect (× 10)		−.10 (−.18)*		.04 (.10)*		.05 (.20)*		.06 (.16)*
R^2	.04	.10	.03	.07	.04	.14	.04	.11

[a]Reference group (excluded category) is semi- and unskilled blue-collar workers.
*p <.05.

199

tunity. Of the measures of beliefs about how the stratification order works in fact, explanations of poverty have the strongest and most consistent effects on all aspects of beliefs about blacks' opportunity. Neither the assessment of personal opportunity nor individual explanations of wealth have significant effects on these beliefs. Structural explanations of wealth have statistically significant effects on the perceived extensiveness of preferential treatment and perceived reverse discrimination only.

Consistent with expectations, the more individual and the less structural are beliefs about the causes of poverty: (1) the less the perceived discrimination; (2) the greater the perceived improvement in opportunity for blacks; (3) the more the perceived preferential treatment; and (4) the greater the likelihood of perceiving reverse discrimination. Contrary to expectation, however, the more that wealth is attributed to structural factors—net of the effects of explanations of poverty and other variables—the more extensive preferential treatment is perceived to be and the greater the likelihood of holding a belief in reverse discrimination. This may indicate that some whites displace against blacks anger or frustration over the failure of the stratification order to function as it should ideally (Kluegel & Smith, 1982), or that preferential treatment is viewed primarily by whites as a structural barrier that prevents whites from attaining wealth.

Summary

The evidence presented in this chapter and earlier (Chapter 3) quite clearly shows that most Americans believe that blacks no longer face barriers to achieving economic parity with whites. Most Americans appear to see limits to opportunity as a matter of the American past, strictly associated with individual race prejudice. Accordingly, there has been a steady increase since the 1960s in the percentage of white Americans who believe that great progress has been made in the opportunity for black Americans to get ahead.

The view white Americans have of blacks' opportunity is also quite different from blacks' assessment of their own opportunity. Blacks perceive that their opportunity is much more limited by discrimination than do whites and view themselves as the beneficiaries of preferential treatment much less often than do whites. Black Americans' overall assessment of improvement in their opportunity over the last two decades is considerably less optimistic than that of whites.

In general, the data we have reviewed support our assertion that there has been no corresponding increase in recognition of structural limitation of blacks' opportunity, paralleling the marked decline of traditional racial prejudice among whites. Over-time data show an increase in the percentage of Americans who beleive that blacks no longer experience unfair employment practices. Age-groups differ little or not at all in the perceived chances of blacks to get ahead (Chapter 3), in the perceived extent of discrimination and preferential treatment, and in the assessment of progress in opportunity for blacks. However, younger people are more likely than older ones to attribute existing race differences in socioeconomic status to discrimination. We speculate that this seeming exception to our assertion of no increase in perceived structural limitation to blacks' opportunity may not be one in fact. It may be that younger people more often attribute current race differences in socioeconomic status to *past* racial discrimination but do not see race discrimination as currently placing limits on opportunity for blacks to any greater degree than older people.

Results of our regression analyses also support our assertion that prevalent beliefs about how the stratification order works in fact act to block recognition of limits to blacks' opportunity. Net of the influence of sociodemographic characteristics and racial affect, beliefs about the causes of poverty consistently affect aspects of whites' beliefs about blacks' opportunity. Consistent with the prevalent and stable tendencies of white Americans to deny structural causes and to attribute poverty to individual failings, it seems quite clear that most whites do not see black poverty as an important part of the "race problem." To most white Americans the fact that blacks make up a disproportionate share of the poor because of past race discrimination (if this fact is recognized at all) does not constitute a problem in need of a solution, because most white Americans do not believe that poverty itself presents any structural limits to opportunity.

AFFIRMATIVE-ACTION ATTITUDES

Because equal opportunity policy, commonly referred to collectively in popular media as "affirmative action," has been a matter of much controversy, it also has been the subject of much opinion polling. These poll results and other surveys make it possible to construct a thorough description of how the American public views equal opportunity policy for blacks.

Lipset and Schneider (1978) present an overview of poll data, from which the following observations may be made:

1. The majority of white Americans express support for programs to help blacks acquire training necessary to compete for jobs on an equal basis with whites. Approximately 80% of white Americans (in 1972) expressed support for government job-training programs. Roughly 60% of white Americans approve of requiring large companies to set up

special training programs for members of minority groups and approve of colleges giving special consideration to the best minority applicants to help more of them get admitted.

2. White Americans strongly reject programs they view as promoting preferential treatment favoring blacks. Only about 10% of whites favor preferential treatment for blacks in jobs and college admissions to make up for past discrimination, against the alternative of basing access strictly on evidenced ability. Of whites, 60% disapprove of requiring businesses to hire a certain number of minority workers. Approximately 80% of whites oppose giving preference to a black worker for a promotion over a white worker when both have equal ability.

3. Higher percentages of blacks than whites favor all equal opportunity programs. All proposed programs have majority support among blacks, except favoring preferential treatment over access strictly on evidenced ability (70% of blacks favor access on evidenced ability).

Responses to questions about equal opportunity programs asked in our survey, in the National Election Surveys (1972 and 1982), and in the 1980 General Social Survey are given in Table 7.7. Age-group differences in responses to these questions are presented in Table 7.8.

The first four questions (asked in our survey) show a pattern of support consistent with that found in poll data. Roughly three-quarters of whites agree that programs that simply help blacks to get ahead should be supported. Roughly two-thirds of white Americans believe that

TABLE 7.7. Affirmative-Action Attitudes

	White		Black	
	Percentage	(f)	Percentage	(f)
Affirmative-action programs that help blacks and other minorities to get ahead should be supported (Help)[a]				
Strongly agree	6	(81)	26	(137)
Agree	70	(892)	70	(364)
Disagree	21	(262)	4	(21)
Strongly disagree	3	(41)	0	(2)
College and universities should set aside a certain number of positions to admit qualified blacks and other minorities (College)[b]				
Strongly agree	5	(26)	10	(24)
Agree	55	(304)	74	(173)

Continued

TABLE 7.7. (Continued)

	White		Black	
	Percentage	(f)	Percentage	(f)
Disagree	30	(197)	13	(31)
Strongly disagree	5	(27)	3	(6)
Employers should set aside a certain number of places to hire qualified blacks and other minorities *(Business)*[e]				
Strongly agree	3	(24)	16	(46)
Agree	48	(350)	57	(162)
Disagree	40	(289)	24	(67)
Strongly disagree	9	(64)	3	(8)
Do you personally feel that such preferential treatment (for blacks) is/would be: *(Preferential)*[d]				
Fair	35	(434)	42	(202)
Unfair	65	(789)	58	(284)

Some people feel that the government in Washington should make every possible effort to improve the social and economic position of blacks and other minority groups, even if it means giving them preferential treatment. (Suppose these people are at one end of the scale at point 1.) Others feel that the government should not make any special effort to help minorities because they should help themselves. (Suppose these people are at the other end, point 7.) And of course, some other people have opinions somewhere in between (at points 2, 3, 4, 5, or 6). Where would you place yourself on this scale, or haven't you thought much about this? (SHOULD HELP)[e]

	1972[f]	1980[e]		1982[f]
		White	Black	
1. Government should help	7%	3	22	4
2.	6	4	12	4
3.	12	10	6	10
4.	22	23	24	26
5.	11	17	9	15
6.	12	15	5	16
7.	18	21	10	11
0. Haven't thought much	12	7	12	14
(N)	(1965)	(1314)	(145)	(1214)

[a] $\chi^2 = 197.20$; $p < .001$.
[b] $\chi^2 = 48.30$; $p < .001$.
[c] $\chi^2 = 77.79$; $p < .001$.
[d] $\chi^2 = 5.24$; $p < .05$.
[e] Source: 1980 General Social Survey (Davis, 1982)
[f] Source: 1972 and 1982 National Election Surveys. Wording in 1972 and 1982 omits "even if it means giving them preferential treatment." Whites only.

TABLE 7.8. Age-Group Differences in Attitudes toward Affirmative Action by Race

	Percentage agree				Should help		
Age-group	Help	College	Business	Preferential	1,2	3–5	6,7
White							
18–29	77	65	51	35	10	57	33
30–39	80	55	53	37	8	55	37
40–49	74	54	38	33	4	53	44
50–59	72	52	46	34	8	52	40
60+	77	64	66	38	5	52	43
	$(p < .4)$	$(p < .1)$	$(p < .01)$	$(p > .5)$		$(\chi^2 = 15.35; p < .10)$	
Black							
18–29	92	85	84	44	39	56	6
30–39	99	89	70	39	36	44	20
40–49	96	85	64	39	47	35	18
50–59	94	73	64	38	32	41	27
60+	97	89	74	45	43	33	24
	$(p > .05)$	$(p > .2)$	$(p < .05)$	$(p > .5)$		$(\chi^2 = 7.43; p > .4)$	

preferential treatment is unfair.[8] Proposals to set aside positions in colleges and businesses for qualified minorities are supported at levels intermediate to support for simple help and preferential treatment. Responses to these questions and poll data suggest that most Americans hold the following view: "the government should help blacks get the skills and training needed to compete equally with whites in the labor force, but the government should directly intervene little or not at all in the workplace."

A question asked in the 1980 General Social Survey and a close variant (without a reference to preferential treatment) asked in 1972 and in 1982 in National Election Surveys, asks respondents to choose between strong government action to improve the socioeconomic status of blacks and no government assistance, with blacks making progress toward parity by virtue of their efforts as individuals alone.[9] Responses to these questions in general argue that most white Americans favor a compromise between government action and individual effort, with the latter given more weight than the former. The tendency to favor individual effort over government assistance is especially pronounced when the possibility of government assistance involving preferential treatment is involved (1980 General Social Survey question).

Since the question does not refer to specific equal opportunity programs, we can only speculate about what kind of programs respondents have in mind when they opt for an alternative half-way between maximum government assistance and self-help alone. One such compromise, we suggest, is provided by government financed programs to "help minorities help themselves." Again, here as in more direct questions about policy preference, most Americans appear to favor educational and job-training programs and to oppose programs that involve

---

[8]More people consider preferential treatment fair (about 35%) than favor it (about 10%). This difference suggests that people make a distinction between the fairness of preferential treatment and its desirability.

[9]Kuklinski and Parent (1981) argue that this measure must be employed with caution since it is contaminated by distrust and cycnicism toward big government. Their argument implies that some people who otherwise support equal opportunity policy will respond negatively to this question out of anti-federal-government sentiment. They do not provide an estimate of how strongly contaminated this measure is, but two considerations lead us to speculate that it is not substantial. First, the distribution of responses to this measure is consistent with the sentiment about equal opportunity programs expressed in other survey and poll data. Second, although it is plausible that a respondent who strongly favors such programs might indicate a score in the middle of the response continuum as a result of also having high anti-big-government sentiment, it is not plausible that such an individual would endorse the statement, "the government should not make any special effort to help minorities because they should help themselves," as a result of simple distrust of the federal government.

direct government intervention in the hiring and promotion practices of employers.

The over-time comparison (1972–1982) in Table 7.7 and age-group comparison in attitudes toward equal opportunity policy in Table 7.8 tell much the same story. There is little or no evidence that support for equal opportunity policy has changed in recent years. Between 1972 and 1982 the distribution of responses to the question concerning the involvement of the federal government in ensuring equal opportunity changed little. Other than an increase in the proportion of the population who indicate that they "haven't thought much" or "don't know" about government involvement, there has been only small change, from the categories involving the extreme choices to more moderate positions on the continuum of support for federal government support for equal opportunity programs.

Earlier in this chapter we proposed that the tendency of younger age groups to attribute the race difference in average socioeconomic status to racial discrimination may indicate only a growing belief that racial discrimination operated in the recent American past and not an increasing belief that at present blacks suffer from structural limitation of their opportunity. The lack of age-group differences in support for both government assistance in general and for specific policies that are even roughly comparable to corresponding age-group differences in attributing the black–white economic gap to racial discrimination argues that our earlier speculation is valid. If the perceived structural limitation of blacks' current opportunity was becoming more prevalent, then increased support of equal opportunity programs seems to follow logically, and we have no evidence that it has in fact.

Determinants of Whites' Affirmative-Action Attitudes

Tables 7.9 and 7.10 give regression analysis results for the determinants of attitudes toward equal opportunity programs that parallel previously reported analyses of the determinants of whites' beliefs about blacks' opportunity. Table 7.9 gives results for the effects of sociodemographic characteristics alone in both the representative sample and in the sample of full-time workers only (right-hand column). Table 7.10 gives results for the effects of stratification beliefs and racial affect net of sociodemographic characteristics for both the representative sample and full-time workers alone (right-hand column).

As in the analyses of the determinants of beliefs about blacks' opportunity, results concerning whites' attitudes toward affirmative-action programs show that beliefs about how the American stratification order

TABLE 7.9. Partial Regression Coefficients for the Effects of Sociodemographic Characteristics on Whites' Attitudes toward Affirmative Action[a,b]

	Help		College		Business		Preferential	
Age (10 years)	.00 (.00)*	−.03 (−.06)	−.01 (−.03)	−.08 (−.15)*	.01 (.03)	.00 (.00)	−.01 (−.02)	−.01 (−.04)
Region (1 = South)	−.07 (−.05)	−.08 (−.06)	−.09 (−.06)	−.03 (−.02)	−.05 (−.03)	−.05 (−.03)	.05 (.04)	.05 (.05)
Sex (1 = male)	−.10 (−.09)*	.00 (.00)	−.15 (−.12)*	−.15 (−.11)*	−.11 (−.08)*	−.13 (−.09)*	−.05 (−.06)	−.05 (−.05)
Income (log)	.01 (.01)	.02 (.02)	−.03 (−.03)	−.01 (−.01)	−.12 (−.13)*	−.08 (−.07)	−.01 (−.01)	−.02 (−.03)
Education	.02 (.11)*	.02 (.11)*	.01 (.01)	.01 (.05)	−.00 (−.01)	.01 (.05)	.01 (.05)	.01 (.08)
Upper middle class		.28 (.23)*		−.20 (−.14)*		−.12 (−.08)		.02 (.03)
Lower middle class		.12 (.08)		−.18 (−.11)*		−.14 (−.08)		−.03 (−.03)
Upper working class[c]		.02 (.02)		−.25 (−.14)*		−.12 (−.06)		−.09 (−.07)
Occupational segregation		−.13 (−.18)*		.01 (−.01)		−.07 (−.08)		−.02 (−.04)
Individual segregation		−.01 (−.01)		−.05 (−.04)		.03 (.03)		−.01 (−.01)
R^2	.02	.05	.02	.06	.03	.04	.01	.02

[a]Left-hand column coefficients estimated in the total representative sample, and right-hand column coefficients estimated in the sample of full-time workers only.
[b]Values in parentheses are standardized regression coefficients.
[c]Reference group (excluded category) is semi- and unskilled blue-collar workers.
*$p < .05$.

TABLE 7.10. Partial Regression Coefficients for the Effects of Stratification Beliefs and Racial Affect on Whites' Attitudes toward Affirmative Action[a]

	Help		College		Business		Preferential	
Relative deprivation	−.05 (−.14)*	−.05 (−.12)*	−.03 (−.08)*	−.03 (−.07)	−.05 (−.12)*	−.07 (−.15)*	−.02 (−.06)*	−.01 (−.04)
Opportunity trend	.00 (.00)	−.01 (−.01)	.00 (−.03)	.00 (.00)	.05 (.03)	.05 (−.03)	−.02 (−.02)	−.10 (−.10)*
Discrimination	.08 (.11)*	.07 (.10)*	.11 (.15)	.09 (.12)*	.12 (.12)*	.05 (.06)	.02 (.04)	.02 (.03)
Individual poverty	−.03 (−.05)	−.05 (−.08)*	.04 (.06)	.04 (.05)	.02 (.04)	.02 (.03)	−.02 (−.05)	−.01 (−.03)
Structural poverty	.08 (.13)*	.09 (.15)*	.09 (.15)*	.17 (.25)*	.13 (.18)*	.16 (.22)*	.04 (.08)*	.06 (.13)*
Individual wealth	.01 (.02)	.04 (.06)	−.01 (−.02)	−.03 (−.04)	−.06 (−.08)*	−.10 (−.14)*	.02 (.04)	.03 (.06)
Structural wealth	.00 (.00)	.04 (.06)	−.01 (−.02)	−.11 (−.16)*	.00 (.00)	−.02 (−.03)	−.02 (−.05)	−.03 (−.07)
Egalitarianism	.16 (.13)*	.17 (.13)*	.20 (.15)*	.18 (.12)*	.27 (.19)*	−.33 (.22)*	.06 (.06)	.01 (.01)
Inegalitarianism	.04 (.02)	.01 (.01)	−.03 (−.02)	.07 (.04)	.03 (.02)	.07 (.04)	−.02 (−.05)	−.02 (−.06)
Racial affect (× 10)	−.11 (−.30)*	−.11 (−.30)*	−.11 (−.27)*	−.12 (−.28)*	−.08 (−.20)*	−.08 (−.19)*	−.05 (−.16)*	−.05 (−.18)*
R^2	.22	.27	.21	.27	.22	.23	.07	.12

[a]All effects of net sociodemographic characteristics (see Table 7.9). Left-hand column coefficients estimated in the representative sample, and right-hand column coefficients estimated in the sample of full-time workers only.
*$p < .05$.

208

does work significantly affect whites' support for these programs net of the influence of economic self-interest and racial affect (Table 7.10). Opposition to all programs in part rests in the tendency of most Americans to deny the importance of structural causes of poverty.

Opposition to affirmative-action programs also stems from the prevalent tendency of the American public to deny that a more egalitarian distribution of income has benefits. Thus there is evidence that many white Americans oppose affirmative-action programs because they are perceived to promote equality of economic outcomes.

As expected, negative affect (both directly racial in character and stemming from perceived relative deprivation) substantially underlies white opposition to affirmative-action programs. Racial affect is the strongest single determinant (here the largest standardized partial regression coefficient) of support for programs simply to help blacks get ahead, a program to set aside positions in college for qualified blacks, and of the perceived fairness of preferential treatment. The sense that one is part of a group overlooked by the government is significantly associated with opposition to all the proposed methods for achieving black–white economic parity.

Racial affect, however, is not the strongest single determinant of support for a program to set aside jobs for qualified blacks. In this case the effects of both structural explanations of poverty and egalitarianism are roughly equal to that of racial affect. Furthermore, individualist explanations of wealth have a statistically significant effect on support for this program that is not present in the other cases.

In general there are few consistent differences in affirmative action attitudes among different sociodemographic groups. Regressions for the total effects of sociodemographic variables (Table 7.9) show no statistically significant differences in support for these programs by region or age group. Higher income is associated with opposition to a program to set aside positions in business only. More highly educated respondents tend to favor programs to simply help blacks get ahead, but this effect is not present for attitudes toward other programs. In general women express a higher average level of support for equal opportunity programs than do men.

According to the competitive threat that equal opportunity programs pose to white workers, one might expect that whites in occupations with a high percentage of black co-workers would oppose these programs more often than whites in occupations with a low percentage of black co-workers. Furthermore, since the average years of formal education for blacks is lower than that for whites (U. S. Bureau of the Census, 1983) programs to further opportunity for blacks may present more of a competitive threat to white blue-collar workers, because formal educational credentials play a less important role in screening for these jobs.[10]

The results of our regression analyses (Table 7.9) give some evidence of a competitive threat influence on attitudes toward equal opportunity programs. As expected, blue-collar workers express more opposition to programs to simply help blacks get ahead than do white-collar workers, and especially middle to upper level white-collar workers. White-collar workers and skilled blue-collar workers express more opposition to a program to set aside positions in college for qualified blacks. Since people from these groups have a substantially higher likelihood of sending their children to college than do unskilled or semiskilled workers (Featherman & Hauser, 1978), the potential cost to them may be more salient.

However, in general the threat that affirmative-action programs seem to pose to an individual's direct economic self-interest has a substantially smaller impact than that of racial affect or beliefs about social inequality. Our indicators of direct economic self-interest account for a much smaller share of the explained variation in affirmative-action attitudes than do other factors (compare Tables 7.9 and 7.10)[11] Furthermore, there are no significant effects of our measures of competitive threat on support for a program to set aside positions in businesses or on the perceived fairness of preferential treatment. Finally, one indicator of competitive economic threat has a significant effect opposite that expected. Net of the effects of occupation category and other sociodemographic variables, the higher the percentage of black co-work-

[10]Between 1960 and 1982 the black–white gap in median years of education declined dramatically, from a difference of 2.9 years (10.9 for whites versus 8.0 for blacks) to a difference of .4 (12.6 for whites versus 12.2 for blacks) in 1982 (U.S. Bureau of the Census, 1983). However, since most of the gain in educational credentials for blacks has come in recent years the "threat" that these gains pose to whites in white-collar jobs is minimized by its high concentration among younger cohorts of workers. Furthermore, much of the decline was produced by a gain in the percentage of blacks completing high school. Blacks still lag behind whites in percentages attending and graduating from colleges and universities.

[11]Our measures of competitive threat are indirect—based on the assumption that whites in industries or occupations with a high percentage of black co-workers will see equal opportunity programs for blacks as a greater actual or potential threat to their economic well-being than will whites in industries or occupations with a low percentage of black co-workers. Research employing more direct measures of competitive threat at the level of specific firms or jobs may find evidence, of course, of stronger competitive threat than present in our analyses. Such measures were not available in our study, nor are they present in other nationally representative surveys that also contain information on whites' beliefs about blacks' opportunity or their attitudes toward equal opportunity policy.

ers in an occupation the greater is the support of white workers for programs to simply help blacks get ahead.

CONCLUSIONS

In recent years scholars have offered explanations of the puzzle presented by the persistence of controversy and prevalent opposition to policy for racial change in the face of indications of declining traditional racial prejudice. Broadly speaking, these explanations are of two major kinds. Some scholars, as noted previously, have emphasized the affective basis of negative attitudes toward policy for racial change, calling attention to persistent sources of antiblack hostility (Sears & McConahay, 1973; McConahay & Hough, 1976; Kinder & Sears, 1981). Other scholars have emphasized the cognitive basis of such attitudes, especially the threat that racial policy poses to whites self-interest, narrowly or, more often, broadly construed (Wellman, 1977; Bobo, 1983; Jackman & Muha, 1984).

The research results presented in this chapter support certain claims made by both sets of scholars. As we have seen, in accordance with the symbolic-racism perspective, attitudes toward affirmative action are substantially shaped by racial affect. Also consistent with arguments made by the proponents of the symbolic-racism perspective, we have found that the influence of economic self-interest, narrowly defined by the threat that affirmative-action policies seem to pose to one's economic status, is substantially weaker than that of racial affect.

Pettigrew (1985) has criticized the symbolic-racism framework for employing a narrow and restrictive definition of self-interest. By defining self-interest only in terms of the objective or direct threat that a program poses to an individual's position of relative privilege, researchers within this framework have been able to readily demonstrate the weak effects of self-interest relative to racial affect. Implicitly, proponents of the symbolic-racism perspective have thus downplayed the importance of cognitive (nonaffective) sources of attitudes toward racial policy (though symbolic-racism theory may now be developing in this direction; see Sears et al., 1986). Our results support the assertion (Bobo, 1983; Pettigrew, 1985) that this perspective has too easily dismissed the influence of cognitive factors. As we have seen throughout the analyses presented in this chapter, the influence of dominant-ideology beliefs is as strong or stronger than that of racial affect. There is clear evidence here that beliefs about social stratification do play a major role, independent of the impact of both racial affect and direct self-interest, in shaping white Americans' response to equal opportunity policy.

More than a response to direct threat to white Americans' pocketbooks, and at least as much as a result of racial animosity toward blacks, *opposition to equal opportunity programs stems from the threat these programs present to an economic order that is believed to be just in principle and to work well in fact.* In this regard, our findings quite strongly support Bobo's (1983) claim that whites need not hold blatantly stereotyped beliefs or animosity toward blacks to justify to themselves or others resistance to black demands for social change, including, of course, opposition to equal opportunity programs. White Americans also oppose policy on the grounds of the threat they perceive it presents to a stratification system they believe benefits themselves personally or American society more generally.

In Chapters 1 and 2 we proposed that social policy meets with public acceptance to the degree that it is consistent with the dominant ideology. This clearly seems to hold for whites' attitudes toward equal opportunity programs. Stratification beliefs have their strongest net impact on support for a program to intervene directly in businesses by requiring them to set aside a certain number of positions for qualified blacks. This type of program presents a greater challenge to dominant-ideology beliefs than do job-training programs or programs to help blacks acquire needed educational credentials. First, it challenges the assumption that getting the required job training or educational credentials is enough to guarantee plentiful opportunity in the workplace. Second, setting aside jobs has more of an element of directly promoting equality of outcomes than do job-training or educational programs. The latter programs may be viewed as furthering the competition for scarce resources that most Americans believe benefits the collectivity as a whole, while the former program may be seen as decreasing competition.

More generally, findings from our survey and several other surveys and polls show a pattern of majority support for programs that involve changing individuals to fit the existing stratification order and majority opposition to programs that appear to call for change in the stratification order itself.[12] To the extent that programs such as hiring quotas involve direct promotion of equality of outcomes, they call for change in the

---

[12]Wellman (1977) found in in-depth interviews of a small nonrandomly selected sample of white residents of San Francisco a marked preference for individualistic solutions to race-related problems; individualistic in the sense of changing the attitudes and behaviors of prejudiced whites or in the sense of educating blacks to have the proper skills and work-related values, rather than calling for basic structural changes. Our results suggest that Wellman's conclusions apply more generally to the American public. In general, Wellman offers several propositions about whites' beliefs about race differences in economic status and related policy attitudes that are similar to the conclusions we have reached based on analyses of much larger, more representative samples than the one he employed.

present functioning of the stratification order. Consistent with the emphasis Americans give to equity as a fair criterion for the distribution of income, Americans strongly oppose quotas and preferential treatment as means to achieve black–white economic parity. Indeed, a substantial majority of black Americans also oppose these means. As we found in Chapter 5, the majority of black Americans share whites' emphasis on equity; that is, hold similar beliefs about how the stratification order should work in principle. However, blacks more than whites are suspicious of how fairly the stratification order does work in fact. Consequently blacks more than whites support programs to directly intervene in the workplace; to have safeguards that if they "play by the rules" (e.g., obtain the necessary qualifications for jobs) the rules will be applied fairly. Whites much more than blacks believe that the rules are currently being applied fairly—that there are no structural barriers to opportunity in America.

8

OPPORTUNITY FOR WOMEN

In recent years the women's movement has made impressive progress in placing the issue of women's social and economic equality on the national political agenda through such efforts as the unsuccessful struggle to pass the Equal Rights Amendment (ERA). Our society seems to be moving from the assumption that women's place is in the home toward the implementation of equal opportunity for the sexes. The recent past has seen widespread public debate and media attention to sex discrimination, equal opportunity, and affirmative-action programs for women. Have public attitudes on issues related to sexual equality of opportunity responded to these changes, or are beliefs and attitudes rooted in stable elements of the dominant ideology? What is the current level of support for political moves toward equal opportunity, such as the ERA?

In this chapter we consider many of the same issues dealt with (with regard to blacks) in Chapter 7. They include the perceived extent of discrimination and preferential treatment, overall opportunity for women, and the fairness of preferential treatment. Issues specific to women include attitudes of sex-role traditionalism and support for the ERA. As in Chapter 7 we begin by examining the current distribution of opinions and over-time trends to see whether the recent history of the women's movement has influenced the public. We then turn to analyzing the determinants of beliefs and attitudes to test our predictions that self-interest, the dominant ideology, and intergroup affect will be influential. A final section compares the results for women and for blacks and discusses the factors that may contribute to both similarities and differences in public views on blacks and women.

DESCRIPTION OF BELIEFS ON WOMEN'S OPPORTUNITY

Our ability to show clear over-time changes in public opinion is limited by the fact that there is little previous research on perceptions of women's opportunity or sex discrimination. Available data on beliefs and attitudes about women's opportunity are largely limited to assessments of support for the ERA and of sex-role traditionalism. The latter is the opinion that men and women should have separate spheres of endeavor (roughly, the world of work and politics versus the home and family). The data show that sex-role traditionalism is on the decline. The proportion stating that they would be willing to support a qualified woman for president if she were nominated by their party increased from about 60 to 87% from 1958 to 1983 (Figure 8.1). Most of the change appeared to occur between about 1969 and 1974, a period of widespread publicity for the women's movement.

In more recent years, further decreases in traditional attitudes are evident, though the pace of change seems slower. The proportion agreeing that "women should take care of running their homes and leave running the country up to men" decreased from 36 to 23% between 1974 and 1983. And the proportion approving of women having "an equal role with men in running business, industry, and government" increased from 47 to 56% between 1972 and 1978 (Table 8.1).

The ERA has been a controversial political issue only since the late 1970s, so there are not extensive time-series data on it. One survey from 1977 shows almost precisely the same response distribution as our 1980 results despite some differences in wording; there is thus some indication of stability of the public approval of the ERA (Table 8.1).

In the absence of over-time data, we turn to analyses of age-group differences, shown in Figure 8.2, on the items related to women's opportunity. Consistent with the strong over-time trend, sex-role traditionalism shows a strong and linear age effect, with older respondents being more traditional in orientation. Older people also perceive less discrimination against women and are less favorable to the ERA. In contrast, older respondents tend to see preferential treatment for women as more fair than younger respondents do. Other measures show no consistent age-related trends.

These age-related findings are consistent with the available over-time data and with the data on changes in beliefs and attitudes regarding blacks, and suggest three conclusions: (a) Very limited data imply stability or only weak trends in perceptions of women's opportunity, as in the case of black opportunity. There may be some tendency for the young to see more prevalent discrimination against women. (b) Trends on such political attitudes as support for the ERA are also weak or nonexistent. (c) On the other hand, there has been a fairly strong trend away from traditional sex-role attitudes and toward denial of the legitimacy of differential treatment by sex in economic matters, conceptually parallel to the trend away from racial segregationist sentiment (Chapter 7). Overall, there has been a trend toward a more liberal viewpoint on the role women *should* play in society, without a cor-

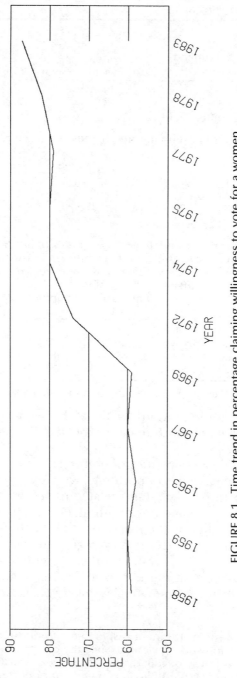

FIGURE 8.1. Time trend in percentage claiming willingness to vote for a women for president.

TABLE 8.1. Beliefs and Attitudes about Women's Opportunity: Over-Time
Trends (in Percentage)[a]

Support of Equal Rights Amendment	Strongly favor	Favor	Oppose	Strongly oppose
1980	19	53	22	6
1977 General Social Survey	23	51	17	10
(Note: Wordings differ slightly)				

Women should take care of running their homes and leave running the
country up to men.

	Agree	Disagree
1978 General Social Survey	32	68
1977 General Social Survey	38	62
1975 General Social Survey	36	64
1974 General Social Survey	36	64

Recently there has been a lot of talk about women's rights. Some people
feel that women should have an equal role with men in running business,
industry, and government. Others feel that women's place is in the home.
Where would you place yourself on this scale?

	Equal role (1–3)	Midpoint (4)	Women in home (5–7)
1978 National Election Survey	56	16	22
1976 National Election Survey	50	18	24
1974 National Election Survey	49	18	29
1972 National Election Survey	47	19	29

[a]Many percentages restated to exclude "don't know" responses.

respondingly strong trend toward the belief that women are in fact the
victims of discrimination, which remains around 30% in every age group
except the oldest.

To give a more detailed picture of both men's and women's views
on issues related to women's opportunity, we present Table 8.2. Compared with the corresponding items related to blacks, substantial recognition of barriers to women's opportunity is evident in the data. In
figures that do not differ by the respondent's sex, about 39% feel that
women's opportunity is worse than average, whereas only 14% see it
as better than average.[1] The reason for this perception is clear. Of the
sample, 29% respond that there is "a lot" of discrimination against
women, and less than 20% (more males than females) see just "a little"

---

[1]Note that our question, to orient respondents to our intended meaning,
specifies opportunity for *working* women while the comparison question about
blacks' opportunity is not so qualified. The difference in wording may account
partially for the difference in public perceptions of opportunity, if women's
opportunity is perceived as worse than blacks' specifically in the workplace
but not elsewhere.

or "none." A substantial proportion of the population thus perceives women as the victims of at least some opportunity-related discrimination. However, as in the case of blacks, there is a very widespread perception that the situation has improved in the recent past: Almost 60% of respondents see great improvement, implicitly acknowledging that discrimination was even more pervasive in earlier times.

Turning to the issue of preferential treatment that favors women, 64% see at least "some" preferential treatment, and 11% see "a lot." Sex differences on this question are quite small, essentially limited to the greater tendency of men than women to see "a lot" of preferential treatment (13 versus 9%, respectively). Opinion about the fairness of such treatment is split, with 42% seeing it as fair and 58% as unfair; again, the respondent's sex makes no substantial difference.

Support for the ERA is obtained from a majority of our sample (as from other recent data, as Table 8.1 showed). Slightly more men than women express support (75 versus 70%, respectively), while women's support is more likely to be strong than men's. Finally two items constitute our measure of sex-role traditionalism. Almost one-half the respondents agree with the traditional view that "men will always be the basic breadwinners," while on the other item, only 25% hold the position that women should not "have the right to compete with men" in any area. Sex differences appear on both items. On the first, overall agreement/disagreement does not differ by sex, but women are more likely to disagree *strongly* than men. On the second item, men are considerably more likely to hold the nontraditional position (accepting women's right to compete) than women are.

In summary, there is substantial recognition of opportunity-related barriers affecting women. Both those who see women's opportunity as below average and those who do not are likely to perceive great improvement in the recent past, implicitly acknowledging past discrimination. And ERA support is widespread. In contrast to the large black–white differences found in Chapter 7, perceptions of women's opportunity and related attitudes differ by sex only infrequently and in inconsistent directions. While women are more likely to see at least some antiwoman discrimination, men are less likely to hold traditional views on sex roles and more likely to support the ERA. There is no sex difference on approval of preferential treatment for women nor on perceptions of the overall level of women's opportunity.

DETERMINANTS OF BELIEFS CONCERNING WOMEN'S OPPORTUNITY

Our general perspective and our findings on views of blacks' opportunity suggest that three factors may influence beliefs and attitudes about women's opportunity: self-interest, general stratification beliefs,

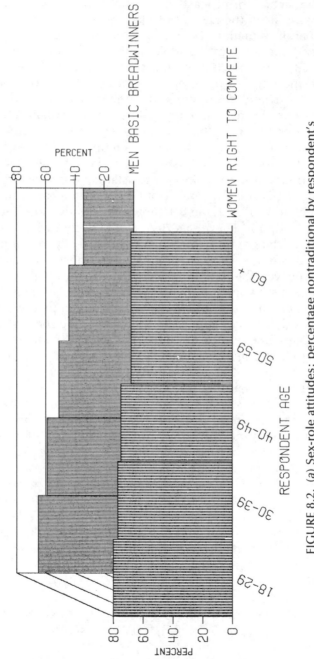

FIGURE 8.2. (a) Sex-role attitudes: percentage nontraditional by respondent's age; (b) perceptions of women's opportunity by respondent's age.

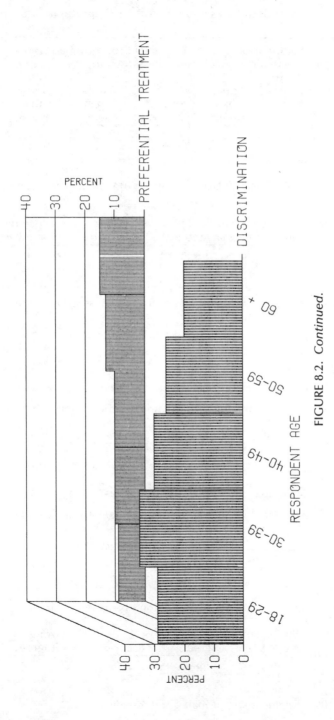

FIGURE 8.2. Continued.

TABLE 8.2. Beliefs and Attitudes about Women's Opportunity Broken Down
          by Sex

Do you think that the chance of getting ahead for a woman who works full-
time, compared with a man working at the *same* job, is . . .

Sex	Much better than average	Better than average	About average	Worse than average	Much worse than average	(N)
Male	3	13	46	37	1	(654)
Female	2	12	47	38	2	(804)
Total	2	12	46	37	2	(1458)

Do you think that during the last 10–20 years the chances for women to get
ahead have . . .

Sex	Improved greatly	Improved somewhat	Stayed about the same	Become worse	Become much worse	(N)
Male	62	34	3	1	0	(670)
Female	52	39	4	1	0	(826)
Total	58	37	4	1	0	(1496)

How much discrimination do you feel there is against women in any areas
of life that *limits* their chances to get ahead?

Sex	A lot	Some	A little	None	(N)
Male	29	50	17	4	(664)
Female	28	56	10	5	(818)
Total	29	53	14	4	(1482)

($p < .01$ for comparison of males and females)

How much preferential treatment for women is there that *improves* their
chances to get ahead?

Sex	A lot	Some	A little	None	(N)
Male	13	51	31	5	(658)
Female	9	55	30	6	(803)
Total	11	53	30	6	(1461)

($p < .05$ for comparison of males and females)

Do you personally feel that such preferential treatment (is/would be) fair or
unfair?

Sex	Fair	Unfair	(N)
Male	44	56	(646)
Female	41	59	(785)
Total	42	58	(1431)

The Equal Rights Amendment, guaranteeing no sex discrimination, should
be passed.

Sex	Strongly agree	Agree	Disagree	Strongly disagree	(N)
Male	16	59	20	5	(361)
Female	22	48	24	7	(453)
Total	19	53	22	6	(814)

($p < .05$ for comparison of males and females)

Continued

TABLE 8.2. (Continued)

It is all right for women to work, but men will always be the basic breadwinners.

Sex	Strongly agree	Agree	Disagree	Strongly disagree	(N)
Male	9	37	42	12	(667)
Female	9	38	33	19	(823)
Total	9	38	37	16	(1490)

($p < .001$ for comparison of males and females)

Women should have the right to compete with men in every sphere of activity.

Sex	Strongly agree	Agree	Disagree	Strongly disagree	(N)
Male	20	65	12	2	(671)
Female	17	49	30	4	(825)
Total	18	56	22	3	(1456)

($p < .001$ for comparison of males and females)

and other beliefs and attitudes based in personal experiences or intergroup affect. However, there are several reasons for these factors' having different effects on beliefs about women and blacks.

Self-interest in identifying and removing barriers to women's opportunity should be widespread, because of the large numbers of women (compared to blacks) and also self-interest in women's opportunity gains on the part of married men with working wives. Among the latter, beliefs and attitudes concerning women's opportunity should have a basis in cooperative self-interest. This cooperative self-interest has little parallel in the case of blacks and whites, and in fact it may partially account for the lack of sex differences in views of women's opportunity.

However, competitive self-interest that pits men against women should also be influenced by the large numbers of women. Because of their numbers, women presumably present an important competitive threat to men under conditions of equal opportunity. Thus both cooperative and competitive self-interest should influence views on women's opportunity more than in the case of blacks.

Beliefs about women's opportunity and attitudes toward equal opportunity policy for women should also be substantially shaped by *general stratification beliefs,* including the dominant ideology. For example, views of the causes of poverty and preferences for equal or unequal income distributions should contribute to evaluations of policies promoting equal opportunity for women, as they do for blacks. Those seeing individual (rather than structural) causes of economic position and favoring inequality should tend to oppose policies (such as the ERA) that are based on the presumption that discrimination exists and moves toward greater equality would be beneficial.

Finally, beliefs and attitudes derived from current political discourse and the media may also influence views on women's opportunity. Particularly important influences in this case should be beliefs derived from personal experiences and intergroup affect. *Personal experiences* of unfavorable treatment based on sex may be widespread, because women constitute over one-half of the population. In addition, the frequent contact between women and men should result in indirect awareness of sex discrimination on the part of many men. Because of racial segregation, intergroup contacts that would allow whites to learn of blacks' experiences of unequal opportunity are much rarer. Personal experiences are also influenced by one's work, and Crosby (1982) found that working women (particularly those with higher status jobs), who have more chances to experience discriminatory treatment, were more likely than housewives to view women's opportunity as poor.

Intergroup affect may be a final major influence on beliefs and attitudes concerning a social group. However, the form taken by this factor is theoretically and empirically less clear in the case of women than in the case of blacks. Specifically, sex-role traditionalism is a potentially powerful influence on beliefs and attitudes concerning women's opportunity. In our data, substantial minorities endorse the traditional position on each of our two items. Sex-role traditionalism thus may work against policies designed to achieve equal opportunity for women and may also reduce the recognition of sex-based limits to opportunity or at least the application of the label "discrimination." Sex-role traditionalism itself is presumably a product of early socialization, so it should be related to such variables as age and education; younger respondents and those with more education (perhaps especially women) would be expected to be less traditional.

The relationship of sex-role traditionalism to negative intergroup affect like that discussed in the previous chapter is, however, unclear. Conceptually, sex-role traditionalism is somewhat parallel to "old-fashioned racism" (McConahay & Hough, 1976), in that it favors *a priori* limits to opportunity for members of a particular group, based on attributed (stereotyped) characteristics. However, as we have seen, such attitudes have all but died out in the racial realm, while sex-role traditionalism is quite widespread. Negative racial affect is presently theoretically said to take the form of symbolic racism (McConahay & Hough, 1976), which involves views that on the surface are not racist, linking blacks to violations of cherished values by their presumed lack of the work ethic, propensity to street crime and violence, etc. (It might be possible to construct a comparable measure of "symbolic antiwoman" views, involving such items as "Careers for women are the cause of the rising divorce rate," but nobody seems to have attempted this.)

The parallels between sex-role traditionalism and old-fashioned antiblack prejudice imply that both reflect negative intergroup affect. However, there are also clear differences in the quality of affective responses to blacks versus women. Most notably, conceptualizations of intergroup affect in social distance terms (Bogardus, 1925) are very common. Though we know of no relevant data, if seems clear that desired social distance for the sexes is much less than that for the races, implying less intense negative affect in the case of women. Yet other types of evidence (e.g., public support or opposition to civil rights versus women's rights groups) show similar overall public responses.

Further research, using more conceptually and operationally parallel measures of sentiment toward racial and sexual groups, is required for the full understanding of the roles of negative intergroup affect and specific, content-laden beliefs in shaping responses to particular groups. Our measures deal more with group-specific issues of content than with the possibly similar underlying affective dynamics. In presenting and interpreting results in this chapter, we refer to sex-role traditionalism under its own name rather than terming it a measure of intergroup affect. Conclusions about the role of affect in shaping responses to blacks and women must be somewhat tentative until differently designed studies are carried out, but our current conclusions will be presented at the end of this chapter, based on the overall patterns of results in Chapters 7 and 8 rather than on the results of just one or two measures.

In summary, beliefs about women's opportunity and attitudes on related policies should be shaped generally by the same influences that affect views on redistribution and on blacks' opportunity. Those factors are self-interest of various kinds, general beliefs and attitudes about inequality (i.e., the components of the dominant ideology), and other beliefs and attitudes including personal experiences and intergroup affect. The form of the latter that is relevant to the case of women is sex-role traditionalism: the view that women are properly restricted to the home role and should not expect nondiscriminatory treatment in the work world.

Analyses predicting sex-role traditionalism and perceptions of the extent of discrimination against women, preferential treatment favoring women, and the overall state of women's opportunity relative to men's are summarized in Tables 8.3 and 8.4. The independent variables are our standard set of sociodemographic items (sex, age, race, education, family income, and residence in the South region), with additions that are specifically relevant to issues of women's opportunity: *marital status* and, for analyses focusing on workers only, the *proportion female in the respondent's occupation*. The latter measures conceptually different dimensions for men and women. For men, it measures the economic threat to self-interest that might be posed by equalizing women's op-

TABLE 8.3. Sex-Role Traditionalism and Perceptions of Women's
         Opportunity: Regressions on Sociodemographic Variables

Independent variable	Sex-role traditionalism	Discrimination	Preferential treatment	Opportunity
Sex (female)	1.03*	.10	−.10	.70*
	(.40)	(.07)	(−.07)	(.44)
Age (10 years)	.13*	−.03*	.00	−.00
	(.17)	(−.07)	(.00)	(−.01)
Race	.08	.26*	.10	.16*
(nonwhite)	(.02)	(.11)	(.05)	(.07)
Education	−.06*	.02*	−.03*	.01
(years)	(−.12)	(.07)	(−.12)	(.03)
Income (log)	−.16	−.03	−.11	−.13
	(−.04)	(−.01)	(−.05)	(−.05)
South	.10	−.04	.08	.08
	(.04)	(−.03)	(.05)	(.04)
Married man	.16	.09	.00	.08
	(.05)	(.05)	(.00)	(.05)
Married	.32*	.00	.02	.01
woman	(.11)	(.00)	(.01)	(.01)
Sex-education	.08*	—	—	.06*
interaction	(.42)			(.49)
R^2	.11	.03	.03	.03
(N)	(1305)	(1305)	(1305)	(1305)

*$p < .05$.

portunity—if there are only a few women in the occupation they are
less of an immediate threat than if there are many. And for women, it
measures the "traditional" versus nontraditional nature of the occupation, in the sense that nurse, secretary, and schoolteacher are traditional women's occupations and steelworker and truck driver are not.

Sex-role traditionalism is significantly related to the respondent's age,
women's marital status, and a sex–education interaction (Table 8.3).
The old are more traditional than the young, and married women are
more traditional than single. The liberalizing effect of education is considerably stronger for women than for men; below about 12 years of
education women are more traditional, but above that point men are.
These results are in general agreement with those of prior work on
sex-role attitudes (Mason, Czaja, & Arber, 1976; Thornton & Freedman,
1979; Mason & Bumpass, 1975; Cherlin & Walters, 1981).

In accordance with the causal model presented in the introduction
to Part II, the analyses of beliefs about women's opportunity presented
next (Table 8.4) will include as predictors, besides the sociodemographic
variables, measures of belief in the dominant ideology, sex-role traditionalism, and relative deprivation.

For perceptions of discrimination, Table 8.3 shows that among the

TABLE 8.4. Perceptions of Women's Opportunity: Regressions on Sociodemographic Variables and Dominant Ideology

Independent variable	Discrimination	Preferential treatment	Opportunity
Sex (female)	.06	−.11	.62*
	(.04)	(−.08)	(.40)
Age (10 years)	−.00	−.00	−.02
	(−.00)	(−.01)	(−.04)
Race (nonwhite)	.16*	.03	.18*
	(.07)	(.02)	(.08)
Education (years)	.01	−.01	.02
	(.04)	(−.05)	(.05)
Income (log)	−.01	−.08	−.15*
	(−.00)	(−.04)	(−.06)
South	−.02	.07	.06
	(−.01)	(.04)	(.04)
Married man	.11	−.02	.07
	(.07)	(−.01)	(.04)
Married woman	.05	−.00	−.00
	(.03)	(−.00)	(−.00)
Sex–education interaction	—	—	.05*
			(.43)
Structural wealth	.06*	.02	−.06*
	(.07)	(.03)	(−.08)
Individual wealth	−.02	.02	.04
	(−.03)	(.03)	(.05)
Structural poverty	.12*	.08*	.02
	(.16)	(.11)	(.02)
Individual poverty	−.01	.04	.05
	(−.01)	(.05)	(.06)
Egalitarianism	−.07	.07	.09
	(−.05)	(.05)	(.06)
Inegalitarianism	−.11	.13*	.13*
	(−.06)	(.07)	(.07)
Sex-role traditionalism	−.15*	.05*	.04*
	(−.26)	(.09)	(.07)
Relative deprivation	−.00	.00	−.01
	(−.01)	(.01)	(−.02)
R^2	.13	.07	.06
(N)	(1305)	(1305)	(1305)

* $p < .05$.

sociodemographic variables the effects of age, race, and education are significant. More discrimination against women is perceived by the young, nonwhites, and the more educated. Marital status makes little difference, and there are no effects of region, income, or sex. In Table 8.4, among the belief and affect variables, effects of structural explanations and sex-role traditionalism are found. Those who perceive structural reasons for wealth or poverty or hold nontraditional views on sex roles tend to see more discrimination against women. These relationships are quite reasonable, in that discrimination is one important form of structural barrier to achievement, to which one might expect those with traditional sex-role attitudes to be less sensitive.

For perceptions of preferential treatment favoring women, only one sociodemographic variable attains significance: The less educated see more prevalent preferential treatment. Among the belief variables, there are effects of structural explanations for poverty, inegalitarianism, and sex-role traditionalism. Those preferring income inequality, those perceiving structural reasons for poverty, and sex-role traditionals see more preferential treatment. Again, the relationship with structural explanations is understandable in that preferential treatment for women is one structural force influencing opportunity. Inegalitarians and those with traditional sex-role attitudes, on the other hand, presumably see prevalent preferential treatment because they disapprove of it and are therefore sensitive to its possible presence.[2]

Perceptions of overall opportunity for women relative to men are significantly influenced by a sex-education interaction and by race, among the sociodemographic variables. There is essentially no effect of education for men but more educated women see women's opportunity as poor (the means for males and females cross over at around 12 years of education). Nonwhites see women's opportunity as relatively good. Adding the belief variables, those with structural explanations for wealth see women's opportunity as relatively worse than average. People evidently perceive limits on women's opportunity in terms of preventing women from attaining wealth more than as preventing them from moving out of poverty. In addition, inegalitarians and those with traditional sex-role attitudes see women's opportunity as relatively good, in effects paralleling those on perceived preferential treatment.

[2]It might be argued that preferential treatment has quite different meanings for those who view it as fair versus those who view it as unfair (i.e., as "reverse discrimination"). To check this possibility, we repeated this analysis separately for these two groups of respondents. There are only two significant differences between the relationships for those viewing it as fair ($N=547$) and as unfair ($N=758$). One is that among those viewing it as unfair, the old tend to see less preferential treatment than the young, while this relationship is absent among those seeing it as fair. Also, the effect of structural explanations for wealth is different. Those holding such explanations see more preferential treatment if it is unfair, but this relationship is near zero for those seeing it as fair. It seems that *unfair* preferential treatment ("reverse discrimination") is linked in people's thinking to structural barriers that prevent some people from attaining wealth; perhaps this is why it is seen as unfair. Other effects in the data are similar for both groups. The results, then, are not too divergent in the two groups, indicating that the determinants of perceptions of preferential treatment are relatively similar whether it is viewed as fair or unfair.

In summary, age, education, sex-role traditionalism, and dominant-ideology beliefs are the most consistent predictors of perceptions of women's opportunity. Older, less educated people with traditional views about sex roles and a firm adherence to the dominant ideology are generally likely to see little sex discrimination, much preferential treatment that favors women, and generally good opportunity for women overall.

DETERMINANTS OF POLICY ATTITUDES

We turn next to analyses of the determinants of attitudes toward the most widely recognized policy to implement equal opportunity for women, the ERA. Given the prevalence of opinions that women do experience discrimination and unequal opportunity, we should expect antidiscrimination measures like the ERA to be heavily favored. In fact, the ERA does command majority support, like programs of simple help (e.g., job-training programs) for blacks. (On the other hand, Table 8.2 shows that preferential treatment for women is less popular, as it is for blacks.)

We further expect the determinants of policy attitudes to include those that influenced the attitude measures in Chapter 7. The independent variables include the perception of discrimination against women as well as the other predictors included in Table 8.4. One additional measure of personal experience with sex discrimination is a yes/no item reflecting a person's perception of *having been held back by her sex*, a recoded version of a measure discussed in Chapters 3 and 4.

Table 8.5 presents the results. ERA support is influenced only by region and race, among the sociodemographic variables. Residents of the South tend to favor the ERA less than others, while nonwhites support it. When the belief variables are added to the model, significant effects are for more support of ERA among those who use individual explanations for wealth and do *not* use individual explanations for poverty and those high on egalitarianism. In addition, support is higher among those with nontraditional views on sex roles and those who see much sex discrimination. Though there are a few discrepancies, our results are in general agreement with those of Huber, Rexroat, and Spitze (1978) who investigated the determinants of ERA support in an Illinois sample using a somewhat different set of independent variables.

Interpreting the results, support for the ERA is found among those with nontraditional sex-roles attitudes and those who see much discrimination against women. Such individuals might well favor it on the grounds that it will eliminate or compensate for the inequitable treat-

TABLE 8.5 Equal Rights Amendment (ERA) Support: Regressions on Sociodemographic Variables, Dominant Ideology, and Perceptions of Women's Opportunity

Independent variable	Support ERA	Support ERA
Sex (female)	.10	.06
	(.06)	(.04)
Age (10 years)	−.02	.01
	(−.04)	(.03)
Race (nonwhite)	.25*	.16[†]
	(.10)	(.06)
Education (years)	.01	−.00
	(.04)	(−.01)
Income (log)	.01	.04
	(.01)	(.02)
South	−.16*	−.11[†]
	(−.09)	(−.06)
Married man	.03	.04
	(.02)	(.02)
Married woman	−.14[†]	−.06
	(−.08)	(−.04)
Structural wealth		.00
		(.00)
Individual wealth		.06*
		(.08)
Structural poverty		.05
		(.06)
Individual poverty		−.09*
		(−.11)
Egalitarianism		.25*
		(.15)
Inegalitarianism		−.00
		(−.00)
Sex–role traditionalism		−.23*
		(−.38)
Relative deprivation		.01
		(.03)
Held back by sex		.09
		(.02)
Discrimination		.11*
		(.11)
$R^2/(N)$	.03/(738)	.24/(761)

*$p < .05$; [†]$p < .10$.

ment of women that they perceive in the workplace. This interpretation fits with the effects of egalitarianism and explanations for poverty. The ERA is supported by those who prefer more equality and deny that the poor are individually responsible for their fate. It seems to be taken, overall, as an issue of the equalization of opportunity.

Sex Differences

The structure and determinants of attitudes concerning women's opportunity might be expected to differ between men and women. To test this possibility, the above analyses were repeated for the two sexes separately. Here the points at which the results differed significantly will be mentioned; in other respects the results can be assumed to be essentially the same for men and for women.

Some sex differences have already been incorporated into the above analyses: the interactions of sex with education that influence sex-role traditionalism and perceptions of women's opportunity. These interactions reflect larger effects of education for women than for men and have already been presented. There is only one other significant sex difference in the regression coefficients. The effect of individual explanations for wealth on ERA support (Table 8.5) is positive for females and near zero for males. Perceiving structural barriers to the attainment of wealth leads women to support improvements in women's opportunity, whereas this relationship is absent for men. Thus, attitudes toward sex-related policies may be more closely linked to perceived economic opportunity for women than for men.

Effects of Occupational Sex Composition

In analyses focusing only on employed respondents, we can examine the effects of occupational sex composition, the percentage of females in the respondent's occupation. Such analyses should reveal *(a)* for women, effects of being in a "nontraditional" occupation; that is, an occupation with a low proportion of women overall; and *(b)* for men; effects of potential female competition for pay and promotions. Significant effects, however, are few. In analyses controlling all the individual-level characteristics included in the earlier tables, occupational composition affects only sex-role traditionalism (for both sexes) and perceived women's opportunity (for men).

For men, a higher proportion of females in the occupation is associated with *decreased* sex-role traditionalism [$b = -.06 (-.09), p < .05$] and perceptions of *worse* than average women's opportunity [$b = -.03 (-.07), p < .05$]. These relationships are the opposite of those predicted by the competitive threat hypothesis, that men in occupations where women might pose a greater threat would be more opposed to women's equality. In fact, it might be appropriate to invert that hypothesis and to state on the basis of our findings that men in occupations with *few* women may be more sensitive and potentially upset about the threat that female competition is imagined to present.

For women, being in a more "traditional" (i.e., female-dominated) occupation is associated with increased sex-role traditionalism [b = .05 (.15), $p < .01$]. Of course, this relationship might reflect either *(a)* selection, where women with nontraditional attitudes seek nontraditional occupations or *(b)* an effect of the occupational context on attitudes. To disentangle these explanations unambiguously would require longitudinal data which we do not possess. However, a rough answer may be obtained from an examination of the relationship separately for younger and older women. If it reflects selection we would expect the relationship to be stronger among younger women, for whom the occupational choice is more recent and subsequent attitude change is less likely to have occurred. If it reflects an occupational effect, then the relationship might be the same regardless of age or might even be stronger for older women, for whom the occupational context has had a longer time to have an influence. In fact, the relationship is similar in size among women under and over 40 years of age, if anything stronger among older women [b (standardized b) = .06 (.16) versus .09 (.26)]. We tentatively conclude that it represents primarily an effect of the occupational context on attitudes rather than a selection effect; this conclusion is in line with recent work on reciprocal effects of psychological variables and occupations in general (Kohn & Schooler, 1983).

SUMMARY: THE PUBLIC VIEW OF WOMEN'S OPPORTUNITY

Both men and women substantially agree in recognizing barriers to women's opportunity, largely in the form of sex discrimination. Both men and women are also coming increasingly to feel (as over-time data show) that *a priori* limitations of women's opportunity, based on the idea that "women's place is in the home," are inappropriate. Consistent with these observations, in our sample a large majority supports the ERA to the Constitution. Our findings on the determinants of these attitudes will be summarized in terms of the major theoretical influences discussed above.

Self-Interest Effects

Self-interest in women's opportunity issues is potentially measurable by sex (to be discussed below) but also by family status and income. Such effects on the perception and policy variables were generally nonsignificant. Married men do *not*, as might be predicted from their self-interest, support women's opportunity more than single men do. Furthermore, as noted above, the effects of occupational sex composition for men are in the opposite direction to that predicted on the basis of a competitive threat hypothesis: men who objectively seem to have more to fear from female job-related competition are in fact more likely to reject traditional sex roles.

Thus, in cases where potential self-interest effects can be identified, they seem to be weak and inconsistent. The weakness of self-interest effects is consistent with our findings on whites' attitudes toward affirmative-action programs for blacks (Chapter 7). In those analyses self-interest measures produced weaker effects than measures of racial affect and general beliefs about inequality.

These findings are also consistent with others in the current literature (e.g., Kinder & Sears, 1981; Lau & Sears, 1981), where the general emphasis is on the strength of effects of "symbolic racism" and other affect-laden, early socialized beliefs and attitudes compared to self-interest. Extending this logic and our findings to the case of women would imply that beliefs and attitudes about women's opportunity reflect general beliefs about society (stratification beliefs) and attitudes about women's place in it (sex-role traditionalism) more than they reflect considerations of one's personal situation and likely losses or gains from changes in women's position.

Sex Comparisons

One of the most notable points about the results is the nature of sex effects. In the regression results, sex never has an across-the-board effect. For sex-role traditionalism and women's opportunity perceptions, sex effects take the form of a sex-education interaction, with crossover points near 12 years, the U.S. median level of education. Below that level, men are more "liberal" on both of these variables, while above that point women are. The meaning of education in terms of its effects on beliefs about women's roles and women's opportunity is thus notably different for men and women. The same point has emerged in earlier chapters, where we noted repeatedly that education's role in increasing status (and hence generally conservative views) was greater for white men than for women or blacks. Education is more likely to have a liberalizing effect (or at least weaker status-based effects) for the latter groups.

However, main effects of sex that are not qualified by a sex–education interaction of this form are completely absent. Even in bivariate analyses (Table 8.2), most variables show only small sex differences in the distributions. These results disconfirm the notion that competitive self-interest should be preeminent in determining such political opinions, with women in general holding beliefs and supporting policies that would materially benefit them. Instead, both men and women seem to derive their views on sex-related issues from their general beliefs about inequality and their sex-role attitudes in similar ways. Perhaps the reason many people gather the impression that women favor these policy issues more than men is that they are exposed (through personal acquaintance or through observing those who write or contribute to the media) primarily to samples of highly educated individuals, among whom women are more liberal.

Effects of General Beliefs about Inequality

The results show that people derive their beliefs about women's opportunity and related attitudes in major part from their general stratification beliefs, as they do beliefs about blacks (Chapter 7). Individuals' views of the general workings of the system of inequality are crucial determinants of their perceptions of women's opportunity and their attitudes on opportunity-related policy issues. Belief in the dominant ideology (high individualism and inegalitarianism, low structuralism and egalitarianism) generally leads to perceptions of little discrimination and to opposition to the ERA. The dominant-ideology tenet of personal causation denies the prevalence of discrimination, so that no programmatic remedy is necessary. Equal opportunity policies may even be viewed as undesirable because of the perceived benefits of inequality.

Effects of Other Beliefs and Attitudes

A third category of influence on beliefs and attitudes, in our theory, is beliefs derived from recent political and media debate or from personal experiences. Reports of personal experiences with the stratification system (having been held back by sex) have no significant effects on policy attitudes (Table 8.5). It is interesting to compare the near-zero effects of having *personally* experienced sex-based opportunity limitations with the stronger effects of perceiving discrimination *in general*. Generalization from personal experience may not be important in determining patterns of reaction to women's opportunity issues in general. As noted in Chapter 3, explanations will play a crucial role in the generalization process: Many people who perceive barriers to achievement in their own lives may not identify them as sex-linked or indeed in any other but the most specific and personal terms. Even those women—under 2% of the sample—who do report that they were held back by sex do not seem to draw wide-ranging consequences for their beliefs and attitudes. These findings parallel others on the weakness of personal experiences and interests, in comparison with societally referenced "sociotropic" beliefs, in predicting general attitudes (e.g., Kinder & Kiewiet, 1979).

Finally, intergroup affect enters into the results in the specific form of sex-role traditionalism, which has consistent and powerful effects.

It leads to perceptions of little discrimination, much preferential treatment, and good opportunity for women, and to opposition to the ERA. However, relative deprivation has no significant effects on any of the variables considered in this chapter, in contrast to Chapter 7. Women, unlike blacks, do not appear to be a popular target for hostility from individuals who feel themselves overlooked by the government.

Conclusions

The major influences on beliefs and attitudes on women's opportunity are beliefs in the dominant ideology, or alternative beliefs about the workings of inequality in general, and the attitude of sex-role traditionalism, or views of the proper role of women in society. Self-interest effects, including even the effect of sex itself, are quite weak and narrow. Intergroup affect (in the form of relative deprivation effects) is also not a major influence. The picture is rather different from that drawn in Chapter 7, where affective influences were strong and race itself the most important predictor of beliefs and attitudes. We turn, then, to comparing the public view of blacks and women in an attempt to draw conclusions from the observed differences.

COMPARISON WITH VIEWS ON BLACKS

Beliefs about Opportunity

As we observed in the introduction to Part II, the logical structure of issues related to women's opportunity and blacks' opportunity is essentially the same. The parallelism of the issues in the cases of blacks and women is reflected in use of many parallel questions in our survey, facilitating comparisons. In this section we discuss such comparisons in some detail, as they prove highly informative about the dynamics of publics views on opportunity and related policy issues.

To begin with, Table 8.6 presents some marginals drawn from Chapter 7 and this chapter in the form of means for easier comparisons. Both men and women hold more negative views of women's opportunity than whites do on corresponding items related to blacks. The means show perceptions of slightly more discrimination against women than against blacks, more preferential treatment favoring blacks than favoring women, and as a result more general opportunity for blacks than for women. In the latter two cases, both men's and women's views on women are more pessimistic than either whites' *or blacks'* views on blacks. Some of the differences between public perceptions of the situations of blacks and women are quite large. For example, the proportion of whites who see blacks as beneficiaries of "a lot" of unfair

TABLE 8.6. Means and Standard Deviations for Beliefs Concerning Women's
Opportunity, by Sex, with Beliefs Concerning Blacks'
Opportunity, by Race

	Target group:			
	Women		Blacks	
	Respondents			
Item	Males	Females	Whites	Nonwhites
Extent of discrimination	3.04	3.08	2.01	3.32*
(1 = none, 4 = a lot)	(.79)	(.76)	(.88)	(.81)
Extent of preferential	2.73	2.67	3.11	2.77*
treatment (1 = none,	(.75)	(.73)	(.75)	(.83)
4 = a lot)				
Opportunity compared to	2.80	2.73	3.06	2.81*
average (1 = much	(.79)	(.76)	(.89)	(.93)
worse than average,				
3 = average, 5 = much				
better than average)				
Trend of opportunity	4.57	4.49*	4.57	4.02*
(1 = become much	(.60)	(.65)	(.59)	(.97)
worse,				
3 = stayed same,				
5 = improved greatly)				
Sex-role attitude scale	−0.59	−0.42*	—	—
(range = −3 to 3;	(1.21)	(1.37)		
higher = traditional)				
Favorability to ERA	2.86	2.85	—	—
(1 = strongly disagree,	(.74)	(.83)		
4 = strongly agree)				
Favorability toward women's	3.41	3.28*	3.24	3.95*
rights/civil rights	(1.08)	(1.19)	(1.15)	(1.04)
organizations (1 = very				
unfavorable, 5 = very				
favorable)				
Fairness of preferential	44%	41%	35%	38%
treatment (percentage				
saying "fair")				
Reverse discrimination	8%	6%	24%	14%*
(percentage seeing)				
(N) for column:	(664)	(818)	(1274)	(192)

*$p < .05$ for difference between males and females or whites and nonwhites.

preferential treatment ("reverse discrimination"), over 20%, is three
times as large as the proportions of either women or men who hold
the same view regarding women.

Evidence from other data sets as well relates to comparisons of popular views of women and blacks, giving them an over-time dimension.
Table 8.7 presents some details. The only question on which extensive
time-series data are available is a measure of verbally expressed will-

TABLE 8.7. Comparisons of Public Beliefs and Attitudes on Women and Blacks[a]

Percentage expressing willingness to vote for minority group member for President	Woman	Black
1978 General Social Survey	79	81
1977 General Social Survey	77	74
1975 General Social Survey	78	77
1974 General Social Survey	77	80
1972 General Social Survey	70	69
1969 Gallup Poll	55	67
1967 Gallup Poll	57	54
1963 Gallup Poll	56	47
1959 Gallup Poll	58	46
1958 Gallup Poll	55	38
Percentage seeing discrimination against group members		
1980	82	76
1976 National Election Survey	64	30
Percentage saying group members should organize rather than deal with discrimination as individuals		
1980	54	53
1976 National Election Survey	53	20

[a]Note: N.E.S. question wordings differ from those in 1980 survey and differ between women and blacks.

ingness to vote for a woman or black for president (cf. Ferree, 1974). The results appear anomalous. In the early years shown the public was more accepting of a woman than of a black, but the difference diminished sharply around 1967 and has been near zero since 1972. It appears that this question does not tap the same dimensions of public reactions to women and blacks that opportunity-related items do. Other items (whose interpretation is clouded by wording differences) show that the current perception of more discrimination against women than against blacks was also found in 1976. In addition, in 1976 (but not in 1980) more people approved of organized efforts to combat discrimination by women than by blacks.

What are some possible explanations for the differences between views of women and blacks? In objective terms it is difficult to argue that the popular view of women as more disadvantaged than blacks is justified. In educational credentials, in unemployment rates, and in their proportional representation beyond the "token" level in positions of power in most areas of society, women currently fare considerably better than blacks.

We argued in Chapter 7 that whites' unrealistic views of blacks' opportunity are in part a product of segregation in American society, as whites largely lack any day-to-day contact with blacks that might give them a more realistic picture. The differences observed here support that claim, as the lesser effects of segregation on public views of women's opportunity would make them generally more realistic (though perhaps not completely so). There is clearly more widespread personal experience by women themselves (because of their greater numbers) than by blacks of any actual barriers to opportunity, and also indirect experience by married men. Men in general obviously have more social contacts with women than whites do with blacks, which can lead to their obtaining information about the realities of discrimination. In addition, cooperative self-interest should lead married men as well as women to perceive and oppose limits to women's opportunity. However, these factors are probably not the keys to understanding the differences between public views of the situations of women and blacks, because our analyses in this chapter showed that neither personal experiences nor self-interest account for a major portion of the variance in attitudes related to women.

One difference between the public view of blacks and women is evident in comparisons of the influence of explanations for wealth and poverty between Chapter 7 and this chapter. Some effects, of course, are similar. Holding more structural and less individual explanations for poverty leads to perceptions of more discrimination and to support for equal-opportunity policies in both cases, as would be expected from our theory concerning the dominant ideology's influence on policy attitudes.

However, some effects of explanations for wealth are different. Structural explanations for wealth lead to an unsympathetic view of blacks (seeing more preferential treatment) but a sympathetic view of women (seeing more discrimination and worse opportunity). And individual explanations for wealth lead to opposition to one policy (business hiring) for blacks but to support for the ERA for women. These differences can be interpreted as indicating that respondents take different perspectives when considering the situations of blacks versus women. When considering blacks, white respondents evidently consider preferential treatment and other policies as *barriers* that prevent whites from attaining wealth (i.e., they link them to structural explanations for wealth). On the other hand, in considering women, both male and female respondents seem to identify sympathetically with women as the victims of discrimination, viewing equal-opportunity programs with favor if they perceive structural barriers.

In summary, perhaps because of more widespread access by the public to information about women than about blacks (because of the absence of social and residential segregation), perceptions of women's opportunity are more negative than are corresponding perceptions about blacks. We turn next to examining whether policy attitudes show similar patterns of more support for equal opportunity for women than for blacks.

Policy Attitudes

The only policy question asked in identical form about blacks and women concerns the fairness of preferential treatment. On this policy, respondents favor preferential treatment for women more than for blacks, but by a narrow margin (42 versus 35% approving). However, the ERA is favored by 72% of respondents, a higher percentage than any of the programs for blacks that were discussed in Chapter 7 except simple help. Equal opportunity programs for women are viewed more favorably by the public than corresponding programs for blacks.

How can these differences in policy attitudes be explained? As Chapter 7 noted, the ideal of equal opportunity for both blacks and women is generally supported by the public; it is consistent with the dominant-ideology belief of individualism, which implies that people should be given equal starting points in the competitive individualistic struggle for advancement. *However, whites believe that blacks currently have equal opportunity while women do not.* The civil rights movement therefore is seen as striving to go beyond equal opportunity, which is generally accepted, to demand equality of *outcomes* in such areas as racial quotas in hiring. Such demands are generally perceived as illegitimate by whites, partly because of racial animosity but also partly because they violate principles of the dominant ideology including individualism and equity. The modern women's movement, on the other hand, which started roughly 10 years after the civil rights movement (in the early 1970s compared to the early 1960s), is not yet perceived as making such demands. The women's movement in 1980 was still, in a sense, at the "civil rights" stage (comparable, say, to the year 1965 in race relations), when demands center on equal opportunity and are accepted by a majority of Americans; the dissenters are mainly those who hold strongly traditional sex-role attitudes (or traditional white supremacist views). Should the women's movement be seen as going beyond equal opportunity goals toward demands for equality of outcomes, it may lose some popular support as the civil rights movement has, by colliding in many people's minds with basic tenets of the dominant ideology. Recent demands for "equal pay for comparable work," among other things, may trigger the public perception that the women's

movement is now entering this stage, pitting public desires for individual-level pay equity against distrust of government-enforced equality.

The other crucial factor distinguishing reactions to blacks and women
seems to be the role of negative racial affect in adversely influencing
whites' views of blacks. Though it is possible to view sex-role traditionalism conceptually as reflecting negative affect toward women, affective responses toward blacks seem to be stronger, based on several
types of evidence.

a. First, Chapter 7 demonstrated that relative deprivation, a feeling
of frustration at being overlooked by the government in its attention
to the problems of others, was a major force leading to reduced white
sympathy for blacks' problems. This variable never influences attitudes
regarding women. Clearly, hostility engendered by relative deprivation
is channeled more readily into antiblack than antiwomen sentiment.

b. As Table 8.6 shows, black–white differences on issues related to
blacks are uniformly larger than male–female differences on issues related to women. Rough calculation based on the table shows that the
seven male–female differences average only .09 standard deviation on
the attitude and belief measures, while the five black–white differences
average a huge .54 of a standard deviation. Moreover, the black–white
differences are all consistent in direction (blacks being more pessimistic
about current opportunity and more favorable to change), while the
male–female differences are inconsistent, with males being lower on
sex-role traditionalism. These findings all imply that black–white differences are more consistent within groups and more differentiated
between groups, suggesting that they are largely shaped by group
identification and between-group conflicts and hostility.

Countervailing Factors. Two factors might be expected to work
against the greater support for women's opportunity than for blacks'.
One is the prevalence of the attitude of sex-role traditionalism. This
attitude legitimates differential treatment of men and women in the
area of economic opportunity, since "men will always be the basic
breadwinners." So its prevalence should work against recognition of
limits to women's opportunity as "discrimination" and hence as unfair.
Corresponding attitudes related to blacks, which would *a priori* deny
them opportunity in certain spheres, are part of the attitudinal cluster
which has been called "old-fashioned racism" and has almost completely died out in the present era (see Chapter 7). This factor, then,
disadvantages women as compared to blacks. However, traditional sex-
role attitudes are changing in the direction of more liberalism, so the
effect of this factor might be expected to diminish in the future, leading
to an even greater disparity between popular views of women and
blacks.

The second factor working toward *less* favorability to equal opportunity for women than for blacks is the presumed greater competitive self-interest of men in denying legitimacy to improvements for women because of their greater numbers and potentially greater competitive threat than blacks. However, the results were in the opposite direction, both in the overall comparison of views about blacks and women and in the specific relationship of occupational sex composition to men's sex-role attitudes. We speculate that the numerical differences between women and blacks actually serve for whites to make racial group membership and thus *competitive* self-interest more salient than cooperative. Social–psychological research has shown that group membership becomes much more salient for members of small minorities [e.g., a solo female in a mostly male work group (Taylor *et al.*, 1978)]. Once this process leads to the salience of group membership for blacks, the framing of attitudes and decisions in terms of the in-groups/out-group dimension may follow. Cooperative self-interest may be more salient for women, because of their larger numbers and the resulting lesser degree of salience of the group membership (Gurin *et al.*, 1980), the general lack of segregation, and, probably most important, the lack of negative affect such as prevails between whites and blacks.

Correlations between Views about Women and Blacks. While the above discussion has focused on the mean differences between perceptions of women and blacks, our theory implies that there should be some similarities between beliefs concerning these groups. It is possible to test this idea by examining the correlations shown in Table 8.8. The median correlation between the corresponding variables for women and for blacks is around .30, a highly significant value. This suggests that many people organize their attitudes *not* by group (potentially holding one general belief about the position of women in society and a different belief about blacks), but by topic, tending to see a particular level of discrimination or opportunity (for example) as applying to both women and blacks.

TABLE 8.8. Intercorrelations of Beliefs and Attitudes on Women's Opportunity with Those on Blacks' Opportunity

Variable	Correlation between item for women and blacks
Discrimination	.30*
Extent of preferential treatment	.13*
Overall opportunity	.24*
Preferential treatment fair	.31*
Support women's rights/civil rights organizations	.49*

*$p < .05$.

These beliefs in turn are linked to a person's overall sense of the current working of the stratification system (e.g., structural explanations for poverty or egalitarianism/inegalitarianism). Evidence appeared in Tables 8.4, 8.5, and 7.7. Thus basic orientations to the stratification system influence people's responses about specific groups, though undoubtedly differentiating factors (e.g., sex-role traditionalism) also enter into such judgments. This line of reasoning is consistent with the findings of Ferree (1974), who found that attitudes toward women were becoming more closely related over time to attitudes toward blacks.

SUMMARY

Processes shaping beliefs and attitudes about inequality can produce both similarities and differences in views on women and blacks. General beliefs about stratification have substantial linkages to beliefs and attitudes about women's opportunity; the latter are part of a person's overall view of inequality in society rather than a separate issue, a point further illustrated by the correlations between beliefs about women's and blacks' opportunity. To a major extent, the important distinctions are between those high and low on individualism, egalitarianism, etc., with specific views on the prevalence of sex discrimination and the desirability of the ERA derived as consequences of those basic belief patterns. In addition, our analyses showing linkages between women's opportunity and general economic beliefs imply that "women's issues" may continue to move toward a place of greater centrality in political debate. The much discussed and historically unprecedented "gender gap" (the tendency of women to vote Democratic more than men in 1980, 1982, and 1984) may be one sign of this new issue polarization. Americans may be coming to perceive issues affecting women in a wider context of the general structure of inequality in society. The identification of women as a *group* with common political interests may also be increasingly, though our discussion above cited reasons for believing that it is not currently so strong as group identification among blacks.

However, there are also important factors that distinguish views of women's opportunity from views on blacks. Sex-role attitudes (views of the legitimacy of limiting women's opportunity) influence political opinions about women's opportunity to their disadvantage, but such traditional attitudes are considerably less prevalent among the young than among the old. The greater numbers of women may work in their favor by resulting in greater competitive and cooperative self-interest in improving women's situation (the former among women themselves, the latter among men married to working women), more widespread exposure to realities of sex discrimination, and perhaps a greater salience of cooperative rather than competitive self-interest (as compared to whites' reactions to blacks).

Our analyses also revealed different linkages between views of the way the stratification system works (particularly explanations for wealth and poverty) and views about blacks' and women's opportunity. The effect of these differences is that belief in the dominant ideology seems to generate more negative views of programs to aid blacks (e.g., individual explanations for wealth lead to opposition to such programs) but more positive views of programs to aid women. Helping blacks is somehow seen as distorting the proper workings of the system, while helping women is seen as properly rectifying the effects of discrimination. As noted above, these differences may flow in part from the perception that the black civil rights movement is now demanding equality of outcomes rather than simple equal opportunity, while the women's movement is still seen to be in an earlier stage, seeking equal opportunity.

The other important factor in women's favor seems to be the lesser degree of negative intergroup affect which is so important in shaping views that whites hold about blacks. The affect results in blacks (but not women) becoming a target for anger engendered by feelings of relative deprivation and in strong black–white differences on attitudes related to blacks and only weak male–female differences in attitudes concerning women. Antiwoman affect may be considered to take the form of sex-role traditionalism, as discussed above, but we have no direct evidence for this conceptual connection. In any case, this factor seems to be lesser in magnitude than negative racial affect, and it is diminishing, as over-time data show.

III

CONSEQUENCES OF BELIEFS
ABOUT INEQUALITY

The previous chapters have dealt mainly with relationships among different beliefs and attitudes and with the dependence of beliefs and attitudes on sociodemographic variables such as age, race, or education. The skeptic might question the importance of such investigations, asking whether beliefs and attitudes toward various policies actually have much practical importance. Do people's beliefs or attitudes concerning inequality have any concrete consequences, or are they epiphenomena that are only of academic interest and the subject of mild popular curiosity (as shown by the number of published opinion polls)?

The skeptic can support his or her position by several lines of argument. It is frequently noted that the public is notoriously ill-informed and uninterested in many issues. Pollsters' tests of elementary knowledge of government structure and policies often imply widespread ignorance of these matters among the general public. Why should we pay any attention to uninformed opinions? The answer here must be that on the occasions when opinions *do* make a difference in people's behaviors—when they vote, join pressure groups, or take to the streets in sufficient numbers to bring about or block policy changes (in Selma, Alabama in the 1960s or South Boston in the 1970s)—they do so with the same level, or lack, of information. It seems clear that the types of knowledge on which people rely as the basis of their political attitudes and behaviors include many other things besides textbook civics knowledge. Indeed, the research reported in this book can be seen as an attempt to answer some questions about the principles on which people's political thinking is based—the ways in which it does make sense and has logical structure. When these principles are better understood, the public's lack of textbook civics knowledge may seem less crucial.

The skeptic can also cite some social–psychological research (e.g., Wicker, 1969) in support of the argument that attitudes do not predict behavior and therefore are irrelevant to any actual, concrete consequences. However, more recent research has reversed this negative conclusion. When attitudes and behaviors are properly and reliably measured (Fishbein & Ajzen, 1975; Ajzen & Fishbein, 1977), when the attitudes are based on direct experience with the attitude object (Fazio & Zanna, 1978), and when the individual has a vested interest in the attitude object (Sivacek & Crano, 1982), attitudes do reliably and strongly predict the relevant behaviors. In short, attitudes that matter to the individual—those related to direct experiences and held with high personal involvement—are the ones that govern behaviors (Kelman, 1974). Examples are manifold, but perhaps the clearest are in the field of political behavior. As Chapter 1 noted, public attitudes influence the passage of legislation and the formulation of government policy (e.g., Burstein, 1979), at least on issues where the public is interested and involved—such as the issues surrounding welfare, race, and gender dealt with in Chapters 6–8. In addition, standard models of voting choice are based primarily on attitudes of the citizen: identification with a political party and attitudes toward the candidates themselves.

In this section, then, we will expand our focus beyond attitudes toward various policies to examine more concrete consequences of beliefs and attitudes concerning inequality. Chapter 9 takes the hint suggested by the paragraph above and examines the effects of beliefs and attitudes about economic inequality on political partisanship and the 1980 presidential vote. We also examine beliefs and attitudes of certain elite groups that have disproportionate political power.

Chapter 10 examines more personal but equally significant consequences of beliefs about inequality in individuals' emotional reactions to their lot in life. Explanations for success and failure have profound consequences for satisfaction and other emotional reactions, at least in laboratory studies. Here we extend this analysis to the general public. Will people who believe that they are personally responsible for their economic positions be more satisfied with their lives overall, or will this only hold for the relatively well-off? Will external or structural explanations be linked to feelings of frustration and anger and hence possibly to mental health problems like stress and depression? If such relationships appear, they will constitute another reason for viewing people's beliefs and attitudes about inequality as central and consequential for their lives.

9

THE POLITICAL SIGNIFICANCE OF
STRATIFICATION BELIEFS

In this chapter we examine two avenues of the potential political impact of dominant-ideology beliefs. First, although it is possible to question whether the beliefs and attitudes held by the American public in general have much political significance, there is much less doubt about the significance of the beliefs and attitudes held by certain subgroups. Here we explore the beliefs about economic inequality and attitudes toward related policy held by two such subgroups: those who own or control economic resources, and the most highly educated Americans.

Second, with the exception of occasional political referenda, the American public does not directly make social policy. But it does vote, of course, for representatives who do make policy. In this chapter we examine the impact of dominant-ideology beliefs and related policy attitudes on the 1980 presidential vote. Because the president strongly shapes the social policy agenda, knowledge of the role played by public beliefs and attitudes in presidential elections is of interest. The election of Ronald Reagan, a strong advocate of dominant-ideology beliefs, and his subsequent efforts to markedly change or eliminate inequality-related social policy established in the previous three decades (Nathan, 1983) makes analysis of the 1980 presidential election outcome of especially compelling interest.

BELIEFS AND ATTITUDES OF POLITICALLY IMPORTANT SUBGROUPS

Owners and Managers

There are many reasons for arguing that people who own or control economic resources—through ownership of businesses and stocks and the exercise of managerial authority—exercise disproportionate control over the polity. Although the extent of this control is a subject of debate (see Hamilton, 1972; Domhoff, 1978), few would disagree with the assertion that members of the economic elite are very important political actors. Their control over economic resources gives them at least the strong potential for shaping candidate selection and electoral outcomes through campaign contributions. Furthermore, in part because of the monetary cost of running for national office and other resources (such as time) needed, the wealthy are very disproportionately represented among candidates for and incumbents of national office (Domhoff, 1978).

Given the disproportionate influence that people who own or control economic resources may exert over social policy through electoral outcomes, their beliefs about social and economic inequality are of special interest. To examine these differences we make use of data from the over-sample of the affluent. The use of these data in conjunction with the representative sample permit more reliable comparisons among people who exercise different amounts of control over economic resources and people at different levels of wealth ownership than is possible with data from any strictly representative survey of 1500 respondents or so.

We asked a series of questions that permit us to define five classes of control over economic resources: (1) workers—people who neither own their business nor exercise any supervisory authority; (2) first-line managers—those who exercise authority directly over workers but do not own their business; (3) middle managers—persons who are at a position in the authority hierarchy of their place of employment one or more levels removed from workers;[1] (4) small business owners—people who own their business and employ two or fewer other people; and (5) large business owners—people who own their business and employ three or more other people. We also asked respondents to indicate the value of their investments (other than home ownership) in categories ranging from none to $50,000 or more.[2] Table 9.1 gives mean values for measures of beliefs about how the stratification order does and should work and for racial affect and sex-role traditionalism by categories of control and wealth ownership.[3]

Several conclusions may be drawn from Table 9.1. First, in general, the greater the control exercised in the workplace and the more extensive is wealth ownership the stronger is adherence to dominant-

---

[1] Employees (not self-employed) who said they supervised someone who supervised someone else are classified as middle managers.

[2] Respondents were asked: "At present do you (or other members of your household) have any investments—such as savings accounts, stockholdings, bonds, trusts, or property holdings *other than your home?*"

[3] To avoid confounding differences among categories of workplace control and wealth ownership with race differences we restrict these analyses to whites only. Nonwhites are much more disproportionately represented among workers and first-line managers and rarely occupy the higher wealth categories.

TABLE 9.1. Means for Beliefs about Economic Inequality, Racial Affect, and Sex-Role Traditionalism by Categories of Control and Wealth Ownership (Whites Only, Combined Representative and Affluent Samples)

	$(N)^a$	General opportunity	Structural poverty	Individual poverty	Structural wealth	Individual wealth	Egalitarianism	Inegalitarianism	Racial affect	Sex-role Traditionalism
Workplace control										
Worker	(793)	3.72	−.14	−.04	−.03	−.02	2.40	2.80	45.60	3.50
First-line	(331)	3.96	−.24	−.20	−.21	.03	2.34	2.79	44.53	3.32
Middle manager	(210)	4.04	−.54	−.32	−.35	.05	2.10	2.80	43.50	3.02
Small owner	(104)	4.05	−.37	−.05	−.14	.35	2.15	2.97	47.21	3.57
Large owner	(90)	4.12	−.73	.09	−.69	.39	2.09	2.90	47.86	3.48
η		.16*	.19*	.12*	.18*	.13*	.25*	.11*	.07*	.13*
Wealth ownership										
None	(405)	3.58	.14	.03	.14	−.12	2.54	2.78	47.88	3.61
Less than 1000	(177)	3.73	−.08	.01	.01	.00	2.37	2.85	45.53	3.32
1000–9999	(377)	3.88	−.18	−.16	−.08	.06	2.35	2.79	43.28	3.23
10,000–24,999	(211)	3.93	−.33	.01	−.18	.05	2.29	2.84	44.81	3.22
25,000–49,999	(129)	4.13	−.35	.00	−.34	.19	2.21	2.87	45.61	3.44
50,000+	(204)	4.12	−.59	−.04	−.61	.46	2.09	2.94	46.14	3.43
η		.21*	.24*	.07	.24*	.19*	.29*	.13*	.08	.12*

^{a}Full-time workers only.

* = $p < .05$.

ideology beliefs and the less likely is a person to express beliefs that potentially challenge the dominant ideology. Second, the previously observed pattern (Chapters 4 and 5) of stronger differences among groups in areas of belief that potentially challenge the dominant ideology than in aspects of the dominant ideology itself holds for both control and wealth ownership. People in different categories of control over economic resources and at different levels of wealth ownership display stronger differences (as reflected in the value of η) in structural explanations for wealth and poverty and egalitarianism than in individual explanations for wealth and poverty, inegalitarianism, and the perceived general availability of opportunity. Third, there are no statistically significant differences among groups differing in workplace control or wealth in our measure of racial affect. Finally, while there are statistically significant differences among these groups in sex-role traditionalism, they do not follow a linear pattern as is generally the case for beliefs about aspects of economic inequality. Owners and workers have the highest levels of sex-role traditionalism. People who own no wealth express the greatest sex-role traditionalism, followed by those in the two highest wealth ownership categories.

Wealth ownership and control in the workplace overlap, and both of these factors are correlated with socioeconomic status. Do wealth ownership and control affect beliefs net of their association with each other and with socioeconomic status? Table 9.2 gives partial regression coefficients for the effects (among full-time workers) of workplace control and wealth ownership on beliefs about economic inequality, racial affect, and sex-role traditionalism.

The statistically significant differences in beliefs about economic inequality by wealth observed in Table 9.1 (except those in inegalitarianism) persist net of the effects of socioeconomic status and workplace control. With the exception of the tendency for middle-level managers to perceive less benefit to greater equality in the distribution of rewards than workers and first-line supervisors, there are no statistically significant differences in beliefs about economic inequality among these three groups. In general, the self-employed express stronger individual and weaker structural explanations for economic outcomes (with some differences between small and large owners) and less perceived benefit to greater equality than do employees.

These findings suggest that ownership, both in the qualitative sense of "being one's own boss" and the quantitative sense of amount of wealth owned, shape beliefs about how the stratification order does and should work. However, the exercise of control, aside from the control inherent in ownership and the higher socioeconomic status it brings, has little such influence. Owners in both senses more often endorse dominant-ideology beliefs and more frequently deny proposed

TABLE 9.2. Partial Regression Coefficients for the Effects of Sociodemographic Characteristics, Wealth Ownership, and Category of Workplace Control on Beliefs about Economic Inequality, Racial Affect, and Sex-Role Traditionalism (Whites Only, Full-Time Workers, Combined Representative and Affluent Samples)[a]

	General opportunity	Structural poverty	Individual poverty	Structural wealth	Individual wealth
Age (× 10)	.04 (.05)	−.05 (−.06)*	.07 (.09)	−.03 (−.03)	−.01 (−.01)
Education	.05 (.14)*	−.07 (−.20)*	−.10 (−.29)*	−.08 (−.23)*	−.01 (−.04)
Sex (1 = male)	.14 (.07)*	−.17 (−.08)*	−.07 (−.04)	−.18 (−.08)*	.12 (.06)*
Income (log)	.12 (.08)*	−.03 (−.02)	−.03 (−.02)	−.06 (−.04)	.13 (.09)*
Wealth	.07 (.12)*	−.08 (−.13)*	.01 (.02)	−.06 (−.09)*	.08 (.13)*
Worker[b]	−.12 (−.06)	.05 (.03)	.11 (.05)	.08 (.04)	.02 (.01)
Middle Manager	−.04 (−.01)	−.11 (−.04)	.06 (.02)	.02 (.01)	.00 (.00)
Small Business	.13 (.04)	−.11 (−.03)	.04 (.01)	.06 (.01)	.27 (.07)*
Large Business	−.07 (.02)	−.20 (−.05)	.27 (.07)*	−.27 (−.07)*	.16 (.04)
R^2	.10	.12	.11	.12	.05

	Egalitarianism	Inegalitarianism	Racial affect	Sex-Role traditionalism
Age (× 10)	−.01 (−.03)	−.00 (−.02)	1.02 (.08)*	.13 (.12)*
Education	−.02 (−.21)*	−.16 (−.12)*	1.49 (−.26)*	−.10 (−.23)*
Sex (1 = male)	−.03 (−.03)	.07 (.08)*	2.21 (.16)*	.18 (.07)*
Income (log)	−.09 (−.12)*	.10 (.16)*	.08 (.00)*	−.16 (−.08)*
Wealth	−.03 (−.11)*	.01 (.03)	.56 (.06)	.02 (.03)
Worker[b]	.00 (.00)	.04 (.06)	1.06 (.03)	.00 (.00)
Middle Manager	−.16 (−.11)*	.01 (.01)	−.40 (−.01)	−.21 (−.06)
Small business	−.20 (−.11)*	.17 (.11)*	−.73 (−.01)	.12 (.02)
Large business	−.11 (−.06)	.04 (.03)*	.75 (.01)	.14 (.03)
R^2	.17	.05	.08	.10

[a]Values in parentheses are standardized regression coefficients.
[b] Reference category (excluded group) is first-line managers.
* = $p < .05$.

structural reasons for wealth and poverty and proposed benefits to greater equality. However, neither ownership nor authority level significantly affects racial affect or sex-role traditionalism, net of the effects of other factors. People who exercise substantial control over economic resources are more conservative than others in their view of the sources and consequences of economic inequality, but they do not express more conservative racial or sex-role beliefs.

Beliefs of the Economic Elite

Any usual-sized representative survey of the American population conducted by the standard sampling procedures has only the smallest likelihood of including someone from the group of people at the apex of economic power. Although we cannot offer data concerning the beliefs of this group, our over-sample of affluent Americans does permit us to give a reliable characterization of the beliefs held by people in the upper 5% of the combined income and wealth distribution. This is a somewhat broader definition of elite status than some scholars use, but it is frequently employed. At a minimum those in this upper 5% have the potential to exercise disproportionate political power stemming from their substantial discretionary income and potential contributions to parties and politicians.

In our data the upper 5% of the combined wealth and income distribution is approximately defined by making $40,000 or more family income (in 1979) and having investments (aside from home ownership) worth $50,000 or more.[4] To characterize the perspective of the economic elite we array in Table 9.3 percentages for responses to selected items from our composite measures of beliefs about economic inequality for elites (as defined above) and nonelites. Table 9.4 gives percentages for responses to racial affect and sex-role traditionalism items for economic elites and nonelites.

Perhaps the most striking aspect of Table 9.3 is the very pronounced tendencies for the economic elite to deny the influence of factors that question and to affirm the influence of factors that support the legitimacy of their highly privileged position. Roughly 75% of this group deny that wealth is to any degree the product of exploitation, almost 90% explain wealth by the willingness of the rich to take risks, and

---

[4]The economic elite as we define it here: (1) averages 2 years more formal education than the U. S. population in general (approximately 15 versus 13 years); (2) has a family income of roughly $70,000 on average; (3) has an average age of about 45 years; and (4) is 58% male. Politically, 45% identify with the Republican party, and an additional 34% are Independents. Among those who intended to vote and knew whom they were going to vote for, 67% opted for Reagan and 15% indicted an intention to vote for Anderson.

TABLE 9.3. Elite versus Nonelite Beliefs about Economic Inequality (in Percentage)[a]

	General opportunity very or good[b]	Poverty jobs[b]		Poverty schools[c]		Poverty effort[d]		Poverty thrift[e]	
		V.I.	N.I.	V.I.	N.I.	V.I.	N.I.	V.I.	N.I.
Elite (N = 102)	76	7	58	32	33	59	13	66	8
Nonelite (N = 1401)	66	28	29	41	28	52	9	62	7

	Wealth dishonest[b]		Wealth exploit poor[b]		Wealth risk[b]		Wealth ability[b]	
	V.I.	N.I.	V.I.	N.I.	V.I.	N.I.	V.I.	N.I.
Elite	17	60	9	75	88	1	65	4
Nonelite	23	34	24	36	66	4	46	11

	Reduce conflict agree[b]	Equal contribution agree[b]	Motivate work agree[b]	Equality means socialism agree[b]
Elite	33	8	84	85
Nonelite	51	35	75	75

[a]V.I. = very important, N.I. = not important.
[b]p < .01.
[c]p > .20.
[d]p > .10.
[e]p > .30.

253

TABLE 9.4. Elite versus Nonelite Beliefs about Race-Relations and Sex-Roles (in Percentage)

	NAACP Attitude[a]		Black movement[b]	
	Favorable	Unfavorable	Too fast	Too slow
Elite	41%	33	25	29
Nonelite	50	25	30	18
	Right to compete (Agree)[c]		Men as breadwinners (Agree)[d]	
Elite	78		53	
Nonelite	77		56	

[a]$p > .25$.
[b]$p < .05$.
[c]$p > .65$.
[d]$p > .70$.

nearly 60% deny that poverty is produced to any degree by the failure of industry to provide jobs. This group likewise shows a strong tendency to affirm the necessity and beneficial nature of economic inequality and to deny that greater equality is just or beneficial.

The economic elite on the whole express more unambivalent support of the justice of the existing stratification order than do other Americans. Elites and nonelites do not differ substantially in the level of adherence to dominant-ideology beliefs. Individualist explanations for wealth and poverty predominate in both groups, and substantial majorities of each group see economic inequality as necessary and desirable. However, elites, unlike the general American public, do *not* simultaneously hold beliefs that potentially question the explanation of how the stratification order does and should work provided by the dominant ideology. For example, whereas most Americans are willing to attribute part of the responsibility for poverty to the failure of private industry to provide jobs, our data suggest that the clear majority of the economic elite attribute little or no such responsibility to private industry.

As evident in Table 9.4, elites and nonelites essentially do not differ in their responses to our indicators of racial affect and sex-role traditionalism. Thus while economic elites hold a consistently conservative view of how the American stratification order does and should work, it seems that both economic elites and nonelites have been equally influenced by the trend toward more liberal beliefs about race and sex during the last two decades. To the degree that this group demands that candidates for political office express support for dominant-ideology beliefs in return for economic support, it presents a strong force for conservative politics. That the economic elite does not differ from the general American public in the level of racial affect or sex-role traditionalism suggests, however, that they may not oppose at least certain kinds of race and sex-related social programs (i.e., a certain amount of "social liberalism").

A New Class?

One major conclusion drawn from our examinations of age-group differences and available over-time data in Chapters 3, 4, and 5 was that Americans' adherence to dominant-ideology beliefs has remained nearly constant over recent decades. Of course the lack of change in the population as a whole does not necessarily mean that no subgroups have changed. Stability at the aggregate level may be due to opposing changes among different subgroups. Even large changes in a small subgroup may not be noticeable in an examination of change over time for the aggregate.

The so-called "new class" thesis about change in American politics suggests that these considerations about the lack of change in the aggregate may hold for the dominant ideology. Proponents of the new class thesis in its various forms (Inglehart, 1977, 1981; Ladd, 1978; Lipset, 1979) hypothesize that education in the last two decades, and perhaps especially in the period from the mid-1960s to the mid-1970s, has been a substantially more "liberalizing" force than in previous times.[5] From the Free Speech Movement to the era of anti-Vietnam war protest, the "1960s" was a period of widespread liberal politics on American college campuses. The new class thesis proposes that this period produced a group of especially liberal, college-educated people who now have assumed upper middle-class occupations.

If this new class does hold dominant-ideology beliefs less strongly, then it presents a disproportionately strong potential force for liberal programs and policy to change aspects of economic inequality. Like the economic elite, the college educated have more time, more discretionary income, and other resources that contribute to one's political influence. Does the hypothesized liberalism of the new class involve greater rejection of the dominant ideology than found among other groups? Has change toward less adherence to the dominant ideology taken place among the college educated that was not manifest in our examinations of aggregate change?

Table 9.5 presents means of beliefs about economic inequality by age group separately for college-educated people (16 plus years of ed-

[5]Other variants of the new class thesis employ occupation or other non-education-based criteria for designating new class membership (for a review of new class formulations see Brint [1984]).

ucation) and others (noncollege educated). The age-group differences in this table offer little support for the new class thesis in regard to beliefs about how the stratification order should and does work. Age boundaries for the new class may be defined variously, but a liberal definition specifies that this group is contained within the age range from 26 to 45 years old in 1980.[6] Neither college-educated people in this range broadly, nor any specific 5-year age group of people within it, show beliefs about inequality that are substantially more liberal than the noncollege educated of the same ages. Although among the college-educated younger age groups are more liberal, with the exception of individualist explanations for poverty, adherence to the dominant ideology is as or more widespread among college-educated younger people as it is among the noncollege educated overall.

Evidence much more consistent with the new class thesis is found in Table 9.6. Here we array mean values for measures of racial affect, sex-role traditionalism, and social policy attitudes by age-group separately for college-educated and other respondents. College-educated younger age people, especially those in the 31–40-year-old range, have beliefs and attitudes about race, sex, and social policy that are as liberal as or more liberal than any other group.

This evidence argues that higher education in recent decades, and perhaps especially in the 1960s, did produce a new class of liberals, but this liberalism is largely limited to the areas of race relations, sex-role beliefs, and their implications for policy attitudes. In addition to expressing the lowest levels of negative racial affect and sex-role traditionalism, younger college-educated people have the highest relative levels of support for welfare, affirmative-action programs for blacks, and the ERA and are most likely to believe that preferential treatment for blacks and women is fair. The liberalism of this new class, however, does not extend to challenging dominant-ideology beliefs about how the stratification order does and should work.

Summary

The politically important subgroups that we have examined here are generally characterized by the same pattern of social liberalism and economic conservatism we have commented on throughout this book.

---

[6]College-educated people from 26 to 45 years of age in 1980 have attended college in the period between the civil rights era of the early 1960s and the end of the Vietnam era in the early to mid-1970s. This, of course, was a period of marked political and social activism on college campuses, especially marked in contrast to the relative quiescence experienced by students attending prior to this period (those over 45) and subsequently (under 26 in 1980).

TABLE 9.5. Age-Group Differences in Beliefs about Economic Inequality (Means) by Level of Education; College (16+ years) versus Noncollege-Educated Whites (Combined Representative and Affluent Samples)

Age group	General opportunity		Structural poverty		Individual poverty		Structural wealth	
	College	Noncollege	College	Noncollege	College	Noncollege	College	Noncollege
18–25	3.91	3.67	−.27	.05	−.35	−.13	.07	−.03
26–30	3.87	3.75	−.40	.07	−.53	−.09	−.30	.18
31–35	3.99	3.70	−.50	−.14	−.58	−.08	−.45	.00
36–40	4.10	3.98	−.51	−.30	−.66	.02	−.75	−.16
41–45	4.05	3.57	−.71	−.16	−.40	.05	−.53	−.06
46–50	4.10	3.89	−.79	−.16	−.28	.25	−.55	.15
51–55	4.18	3.81	−.64	−.06	−.55	.38	−.62	−.01
56–60	4.10	3.89	−.92	−.01	.02	.33	−.49	−.07
61+	4.31	3.91	−.58	−.06	.17	.32	−.72	−.09
η	.15	.12*	.17	.11	.23*	.21*	.23*	.10

Age group	Individual wealth		Egalitarianism		Inegalitarianism		(N)	
	College	Noncollege	College	Noncollege	College	Noncollege	College	Noncollege
18–25	−.42	−.13	2.38	2.47	2.72	2.80	(32)	(239)
26–30	−.04	.03	2.22	2.45	2.68	2.82	(90)	(142)
31–35	.02	−.09	2.22	2.35	2.70	2.91	(86)	(106)
36–40	.00	.22	2.06	2.28	2.82	2.91	(50)	(108)
41–45	.25	.13	2.01	2.33	2.90	2.83	(39)	(91)
46–50	−.04	.12	2.07	2.34	2.74	2.98	(30)	(70)
51–55	.09	.12	1.98	2.40	2.83	2.82	(28)	(105)
56–60	.43	.03	1.94	2.37	2.92	2.88	(22)	(80)
61+	.45	.26	2.10	2.53	2.92	2.85	(41)	(227)
η	.23*	.15*	.24*	.17*	.18	.11		

* = $p < .05$.

TABLE 9.6. Age-Group Differences in Racial Affect, Sex-Role Traditionalism, and Attitudes toward Inequality-Related Social Policy (Means) by Level of Education (Whites Only)

Age group	Racial affect		Sex-role traditionalism		Welfare		Redistribution	
	College	Noncollege	College	Noncollege	College	Noncollege	College	Noncollege
18–25	36.13	45.28	2.47	3.24	6.07	5.25	3.91	3.98
26–30	39.15	46.18	2.72	3.28	5.30	4.93	3.27	3.77
31–35	35.94	47.45	2.80	3.35	6.01	4.64	3.39	3.59
36–40	35.40	47.34	2.56	3.54	5.96	5.05	3.10	3.56
41–45	43.91	46.01	3.37	3.55	4.97	5.10	2.61	3.40
46–50	42.78	51.21	2.93	3.54	5.48	5.54	2.79	3.42
51–55	39.60	50.12	3.36	3.77	5.23	5.10	3.19	3.48
56–60	46.81	48.66	3.36	3.77	4.94	5.06	2.70	3.76
61+	46.62	48.73	3.40	4.13	5.26	5.29	2.90	3.65
η	.25*	.11	.25*	.25*	.18*	.11	.24*	.16*

Age group	Affirmative action		E.R.A.		Preference black		Preference women	
	College	Noncollege	College	Noncollege	College	Noncollege	College	Noncollege
18–25	2.97	2.79	2.82	2.80	.43	.32	.28	.35
26–30	2.86	2.71	2.76	3.00	.30	.33	.34	.39
31–35	2.91	2.77	2.92	2.96	.56	.24	.49	.39
36–40	2.98	2.73	3.04	2.81	.59	.30	.48	.41
41–45	2.82	2.75	2.52	2.75	.44	.32	.69	.42
46–50	2.97	2.70	2.70	2.55	.36	.21	.41	.30
51–55	2.86	2.74	3.06	2.68	.30	.37	.42	.37
56–60	2.73	2.81	2.86	2.92	.19	.34	.54	.43
61+	2.76	2.77	3.06	2.70	.33	.37	.34	.52
η	.12	.06	.19	.16*	.26*	.10	.22*	.13*

* = p < .05.

258

The gap between beliefs in these two areas, however, is more pronounced in these subgroups than it is among the general population. Members of the new class are more socially liberal than other segments of the population but are equally conservative in their support for the dominant ideology. Business owners and members of the economic elite express a level of social liberalism equal to that of the American population in general, but they are somewhat stronger and more consistent (i.e., less ambivalent) supporters of the dominant-ideology explanation of economic inequality than are other groups.

VOTING

Partisanship and Stratification Beliefs

The strongest and most consistent predictor of voting choice, especially in congressional and presidential elections, is political party identification. Party affiliation is complexly determined, reflecting familial influences, economic self-interest, the influence of political leaders, and historical events (Fiorina, 1981). Beliefs about economic inequality, of course, may also contribute to partisanship.

During the last three decades most legislation involving attempts to change aspects of social and economic inequality has been proposed and most strongly supported by Democratic legislators. Some of it, such as welfare for the poor and equal employment opportunity legislation, as we have seen in previous chapters, seems to be widely perceived as opposing dominant-ideology beliefs. We might expect therefore that the dominant ideology plays a role in partisanship, at the least in leading people who on other grounds might identify with the Democratic party to not do so.

Estimating the causal effect of beliefs about economic inequality on partisanship is a difficult task in the face of the multiple causes of partisanship and the ambiguities of causal ordering involved. Since we lack the requisite data, we do not attempt to do so here. Instead we simply look at differences in stratification beliefs and policy attitudes by party identification. As is the case with much causal inference in the social sciences, the absence of association between party identification and beliefs and attitudes presents stronger evidence for little or no causal effect than the presence of substantial association offers for the existence of a significant causal influence.[7] Table 9.7 presents values of means for these beliefs and attitudes by three categories of

_____

[7]Specifically, patterns of intervariable relationships resulting from spuriousness seem to be empirically more common than patterns resulting from suppressor effects.

TABLE 9.7. Means for Beliefs about Economic Inequality and Policy Attitudes by Party Identification (All Respondents, Representative Survey)

	Democrat	Independent	Republican	η
General opportunity	3.63	3.74	3.98	.14*
Structural poverty	.25	−.07	−.24	.20*
Individual poverty	−.01	−.05	.06	.04
Structural wealth	.12	.01	−.21	.13*
Individual wealth	−.06	.00	.16	.09*
Egalitarianism	2.55	2.40	2.32	.18*
Inegalitarianism	2.73	2.79	2.91	.18*
Racial affect[a]	45.79	44.98	46.33	.03
Sex-role traditionalism	3.58	3.37	3.56	.07*
Welfare	5.88	5.40	4.88	.18*
Redistribution	4.05	3.78	3.31	.22*
Affirmative action	2.91	2.83	2.76	.09*
Preference blacks	.40	.36	.31	.07*
ERA	2.82	2.90	2.74	.10*
Preference women	.44	.41	.43	.03
(N) Percentage	(521) 38.1	(511) 37.3	(337) 24.6	

[a]Mean values for racial affect based on white respondents only.
* = $p < .05$.

political partisanship. Table 9.8 gives percentages for selected items from our composite scales to help give a sense of the magnitude of average differences among people differing in party affiliation.

Republicans, as evident in Table 9.7, are stronger supporters of the dominant ideology than Independents or Democrats. They express both higher levels of support on the average for dominant-ideology beliefs and lower levels of adherence on the average to beliefs that potentially challenge them. Overall, Independents have an average level of endorsement of dominant-ideology beliefs that is roughly the same as Democrats. Among Independents the average values for beliefs that potentially challenge the dominant ideology are between Democrats and Republicans.

Republicans express the most conservative attitudes toward policy concerning economic inequality. The largest differences among the three groups concern attitudes toward welfare and income redistribution—the old "New Deal" economic issues that still most clearly distinguish the two parties. There are no statistically significant differences in racial affect on average among these groups. Democrats and Republicans have nearly equal levels of sex-role traditionalism, on the average, and Independents are less traditionalist, on the average, than adherents of either party.

Although Democrats hold more liberal beliefs about economic inequality and related policy than Republicans, as seen in Table 9.8 the

TABLE 9.8. Selected Items from Composite Measures of Beliefs about Economic Inequality and Policy Attitudes by Party Identification (All Respondents)

Item	Democrat	Independent	Republican
General opportunity (very good or good)	59	61	74
Poverty jobs (V.I./N.I.)[a]	41/16	31/31	27/32
Wealth exploit poor (V.I./N.I.)	36/27	28/31	21/44
Wealth risk (V.I./N.I.)	57/8	62/5	72/2
Equal contribution (agree)	45	38	34
Equality means socialism (agree)	70	73	82
Guaranteed job (agree)	69	65	47
Minimum income (agree)	60	43	36
Maximum income (agree)	26	21	16
Welfare spending too much (agree)	73	79	89
Welfare dishonest (agree)	71	74	76
Affirmative action (agree)	84	77	73
ERA (agree)	76	73	66
Right to compete (agree)	73	78	72

[a]Very important (V.I.); not important (N.I.).

difference between these groups is not substantial. In all three groups clear majorities view opportunity for the average American as plentiful, explain wealth by superior individual characteristics and poverty by inferior ones, and embrace the necessity and desirability of economic inequality. People who express beliefs that potentially challenge the dominant ideology are in the minority in each group.

In keeping with their lower levels of endorsement of dominant-ideology beliefs, Democrats are more supportive of welfare spending and of placing an upper limit on earnings. The average Democrat, however, is scarcely a "liberal" on these issues. Of Democrats, 70–75% believe that too much is being spent of welfare and oppose an income ceiling. The average Democrat, on the other hand, is a liberal on floor limits on earnings and government-guaranteed jobs. In contrast, the average Republican identifier is a conservative on these same issues; the majority of Republicans oppose each policy.

Although the average Republican takes a more conservative stance on policy involving equal opportunity for blacks and women than the average Democrat, Republicans resemble Democrats in the pattern of support for different policies, and the difference in level of endorsement between the two groups is not large. In both groups (and among Independents) clear majorities support both programs to help blacks get ahead and the ERA and see preferential treatment for blacks and women as unfair.

With the exception of support for job guarantees and minimum incomes for workers—perhaps reflecting the historical identification of the Democratic party as the "party of the common man"—neither beliefs about economic inequality nor related policy attitudes seem much to influence the choice of party affiliation. There is a similar lack of apparent impact of racial affect and sex-role traditionalism on this choice. Put another way, among Democratic party affiliates many people are quite conservative on issues involving economic inequality—that is, hold beliefs that justify existing inequality and oppose policies to modify it—but maintain an identification with the Democratic party despite this conservatism. Some Republican identifiers express liberal views on these issues—substantially more for equal opportunity policy for blacks and women than for beliefs challenging the dominant ideology—but maintain an identification with the Republican party.

Moreover, in one respect the results presented in Tables 9.7 and 9.8 may overstate the influence of dominant-ideology beliefs and related policy attitudes on party identification. As we have seen in previous chapters, blacks express substantially more liberal beliefs and attitudes that do whites. Because blacks are predominantly Democratic party identifiers, they influence the average value much more among Democrats than among the other two groups. In our survey blacks make up close to one-fifth of democratic party affiliates. In contrast, they constitute but 5% of Independents and 1% of Republicans.

Tables 9.9 and 9.10 give comparisons of beliefs and attitudes between black and white Democrats that parallel those among parties in Table 9.7 and 9.8. Tables 9.9 and 9.10 show very substantial race differences among Democrats. Indeed, the race gap within the group of Democratic party affiliates is generally larger than the difference between white Democrats and Republicans (who are 97% white). If comparison is restricted to white Americans, there is even weaker support for the hypothesis that beliefs about economic inequality affect party identification.

TABLE 9.9. Means for Beliefs about Economic Inequality and Policy Attitudes Among Democrats by Race

Item	Black	White
General opportunity	3.40	3.74*
Structural poverty	.73	.10*
Individual poverty	−.03	−.01
Structural wealth	.36	.00*
Individual wealth	−.22	−.02*
Egalitarianism	2.75	2.49*
Inegalitarianism	2.67	2.75*
Racial affect	—	45.79
Sex-role traditionalism	3.67	3.57
Welfare	6.91	5.65*
Redistribution	4.52	3.88*
Affirmative action	3.22	2.83*
Preferential blacks	.43	.38
ERA	3.00	2.86
Preferential women	.44	.42
(N)	(350)	(409)

* = $p < .05$ for the difference between means.

TABLE 9.10. Selected Beliefs about Economic Inequality and Policy Attitudes of Democrats by Race (in Percentage)

Item	Black	White
General opportunity (very good or good)	49	63
Poverty jobs (V.I./N.I.)[a]	61/7	35/17
Wealth poor (V.I./N.I.)	51/17	30/32
Wealth risk (V.I./N.I.)	57/8	63/5
Equal contribution (agree)	65	41
Equality means socialism (agree)	71	71
Guaranteed job (agree)	83	66
Minimum income (agree)	84	54
Maximum income (agree)	34	20
Welfare spending too much (agree)	57	77
Welfare dishonest (agree)	68	73
Affirmative action (agree)	96	82

[a]Very important (V.I.); not important (N.I.).

The 1980 Presidential Election

Viewed in light of social liberalism (i.e., the substantial liberal trends in the areas of race relations and sex role beliefs), the election of Ronald Reagan to the presidency in 1980 is somewhat puzzling. Though he made an effort to deflect charges of being "antiblack" and "antiwomen," he took no positive efforts to indicate that he supported policy consistent with social liberalism and maintained positions such as opposition to the ERA that seemed to offer evidence for these charges. How did Reagan succeed in winning the presidency in the face of his at least passive opposition to liberal trends in race relations and sex-role beliefs?

One intuitively plausible answer is that the American public simply did not base their vote on racial or sex-role beliefs. For most white Americans, the problems faced by blacks have little personal significance. The same claim may not be made strictly for women's issues, but it may be made for men and for women in circumstances where legislation such as the ERA holds little promise of immediate gain. More tangible interests may override abstract considerations of justice and progress in shaping voting. A large literature has established that "economic voting" does influence electoral outcomes (Tufte, 1978). Since both unemployment and inflation were at postwar highs, "pocketbook voting" may have been especially strong in 1980, dwarfing potential effects of social liberalism.

Another explanation for Reagan's success lies in the widespread endorsement of dominant-ideology beliefs across political party lines and other potential bases of group divisions. If people vote on the basis of their beliefs about economic inequality, then Republican candidates for president appear to have an ideological advantage over Democrats. The more that a Republican candidate is able to identify a Democratic opponent (or the more a Democratic candidate is self-identified) with programs such as welfare for the poor and racial quotas in employment that challenge dominant-ideology beliefs, the more the Republican should benefit by the prevailing adherence to dominant-ideology beliefs. Reagan quite visibly championed dominant-ideology beliefs and charged Democrats, and by implication his immediate opponent, with opposing them. This position was clearly implicit if not explicit in his antiwelfare spending and antiracial quota campaign rhetoric. Reagan may have gained votes from his efforts to identify himself as the candidate of the dominant ideology. Furthermore, his gains in this regard may have functioned to offset losses from social liberalism.

Mean values for beliefs about economic inequality and related policy attitudes by voting intention in the 1980 election are arrayed in Table

TABLE 9.11. Means for Beliefs about Economic Inequality and Related Policy Attitudes by Voting Intention in the 1980 Presidential Election (Whites Only)

	Carter	Anderson	Reagan	No vote	Do not know	Eta
General opportunity	3.84	3.79	3.92	3.52	3.66	.23*
Structural poverty	.00	− .15	− .31	.10	.07	.17*
Individual poverty	− .04	− .45	.17	− .01	.31	.22*
Structural wealth	− .09	− .11	− .10	.04	.07	.07
Individual wealth	.00	− .02	.18	− .08	.00	.11*
Egalitarianism	2.43	2.36	2.33	2.51	2.45	.14*
Inegalitarianism	2.75	2.78	2.91	2.74	2.85	.19*
Racial affect	44.20	37.31	49.04	46.96	47.52	.25*
Sex-role traditionalism	3.48	2.93	3.60	3.55	3.83	.19*
Welfare	5.69	5.71	4.69	5.49	5.31	.21*
Redistribution	3.82	3.64	3.38	3.95	3.76	.18*
Affect	2.76	2.99	2.67	2.80	2.75	.19*
Preferential blacks	.42	.47	.28	.32	.33	.15*
ERA	2.82	3.08	2.68	2.93	2.72	.18*
Preferential women	.45	.47	.41	.37	.38	.07
Education	12.76	14.16	12.97	12.13	12.78	.23*
Age	42.57	37.18	44.44	37.81	50.15	.22*
(N) Percentage	(280) 23.8	(188) 16.0	(414) 35.1	(210) 17.8	(86) 7.3	
Percentage of decided voters	31.7	21.3	46.9			

$* = p < .05$.

9.11. Because we conducted our survey in the several months prior to the 1980 election, we have data on voting intentions only. Intentions, of course, are not always acted on. People may have voted for another candidate than indicated at the time of our survey or not voted at all when they indicated an intention to do so.[8] Also, at the time of our survey the independent candidate, Anderson, was favored by approximately 20% of respondents who said they intended to vote and knew who they were going to vote for. Anderson received only 6% of the actual vote. Thus although it seems plausible that intentions during the summer and early fall of 1980 are good indications of the actual vote

[8] In our survey approximately 21% of respondents reported that they did not intend to vote. Since slightly over twice that many, 45%, in fact did not vote (U.S. Bureau of the Census, 1981), apparently about 25% of our respondents who indicated an intention to do so in fact did not vote.

in 1980, caution must be exercised in making inferences about the determinants of the vote in the actual election from our results.[9]

In its favor, the study of voting intentions does permit an assessment of actual candidate preferences in the 1980 presidential election, preferences not compromised by voters turning to either Carter or Reagan out of the practical concern, which increased as the election neared, that a vote for Anderson would be wasted. By studying intentions during the summer months before the election we are able to explore the bases of support for Anderson—who judged by the policies he advocated appeared to be carrying the banner of compromise between social liberalism and the dominant ideology.

From Table 9.11 we see that Anderson supporters expressed beliefs and attitudes that on the whole more closely resembled Carter supporters than Reagan supporters. Carter and Anderson supporters had approximately equal mean values for individual and structural explanations for wealth, for the perceived availability of opportunity in America, and for inegalitarianism. Anderson supporters were less egalitarian and attached less importance to structural causes of poverty on the average than Carter supporters, but they were also less likely to attribute poverty to individual failings of the poor.

In general Anderson was the candidate of social liberalism and the new class as discussed earlier. Respondents who indicated an intention to vote for him expressed more positive racial affect and less sex-role traditionalism than either (white) Carter or Reagan supporters. Accordingly, Anderson supporters expressed the highest levels of support for equal opportunity policy for blacks and women. Consistent with the hypothesis that Anderson was the candidate of the new class, his supporters were on the average 5 and 7 years younger than Carter and Reagan voters, respectively, and were well educated—over 1 year more on the average than supporters of either Carter or Reagan. It seems that Anderson support resulted from the clash between social liberalism and the economic conservatism of the dominant ideology that we have

[9]Our results match those from Gallup polls of voting intentions during the summer months preceding the 1980 election (Gallup, 1981). Averaged over the five surveys from the June–August period, Reagan, for example, was the choice of 39% of registered voters and of 42% of voters who had formed a preference for a candidate. Judging from poll results over the preelection survey, we estimate that roughly 60% of early Anderson supporters who switched voted for Carter. Furthermore, it appears that in the end most of the "undecided" voted for Reagan. Note also from Table 9.11 that among our survey respondents who indicated they did not know whom they were going to vote for, the average age was approximately 50 years. Older voters, as indicated in Table 9.12, favored Reagan.

discussed throughout this book. It also appears that in the end, as evidenced in the election results, economic conservatism had the upper hand in determining voting.

From Table 9.11 we also see that people who indicated an intention to vote for Reagan were on average stronger adherents to dominant-ideology beliefs, stronger opponents of related social policy, expressed more negative racial affect and more sex-role traditionalism than either Carter or Anderson supporters. The overall conservatism of Reagan supporters in these regards, of course, is not surprising, nor does it of itself establish that support for or opposition to Reagan's candidacy was produced by these beliefs and attitudes. To offer stronger evidence concerning the effects of beliefs and attitudes about economic inequality and social liberalism we ran regression analyses of the intention to vote for Reagan or not, with the results given in Tables 9.12 and 9.13.

Making definitive claims about the causes of voting choice is a difficult matter. As a lengthy research literature attests (Page, 1978) there are potentially many ephemeral as well as longer term factors that shape the vote. Most analyses of voting are subject to some degree to the error of spuriously attributing an observed effect to a factor that is correlated with the variable one makes a causal inference about but is excluded from a study. There are also potential ambiguities of causal ordering. Voters may adopt certain beliefs and attitudes because a candidate they favor on other grounds expresses them, rather than favoring a candidate because he or she expresses beliefs and attitudes consistent with those already held by voters.

In each estimated regression equation we include sex, age, education, income, and region. Also, as a control for the effect of economic conditions during the period before the election, we included a measure of perceived loss in the standard of living for one's family due to inflation.[10] Thus we are able at least partially to rule out spuriousness in causal inference potentially due to effects of sociodemographic characteristics and economic voting.

We have little reason to doubt that the direction of potential causal influence is from racial affect and sex-role traditionalism and from beliefs about economic inequality to voting choice. Beliefs in these areas seem to have been so strongly the product of events outside the political sphere that there is little possibility that politicians have much effect

---

[10]In the context of several questions about the respondent's financial situation in recent years, respondents were asked to assess if inflation had hurt their financial situation: (1) a great deal; (2) somewhat; (3) not much; or (4) not at all.

TABLE 9.12. Partial Regression Coefficients for the Effects of Beliefs about Economic Inequality and Other Factors on the Intention to Vote for Reagan (Whites Only)[a]

	All voters (N = 932)		Democrats (N = 285)		Republicans (N = 269)		Independents (N = 328)	
Sex (1 = male)	.06	(.06)[+]	.01	(.01)	-.01	(-.01)	.09	(.09)[+]
Education	-.01	(-.03)	-.00	(-.04)	-.00	(-.02)	.00	(.01)
Age (× 10)	.02	(.06)[+]	.00	(.02)	.01	(.06)	.03	(.10)[+]
Income (log)	.03	(.05)	-.02	(-.04)	.07	(.13)*	.05	(.07)*
Wealth	.01	(.03)	.02	(.06)	-.00	(-.01)	.00	(.00)
Northeast[b]	.03	(.02)	.06	(.06)	-.07	(-.07)	.09	(.09)*
South	.07	(.06)[+]	.05	(.06)	.01	(.01)	.14	(.13)[+]
West	.13	(.10)[+]	.08	(.07)	.06	(.06)	.19	(.15)[+]
Inflation impact	.05	(.07)[+]	.05	(.10)[+]	.01	(.01)	.06	(.09)[+]
Racial affect (× 10)	.05	(.16)[+]	.06	(.22)[+]	.03	(.13)[+]	.05	(.19)[+]
Sex-role traditionalism	.02	(.06)[+]	.00	(.00)	.04	(.12)[+]	.04	(.10)[+]
Structural poverty	-.03	(-.07)[+]	.00	(.00)	-.05	(-.12)[+]	-.03	(-.07)
Individual poverty	.05	(.11)[+]	.01	(.02)	.03	(.08)	.09	(.20)[+]
Egalitarianism	.04	(.04)	.01	(.01)	.07	(.08)	.09	(.09)*
Inegalitarianism	.07	(.06)[+]	.19	(.18)[+]	.01	(.01)	.01	(.01)
Democrat[c]	.20	(-.19)[+]	—	—	—	—	—	—
Republican	.35	(.31)[+]	—	—	—	—	—	—
R² (percentage Reagan)	.31	(46.9)	.11	(22.8)	.09	(78.2)	.21	(41.8)

[a]Values in parentheses are standardized regression coefficients.
[b]Reference category (excluded group) is Midwest.
[c]Reference category (excluded group) is Independents.
* = $p < .10$.
[+] = $p < .05$.

268

TABLE 9.13. Partial Regression Coefficients for the Effects of Policy Attitudes and Other Factors on the Intention to Vote for Reagan (Whites Only)[a]

	All voters (N = 932)		Democrats (N = 285)		Republicans (N = 269)		Independents (N = 328)	
Sex (1 = male)	.06	(.06)†	.02	(.03)	.00	(.00)	.07	(.07)*
Education	-.01	(-.07)†	-.01	(-.08)	-.01	(-.04)	-.01	(-.07)*
Age (×10)	.03	(.10)†	.01	(.03)	.03	(.13)†	.05	(.15)†
Income (log)	.03	(.04)	-.01	(-.01)	.07	(-.12)	.01	(.02)
Wealth	.01	(.05)	.03	(.10)	-.00	(-.01)	.00	(.01)
Northeast[b]	.04	(.03)	.06	(.06)	-.07	(-.07)	.12	(.11)*
South	.10	(.09)†	.08	(.09)*	.01	(.01)	.19	(.17)†
West	.12	(.10)†	.09	(.09)*	.07	(.07)	.16	(.13)†
Inflation impact	.05	(.07)†	.06	(.11)†	.00	(.00)	.07	(.10)†
Welfare	-.03	(-.13)†	-.03	(-.12)†	-.01	(-.06)	-.06	(-.26)†
Redistribution	.00	(.00)	-.01	(-.01)	-.02	(-.09)	-.01	(-.03)
Affirmation action	-.09	(-.11)†	-.11	(-.15)†	-.05	(-.07)	-.03	(-.04)
Preference fair	-.08	(-.08)†	-.05	(-.05)	-.10	(-.11)*	-.16	(-.15)†
ERA	-.04	(-.05)*	.03	(.04)	-.07	(-.10)*	-.07	(-.08)*
Democrat[c]	-.20	(-.19)†	—	—	—	—	—	—
Republican	.35	(.31)†	—	—	—	—	—	—
R²	.31		.08		.08		.23	

[a]Values in parentheses are standardized regression coefficients.
[b]Reference category (excluded group) is Midwest.
[c]Reference category (excluded group) is Independents.
* = $p < .10$.
† = $p < .05$.

on them over the several months of a campaign for office. The very stability of adherence to dominant-ideology beliefs argues against their malleability by any single politician in a short period of time. And since change in race and sex-related beliefs and affect have been produced by two decades of educational, economic, and broader social change, it does not seem plausible that isolated political rhetoric can do much to affect these deeply rooted beliefs and sentiments.

We have more reason to question an assumed simple one-way causation from policy attitudes to voting. As products (in part) of the dominant ideology and race and sex-related beliefs, policy attitudes, at least in rudimentary form, are determined outside of the political sphere and thus may be viewed as determinants of voting choice. On the other hand, public knowledge about social policy and programs is doubtless sketchy at best. Politicians potentially have considerable latitude in defining what a program entails and in characterizing how much it has succeeded or failed. Although a person's basic assessment of the necessity and desirability of a program may predate any given political campaign, politicians may add to this assessment by advancing their view of the nature of a program and its failures or accomplishments. The public's assessment of welfare spending for the poor provides an example of the interchange between the impact of the dominant ideology and political rhetoric. The negative attitude toward welfare spending that in part is the product of widespread individualist explanations for poverty has been added to by nearly two decades of anti-welfare political rhetoric. This rhetoric seems to have given welfare spending the proportions of much larger items in the federal budget in the minds of most Americans and led them to believe that welfare spending is now among the leading causes of poverty.

The ability of a politician to create an attitude in the public during a campaign is in likelihood much stronger for issues that are newly raised, that lack much history of concern before a campaign, that require an urgent solution (e.g., rapidly growing inflation), or that are (or are seen as) technically complex. The policy and programs involving economic inequality that we have been examining are largely not of these kinds. Welfare has been an issue for roughly two decades. Affirmative action and the ERA had been political issues for several years prior to the 1980 election. None of these programs seems technically complex, nor were the times calling for urgent solutions to poverty, sex, or race-related problems. For these reasons we think it reasonable to assume that most voters' attitudes on inequality-related policy were set before the campaign in 1980, and therefore that the predominant direction of causal influence is from policy attitudes to the reported voting intention.

Regressions for the intention to vote for Reagan or not were run for all respondents who indicated they were going to vote, and separately among Democrats, Republicans, and Independents. Separate regressions were run to explore possible differences in effects of beliefs and attitudes by party affiliation. Since only about 10% of black respondents (who intended to vote) intended to vote for Reagan, we estimate the regression equations among whites only.

The results given in Table 9.12 argue that voting in the 1980 presidential election was affected by both social liberalism and by Americans' beliefs about how the stratification order should and does work. The effects of each were on the whole counterbalancing. Given the majority adherence to liberal race and sex-related beliefs, social liberalism on the whole (see the "All voters" column) encouraged people to vote against Reagan. The majority adherence to dominant-ideology beliefs, on the other hand, worked to his benefit.

Among all three groups, the more negative the racial affect the more likely the intention to vote for Reagan. However, support for traditional sex roles did not affect the intention to vote for Reagan among Democrats, while it did affect the intention to vote for Reagan among Republicans and Independents. While explanations for poverty affected the Reagan vote among Republicans and Independents, they did not do so among Democrats. Among Democrats only, the stronger the belief in the necessity and desirability of economic inequality, the more likely was the intention to vote for Reagan.

The pattern of counterbalancing effects seen in Table 9.12 are also visible in regression analyses employing measures of policy attitudes (Table 9.13). Reagan benefited from the prevailing antiwelfare and antipreferential treatment sentiment but lost votes on the liberal issues of support for programs to simply help blacks get ahead and the ERA. Attitude toward income redistribution does not have a statistically significant partial effect. In part, this lack of effect may be because economic redistribution was not a campaign issue. Also, recall that the most sizable differences among party affiliates (Table 9.7 and 9.8) involved attitudes toward redistribution benefiting low-income workers. To the degree that those and other beliefs and attitudes influence party identification, they have indirect effects on voting that are not shown in Tables 9.12 and 9.13, which give the direct effects net of party identification (and other factors) only.

Based on the party-specific partial regression effects, we offer the following accounting for the impact of the stances Reagan took vis-à-vis social liberalism and the dominant ideology. In this accounting we assume—consistent with interpretations of party identification as based on a party's history of benefiting a person or of supporting a person's ideology (Fiorina, 1981)—that a party affiliate begins with an intention to vote for his or her party's candidate and must be convinced to do otherwise.

Reagan's passive opposition to race-relevant policy gained him support among Democrats with high negative racial affect but lost more support among socially liberal Republicans and Independents. Reagan's stance on sex-relevant issues gained him no support among Democrats but lost support among Republicans and Independents. Perhaps, because of the larger number of highly educated women among Republican identifiers and Independents, sex-role issues had greater salience for these two groups on average than for Democrats.

Reagan's antiwelfare position appeared to net him Democrats and, especially, Independents. The gains among Democrats, however, are better attributed to race beliefs, since it is only among Independents that individualist explanations for poverty affect voting. Perhaps because Democrats on the average attach more importance to structuralist causes of poverty than others, Reagan's antiwelfare message was less well received. Democrats may see enough benefit to themselves from the success of the party in general to override antiwelfare sentiment, whereas Independents lacking such perceived benefit have nothing to check the expression of this sentiment in voting. Finally, Reagan gained support from Democrats who strongly believed in the necessity and desirability of economic inequality. The lack of a parallel effect among Independents leads us to speculate again that education level may have played a role. Reagan's appeal to the need for less restriction on the ability to accrue wealth as a spur to the economy (i.e., his emphasis on the "trickle down" model of long-run economic gain) may have been more influential among the less educated who adhere to this document-ideology belief than among the more highly educated, who tend to reject it.

CONCLUSIONS

The results of the analyses presented in this chapter speak to the political significance of dominant-ideology beliefs in two major respects. First, we have seen that amid differences among subgroups in society—defined by economic ownership and control or by political partisanship—there is shared adherence to the dominant ideology. Such agreement means that contention between different political groups over inequality-related social policy is likely to begin with both parties favoring policy that does not challenge the dominant ideology. Thus, the American political debate over potential social policy covers a narrow range anchored by agreement on the dominant-ideology interpretation of how the stratification order should work.

We have also seen that there is little difference among politically important subgroups in racial affect and sex-role traditionalism. Furthermore, one element of the political elite, younger (under 40) college-educated people, expresses consistently more liberal attitudes toward race and sex-related policy than other elements of the American public. It appears that none of the three important political actors we have examined in this chapter (political parties, economic and educational elites) holds beliefs about race or sex-roles that predispose opposition to all proposed policy to change racial or sexual inequality. Thus, although proposed race and sex-related policy in recent decades has commonly been brought to the political arena by the Democratic party, it has some potential for garnering support or at least avoiding opposition by groups who have disproportionate influence on policy. Yet, because these groups, especially the economic elite, are strong and undoubting adherents to the dominant-ideology explanation of how the stratification order does and should function, their opposition can be avoided only if the proposed policy is consistent with dominant-ideology beliefs in ways we have identified in previous chapters.

Second, we have seen that social liberalism and dominant-ideology beliefs were part of the currents that shaped the 1980 presidential election. One aspect of their influence was seen in the Anderson candidacy, which was primarily the vehicle of younger, highly educated citizens with socially liberal attitudes. As we have also seen, majority adherence to dominant-ideology beliefs across political party lines provided enough votes for Reagan as the candidate of the dominant ideology to offset those lost by his stance of at least passive opposition to social liberalism issues. We do not argue that the effect of dominant ideology was large enough that its absence would have led to the election of Carter. Our analysis shows that Reagan benefited from "economic voting"—people whose standard-of-living declined due to inflation voted against Carter—and other analysis (Markus, 1982) has argued that Carter suffered from perceived mishandling of foreign affairs (most notably the Iranian hostage situation). Yet, the impact of dominant-ideology beliefs did contribute to the election of a president who on taking office acted to sharply reduce federal spending on policy related to economic inequality and in other ways moved to reduce its viability.

10

PERSONAL CONSEQUENCES OF BELIEFS
ABOUT INEQUALITY

Beliefs about inequality may have consequences for an individual's personal life, as well as for political and social attitudes and behaviors, discussed in previous chapters. The consequences at the societal level of widespread belief in the dominant ideology include unsympathetic attitudes toward the poor and racial minorities, for they are blamed for their own lack of progress. But the individual-level consequences may be more benign. In this chapter we examine the effects of beliefs about inequality on people's emotional reactions to their life situations. Laboratory-based research on the emotional consequences of causal beliefs has demonstrated that people with different perceptions of the causes of short-term successes or failures react with characteristic emotional patterns (of anger, pride, shame, thankfulness, etc.). For example, confidence is felt when successes are caused by one's own ability or effort. People's beliefs about the causes of their overall economic situation, therefore, might influence the overall tenor of their emotional reactions, shaping positive or negative reactions and potentially having an effect on mental health and life satisfaction.

Clearly, emotional responses like satisfaction and happiness versus worry and frustration might be influenced by a person's objective circumstances, such as income levels: It is well known that general mental health and life satisfaction are higher among the more well-off (Campbell, Converse, & Rodgers, 1976). However, more subjective elements also influence emotional responses. Specific possibilities are suggested by recent research in social psychology on the effects of psychological control. Perceiving that one has control over one's outcomes seems to have good consequences across a wide range of variables—cognitive, motivational, and emotional. This relationship holds cross-culturally, even when the culture itself generally teaches external rather than internal explanations [as in Mexico (Mirowski & Ross, 1984)]. Indeed, as Chapter 2 noted, these effects seem to be biologically based and are found even in subhuman organisms like rats (Maier & Seligman, 1976).

It is easy to imagine that people who are rich or at least relatively comfortable will feel better if they explain their position in terms of their own abilities and efforts (i.e., internal explanations) than if they use external explanations. However, will the benefits of psychological control hold even for the poor and disadvantaged? Can it actually be psychologically beneficial to hold oneself causally responsible for undesirable outcomes? Our analyses examine this issue by investigating whether explanations (internal versus external) interact with outcomes in predicting emotions—that is, whether the effect of explanations on emotions is the same across the range of economic circumstances from rich to poor.[1]

Specific investigations of the relationships of emotions to explanations have been conducted by Weiner and his associates (Weiner, 1980; Weiner, Russell, & Lerman, 1978, 1979; Russell, 1980). Weiner's theory of emotional responses involves two steps, beginning with the experience of a good or bad outcome of some sort (e.g., good or poor economic outcomes). "Outcome-dependent emotions" such as happiness or unhappiness follow such outcomes. As the second step, the individual may seek an attribution for the outcome, explaining it in some way, and further emotions may be stimulated by the attribution. Anger is felt in response to failure caused by other people's actions, for example, or surprise in response to outcomes caused by luck. This theory furnishes important hypotheses about attribution–emotion links that can be applied to our analyses of the effects of real-life outcomes, explanations, and emotions (cf. Smith & Kluegel, 1982).

DISTRIBUTION OF EMOTIONS

In these analyses, we consider four positive and four negative affects: thankful, happy, proud, confident, worried, frustrated, disappointed, and guilty, as well as a measure of overall life satisfaction. We also

[1]Research on emotion and attributions has often been conceptualized in terms of explanations for "success" and for "failure," largely because the laboratory-based studies within this tradition have often manipulated outcomes in this simple dichotomous manner. We take the more realistic view that outcomes in real life vary continuously (for economic outcomes, people can report using our measure that they are affluent, comfortable, just able to get along, or poor). Thus, it is impossible to analyze the effects of explanations on emotions separately for "success" and "failure" conditions. Instead, to account for the possibility that the effects of explanations may differ between people at different outcome levels, interactions between explanations and the outcome variable are tested within the regression models. If an interaction is significant, say for the dependent variable happiness, this would mean that internal explanations increase happiness more for the affluent than for the poor, with the other outcome groups lining up in between. This could be loosely restated in (perhaps more familiar) terms as: Internal explanations for success increase happiness more than internal explanations for failure.

employ two composite affect measures: the sum of the five positive affects (including satisfaction) and the sum of the four negative ones.

Eight emotions were measured with the same response scale: "We'd like to know generally how you have been feeling recently. Do you feel (happy) almost always, just sometimes, or almost never?" The more positive emotions were also the more commonly claimed by respondents. Of the eight, the order from most to least prevalent is thankful, happy, proud, confident, worried, frustrated, disappointed, and guilty. Note in Table 10.1 that every positive emotion is more widely acknowledged than any negative one.

TABLE 10.1. Emotional Responses: Marginals by Sex

	Percentage reporting feeling emotion		
	Almost always	Just sometimes	Almost never
Thankful			
Males	58	29	4
Females*	81	18	1
Total	75	23	2
Happy			
Males	63	35	2
Females*	68	29	2
Total	66	32	2
Proud			
Male	62	31	7
Females	62	30	7
Total	62	30	7
Confident			
Males	48	41	11
Females	45	43	12
Total	46	42	11
Worried			
Males	9	54	37
Females*	12	60	29
Total	10	57	33
Frustrated			
Males	7	61	32
Females	9	62	29
Total	8	61	30
Disappointed			
Males	3	55	42
Females	4	58	38
Total	4	56	40
Guilty			
Males	1	16	82
Females	1	21	78
Total	1	19	80

*$p < .05$ for comparison of males versus females.

Life satisfaction was measured with different wording: "We have talked about various parts of your life. Now I want to ask you about your life as a whole. How satisfied are you with your life as a whole these days? Are you completely satisfied, pretty satisfied, slightly satisfied, neutral, slightly dissatisfied, pretty dissatisfied, or completely dissatisfied?" Only 9% of respondents fall on the dissatisfied side of the neutral point, and 6% were neutral. "Slightly satisfied was given by 12%," 51% were "pretty satisfied," and 21% were "completely satisfied." These figures, showing a strong overall bias toward the positive end of the scale, do not differ significantly between males and females.

These data do show some variation in emotional experience, though. Almost 10% of the respondents reports being "dissatisfied" with life in general on the satisfaction measure, while about 33% say they feel happy only sometimes and 2% say "almost never." Generally, a minority of respondents do not experience positive emotions and claim that the negative emotions almost always characterize them. Perhaps investigation of the dependence of emotions on people's outcomes and their causal interpretations will help identify these individuals, who may be at risk for a variety of physical and mental symptoms (Bradburn, 1969).

RELATIONS OF EMOTIONS TO SOCIODEMOGRAPHIC FACTORS AND BELIEFS

In these analyses, we include our standard set of sociodemographic variables including whether the respondent works full-time, region of residence, and religious affiliation, as well as two measures of explanations for the respondent's own position. They are an item explaining one's position by effort and ability versus luck or other factors and an item giving the respondent's perception of having been held back versus having had a fair chance to achieve in life (both analyzed in Chapter 4).

For interpretation, the respondent's household income will be considered the primary outcome measure. In twentieth-century America, perceived financial success or failure may be among the most central elements of the overall definition of the self as a success or failure. Campbell *et al.* (1976) reported that it is the "preeminent" predictor of overall life satisfaction in their national data, outweighing such variables as perceptions of one's health, friendships, and leisure activities (Campbell *et al.*, 1976, p. 380; Table 11-5). Interactions between the two measures of explanations and income are also entered in the analyses to explore for possible differences in the effects of an explanation for relative success versus failure (see Footnote 1). For example, happiness might be thought to be increased by internal explanations for positive outcomes more than for negative ones. This prediction amounts to an interactive pattern. However, the interaction terms never proved significant in these analyses, so the models without interactions are reported in Tables 10.2–10.4 as the final results.[2]

Thankfulness. Females, the old, those with high incomes, and Protestants and members of other religions (relative to Jews and those with no religion) report more thankfulness. In addition, those who have not been held back are more thankful. This in part reverses Weiner's (1980) prediction that external causes should lead to thankfulness, as those who feel they have had a fair opportunity to achieve—and presumably feel individually responsible for their outcomes—are thankful. Perhaps they are thankful for that opportunity itself.

Happiness. Females, whites, the old, residents of the West and Midwest, and those with higher incomes report more happiness, as do Protestants and members of other religions compared with Catholics, Jews, and members of no religion. In addition, those who do not see themselves as having been held back are happier. Thus, positive outcomes (not surprisingly) produce happiness, which is also increased by internal explanations, in accordance with prior findings. Internal explanations for *failure* do not seem to particularly diminish reported happiness; no significant interaction was found. Even the poor are happier if they do not feel they were held back than if they feel that they were.

Pride. The only variables attaining significance for this emotion are the two explanation measures. Those with internal explanations and those who do not feel held back are more proud than others. Interestingly, income does not have an effect (nor does an income–explanation interaction term), so people appear to feel as proud of internally caused poor outcomes as of internally caused good ones.

Confidence. Respondents with more income and education are more confident, and westerners notably exceed residents of all other regions on this measure. Those who use internal explanations and do not feel held back are also more confident. The pattern agrees with Weiner's (1980) predictions.

Total Positive Emotions. A measure combining the four positive emotions plus satisfaction shows higher scores for females, whites, the old, those with high incomes, and those from the West (followed by those from the South and Midwest, with those from the Northeast lowest). Religion also has an effect, with Protestants and other religious

---

[2]The failure to find interactions means (in terms of the "success" versus "failure" dichotomy) that explanations for success have effects that are statistically indistinguishable from explanations for failure. For example, internal explanations for "success" and for "failure" increase happiness equally.

TABLE 10.2. Positive Emotions: Regressions on Sociodemographic Variables and Attributions[a]

Independent variable	Thankful	Happy	Proud	Confident	Total
Sex (female)	.15*	.07*	.04	.02	.36*
	(.15)	(.07)	(.03)	(.01)	(.09)
Age (10 years)	.05*	.02*	−.01	.01	.12*
	(.18)	(.08)	(−.03)	(.01)	(.10)
Race (nonwhite)	.01	−.18*	.02	−.09	−.40*
	(.00)	(−.12)	(.01)	(−.05)	(−.07)
Education (years)	.00	.00	−.00	.02*	.03
	(.00)	(.02)	(−.01)	(.08)	(.04)
Income (log)	.08*	.21*	.08	.26*	.82*
	(.06)	(.14)	(.04)	(.13)	(.14)
Worker	.00	−.00	.05	−.01	.02
	(.00)	(−.00)	(.04)	(−.01)	(.00)
South	.06	.02	.08	.03	.26
	(.06)	(.02)	(.06)	(.02)	(.06)
Midwest	.03	.07	.05	.03	.21
	(.03)	(.06)	(.04)	(.02)	(.05)
West	.03	.09*	.07	.14*	.37*
	(.03)	(.07)	(.05)	(.09)	(.08)
Religion					
Catholic	.00*	.00*	.00	.00	.00*
Conservative Protestant	.10*	.13*	−.08	.02	.20*
Other Protestant	.07*	.11*	.06	.09	.38*
Jew	−.12*	−.04*	.09	.00	−.03*
Other religion	.10*	.08*	−.03	.13	.25*
No religion	−.19*	−.01*	−.03	−.03	−.43*
Own ability	.01	.05	.18*	.09*	.54*
	(.00)	(.04)	(.11)	(.05)	(.11)
Not held back	.08*	.19*	.08*	.22*	.88*
	(.08)	(.17)	(.06)	(.15)	(.21)
R^2	.11	.11	.03	.08	.14

[a]$N = (1443)$.
*$p < .05$.

identifiers being highest, followed by Catholics and Jews, with adherents of no religion by far the lowest. Finally, both explanation measures have effects, as positive emotions are more common among those who use internal explanations and do not feel held back. These summary findings show the power of explanations—internal explanations for outcomes increase positive affects virtually across the board. The absence of any interaction means that such explanations have positive effects regardless of the respondent's income level: Even poor people feel more positive emotionally if they feel responsible for their position than if they explain it externally.

TABLE 10.3. Negative Emotions: Regressions on Sociodemographic Variables and Attributions[a]

Independent variable	Worried	Frustrated	Disappointed	Guilty	Total
Sex (female)	.09*	.09*	.06	.04	.28*
	(.07)	(.08)	(.05)	(.05)	(.09)
Age (10 years)	− .05*	− .07*	− .04*	− .02*	− .19*
	(− .14)	(− .20)	(− .13)	(− .09)	(− .20)
Race (nonwhite)	− .02	− .11*	.01	− .08*	− .04
	(− .01)	(− .06)	(.01)	(− .06)	(− .01)
Education (years)	− .02*	.00	− .00	− .00	− .02
	(− .07)	(.02)	(− .02)	(− .02)	(− .03)
Income (log)	− .09	− .12*	− .14*	.06	− .29*
	(− .05)	(− .07)	(− .09)	(.05)	(− .06)
Worker	.04	.06	.05	.01	.16
	(.03)	(.06)	(.05)	(.01)	(.05)
South	− .05	.03	.07	.02	.07
	(− .04)	(.02)	(.06)	(.02)	(.02)
Midwest	− .13*	− .03	.01	.01	− .13
	(− .09)	(− .03)	(.01)	(.02)	(− .04)
West	− .09	.05	.03	.03	.02
	(− .06)	(.03)	(.02)	(.03)	(.01)
Religion					
Catholic	.00*	.00	.00*	.00	.00*
Conservative Protestant	− .11*	− .08	− .05*	− .05	− .29*
Other Protestant	− .10*	− .03	− .03*	− .00	− .16*
Jew	− .08*	− .14	.19*	− .04	.21*
Other religion	− .03*	− .04	.07*	− .17	− .17*
No religion	− .16*	.06	.05*	.01	− .04*
Own ability	− .03	.02	− .09*	− .05	− .15
	(− .02)	(.01)	(− .06)	(− .04)	(− .04)
Not held back	− .12*	− .14*	− .14*	− .05*	− .45*
	(− .09)	(− .11)	(− .11)	(− .04)	(− .13)
R^2	.06	.08	.06	.03	.08

[a]$N = (1443)$.
*$p < .05$.

Worry. Turning now to the negative emotions, we find that females worry more than males, and worry is more widespread among the young, the less educated, northeastern residents, and Catholics (with Protestants and Jews in the middle and those with no religion worrying least). Those who feel that they have been held back also worry more. Income is not related to worry, so the well-off and the poor worry equal amounts (though perhaps about different subjects). Again, explanations influence affect, with internal causes (not being held back) leading to more positive emotional experience (less worry, in this case).

Frustration. Females, whites, the young, and those with low incomes

TABLE 10.4 Life Satisfaction: Regression on Sociodemographic Variables and Attributions[a]

Independent variable	Satisfaction
Sex (female)	.15*
	(.06)
Age (10 years)	.10*
	(.13)
Race (nonwhite)	− .31*
	(− .08)
Education (years)	.00
	(.00)
Income (log)	.36*
	(.10)
Worker	− .05
	(− .02)
South	.11
	(.04)
Midwest	.06
	(.02)
West	.07
	(.02)
Religion	
Catholic	.00*
Conservative Protestant	.07*
Other Protestant	.09*
Jew	.06*
Other religion	− .06*
No religion	− .34*
Own ability	.42*
	(.13)
Not held back	.61*
	(.21)
R^2	.13

[a]$N = 1443$.
*$p < .05$.

report frustration, and so do those who feel that they have been held back, as would be expected.

Disappointment. The young, those with low incomes, and Jews (relative to all other groups) feel particularly high levels of disappointment, as do those with external explanations and those who feel held back. The effects of explanations imply that the feeling involved is not disappointment in one's own accomplishments but disappointment in not being allowed to achieve to the best of one's abilities.

Guilt. Guilt is reported more often by nonwhites, the young, and those who feel that they have been held back. The results show that internal explanations reduce guilt as much for the poor as for the rich—

people do not seem to feel guilty about a poor personal economic situation that they, themselves, feel responsible for.

Total Negative Emotion. Higher levels of all negative emotions are reported by females, the young, those with low incomes, and Jews (with Catholics and those with no religion in the middle and Protestants having low levels of negative affect). In addition, those who feel held back show more negative emotions.

In most respects this analysis gives a picture that neatly reverses the determinants of positive affects: The young, Jews, and those with low incomes and external explanations have more negative affect, whereas the old, Protestants, and those with high incomes and internal explanations have more positive affect. However, positive versus negative affects are not determined by exactly the same set of independent variables as dominant-ideology beliefs. Females report more of both types of affect, and there are effects of race and region on positive affect that do not show up on the negative affect summary measure.

Satisfaction. As Table 10.4 shows, more overall life satisfaction is reported by females, whites, the old, and those with higher incomes. Religion also makes a substantial difference, with members of any religion expressing more satisfaction than those with no religion; differences among the different religious affiliations were small. Finally, people who use internal explanations and feel they have not been held back report substantially more satisfaction than their counterparts. It appears that positive outcomes (e.g., high income) and internal explanations generate satisfaction, as predicted by Weiner (1980).

SUMMARY

One obvious point about these analyses is the beneficial effects of economic resources (income) on emotion: Five of the eight specific affects, life satisfaction, and both of the summary measures are significantly affected by income. It invariably produces more positive and less negative affect. Income serves as both a psychological reward (evidence that a person has achieved in life, hence valid grounds for happiness and confidence) and a physical protection against many types of problems (with health, for example) that can cause negative emotions.

It is also interesting to note the similarity of the picture of the high-positive/low-negative affect person with that of the pure believer in the dominant ideology as sketched in Chapter 4: an older, white, male, higher income, westerner with internal explanations. It is obviously true that such factors as higher income will tend to cause increases in both positive affect and dominant-ideology beliefs. One might also speculate that the similarity of one's ideological beliefs to the general context of our society improves one's chances of experiencing positive rather than negative affects—but recall that the same pattern of internal explanations increasing psychological well-being holds in Mexico, where external explanations are more culturally normative (Mirowski & Ross, 1984).

But the most fundamental message of these findings is the benefits of psychological control. The most obvious evidence on this point is that one or both of the explanation variables attains significance in each of the 11 analyses. These effects, like those of income, are also invariable in direction: Internal explanations (or not feeling held back) increase all positive affects and decrease all negative ones. No significant interactions with income are found, leading to the interpretation that internal explanations even for relatively *poor* economic outcomes are more psychologically beneficial than external ones. The benefits of psychological control (using preponderantly internal explanations for one's outcomes) have been demonstrated in a variety of contexts (e.g., Langer, 1983; Folkman, 1984; Langer & Rodin, 1976) and referred to in Chapter 2, and these results further amplify them. People who feel that they are personally responsible for their outcomes in life are better off psychologically than those who give external explanations or feel held back, even if their objective outcomes are not very good.

The benefits of psychological control have obvious implications for the design of social policies related to welfare and equal opportunity for minority groups. The programs should attempt to give the beneficiaries feelings of personal control over their outcomes, perhaps by providing subsidized jobs and child care so that people can work, rather than giving simple external help or "handouts," however generous. It is not irrelevant that programs of this type are also less likely to suffer from the adverse public reaction that welfare receives (Chapter 6). A program's consistency with some elements of the dominant ideology may not only minimize psychological damage to recipients but also minimize political backlash.

Among the other independent variables, some have consistent patterns of effects. Women report more of most emotions, both positive and negative, than men. Our data cannot show whether men and women have different cognitive processes in response to outcomes and explanations, whether women are more attentive to emotional experience than men, or whether women are just more willing to report their emotions publicly. We suspect that the second and third of these possibilities are more realistic.

Age has powerful effects, increasing the level of most positive affects and decreasing negative ones. Older people's prevailing positive view of life has previously been noted (Campbell *et al.*, 1976), and it is certainly comprehensible in social–psychological terms. The old must face a great deal of motivational pressure to see their lifetime retrospectively as having been satisfying and filled with worthwhile accomplishments, rather than wasted, disappointing, or frustrating. For the old, the affect questions become much more of a retrospective judgment on one's life.

There are a few significant race effects: Whites feel significantly more satisfaction, happiness, and total positive affect, and less guilt than nonwhites, but they also feel more frustration. There seems to be a general bias toward greater psychological well-being among whites. The differences between the effects of being nonwhite and being female are of some interest. While nonwhites are less satisfied and happy than whites, females are higher than males on both of these measures. And there is no sex effect on guilt, which shows a race difference. It would be easy to understand that the lower societal status and perceived discrimination often faced by nonwhites and women might have emotional consequences, such as reducing happiness, but why would the results differ for the two groups? We speculate that experiencing poor outcomes as a member of a group may have different psychological effects than experiencing them as an individual, much as Vanneman and Pettigrew (1972) demonstrated different effects of egoistic (individual-level) versus fraternal (group-level) relative deprivation. Group identification or group consciousness on the part of minorities or women may shape the responses to their outcomes in ways that differ from what one would expect from a pure individual-level analysis of explanations and outcomes.

Religion has several significant effects. To generalize, Protestants and members of non-Judeo–Christian religions seem to have more of several positive affects, while Catholics (for worry) and Jews (for guilt and total negative affect) experience more negative ones. On satisfaction, every religious category differs from the no-religion category, which is considerably lower on life satisfaction. Religious belief, as a central component of a person's view of the universe in general and his or her place in it, might be expected to have such major effects on affective reactions as are found here.

Finally, there are intriguing regional differences. Westerners seem to report more positive affects (happiness, confidence, and total positive affect) while being low on worry (northeasterners tend to worry more than others do). Is the line from the old song about the West "where never is heard a discouraging word" still applicable today?

In general, explanations contribute independently to explaining individual differences in emotional experience, beyond the effects of both sociodemographic variables and life outcomes such as income levels. Internal explanations, the belief that one is responsible for one's own position—even if it is objectively a poor position, and even if the belief is objectively largely inaccurate—seem to benefit people's emotional health and life satisfaction.

CONCLUSIONS

This chapter has demonstrated that beliefs concerning inequality (specifically, explanations for economic outcomes) have substantial implications for an individual's personal life. Beliefs about inequality exert an influence beyond such related domains as evaluations of governmental policies and political candidates, extending to central aspects of personal life: emotional experiences such as happiness, satisfaction, worry, and frustration.

If the results of these analyses can be summarized in one sentence, it would be that *the belief in internal control, part of the dominant ideology, is adaptive for an individual's personal life.* This belief leads to more positive and less negative emotional experience. The objective *accuracy* of beliefs in pure individualism may well be questioned (as we discussed in Chapters 3–5); such accuracy, however, may be more often the concern of social scientists than of the person in the street. Psychological control—even if not always accompanied by real control of one's important life outcomes—seems to have positive consequences. These consequences in turn may be important in motivating people to maintain a belief in the dominant ideology as a whole in the face of other beliefs and attitudes that may seem to challenge it. They may influence, therefore, the outcomes of society-wide issues such as the design of welfare or race-related programs, as our earlier chapters have illustrated.

11

CONCLUSIONS

In Chapters 1 and 2 we raised a number of questions about the American public's perspective on economic inequality and related social policy. In this final chapter we reexamine these questions in light of the evidence presented in Chapters 3–10. We begin with an overview of how well our results support the major propositions advanced in Chapters 1 and 2. We then discuss the implications of our findings for theories of the root causes of beliefs about economic inequality. We conclude by relating our findings to the prospects for effective social policy to ameliorate problems stemming from economic inequality in America.

SUMMARY OF FINDINGS

Stability of Adherence to the Dominant Ideology

The measurement of beliefs and attitudes is, of course, an imprecise science. We have made efforts in our survey to minimize some sources of error by asking multiple questions to improve reliability and enable some checks on validity and by replicating as closely as possible some questions used in prior research to better assess over-time changes. Yet there remain several potential sources of error—due to question wording, context, question ordering, guessing, and so on (Schuman & Presser, 1981)—and we have not attempted to assess their impact on our findings. Importantly, however, as we have seen (especially in Chapters 4, 7, and 8) comparisons of available results from independent surveys that ask questions about the same topics lead to the same conclusions, despite variation in question wording and response format. Though we do not discount the need for further research to examine the potential impact of these sources of error, this comparability of findings across surveys makes us confident that the major inferences we have drawn cannot be dismissed because of potential errors of measurement.

Within the limits of available evidence, our results support our proposition that the level of public adherence to the dominant-ideology explanation of economic inequality has been stable over the last three decades. Because of the lack of adequate measures for earlier years, our principal source of evidence concerning this proposition is age-group comparisons; therefore this conclusion rests on somewhat less solid ground than others we have drawn. In general, it is based on the lack of substantial age-group differences in our measures of dominant-ideology beliefs. The lack of such differences may be deceiving. It is possible that substantial shifts among people of all ages have taken place equally; such "period" effects would not be evident in age-group differences.

Other evidence supports the inference that the level of adherence to the dominant ideology has been essentially stable. In the areas of race and sex-role beliefs, sizable aggregate differences across time are reflected in substantial differences among age groups. Why should the process of change be substantially different for beliefs about economic inequality? Moreover, data on over-time change in explanations for poverty do not support an hypothesis of substantial period change in these explanations from the late 1960s to 1980. As seen in Chapter 4, our replications of a set of questions asked in 1969 produced a nearly identical distribution of responses in 1980. Furthermore, poll data from the late 1930s onward suggest that individual explanations for poverty have been predominant since researchers first began to survey them (Schiltz, 1970; Gallup, 1985).

Although there are some statistically significant differences among age groups in adherence to dominant-ideology beliefs, they are small and follow a pattern indicative more of life cycle differences than of aggregate change. Available evidence on over-time change (beliefs about the causes of poverty) that indicates stability in the aggregate supports this inference. It appears that as Americans get older they attach more importance to individualistic factors as causes of poverty and wealth and emphasize individual equity over equality or need as a basis for a just distribution of rewards. These changes in belief over the adult years seem to be continuations of developmental patterns observed in research on children's beliefs about economic inequality (Leahy, 1983). The shift from an egalitarian view of justice in early childhood starts in early adolescence and may continue over the life cycle, up to roughly age 60 when people again become somewhat more egalitarian.

We also speculate that there are limited cohort effects involving perceived opportunity. The youngest cohorts (people under 30 in 1980) are somewhat less optimistic about the availability of opportunity in general, because of declining faith in the market value of a college education. Perhaps because they have fully experienced the post-World War II period of substantial growth in the average standard of living,

Americans 55 years of age and older have a more individualistic view of how the stratification order does and should work than expected on grounds of life-cycle position alone. Some of this difference is attributable to the higher average years of education among younger cohorts, but it is among the college educated that we see a qualitatively larger tendency for people over 55 to attribute poverty and wealth to individualistic causes (see Table 9.5). Of course these inferences about change remain tentative in anticipation of future research on aggregate over-time and life-cycle change in beliefs about economic inequality.

Group Divisions

Adherence to the dominant ideology is, as we proposed, widespread. In each of the groups we have examined the majority express agreement with dominant-ideology beliefs. Variation among groups in beliefs about how the stratification order should and does work is found *not* in adherence to the dominant ideology but in beliefs that *potentially* challenge it. The range of expressed doubt is marked. For example, we have seen that whereas 80% of low-status (as defined in Chapter 3) black Americans believe that they are unfairly underpaid, 80% of high-status whites feel that they are fairly paid for the contribution made to society. For the same groups the difference in the perceived size of the American middle class is likewise striking—roughly, 13 versus 70%, respectively. Whereas 55% of low-status Americans respond that they believe that industry's failure to provide jobs is a very important reason why the poor are poor, only 7% of the economic elite share this view.

The largest and most consistent group disparities in expressed doubt about the workings of the American stratification order are those between blacks and whites. People of lower socioeconomic status express more doubt than those of high status, and women express more doubt than men. But neither the disparity by status nor by sex is so large or so consistent across beliefs as that by race. Illustratively, whereas 20% more women that men believe that they have not had a fair chance to make the most of themselves in life (31 versus 25%), almost twice as many blacks as whites believe so (50 versus 26%).

Judged by the black–white gap in beliefs that potentially challenge the dominant ideology, blacks are the group of Americans that come closest to being "class conscious" in the Marxian definition (Lopreato & Hazelrigg, 1972). Black Americans, of course, much more than whites live in circumstances that present the "objective" conditions for class formation (Giddens, 1973). Opportunity for economic advancement has been explicitly denied on the basis of race. Residential, occupational, and other bases of racial segregation persist. Accordingly, blacks do express a greater sense of group consciousness than do members of other social groups [by sex, age, or economic status (Gurin *et al.*, 1980)].

Our research shows, however, that while blacks express very strong doubt about the justice of the American stratification order as it involves them and others, *they stop short of denying the justice of economic inequality in principle and of dismissing the ideas that the rich and the poor as individuals are deserving of their fate.* Thus they lack the element of Marxian class consciousness of rejecting the legitimacy of the premises of the existing stratification order. Black Americans believe strongly that current economic inequality is unjust and favor a more egalitarian distribution of income, but on average they do not favor strict equality as an alternative to the present order. For example, as we have seen in Chapter 5 roughly 60% of black Americans endorse the proposition that income should be distributed mainly on the basis of skill and training rather than on need, and approximately 64% of our black respondents agreed with the proposition that inequality is needed to motivate people to work hard.

Since blacks constitute but 11% of the American public, on numerical grounds alone the challenge that their action as a group might provide to the dominant ideology is limited. Our research argues that the potential for such challenge from action by other groups is even more limited. Marxian and neo-Marxian theory underscores the potential for social change inherent in the working class. Depending upon how inclusive one's definition of the working class is, numerically it presents a potentially large force for change should it act in a concerted fashion. Our findings argue that, to the extent that can be inferred from beliefs about economic inequality, there is little such potential presented by the American working class. First, the American working class shares with other groups majority adherence to dominant-ideology beliefs. Second, there is much variation among members of the American working class in the level of doubt expressed about the workings of the stratification order. Lower income workers indicate more doubt than more affluent ones. Men express less doubt than women. And, of course, black workers question the justice of the status quo much more on average than whites.

On the whole, women express more doubt about the justice of economic inequality than men, but sex differences in beliefs about economic inequality are much smaller than the parallel race differences. Perhaps because of the differences between men and women in opportunity-related experience, women have a less optimistic assessment of the general availability of opportunity, attach more importance to structural causes of wealth and poverty, and have a more pessimistic assessment of their personal opportunity for economic advancement.

One might also surmise that attention to sex-related inequality by the women's movement has made women more aware of inequality of opportunity, and consequently they attribute the above sex differences to this increased awareness. Our findings do not support this interpretation. On average, women do not perceive greater inequality of opportunity for women or other groups, nor perceive less equality of educational opportunity than do men. College-educated women do perceive less equal opportunity for women and other groups than less-educated women; but they do not express less optimism than men about their personal opportunity for economic advancement, nor do they differ from college-educated men in the tendency to ascribe less importance to structural causes of poverty and wealth than do the lesser educated. The less optimistic view of opportunity held by women seems to reflect more the influence of sex differences in work and other circumstances that shape one's view of society than a sensitizing impact of the women's movement. The latter influence seems to be present for college-educated women only, and its effects seem limited to encouraging belief in unequal opportunity for women and other groups alone. In short, our findings in Chapter 8 and those of Gurin *et al.* (1980) argue that compared to blacks, women are much less conscious of themselves *as a group* in relation to inequality in society. Group consciousness may be increasing among women, as indicated by the emergence of a "gender gap" in voting in recent years, but still by all indications it is far below the level of blacks.

Resistance to Challenge

We have seen that most Americans do not believe that all is well with the workings of the American stratification order in fact. Majorities question the fairness of incomes much above or below the average. Most Americans perceive that at least one major group (the poor, women, or blacks) experiences unequal opportunity for economic advancement to some degree. Substantial minorities attribute poverty or wealth to supraindividual factors. Furthermore, many Americans—especially blacks and those of lower status—question the fairness of their personal opportunity and economic status.

Yet, as we have also seen these doubts do not much affect the prevailing beliefs that economic inequality in principle is necessary and beneficial (i.e., just), and that ultimately all Americans are individually responsible for their economic fate. Thus as we proposed, potential challenges to the dominant ideology largely coexist with widespread adherence to it. Our findings and prior research and theory point to three reasons for this coexistence.

First, most Americans have just one or a few reasons to doubt the dominant-ideology explanation. College-educated Americans more often believe that the poor, women, and minorities have unequal opportunity but largely do not doubt that the stratification order works as it should for themselves. Working-class Americans have more doubt about how equitably they are personally treated but express less doubt than the college-educated that other groups (such as minorities or women) have equal opportunity for economic advancement. In light of the strong motivational reasons for believing the dominant ideology that we discussed in Chapter 2 and given only one or a few reasons to question the justice of the current order, believing that one's own experience or that of other groups is exceptional seems to be a common response. "Blacks and women are denied opportunity not because the system malfunctions but because prejudiced or sexist *individuals* act to keep it from performing equitably." "The rich have better opportunity and get more than they deserve relative to their contribution, but their actions don't affect me." "Poverty does make it more difficult to succeed, but the poor can overcome it with individual effort." Our results suggest that beliefs like these are commonplace in Americans' thinking about economic inequality.

Second, the recent history of improvements in the average standard of living and upward social mobility in the United States presents evidence to most Americans about the availability of opportunity to counterbalance doubt and to encourage the hope of success in the future. As we have seen, most Americans are quite optimistic about their personal chances to get ahead, even if they have doubts about the availability of opportunity in general or perceive that they have had blocked opportunity in the past. Americans place strong faith in themselves and therefore consider that they as individuals are exempt from the failings of the stratification order in the aggregate. For example, while doubt about the market value of a college education has been increasing, the young believe that they individually will still benefit greatly from obtaining one. College-educated women see more limited opportunity for women on the average than do other women, but they are also the most optimistic about their personal chances to get ahead; and so on.

Finally, as much contemporary research on social cognition has demonstrated (Chapter 2), beliefs may be held in a nonintegrated or "compartmentalized" fashion as part of independent schemas that are cued in different contexts. Cognitive consistency theory implies the existence of a self-evident, if not innate, "social logic" that leads people to see the inconsistencies or contradictions between or among beliefs and attitudes. Lane (1962) and others (Mann, 1970; Parkin, 1971; Free & Cantril, 1968) have argued that there is no such self-evident logic— that people need an explicitly formulated counterideology before such inconsistencies and contradictions will be recognized. The results of this research are quite consistent with this argument.

Policy Attitudes

As we proposed, rather than policy that challenges dominant-ideology beliefs, the American public tends to support policy that is a compromise between liberal influences that provide the impetus for them and the conservative influence of the dominant ideology. One liberal influence is provided by the recognition of substantial poverty amidst affluence. Although most Americans want to do something about poverty, it has become increasingly clear that this "something" does not include direct-transfer payments. Such payments directly challenge prevailing equity norms. The challenge to the dominant ideology is not the only source of antiwelfare sentiment. As seen in Chapter 6, welfare attitudes contain a lot of symbolic and emotional "baggage." For many people welfare has come to stand for all the perceived ills of American domestic policy. Other antipoverty programs (like government guaranteed jobs) that do not challenge Americans' beliefs about the functional value of economic inequality are not the objects of such strongly negative sentiment.

Our findings suggest that the public evaluates inequality-related policy according to its place on a continuum from equal opportunity to direct-income redistribution. If any government involvement is believed to be needed, the closer it is in content to assuring equal opportunity the greater is the degree of public support. The more it looks like direct redistribution, the greater is the opposition. The ERA, antidiscrimination laws, job-training programs for minorities, and government-guaranteed jobs are equal opportunity assurance programs. Welfare for the poor, hiring quotas for minorities and women, and minimum incomes all shade in some degree toward direct redistribution.

The popularity of equal opportunity assurance programs may stem from several sources. They are less threatening to immediate self-interest. They can be viewed as programs to socialize an out-group in in-group values. But, as our results show, they are also compatible with dominant-ideology beliefs. They emphasize individualistic solutions and so do not question the beliefs of people who deny structural causes: They call for changing the behavior of people who are the source of the problem (race or sex discriminators) or for changing the skills or attitudes of those involved in the problem to allow them to better fit in the current order. They do not violate equity norms by seeming potentially to reduce the motivational value of economic inequality.

Equal opportunity assurance programs are not only compatible with the dominant ideology, but if people are convinced that a group has been systematically denied equal opportunity, then they are mandated. Equal opportunity is a major premise of the logic of opportunity. If it does not hold, it is logical to question the principal conclusion of the logic of opportunity syllogism that current economic inequality is fair. Our data and others reviewed in Chapters 7 and 8 show that currently many Americans believe that at least to some degree women and minorities are victims of discrimination that limits their opportunities for economic advancement.

In this regard, the civil rights and women's movements have provided a force for public support of equal opportunity assurance policy simply by carrying forward and supporting the message that equal opportunity does not exist. As the focus of race policy has shifted from an emphasis on equal opportunity to equal average economic outcomes, however, opposition has become stronger because Americans begin to view race policy in terms of direct income redistribution. As we speculated in Chapter 8, the same fate may await a shift in sex-related policy from an emphasis on equal opportunity to get jobs to equal pay for comparable worth—that is, a shift to a perceived focus on realizing equal economic outcomes.

Recently the issue of comparable worth has been a matter of much attention in the courts, in legislatures, and in the media. At present many opponents of comparable worth cast their criticism of it directly in terms of a choice between equal opportunity assurance programs and direct income redistribution as alternative means to reduce the earnings gap between men and women. One such opponent (Levin,1984), for example, has characterized comparable worth as the "feminist road to socialism." In general, the criticism of comparable worth has the same essential structure of that employed by opponents of affirmative action for blacks. In both cases an effort is made to encourage the public to see these programs as direct economic redistributive efforts and thereby to oppose them for reasons that we have developed throughout this book.

As Verba and Oren (1984) have noted, comparable-worth policy may be viewed as consistent with prevailing equity ideals—that is, with the belief that people should be paid according to the value of their individual contributions. As in the case of affirmative action, however, the involvement of a categorical criterion of justice—that the average income of social groups should be equal—makes the intent of comparable-worth policy somewhat ambiguous. This allows some to characterize it as an egalitarian redistributive program rather than as a program to realize individual pay equity. It remains to be seen which of these two characterizations of comparable worth policy comes to prevail in public opinion.

ULTIMATE DETERMINANTS

In Chapter 2 we discussed the possible impact of several factors that may be seen as the root causes or ultimate determinants of public beliefs about how the stratification order does and should work: self-interest, experience, socialization, and basic social–psychological processes. Strong evidence concerning the impact of certain of these factors requires different kinds of research from that we have conducted. However, we have presented direct evidence concerning the effects of self-interest and experience and can offer informed speculation about the impact of aspects of socialization and basic social–psychological processes.

Self-Interest and Experience

The prevailing tendency for the American public to accept the dominant-ideology justification of current inequality is somewhat weaker among people whose stratification-related experience and economic self-interest may question it. However, even among people who seem to have most reason to deny the dominant ideology, a majority do not. The range of variation in endorsement of the dominant ideology is from simple majority endorsement among poor blacks to nearly unanimous endorsement among white, male members of the economic elite. In contrast, experience and self-interest have a substantially larger effect on beliefs that seem to challenge the assertion that the stratification order is just. Americans at the top and the bottom of the stratification order have markedly different views of the importance of supraindividual causes of wealth and poverty, of their personal past and present chances for economic advancement, of the benefits to greater economic equality, and of the fairness of the actual income distribution to them in general.

Other researchers have noted the pattern of little or no differences by simple economic self-interest or stratification-related experience in expression of some beliefs about economic inequality and substantial differences by self-interest and experience in adherence to others (Mann, 1970; Huber & Form, 1973; Parkin, 1971; Sennett & Cobb, 1972). Since the prior inference that this pattern exists was drawn from small and, to varying degress, unrepresentative samples, one may well have questioned it. Our research quite strongly confirms the existence of this pattern. What accounts for it?

The best answer seems to be, consistent with certain earlier interpretations (Gramsci, 1971; Parkin, 1971), that people's comprehension of inequality is the product of *both* self-interest and experience, on the one hand, *and* socialization and basic social–psychological processes (largely ignored in prior research), on the other hand.

Perhaps because they are learned early, or because the message of individual responsibility is so pervasive in American culture, or because recent history presents plentiful examples of upward mobility, dominant-ideology beliefs seem to be an "anchored" feature of Americans' consciousness of economic inequality. Or, perhaps it is because the individualistic character of the dominant ideology supports using internal explanations that contribute to psychological well-being. Our results show quite clearly that individual self-interest defined by low relative economic status does not of itself lead people to question the necessity and desirability of economic inequality in the ideal, nor does it much dissuade people from the belief that the rich and the poor as individuals deserve their economic fate. Stratification-related experience, of itself, likewise has little impact on these beliefs. As we have seen, the perception that one has not had a fair opportunity for economic advancement does not much affect assessments of the availability or of the equality of opportunity in general. Blocked opportunity is only one type of negative stratification-related experience, and others may have more impact. But, black Americans doubtless encounter many more such experiences on the average than whites, and we have seen they are only slightly more likely than whites to deny dominant-ideology beliefs.

Low relative economic status and experiences that challenge the dominant-ideology explanation of how the stratification order should function do engender a good deal of doubt about the fairness of the existing order and even some sense that a more egalitarian distribution of income might be beneficial to society and just to individuals. How are these doubts and questions accommodated to the seemingly unmovable adherence to the dominant-ideology explanation of inequality? Ultimately, an answer to this question awaits further research.[1] We speculate, however, that people whose self-interest or experience raises such doubts may often construct compromise explanations that blunt their potential challenge. For example, many people may accommodate doubts about whether the stratification order works as it should with the belief in individual responsibility by adopting one of the three following composite explanations:

1. Being raised in poverty does pose barriers to opportunity, but individuals can, should, and do in many instances overcome these barriers.

[1]Hochschild (1981) discusses several ways that people may accommodate ambivalence that arises not only from the challenge that experience may present to the dominant-ideology explanation of how the stratification order should function but from other sources as well. Since these explanations were derived from in-depth interviews of 28 purposively selected respondents, they presently are best viewed as untested hypotheses.

2. There are two types of poor people: (1) the honest, disabled or working poor; and (2) the dishonest, disreputable poor.
3. Poverty is the product of neither individual shortcomings nor faults of the economic system. Rather it is the product of an intermediate level of supraindividual factors (i.e., attributable to characteristics of the family, peers, neighborhoods, drugs).

Our findings suggest that composites 1 and 2 are most often found among lower socioeconomic status Americans, since they most often express the belief that both structuralist and individualist causes are "very important." Composite 3, consistent with Ryan's (1971) speculations about the perspective in which educated Americans view poverty, appears to be most often found among the college educated. This composite explanation fits with the tendency of the college educated to deny more often than other groups that *either* structural or individual factors are "very important" causes of poverty.

Many Americans may also apply composite explanations of why the rich are rich that parallel those for poverty. Americans may believe that the wealthy start with an advantage but may lose it unless they also have great talent and ability. Two populations of the wealthy may likewise be distinguished: those who have inherited it and "self-made" people. Future research should employ direct questioning about these and other potential composite explanations.

Socialization

Our research provides evidence that something other than simple economic self-interest or stratification-related experience produces adherence to dominant-ideology beliefs but not conclusive evidence concerning what specifically this "something" is.

Given the observed widespread adherence to dominant-ideology beliefs, it is reasonable to infer that one source is common socialization. Assessing the impact of this factor calls for methods of research other than an opinion survey. Socialization processes can be most directly understood by examining the social–ideological content of the messages delivered by the media, schools, religious groups, and other socializing insitutions.

Although we cannot offer direct evidence on the impact of socialization agents, we can offer indirect evidence concerning the role of education as one major socializing institution. What inferences might we draw from an overview of its effects on the beliefs and attitudes we have examined in this book?

In general, increasing education is associated with social liberalism and economic conservatism. College-educated Americans express more liberal beliefs concerning issues of race and sex equality than the noncollege educated, but they also express less doubt about the fairness of current economic inequality. The greater social liberalism of the college educated is perhaps more clearly attributable to socialization than is their greater economic conservatism. The latter difference is perhaps more attributable to the fact that education is a status resource than to an explicit teaching of dominant-ideology beliefs. College-educated people earn more money on average, tend to marry other college-educated people, live in middle-class residential areas, work with other middle-class workers, and so on. From the vantage point of middle-class surroundings, the stratification order looks fair; one has little reason to doubt that it works in general as it should.

Perhaps more important than what is explicitly taught in American educational institutions is what is not taught or not received by students. Structurally based criticism of aspects of American economic inequality is selectively available on college campuses. It is largely not taught at secondary schools. Only recently, for example, have high school history texts begun to discuss race differences in terms of discrimination (Fitzgerald, 1979).

One finding does imply that education selectively produces structurally based criticism of the stratification order. Among both blacks and women the college educated are substantially more likely to believe that the poor, women, and blacks have unequal opportunity; among blacks there is a parallel difference in perceived equality of educational opportunity. Two explanations of this finding seem plausible. First, blacks and women (perhaps in response to the fields of study they pursue or perhaps because they seek out "liberal" courses) may be more exposed to courses that teach about structural limits to opportunity. Prior knowledge or experience with race- or sex-related barriers to opportunity and expectations regarding the value of education as a status resource that blacks and women bring to college may guide the curriculum they choose. In contrast to blacks and women, who may seek information that will help them understand the social forces that shape the subordinate economic standing of blacks and women in general, white males more often may view college simply as a resource for acquiring economic privilege.

Second, attending college itself, as well as its consequences for later status, may broaden one's base of information for assessing equality of opportunity. In this regard and throughout the analyses presented in this book there is substantial evidence that a person's view of how the stratification order works in fact is strongly shaped by his or her immediate social world. Thus college education for blacks and women may produce a greater sense of race- and sex-based differences in opportunity by exposing them to more privileged groups. Among lower status (less-educated) blacks and to a lesser extent among lower status women there seems to be an "equality of misery" view of the stratification order that results from overestimating the prevalence of poverty, perhaps due to a lack of much contact with relatively privileged groups.

College education also softens the strong tendency for Americans to blame the poor for their own poverty. This effect of education may be seen as part of the general social liberalism that is acquired at college. The belief that the poor are not personally responsible for their status logically follows from the knowledge that blacks and women disproportionately make up the poor and the perception that blacks and women have limited opportunity due to racial and sexual prejudice.

Even among the college educated, however, individual explanations for poverty prevail, and there is strong antiwelfare sentiment. In part antipoor and antiwelfare attitudes most certainly stem from the individualistic orientation that is communicated to people at all positions in society and reinforced by numerous sources. The American "success story" is retold often by politicians, in the popular media, in biographies of American cultural heroes presented in the teaching of history in schools, and so on (Lewis, 1978). In this respect, the American tendencies to revere our rich as individuals and blame our poor as individuals derive from the same source.

Basic Social–Psychological Processes

Our findings suggest that belief in the dominant ideology is the product of more than the efforts of elites to shape the socialization that takes place in schools and other institutions. Although elites historically (Moore, 1978) and currently encourage images of themselves as superior individuals, the role of basic social–psychological processes is likely more important. We have several reasons for believing this.

First, cross-national studies demonstrate the generality of many of the processes we have described. For example, individual explanations for poverty produce strongly negative attitudes toward welfare throughout the industrialized West (Coughlin, 1980; Lopreato & Hazelrigg, 1972). The evidence includes countries (e.g., Denmark, Italy) with a more pronounced collectivist orientation than the United States, though Americans' antiwelfare attitudes do seem to be relatively extreme. Nowak's (1981) research on the values, beliefs, and attitudes of the Polish people during the time of the demands for change made by the Solidarity movement provides another parallel to our results. The criticism of Polish society prevalent among Poles was not of the justice of socialism in the ideal but of the failure of the Polish government to live up to socialist ideals in reality. Similarly, doubts about the justice of economic inequality in fact do not lead Americans to question the necessity or benefits of economic inequality in the ideal but rather encourage them to support equal opportunity policy to ensure that the economic order works as it should ideally. The cross-national evidence demonstrates that if socialization is solely responsible for the patterns of beliefs and attitudes we observe, it must involve aspects of western culture in general, not some elements specific to the United States.

Second, our findings and the related research discussed in Chapter 2 demonstrate how several specific social–psychological processes directly or indirectly support beliefs in the dominant ideology. The core element of the dominant ideology, individualist explanations for achievement, appears to arise from several processes. People may explain their own accomplishments by their hard work and talents to increase self-esteem (ego-defensive attribution) and to create a sense that poverty afflicts only other, less deserving people (just-world beliefs). Indeed, one interpretation of the tendency of more educated people to find the poor less blameworthy than do the less educated is that they have less need to be ego-defensive. Because the less educated run a greater risk of becoming poor, they need to place more psychological distance between themselves and the poor by labeling the poor as inferior.

The fundamental attribution error, the tendency to see individuals as causes of their own outcomes in general, is likely to contribute to individualist explanations as well. The poor may have highly salient personal characteristics (alcoholism, family instability, a history of unemployment) that become targets for causal inferences as observers attempt to explain their poverty.[2]

Finally, the benefits of psychological control may be important, as Chapter 10 demonstrated. Believing that one causes one's own outcomes avoids the distressing implication that important life outcomes are uncontrollable and thus motivates beliefs in internal explanations in general. As we suggested in Chapter 5, preferences for equity over equality in the distribution of rewards may also be due to the desire for perceived control. Under equity but not equality, one can control one's outcomes by varying the amount of effort one expends.

These processes imply that the poor will generally be blamed for their own poverty. They also appear to lead to views that the wealthy,

---

[2]This attribution error, and perhaps an ego-defensive reaction as well, may account for the otherwise anomalous finding that blacks and whites, on average, equally attribute poverty to individualist factors. Because black Americans live close to the poor residentially, they may have more experience with poor people who have such salient personal problems and thus are affected by the tendency to overattach causal importance to salient objects or events. Because many black Americans also live close to the poor psychologically, they may view the poor as blameworthy out of ego-defensiveness.

as individuals, deserve their positions because they have earned them by their efforts and abilities; such views are quite widespread. However, there are elements of ambivalence in Americans' views of the wealthy, most evident in perceptions of the better-than-average opportunity possessed by the children of the rich (Chapter 3) and the perceived unfairness of average incomes for typical occupations of the wealthy (Chapter 5). These negative perceptions of the wealthy are yet another reason to question the view that Americans' beliefs about inequality arise simply from elite guided socialization.

Social–psychological processes also operate more indirectly to allow people to maintain beliefs in the dominant ideology despite potentially challenging experiences or beliefs. People simply do not display the overall drive toward cognitive consistency that early theories described. Such a drive would imply that potentially challenging beliefs would have to be dealt with or integrated in some way with dominant-ideology beliefs. Instead, people often ignore potential inconsistencies among beliefs, readily responding (for example) on one occasion that everybody has equal opportunity in America and on another that children of the poor actually do not have an equal chance to get a good education or a good job. The different cognitive structures (schemas) and frames of reference that are made salient by different questions are responsible for such seeming inconsistencies, as Chapter 2 outlined. Their consequence is that beliefs that potentially could challenge the dominant ideology, while available to shape some specific responses, often fail to have widespread impact on the perceiver's overall belief system: The dominant ideology retains its powerful and general influence on beliefs, attitudes, and behaviors.

PROSPECTS FOR EFFECTIVE POLICY

The Need for Sustained Commitment

At present the environment of policy addressing economic inequality is confused and somewhat chaotic. Claims that programs have failed or succeeded, that great progress has been made toward equal opportunity by race and sex or that there has been little progress, are made with equal conviction and authority. Such contradictory claims are possible because progress toward ameliorating some aspects of some problems has been made, presenting a situation where evidence may be cited in support of claims by people at either end of the political-ideology spectrum. How much progress has been made? How necessary is it that old policies and programs be continued or that new programs be formulated? Providing detailed answers is beyond the scope of this book, but recent research offering answers to these two questions (Collins, 1983; Farley, 1984; Ferber, 1982; Reskin, 1984) leads us to make the following summary points.

While there are clear indications of progress in certain areas, there are also indications that this progress is uneven, that in some respects it may be illusory, and that in recent years it has begun to erode. From 1960 to the mid-1970s the prevalence of poverty declined (Farley, 1984) and the educational, occupational, and economic status of black Americans relative to whites improved (Featherman & Hauser, 1978). Throughout the 1970s women moved toward parity with men in their level of educational attainment, and women made some gains toward achieving equal representation in certain traditionally male occupations (Beller, 1984).

However, in recent years the prevalence of poverty in general and especially among blacks has increased (U.S. Bureau of the Census, 1983). During the last 10 years the educational gains made by blacks have receded as blacks have lost ground relative to whites in college attendance and completion rates (Darling-Hammond, 1985). The current black middle class is disproportionately the product of expansion of government involvement in social welfare policy and does not reflect gains in white-collar jobs evenly across different sectors of the economy (Collins, 1983). These gains may be threatened by current or future reductions in government support of social welfare programs and policies. Despite gains in educational attainment and some reduction in the sex segregation of occupations there has been virtually no reduction in the wage gap between men and women in earnings (stable at the now somewhat infamous figure that women working full time year-around have earnings that average about 60 of men's).

The long histories of poverty, race, and sex discrimination alone seem to require a commitment to the effort to resolve the problems they represent of more than the approximately two decade history of current inequality-related policy. In the face of the deep embeddedness of these problems in the American social fabric, it is not surprising that the past two decades of inequality-related policy has produced only incomplete, tentative, and somewhat halting progress. The research summarized above indicates that commitment to social policy to alleviate inequality-related social problems should be maintained. Furthermore, this research points to new directions for policy to deal with problems that we are beginning to better understand precisely because of sometimes unsuccessful current and past practice (cf. Auletta, 1982).

Sources of Ambivalence

Throughout this book we have called attention to the ambivalence of American attitudes toward policy to ameliorate problems involving economic inequality. This ambivalence contributes to the instability of public support for current policy and to the controversy that, virtually without exception, surrounds new policy and programs to solve these problems. We conclude with some summary observations about the sources of this ambivalence and a discussion of certain issues involved in resolving it.

Public support for policy to ameliorate problems involving economic inequality essentially derives from two sources. One source is the persistence of marked economic differences among jobs, and by race and sex. The difference in average earnings between blue-collar and white-collar workers and the greater risk of unemployment and poorer chances for career mobility of blue-collar workers are enduring features of American society. There continue to exist large gaps in average socioeconomic status between blacks and whites and between male and female workers. The substantial differences among jobs in earnings and benefits encourage the lesser privileged to seek, in their own self-interest, programs such as unemployment insurance, government-guaranteed jobs, and minimum wage guarantees, to insure workers enough to keep them above the subjective poverty line—enough income to be able to "get along." The continuing demands of blacks and women for equal opportunity programs and policy need little comment.

The second source, social liberalism, is of more recent origin. A key feature of social liberalism, equal opportunity, is in a sense the "Achilles heel" of American stratification ideology (Myrdal, 1962). In response to the civil rights and women's movements, many Americans—and especially the college educated—currently believe that there is now or has been race and sex discrimination that limits opportunity. The simple recognition of race and sex discrimination disposes support for policy to assure equal opportunity, because the presence of unequal opportunity questions the fairness of economic inequality by way of the "logic of opportunity." If Americans become convinced, as a substantial minority have, that others among them lack equal opportunity, then the dominant ideology compels them to support, or at least not oppose, policy to rectify this problem. This aspect of social liberalism, then, has encouraged support for equal opportunity programs and related policy among people who lack direct self-interest for or against such policy.

The force that these two sources provide for support of liberal policy is counteracted by several other factors. One is simple economic self-interest among people in positions of relative economic privilege. However, as we have seen, among the public in general the impact of self-interest is the weakest of the factors we examined. In certain areas, racial affect has a stronger impact than apparent economic self-interest. When policies are identified as benefiting primarily blacks (obviously

for programs like affirmative action, but also welfare) they will be opposed by some whites because of racial animosity. Beliefs about how
the stratification order should work ideally, and does work in fact, have
consistently strong effects on attitudes toward all the policies we have
examined in this book. Most Americans, as our findings have shown,
believe that in principle economic inequality is necessary and desirable
and believe that in the main Americans *as individuals* deserve the income they get, even if viewed in terms of societal equity the jobs they
perform are over- or underrewarded. Thus the prevailing beliefs about
economic inequality dispose most Americans to a conservative view of
social policy.

In general, our research shows that Americans' beliefs about economic inequality restrict the possibilities for solutions to the problems
of poverty and inequality of opportunity. As seen in Chapters 7 and 8,
these beliefs encourage a nonstructural interpretation of these problems. They encourage either a dismissal of the problem by explaining
it in terms of shortcomings of the individuals involved or the view that
the problem is exceptional—that the current order works well except
in a particular case. In the former case opposition to any policy results.
In the latter case only policy that does not challenge the dominant
ideology is supported.

Prevalent beliefs about economic policy encourage the American
public to oppose even short-term income redistribution as a solution
to social problems. For example, while support is given to the poor
out of apparent concern for poor children (Cook, 1979), the amount
provided is generally enough to keep a poor family at a subsistence
level only. Concern for the disincentive to find employment stemming
from the perceived functional value of inequality underlies setting welfare payments at this level. But our findings suggest that the prevalent
tendency to blame the poor as individuals for their circumstances and
other sources of antipathy toward poor adults also serve to keep transfer
payments to the poor at levels that are just high enough to sustain the
poor in their present circumstances but do not provide poor families
with the means to help their children escape poverty.

In addition, the prevalent sense that Americans get what they deserve
as individuals encourages opposition to policies that question the fairness of existing allocation systems. We have seen some evidence indicating that Americans are increasingly critical of schools in this regard.
However, the American public does not have the same suspicion about
the fairness of industry employment and promotion practices. Beliefs
about opportunity for blacks and their attitudes toward equal opportunity policy show Americans' doubt about the need to monitor allocation processes. The majority of Americans seem to believe that all
that is needed to solve any recognized problem involving economic

disparities, such as poverty or race and sex differences in average earnings, is to change individuals to fit into the existing system.

Solutions

The ambivalence of the American public toward inequality-related social policy is certainly not the only contributor to its recent history of alternating advance and retreat. There are other reasons that Americans often appear to offer help with one hand and take it back with the other. Doing so can be the least costly way to look like one is acting to solve a problem without actually doing so. Piven and Cloward (1971), for example, argue that increases in federal support for welfare for the poor has come about in response to elites' desire to have such a cheap solution to race and poverty-related unrest. Inconsistent support for policy also has resulted from the turbulence of presidential politics. With each shift during the last three decades in the party in power we have seen substantial change in the kind of social policy supported and in the funds provided. Because of these many shifts in policy, the long-term stability that may be essential to ameliorate long-standing social problems has not been possible. Since change in political leadership is produced by many nonideological forces—the performance of the economy, foreign affairs, candidate personalities, and so on—some inconsistency in social policy is a by-product of unrelated political events that alternately have brought liberals and conservatives to power.

Because policy is multiply determined, we cannot estimate how much more consistent would be support for effective policy to ameliorate problems of poverty and inequality of opportunity if adherence to at least certain aspects of the dominant ideology changed apace with increasing social liberalism. But we little doubt that if certain elements of the way the public evaluates antipoverty and equal employment opportunity policy in the future remain as stable features, America will not move out of the unhappy equilibrium that currently characterizes this policy. If, for example, many Americans continue strongly to blame the poor for their poverty, then it is likely that Americans will continue to provide near subsistence support for the poor because conscience forbids letting children suffer, but antipathy toward the adult poor forbids doing more.

Public acceptance, of course, is not the only factor that determines the effectiveness of social policy. However, as recent experience involving the public evaluation of affirmative action policy demonstrates, the lack of public acceptance can severely hinder the prospects for success of a policy and reduce support for policy to ameliorate problems involving an aspect of economic inequality in general. For example, currently the public identification of equal opportunity programs with "quotas" raises doubt about the political future of equal opportunity programs for black Americans in general. Whether it is possible to have effective social policy that at present also would be publicly accepted is a question beyond the scope of this book. However, under the assumption that it is possible to do so, the results of this and other research underscore the need to consider public beliefs about how the stratification order should function in the ideal and how it does function in fact.

The American public as we have seen in Chapter 5 strongly adheres to the ideal of individual-level equity and believes that economic inequality is both necessary and beneficial. Policy that is perceived to promote economic equality as an end over these principles of distributive justice stands little chance of public acceptance at present. However, as we have also seen, majorities of Americans do support the principle that no one who works should have an income that falls below that needed to get along—that is, there is majority support for programs to establish a floor on the income distribution *as long as the principle of equity is maintained.* Our findings and those of other research (Cook, 1979) thus suggest that programs targeted to help the "working poor"— day care assistance for working women, subsidized transportation and medical care, and so on—are viable in public opinion. And, as we previously have underscored, programs to train people in the skills needed to compete for unequally rewarded positions also have public acceptance in principle.

Public acceptance of policy in principle, however, does not ensure public acceptance of policy in fact. As we have seen in Chapters 6, 7, and 8, several other factors, including beliefs about how the stratification order works in fact, shape the public's attitudes. The findings of this and other research imply that efforts to win public acceptance must overcome social naiveté—in the form of denial of structural barriers to opportunity for the poor and other groups—self-interest, and racially based and other forms of intergroup hostility.

Perhaps the easiest solution to the problem presented by certain dominant-ideology beliefs is to let time pass. Our results, however, do not hold out much optimism in this regard. In likelihood, liberalizing trends in race relations and sex-role attitudes will continue, if for no other reason than simple cohort replacement. Since current social problems involving economic inequality are also very much race- and sex-related problems, this liberalizing trend presents some hope for more favorable public opinion. As people who oppose policies strictly from traditional racial prejudice or sex-role traditionalism die and are replaced by generally more highly educated people, the impact of racism and sex-role traditionalism will likely diminish.

On the other hand, there is no apparent reason to suspect that adherence to dominant-ideology beliefs will much change if the American economy continues to function as it has in recent decades. As we have seen throughout our analyses the dominant ideology is quite resistant to challenge, even to that presented by the high levels of unemployment and inflation during the 1970s. Our results support Lane's (1962) assertion that the average person remains hopeful as long as he or she believes there is *some* opportunity for economic advancement. Unless economic conditions reach the point where most Americans believe that they have little or no hope of personal economic advancement—a condition, of course, that no one desires—the belief that individuals in America in general get the economic status they deserve is likely to persist. As long as industry presents employees job hierarchies to climb and as long as intergenerational upward mobility is prevalent, most Americans will continue to have experiences that reinforce their belief in the functional benefits of economic inequality.

The clash between liberal social beliefs and conservative economic ones is thus likely to be even sharper in the succeeding decades. With increasing social liberalism and stable adherence to the dominant ideology one might expect public support for compromise programs such as job training or educational grants to increase as well. But, findings in Chapters 7 and 8 suggest that with the passage of time Americans may increasingly believe that race- or sex-related problems no longer exist. As we have seen, many Americans seem to believe that with diminishing individual-level race prejudice or sexism, barriers to opportunity for these groups are also diminishing. The white American public, perhaps in part out of a desire to see the social world as a just place, appears eager to believe that race-related problems are part of the recent past only. As opportunity for better educated women improves, the public may likewise come to view sex-related barriers to opportunity as features of the past.

In both cases the public may come to define as "nonproblems" the more persistent, class-linked, or otherwise structurally based problems such as the poverty of the black underclass (Wilson, 1978) or that of female-headed households with children. The American public often does not look behind these problems to see how race or sex discrimination has produced over history problems that at present look like they are produced by something other than contemporarily practiced race or sex discrimination. The only schema for explaining lack of success (other than barriers erected by prejudiced or sexist individuals) that many Americans have available is lack of effort, ability, or some other character flaw of individuals. As blatant examples of race or sex discrimination become rarer, the attribution of race- or sex-related problems to individual failings of women and minorities may actually increase. Direct effort to change at least some aspects of dominant-ideology beliefs—for example, to encourage a less censorious view of the poor—seems required.

How might one proceed to change Americans' beliefs about economic inequality and, correspondingly, attitudes toward related policy? This question presents a complex issue that goes well beyond the scope of our research. The answer ultimately depends on understanding the root causes of these beliefs. It further involves the question of how much and which beliefs should be changed. Much research, and our findings in Chapter 10 as well, argues that the perception that one lives in an equitable and individually controllable society, that is, in a "just world," benefits people's psychological well-being. Moreover, at the least, beliefs that make up the dominant ideology may be seen as useful fictions, if not accurate descriptions of part of American reality. They encourage the effort to get ahead that in American history has contributed to economic growth and collective improvement in the standard of living. It does not serve the common good to abandon beliefs in the possibility of economic advancement. Neither does it serve us well, however, to allow these beliefs to block possible solutions to America's persisting dilemmas of poverty and inequality of opportunity.

APPENDIX
DATA SOURCES

Detailed information concerning sampling methods and other aspects of data collection for surveys other than the one we conducted are available from the following sources:

National Election Surveys: National Election Survey codebooks published by the Inter-University Consortium for Political and Social Research, Ann Arbor, Michigan.

General Social Survey: General Social Surveys, 1972–1983: Cumulative Data. Davis (1983).

Illinois Survey: Respondents to this representative telephone survey of the state of Illinois were selected by means of random digit dialing; see Form and Hanson (1985).

BELIEFS ABOUT SOCIAL STRATIFICATION SURVEY

Respondents to our survey were interviewed by telephone. Interviews averaged roughly 50 minutes in length. They were conducted by the staff of the Survey Research Laboratory at the University of Illinois at Urbana-Champaign.

A contacted person was considered eligible for the representative sample if he or she were 18 years old or older at the time of the survey, spoke English, and resided in the contiguous 48 states of the United States. Potential respondents were considered eligible for the black sample if they met the above criteria and indicated that they were black in response to a screener question. Potential respondents were considered eligible for inclusion in the affluent sample if they met the criteria for the representative survey and had a family income of $30,000 or more in 1979.

Respondent Selection

A two-stage random-digit-dialing design described by Waksberg (1978) was employed to select phone numbers for potential respondents for the general population (representative) sample. The sampling frame consisted of the AT&T Long Lines Division NPA–NXX Vertical and Horizontal Coordinates tape, that lists all working area-code-exchange combinations in current use. For the black and affluent samples a modification of this design developed by Blair and Czaja (1982) was used.

A total of 10 calls were attempted on each telephone number selected in order to complete an interview. A record of the disposition of each attempted call was kept.

Response Rate

In general, the "response rate" is defined by the ratio of the number of completed interviews to the total number of eligible sample units (Groves & Kahn, 1979). Determining the response rate is straightforward when face-to-face interviewing is used or when telephone numbers are selected from a list of private residences. However, determining the response rate in the case of random-digit dialing involves substantial ambiguity. This ambiguity results from various factors that can make it impossible to determine whether a selected number is that of an eligible respondent. The denominator of the response rate is thus unknown.

Table A.1 gives the distribution of the dispositions of attempted calls. Depending upon assumptions made about the eligibility of persons

TABLE A.1. Dispositions of Attempted Telephone Calls

	General population	Black	Affluent
Screened eligible			
Completed interview	72.7%	59.3	70.8
Refused interview	10.7	15.8	16.4
Noncontact	7.1	11.8	7.9
Unavailable	4.4	7.4	3.5
Partial interview	4.9	5.0	1.2
Other	.2	.7	.2
Number eligible	2074	678	428
Percentage of total attempts	45.6	14.7	13.5
Screened ineligible			
Number ineligible	1564	3344	2329
Percentage of total attempts	34.4	72.4	73.3
Eligibility undetermined			
Refused screener	60.7	47.6	52.6
Noncontact	23.2	34.6	30.2
Unavailable	15.4	16.5	13.6
Other	.1	.1	3.6
Number undetermined	908	599	420
Percentage of total attempts	20.0	13.0	13.2
Completed interviews/ eligible + undetermined	50.5	31.5	35.7

whose eligibility could not be determined, different estimates of the response rate will be obtained. If one excludes cases with undetermined eligibility, then the ratio of completed interviews to the total known eligible defines the response rate. Doing so yields estimated response rates of approximately 73% for the general population, 59% for the black sample, and 71% for the affluent sample. These may be taken as liberal estimates of the respective response rates. On the other hand, if one were to assume that all numbers in the eligibility-undetermined category for the general population sample represent eligible respondents, then a lower bound (conservative) estimate of the response rate in this case is approximately 50%. For the black and affluent samples, this assumption is implausible since high proportions of the eligibility-undetermined numbers are sure to be ineligible because they are not black or are not affluent.

Representativeness

Of more consequence than the "true" response rate is the issue of whether or not nonrespondents differ from respondents in ways that cause this survey to yield substantially biased estimates of the beliefs, attitudes, or other characteristics of the American public. To provide a sense of the potential for such bias we compare here (Table A.2) the distributions for selected sociodemographic and political variables from our Beliefs about Social Stratification survey (BSS) and from two other sources of data for these variables for the same year, the 1980 General Social Survey (GSS), another high-quality sample survey, and the 1980 U.S. Census.

The structure of the 1980 GSS parallels that of our general population survey in the length of interview, population coverage, and sample size. The 1980 GSS differs from our survey in that it involves personal (face-to-face) interviewing rather than telephone interviewing. As generally holds in the comparison of response rates for in-person and telephone interviewing (Groves & Kahn, 1979), the response rate for the 1980 GSS (76% [Davis, 1983]) is higher than even the liberal estimate of the response rate for the BSS study. Thus this comparison gives some indication of the potential bias added by the lower response rate that results from telephone surveying. Census data, of course, are not without potential for nonresponse bias. However, for the reason of their scope of coverage alone, one might view them as the most reliable source of information on sociodemographic variables available.

The comparisons arrayed in Table A.2 lead us to feel confident that the estimates of American's beliefs and attitudes based on the BSS survey are as representative of the "true" beliefs and attitudes held by the American public as may be obtained by state-of-the-art methods

TABLE A.2. Distributions of Selected Sociodemographic and Political
          Characteristics

Characteristic	BSS (1980)	GSS (1980)	1980 Census
Region			
Northeast	22.5	19.9	22.3
North central	28.6	27.8	26.5
South	29.1	33.9	32.5
West	19.8	18.4	18.7
Median education	12.2	12.0	12.5
(persons 25 years +)			
Median family income	$19,996	—	$19,648
Mean age (persons 18+)	41.8	45.0	43.5
Occupation			
Professional, technical	19.2	21.0	17.0
Managers, sales	18.8	19.9	17.0
Clerical	21.3	16.0	18.1
Crafts	12.5	15.0	13.2
Operatives	10.2	10.5	11.2
Laborers	4.2	6.1	8.4
Farm	1.8	2.2	2.8
Service	11.9	9.3	12.1
Sex			
Female	55.2	56.3	52.3
Race			
White	87.3	89.8	87.7
Black	9.0	9.5	10.5
Other	3.7	.7	1.8
Party identification			
Democrat	37.9	38.6	—
Independent	37.5	38.6	—
Republican	24.6	22.8	—
Mean liberalism–conservatism[a]	4.1	4.1	—

[a]Self-rated on a scale from "1" (extremely liberal) to "7" (extremely conservative).

for telephone surveying. The differences among the different estimated distributions for the same variables are not large enough to warrant considering the possibility that they are the product of something other than sampling or measurement error. There is no reason to believe that the BSS study data collection procedures have produced substantially biased results by systematically excluding any particular sociodemographic group or any group along the political spectrum.

Finally, we present (Table A.3) distributions from the black and affluent samples for the same sociodemographic and political characteristics as in Table A.2. With two exceptions, the distributions of these variables among blacks matches that obtained from census data. Respondents in our black sample have a higher average family income than that estimated from 1980 census data ($12,358), and females are

TABLE A.3. Distributions of Selected Sociodemographic and Political Characteristics from the Beliefs about Social Stratification Survey for the Black and Affluent Samples

Characteristic	Black	Affluent
Region		
Northeast	26.1	28.7
North central	20.1	28.1
South	41.5	26.1
West	12.2	17.2
Median education	11.9	14.8
Median family income	$15,010	$39,921
Mean age (persons 18+)	39.6	40.5
Occupation		
Professional, technical	16.1	31.5
Managers, sales	9.9	32.5
Clerical	16.7	15.8
Crafts	8.1	8.9
Operatives	15.9	2.7
Laborers	7.0	.7
Farm	1.3	0.0
Service	25.0	7.9
Sex		
Female	62.9	49.8
Race		
White	—	94.7
Black	100.0	3.3
Other	—	2.0
Party identification		
Democrat	69.1	28.6
Independent	24.2	38.2
Republican	6.7	33.2
Mean liberalism–conservatism[a]	2.2	4.4

[a] Self-rated on a scale from "1" (extremely liberal) to "7" (extremely conservative).

overrepresented relative to the proportion of the black population they comprise (54%). Both of these deviations from representativeness may stem from the known tendency of randomly selected surveys to underrepresent low-income blacks, in general, and low-income black males, in particular.

BIBLIOGRAPHY

Abelson, R. P., Aronson, E., McGuire, W. J., Newcomb, T. M., Rosenberg, M. J., and Tannenbaum, P. H. (Eds.). (1968). *Theories of cognitive consistency: A sourcebook.* Chicago: Rand McNally.

Abelson, R. P., Kinder, D. R., Peters, M. D., and Fiske, S. T. (1982). Affective and semantic components in political person perception. *Journal of Personality and Social Psychology,* 42, 619–630.

Abercrombie, N., Hill, S., and Turner, B. S. (1980). *The dominant ideology thesis.* London: Allen & Unwin.

Adorno, T. W., Frenkel-Brunswik, E., Levinson, D. J., and Sanford, N. (1950). *The authoritarian personality.* New York: Harper.

Ajzen, I., and Fishbein, M. (1977). Attitude-behavior relations: A theoretical analysis and review of empirical research. *Psychological Bulletin,* 84, 888–918.

Allston, J. P., and Dean, K. I. (1972). Socioeconomic factors associated with attitudes toward welfare recipients and the causes of poverty. *Social Service Review,* 46, 13–23.

Alves, W. M., and Rossi, P. H. (1978). Who should get what? Fairness judgements of the distribution of earnings. *American Journal of Sociology,* 84, 541–564.

American National Election Survey Codebook (1972). Ann Arbor, Mich.: Inter-University Consortium for Political and Social Research.

American National Election Survey Codebook (1976). Ann Arbor, Mich.: Inter-University Consortium for Political and Social Research.

Anderson, J. R. (1983). *The architecture of cognition.* Cambridge, Mass.: Harvard University Press.

Apostle, R. A., Glock, C. Y., Piazza, T., and Suelzle, M. (1983). *The anatomy of racial attitudes.* Berkeley, Calif.: University of California Press.

Asch, S. E. (1951). Effects of group pressure upon the modification and distortion of judgments. In H. Guetzkow (Ed.), *Groups, leadership, and men.* Pittsburgh: Carnegie Press.

Auletta, K. (1982). *The underclass.* New York: Random House.

Beller, A. H. (1984). Occupational segregation by sex: Prospects for the 1980's. In B. F. Reskin (Ed.), *Sex segregation in the workplace: Trends, explanations, remedies.* Washington, D.C.: National Academy Press.

Benokraitis, N. V., and Feagin, J. R. (1978). *Affirmative action and equal opportunity: Action, inaction, reaction.* Boulder: Western Press.

Berg, I. (1970). *Education and jobs.* New York: Praeger.

Binzen, P. (1970). *Whitetown USA.* New York: Vintage Books.

Bishop, G. F., Oldendick, R. W., and Tuchfarber, A. J. (1982). Political information processing: Question order and context effects. *Political Behavior,* 4, 177–200.

Blair, J., and Czaja, R. (1982). Locating a special population using random digit dialing. *Public Opinion Quarterly,* 46, 585–590.

Blumberg, P. (1980). *Inequality in an age of decline.* Oxford University Press.
Blumberg, P., and Murtha, J. M. (1977). College graduates and the American dream. *Dissent,* 24, 45–53.
Bobo, L. (1983). Whites' opposition to busing: Symbolic racism or realistic group conflict? *Journal of Personality and Social Psychology,* 45, 1196–1210.
Bogardus, E. S. (1925). Measuring social distances. *Journal of Applied Sociology,* 9, 299–308.
Bowles, S., and Gintis, H. (1976). *Schooling in capitalist America.* New York: Basic Books.
Bradburn, N. (1969). *The structure of psychological well-being.* Chicago: Aldine.
Brewer, W. F., and Nakamura, G. V. (1984). The nature and functions of schemas. In R. S. Wyer and T. K. Srull (Eds.), *Handbook of social cognition* (vol. 1). Hillsdale, N.J.: Erlbaum.
Brickman, P., Folger, R., Goode, E., and Schul, Y. (1981). Microjustice and macrojustice. In M. J. Lerner & S. C. Lerner (Eds.), *The justice motive in social behavior,* pp. 173–202. New York: Plenum.
Brint, S. (1984). "New class" and cumulative trend explanations of the liberal political attitudes of professionals. *American Journal of Sociology,* 90, 30–71.
Burris, V. (1983). The social and political consequences of overeducation. *American Sociological Review,* 48, 454–467.
Burstein, P. (1979). Public opinion, demonstrations, and the passage of anti-discrimination legislation. *Public Opinion Quarterly,* 79, 157–172.
Campbell, A., Converse, P. E., and Rodgers, W. L. (1976). *The quality of American life.* New York: Russell Sage.
Centers, R. (1949). *The psychology of social classes.* Princeton, N.J.: Princeton University Press.
Chaiken, S. (1980). Heuristic versus systematic information processing and the use of source versus message cues in persuasion. *Journal of Personality and Social Psychology,* 39, 752–766.
Cheal, O. J. (1979). Hegemony, ideology and contradictory consciousness. *Sociological Quarterly,* 20, 109–117.
Cherlin, A., and Walters, P. B. (1981). Trends in United States men's and women's sex-role attitudes: 1972 to 1978. *American Sociological Review,* 46, 453–460.
Chesler, M. A. (1976). Contemporary sociological theories of racism. In P. A. Katz (Ed.), *Towards the elimination of racism.* New York: Pergamon.
Clark, M. S., and Fiske, S. T. (1982). *Affect and cognition.* Hillsdale, N.J.: Erlbaum.
Cohen, J. (1969). *Statistical power analysis for the behavioral sciences.* New York: Academic Press.
Collins, R. (1979). *The credential society.* New York: Academic Press.
Collins, S. M. (1983). The making of the black middle class. *Social Problems,* 30, 369–382.
Condran, J. G. (1979). Changes in white attitudes towards blacks: 1963–1977. *Public Opinion Quarterly,* 43, 463–476.
Converse, P. E., Dotson, J. D., Hoag, W. J., and McGee, W. H. (1980). *American social attitudes data sourcebook, 1947–1978.* Cambridge, Mass.: Harvard University Press.
Cook, F. L. (1979). *Who should be helped?* Beverly Hills, Calif.: Sage.
Coughlin, R. M. (1980). *Ideology, public opinion, and welfare policy.* Berkeley: Institute of International Studies, University of California.
Crosby, F. (1982). *Relative deprivation and working women.* New York: Oxford.
Darling-Hammond, L. (1985) *Equality and excellence: The educational status of black Americans.* Santa Monica, Calif.: RAND.

Davis, J. A. (1980). *General social surveys, 1972–1980: Cumulative data.* New Haven, Conn.: Roper Public Opinion Research Center.

Davis, J. A. (1983). *General social surveys, 1972–1983: Cumulative data.* New Haven, Conn.: Roper Public Opinion Research Center.

Davis, J. A. (1984). *General social surveys, 1972–1984: Cumulative data.* New Haven, Conn.: Roper Public Opinion Research Center.

Deutsch, M. (1975). Equity, equality, and need: What determines which value will be used as the basis of distributive justice? *Journal of Social Issues,* 31(2), 137–149.

Domhoff, (1978). *The powers that be.* New York: Vintage.

Downs, A. (1957). *An economic theory of democracy.* New York: Harper.

Duncan, O. D. (1969). Toward social reporting: Next steps. *Social Science Frontiers 2.* New York: Academic Press.

Durkheim, E. (1951). *Suicide.* New York: Free Press.

Evans-Pritchard, E. E. (1937). *Witchcraft, oracles, and magic among the Azande.* New York: Clarendon.

Farley, R. (1984). *Blacks and whites.* Cambridge, Mass.: Harvard University Press.

Fazio R. H., and Zanna, M. P. (1978). On the predictive validity of attitudes: The roles of direct experience and confidence. *Journal of Personality,* 46, 228–243.

Feagin, J. R. (1975). *Subordinating the poor.* Englewood Cliffs, N.J.: Prentice-Hall.

Feather, N. T. (1974). Explanations of poverty in Australian and American samples: The person, society, or fate? *Australian Journal of Psychology,* 26, 199–216.

Featherman, D. L., and Hauser, R. M. (1978). *Opportunity and change.* New York: Academic Press.

Ferber, M. A. (1982). Women and work: Issues of the 1980's. *Signs,* 8, 273–295.

Ferree, M. M. (1974). A woman for president? Changing responses: 1958–1972. *Public Opinion Quarterly,* 34, 275–290.

Fiorina, M. P. (1981). *Retrospective voting in American national elections.* New Haven, Conn.: Yale University Press.

Fishbein, M., and Ajzen, I. (1975). *Belief, attitude, intention and behavior.* Reading, Mass.: Addison-Wesley.

Fitzgerald, F. (1979). *American revised.* Boston: Little, Brown.

Folkman, S. (1984). Personal control and stress and coping processes: A theoretical analysis. *Journal of Personality and Social Psychology,* 46, 839–852.

Form, W. H., and Hanson, C. (1985). The consistency of stratal beliefs. In R. V. Robinson (Ed.), *Research in social stratification and mobility.* Greenwich, Conn.: JAI.

Free, L. A., and Cantril, H. (1968). *The political beliefs of Americans.* New York: Simon & Schuster.

Freeman, R. B. (1976). *The overeducated American.* New York: Academic Press.

Furnham, A. (1982). Explanations for unemployment in Britain. *European Journal of Social Psychology,* 12, 335–352.

Gallup Report. (1985). Poverty seen as worse than official estimates. Report No. 234 (March).

Giddens, A. (1973). *The class structure of the advanced societies.* New York: Harper & Row.

Gilder, G. (1981). *Wealth and poverty.* New York: Basic Books.

Glazer, N. (1975). *Affirmative discrimination.* New York: Basic Books.

Glenn, N. D. (1977). *Cohort analysis.* Beverly Hills, Calif.: Sage.

Gramsci, A. (1971). *Selections from the prison notebooks.* (Q. Heave and G. Nowell Smith, Eds.). London: Lawrence and Wishart.

Greeley, A. (1972). Political attitudes among American white ethnics. *Public Opinion Quarterly*, 34, 43–52.

Greenwald, A. G. (1980). The totalitarian ego: Fabrication and revision of personal history. *American Psychologist*, 35, 603–618.

Groves, R. M., and Kahn, R. L. (1979). *Surveys by telephone*. New York: Academic Press.

Gurin, P., Miller, A. H., and Gurin, G. (1980). Stratum identification and consciousness. *Social Psychology Quarterly*, 43, 30–47.

Hamilton, D. A. (1981). *Cognitive processes in stereotyping and intergroup behavior*. Hillsdale, N.J.: Erlbaum.

Hamilton, R. F. (1972). *Class and politics in the United States*. New York: Wiley.

Hastie, R. (1984). Causes and effects of causal attribution. *Journal of Personality and Social Psychology*, 46, 44–56.

Heclo, H. (1984). *Poverty and policy: Retrospect and prospects*. Institute for Research on Poverty Conference Paper Series, Madison, Wisconsin.

Heider, F. (1958). *The psychology of interpersonal relations*. New York: Wiley.

Hochschild, J. L. (1981). *What's fair?*. Cambridge, Mass.: Harvard University Press.

Huber, J., and Form, W. H. (1973). *Income and ideology*. New York: Free Press.

Huber, J., Rexroat, C., and Spitze, G. (1978). A crucible of opinion on women's status: ERA in Illinois. *Social Forces*, 57, 549–565.

Inglehart, R. (1977). *The silent revolution*. Princeton, N.J.: Princeton University Press.

Inglehart, R. (1981). Post-materialism in an environment of insecurity. *American Political Science Review*, 75, 880–900.

Iyengar, S., Kinder, D. R., Peters, M. D., and Krosnick, J. A. (1984). The evening news and presidential evaluations. *Journal of Personality and Social Psychology*, 46, 778–787.

Jackman, M. R., and Jackman, R. W. (1983). *Class awareness in the United States*. Berkeley, Calif.: University of California Press.

Jackman, M. R., and Muha, M. J. (1984). Education and intergroup attitudes: Moral enlightenment, superficial democratic commitment, or ideological refinement? *American Sociological Review*, 49, 751–769.

Jasso, G., and Rossi, P. H. (1977). Distributive justice and earned income. *American Sociological Review*, 42, 639–651.

Jencks, C. (1972). *Inequality*. New York: Basic Books.

Jencks, C. (1979). *Who gets ahead*. New York: Basic Books.

Johnson-Laird, P. N. (1983). *Mental models*. Cambridge, Mass.: Harvard University Press.

Jones, E. E., and Harris, V. A. (1967). The attribution of attitudes. *Journal of Experimental Social Psychology*, 3, 1–24.

Jones, E. E., and Nisbett, R. E. (1972). The actor and the observer: Divergent perceptions of the causes of behavior. In E. E. Jones, D. Kanouse, H. H. Kelley, R. E. Nisbett, S. Valins, and B. Weiner (Eds.), *Attribution: Perceiving the causes of behavior*. Morristown, N.J.: General Learning Press.

Katz, D. (1960). The functional approach to the study of attitudes. *Public Opinion Quarterly*, 24, 163–204.

Kelley, H. H. (1967). Attribution theory in social psychology. In D. Levine (Ed.), *Nebraska symposium on motivation*. Lincoln, Neb.: University of Nebraska Press.

Kelley, H. H., and Michela, J. (1980). Attribution theory and research. *Annual Review of Psychology*, 31, 457–501.

Kelley, J. (1974). The politics of school busing. *Public Opinion Quarterly*, 38, 23–29.

Kelman, H. (1974). Attitudes are alive and well and gainfully employed in the sphere of action. *American Psychologist*, 29, 310–324.

Kinder, D. (1981). Presidents, prosperity, and public opinion. *Public Opinion Quarterly*, 45, 1–21.

Kinder, D., and Kiewiet, D. R. (1979). Economic discontent and political behavior. *American Journal of Political Science*, 23, 495–527.

Kinder, D. R, and Sears, D. O. (1981). Prejudice and politics: Symbolic racism vs. racial threats to the good life. *Journal of Personality and Social Psychology*, 40, 414–431.

Kluegel, J. R. (1985). The bases of contemporary affirmative action attitudes: "If there isn't a problem you don't need a solution." *American Behavioral Scientist*, 28, 761–784.

Kluegel, J. R., and Smith, E. R. (1981). Stratification beliefs. *Annual Review of Sociology*, 7, 29–56.

Kluegel, J. R., and Smith, E. R. (1982). Whites' beliefs about blacks' opportunity. *American Sociological Review*, 47, 518–532.

Kluegel, J. R., and Smith, E. R. (1983). Affirmative action attitudes: Effects of self-interest, racial affect, and stratification beliefs on whites' views. *Social Forces*, 61, 797–824.

Kohn, M. L., and Schooler, C. (1983). *Work and personality*. Norwood, N.J.: Ablex.

Kornhauser, W. (1939). An analysis of "class" structure of contemporary American society—psychological bases of class divisions. In G. Hartmann & T. Newcomb (Eds.), *Industrial conflict*. New York: McGraw-Hill.

Kriesberg, L. (1979). *Social inequality*. Englewood Cliffs, N.J.: Prentice-Hall.

Kuklinski, J. H., and Parent, W. (1981). Race and big government: Contamination in measuring racial attitudes. *Political Methodology*, 7, 131–159.

Ladd, E. C., Jr. (1978). The new lines are drawn: Class and ideology in America. *Public Opinion*, 1, 48–53.

Lane, R. E. (1962). *Political ideology*. New York: Free Press.

Langer, E. J. (1983). *The psychology of control*. Beverly Hills, Calif.: Sage.

Langer, E. J., and Rodin, J. (1976). The effects of enhanced personal responsibility for the aged. *Journal of Personality and Social Psychology*, 34, 191–198.

Lau, R. P., Brown, T. A., and Sears, D. O. (1978). Self-interest and civilians' attitudes towards the Vietnam war. *Public Opinion Quarterly*, 42, 464–483.

Lau, R. P., and Sears, D. O. (1981). Cognitive links between economic grievances and political responses. *Political Behavior*, 3, 279–302.

Leahy, R. L. (Ed.). (1983). *The child's construction of social inequality*. New York: Academic Press.

Lefcourt, H. M. (1976). *Locus of control*. Hillsdale, N.J.: Erlbaum.

Lerner, M. J., and Miller, D. T. (1978). Just world research and the attribution process: Looking back and ahead. *Psychological Bulletin*, 85, 1030–1051.

Levin, M. (1984). Comparable worth: The feminist road to socialism. *Commentary*, 78, 13–19.

Lewis, M. (1978). *The culture of inequality*. Amherst, Mass.: University of Massachusetts Press.

Lipset, S. M. (1960). *Political man*. New York: Anchor.

Lipset, S. M. (1963). *The first new nation: The United States in historical and comparative perspective*. New York: Basic Books.

Lipset, S. M. (1979). The new class and the professoriate. In B. Bruce-Biggs (Ed.), *The new class?* New Brunswick, N.J.: Transaction Books.

Lipset, S. M., and Schneider, W. (1978). The Bakke case: How would it be decided at the bar of public opinion? *Public Opinion, 1,* 38–44.

Lopreato, J., and Hazelrigg, L. W. (1972). *Class, conflict, and mobility.* San Francisco: Chandler.

McArthur, L. Z. (1981). What grabs you? The role of attention in impression formation and causal attribution. In E. T. Higgins, C. P. Herman, and M. P. Zanna (Eds.), *Social cognition: The Ontario symposium* (vol. 1). Hillsdale, N.J.: Erlbaum.

McConahay, J. B., and Hough, J. C., Jr. (1976). Symbolic racism. *Journal of Social Issues, 32,* 23–45.

McConahay, J. B., Hardee, B. B., and Bates, V. (1981). Has racism declined in America? *Journal of Conflict Resolution, 25,* 563–579.

Maier, S. F., and Seligman, M. E. P. (1976). Learned helplessness: Theory and evidence. *Journal of Experimental Psychology: General, 105,* 3–46.

Mann, M. (1970). The social cohesion of liberal democracy. *American Sociological Review, 5,* 423–439.

Mann, M. (1973). *Consciousness and action among the western working class.* London: Macmillan.

Markus, G. B. (1982). Political attitudes during an election year: A report on the 1980 NES panel study. *American Political Science Review, 76,* 538–560.

Marx, K. *German ideology* (originally published 1845). Excerpted in *Karl Marx,* T. B. Bottomore (Trans.). London: C. A. Watts, 1956.

Mason, K. O., and Bumpass, L. L. (1975). U.S. women's sex-role ideology, 1970. *American Journal of Sociology, 80,* 1212–1219.

Mason, K. O., Czaja, J. L., and Arber, S. (1976). Change in U. S. women's sex-role attitudes, 1964–1974. *American Sociological Review, 41,* 573–596.

Merton, R. K. (1957). *Social theory and social structure.* New York: Free Press.

Miller, D. T., and Ross, M. (1975). Self-serving biases in the attribution of causality: Fact or fiction? *Psychological Bulletin, 82,* 213–225.

Miller, F. D., Smith, E. R., and Uleman, J. (1981). Measurement and interpretation of situational and dispositional attribution. *Journal of Experimental Social Psychology, 17,* 80–95.

Miller, W. E., Miller, A. H., and Schneider, E. J. (1980). *American National Election Study data sourcebook, 1952–1978.* Cambridge, Mass.: Harvard University Press.

Mills, C. W. (1959). *The sociological imagination.* New York: Oxford.

Mirowski, J., and Ross, C. E. (1984). Mexican culture and its emotional contradictions. *Journal of Health and Social Behavior, 25,* 2–13.

Monroe, A. D. (1983). American party platforms and public opinion. *American Journal of Political Science, 27,* 27–42.

Moore, B., Jr. (1978). *Injustice: The social bases of obedience and revolt.* White Plains, N.Y.: M. E. Sharpe.

Myrdal, G. (1962). *An American dilemma.* New York: Harper and Row.

Nathan, N. P. (1983). The Reagan presidency in domestic affairs. In F. I. Greenstein (Ed.), *The Reagan presidency.* Baltimore: Johns Hopkins University Press.

National Election Survey (1972). Inter-University Consortium for Political and Social Research. Ann Arbor, Mich.: Institute for Social Research.

National Election Survey (1982). Inter-University Consortium for Political and Social Research. Ann Arbor, Mich.: Institute for Social Research.

Neustadt, R. E. (1960). *Presidential power: The politics of leadership.* New York: Wiley.

Newcomb, T. M. (1963). Resistance and regression of changed attitudes: Long range studies. *Journal of Social Issues,* 19(4), 3–14.

Nilson, L. B. (1981). Reconsidering ideological lines: Beliefs about poverty in America. *Sociological Quarterly, 22*, 531–548.

Nisbett, R. E., and Ross, L. (1980). *Human inference: Strategies and shortcomings of social judgment.* Englewood Cliffs, N.J.: Prentice-Hall.

Nowak, S. (1981). Values and attitudes of the Polish people. *Scientific American, 245*, 45–53.

Nunnally, J. C. (1967). *Psychometric theory.* New York: McGraw-Hill.

Page, B. I. (1978). *Choices and echoes in presidential elections.* Chicago: University of Chicago Press.

Page, B. I., and Shapiro, R. Y. (1982). Changes in Americans' policy preferences, 1935–1979. *Public Opinion Quarterly, 46*, 24–42.

Parkin, F. (1971). *Class, inequality and political order.* New York: Praeger.

Pennebaker, J. W., Burnam, M. A., Shaeffer, M. A., and Harper, D. C. (1977). Lack of control as a determinant of perceived physical symptoms. *Journal of Personality and Social Psychology, 35*, 167–174.

Pettigrew, T. F. (1979). The ultimate attribution error: Extending Allport's cognitive analysis of prejudice. *Personality and Social Psychology Bulletin, 5*, 461–476.

Pettigrew, T. F. (1981). Race and class in the 1980's: An interactive view. *Daedalus, 110*, 233–256.

Pettigrew, T. F. (1985). New black–white patterns: How to best conceptualize them? *Annual Review of Sociology, 11*, 329–346.

Piven, F. F., and Cloward, R. A. (1971). *Regulating the poor.* New York: Random House.

Pollard, P. (1982). Human reasoning: Some possible effects of availability. *Cognition, 12*, 65–96.

Rainwater, L. (1974). *What money buys.* New York: Basic Books.

Ransford, H. E. (1972). Blue collar anger: Reactions to student and Black protest. *American Sociological Review, 37*, 333–346.

Reskin, B. F. (1984). Sex segregation in the workplace. In *Gender at work: Perspectives on occupational segregation and comparable worth.* Women's Research and Education Institute of the Congressional Caucus for Women's Issues.

Robinson, R. V., and Bell, W. (1978). Equality, success and social justice in England and United States. *American Sociological Review, 43*, 125–143.

Rodin, J., and Langer, E. J. (1977). Long-term effects of a control-relevant intervention with the institutionalized aged. *Journal of Personality and Social Psychology, 35*, 897–902.

Rosenberg, M. J. (1960). An analysis of affective–cognitive consistency. In C. I. Hovland and M. J. Rosenberg (Eds.), *Attitude organization and change.* New Haven, Conn.: Yale University Press.

Ross, L. (1977). The intuitive psychologist and his shortcomings: Distortions in the attribution process. In L. Berkowitz (Ed.), *Advances in experimental social psychology* (vol. 10). New York: Academic Press.

Rule, S. (1983). Report on blacks' opinions plays down class divisions. *The New York Times,* August 2, p. 7.

Rumberger, R. (1981). *Overeducation in the U. S. labor market.* New York: Praeger.

Runciman, W. (1966). *Relative deprivation and social justice.* Berkeley: University of California Press.

Russell, D. (1980). Causal attributions and emotional experience: Towards a cognitive model of emotion in achievement settings. Presented at the American Psychological Association convention, Montreal, Canada, September 2.

Ryan, W. (1971). *Blaming the victim*. New York: Vintage.

Sampson, E. E. (1977). Psychology and the American ideal. *Journal of Personality and Social Psychology, 35*, 767–782.

Schiltz, M. E. (1970). Public attitudes toward social security 1935–1965. Washington, D.C.: U.S. Government Printing Office.

Schuman, H. (1975). Free will and determinism in public beliefs about race. In N. R. Yetman and C. H. Steele (Eds.), *Majority and minority: The dynamics of racial and ethnic relations*. Boston: Allyn & Bacon.

Schuman, H., and Presser, S. (1981). *Questions and answers in attitude surveys*. New York: Academic Press.

Sears, D. O. (1975). Political socialization. In F. I. Greenstein & N. W. Polsby (Eds.), *Handbook of political science, Vol. 2: Micropolitical theory*. Reading, Mass.: Addison-Wesley.

Sears, D. O., and Kinder, D. R. (1985). Whites' opposition to busing: On conceptualizing and operationalizing group conflict. *Journal of Personality and Social Psychology, 48*, 1141–1147.

Sears, D. O., & McConahay, J. B. (1973). *The politics of violence: The new urban blacks and the Watts riot*. Boston, Mass.: Houghton-Mifflin.

Sears, D. O., Huddy, L., and Schaffer, L. G. (1986). Schemas and symbolic politics: The cases of racial and gender equality. In R. Lau and D. O. Sears (Eds.), *Political cognition*. Hillsdale, N.J.: Erlbaum.

Seligman, M. E. P. (1975). *Helplessness: On depression, development, and death*. San Francisco: Freeman.

Sennett, R., and Cobb, J. (1972). *The hidden injuries of class*. New York: Vintage.

Sherman, S. J., and Corty, E. (1984). Cognitive heuristics. In R. S. Wyer and T. K. Srull (Eds.), *Handbook of social cognition* (vol. 1). Hillsdale, N.J.: Erlbaum.

Simmons, R. G., and Rosenberg, M. (1971). Functions of children's perception of the stratification system. *American Sociological Review, 36*, 235–249.

Sivacek, J., and Crano, W. D. (1982). Vested interest as a moderator of attitude–behavior consistency. *Journal of Personality and Social Psychology, 43*, 210–221.

Skinner, B. F. (1948). "Superstition" in the pigeon. *Journal of Experimental Psychology, 38*, 392–413.

Smith, A. W., and Moore, E. G. J. (1981). Continuing trends in white attitudes toward school desegregation, 1954–1980. Paper presented at the annual meetings of the American Sociological Association, Toronto, August.

Smith, E. R. (1984). Model of social inference processes. *Psychological Review, 91*, 392–413.

Smith, E. R., and Kluegel, J. R. (1982). Cognitive and social bases of emotional experience: Outcome, attribution, and affect. *Journal of Personality and Social Psychology, 43*, 1129–1141.

Smith, E. R., and Kluegel, J. R. (1984). Beliefs and attitudes about women's opportunity: Comparisons with beliefs about blacks and a general perspective. *Social Psychology Quarterly, 46*, 81–94.

Snyder, M. L., Stephan, W. G., and Rosenfield, D. (1978). Attributional egotism. In J. H. Harvey, W. Ickes, and W. F. Kidd (Eds.), *New directions in attributional research* (vol. 2). Hillsdale, N.J.: Erlbaum.

Tajfel, H. (1982). Social psychology of intergroup relations. *Annual Review of Psychology, 33*, 1–39.

Taylor, D. G., Sheatsley, P. B., and Greeley, A. M. (1978). Attitudes toward racial integration. *Scientific American, 238*, 42–49.

Taylor, S. E. (1981). The interface of cognitive and social psychology. In J. H. Harvey (Ed.), *Cognition, social behavior, and the environment.* Hillsdale, N.J.: Erlbaum.

Taylor, S. E., and Fiske, S. T. (1978). Salience, attention, and attribution: Top of the head phenomena. In L. Berkowitz (Ed.), *Advances in experimental social psychology* (vol. 11). New York: Academic Press.

Taylor, S. E., and Koivumaki, J. (1976). The perception of self and others: Acquaintanceship, affect, and actor–observer differences. *Journal of Personality and Social Psychology, 33,* 403–408.

Taylor, S. E., Fiske, S. T., Etcoff, N. L., and Ruderman, A. J. (1978). Categorical and contextual bases of person memory and stereotyping. *Journal of Personality and Social Psychology, 36,* 778–793.

Thornton, A., and Freedman, D. S. (1979). Changes in the sex role attitudes of women, 1962–1977. *American Sociological Review, 44,* 831–842.

Thurow, L. (1980). *The zero-sum society.* New York: Basic Books.

Triandis, H. C. (1980). Social psychology. *Handbook of cross-cultural psychology* (vol. 5). Boston: Allyn & Bacon.

Tufte, E. R. (1978). *Political control of the economy.* Princeton, N.J.: Princeton University Press.

U. S. Bureau of the Census. (1980). *Statistical abstract of the United States.* Washington, D.C.: U.S. Government Printing Office.

U. S. Bureau of the Census (1981). *Statistical abstract of the United States.* Washington, D.C.: U.S. Government Printing Office.

U. S. Bureau of the Census (1983). *Statistical abstract of the United States.* Washington, D.C.: U.S. Government Printing Office.

Vanneman, R. D. (1980). U.S. and British perceptions of class. *American Journal of Sociology, 85,* 769–790.

Vanneman, R. D., and Pettigrew, T. F. (1972). Race and relative deprivation in the urban United States. *Race, 13,* 461–486.

Verba, S., and Oren, G. R. (1984). *Equality in America.* Cambridge, Mass.: Harvard University Press.

Waksberg, J. (1978). Sampling methods for random digit dialing. *Journal of the American Statistical Association, 73,* 40–46.

Walster, E., Walster, G. W., and Berscheid, E. (1978). *Equity: Theory and research.* Boston: Allyn & Bacon.

Weber, M. (1959). *The protestant ethic and the spirit of capitalism.* New York: Scribners.

Weidner, G., and Matthews, K. A. (1978). Reported physical symptoms elicited by unpredictable events and the Type A coronary-prone behavior pattern. *Journal of Personality and Social Psychology, 36,* 1213–1220.

Weiner, B. (1980). A cognitive (attribution)–emotion–action model of motivated behavior: An analysis of judgments of help-giving. *Journal of Personality and Social Psychology, 39,* 186–200.

Weiner, B., Russell, D., and Lerman, D. (1978). Affective consequences of causal ascriptions. In J. H. Harvey, W. Ickes, and R. F. Kidd (Eds.), *New directions in attribution research* (Vol. 2). Hillsdale, N.J.: Erlbaum.

Weiner, B. Russell, D., and Lerman, D. (1979). The cognition–emotion process in achievement-related contexts. *Journal of Personality and Social Psychology, 37,* 1211–1220.

Wellman, D. (1977). *Portraits of white racism.* New York: Cambridge University Press.

Wicker, A. W. (1969). Attitudes versus actions: The relationship of verbal and overt behavioral responses to attitude objects. *Journal of Social Issues, 25,* 41–78.

Wilensky, H. L. (1975). *The welfare state and social equality.* Berkeley: University of California Press.

Williamson, J. B. (1974). Beliefs about motivation of poor and attitudes toward poverty policy. *Social Problems, 21,* 634–648.(a)

Williamson, J. B. (1974). Beliefs about welfare poor. *Sociology and Social Research, 58,* 163–175.(b)

Wilson, W. J. (1978). *The declining significance of race.* Chicago: University of Chicago Press.

Wyer, R. S., and Srull, T. K. (1980). The processing of social stimulus information: A conceptual integration. In R. Hastie, T. M. Ostrom, E. B. Ebbesen, R. S. Wyer, D. L. Hamilton, and D. E. Carlston (Eds.), *Person memory.* Hillsdale, N.J.: Erlbaum.

Zajonc, R. B. (1980). Feeling and thinking: Preferences need no inferences. *American Psychologist, 35,* 151–175.

INDEX

A

Abelson, R.P., 15, 18
Abercrombie, N., 75
Accommodation of beliefs, 7,
  28–29, 33, 84, 87–88, 93, 101,
  158
Adorno, T.W., 16
Affirmative-action attitudes
  determinants, 206–211
  polls and surveys on, 201–203
  trends, 191, 200–201
Ajzen, I., 246
Allston, J.P., 154
Alves, W.M., 122
Anderson, J.R., 13, 15
Anderson, presidential candi-
  date, 265–267
Asch, S.E., 20
Attitudes and behavior, 245
Attribution, 13
Auletta, K., 302

B

Belief consensus, 39
Belief dissensus, 40
Beliefs, exceptions to general, 28
Beller, A.H., 302
Benokriatis, N.V., 182
Berg, I., 45
Binzen, P., 146, 183
Bishop, G.F., 16

Blacks opportunity, beliefs about
  determinants, 196–200
  perceived effects
    of ability, 191–192
    of discrimination, 185–191
    of motivation, 191–192
  preferential treatment,
    193–196
  "reverse discrimination", 182,
    193–196
  trends, 191, 200–201
Blair, J., 310
Blumberg, P., 24, 26, 34, 45
Bobo, L., 19, 35, 145, 169, 183,
  211, 212
Bogardus, E.S., 225
Bowles, S., 48
Brewer, W.F., 14
Brickman, P., 110
Brint, S., 255
Burris, V., 45
Burstein, P., 4, 179, 246

C

Campbell, A., 275, 278, 284
Carter, Jimmy, 265–267
Causal assumptions, 147–148
Centers, R., 3, 89, 92
Chaiken, S., 14
Challenges
  to perceived prevalent oppor-
    tunity, 53

Challenges *(continued)*
  to the perceived justice of in-
    equality from perceived in-
    justice in fact, 125
  from poverty, 128
  from stratification-related ex-
    perience, 128
Challenging beliefs, 25–30, 33,
    34, 83–89, 101
Change, inferences about, 38
Cheal, O.J., 23
Cherlin, A., 226
Chesler, M.A., 25
Clark, M.S., 18
Cognitive factors, and attitudes
    toward racial policy, 211–212
Cognitive processes, 12–18, 21,
    25, 35, 157, 241, 275, 299–300
Collins, R., 45
Collins, S.M., 302
Comparable worth, 294
Compromise, *see also* Accom-
    modation of beliefs
  explanations, 296–297
Condran, J.G., 179, 192
Confidence, 279
Cook, F.L., 176, 304, 306
Coughlin, R.M., 23, 25, 32, 75,
    101, 157, 163, 170, 299
Criteria for a just distribution
  age-group differences, 114–115
  distribution, 112–114
  equality, 112
  equity, 113
  fair range of inequality, 121–
    122
  need, 112, 113
Crosby, F., 224
Cross-cutting cleavages, 40

D

Darling-Hammond, L., 302
Davis, J.A., 309, 310
Defensive attribution, 18, 24, 300

Deutsch, M., 20, 112
Disappointment, 282
Discrimination, challenge to
    dominant ideology of 26, 27
Distributive justice
  race and sex differences,
    129–130
  status differences, 135–139
  principles, 20
Domhoff, G.W., 23, 247, 248
Dominant ideology
  and affirmative-action atti-
    tudes, 209–210
  and attitudes toward redistri-
    bution, 152, 157, 163, 166, 174
  and belief in internal control,
    286
  and beliefs
    about blacks' opportunity,
      194
    about women's opportunity,
      234, 239
  as deductive argument, 5
  effects on emotions, 283
  group divisions, 93, 289–291
  policy attitudes, 146, 149, 293–
    294
  policy implications, 31, 305
  political implications, 8, 273
  and Reagan support, 264, 271–
    273
  resistance to challenge, 291–
    293
  social liberalism, 11
  stability of, 27, 287–289, 307
  supporting processes, 22–25,
    295–301
Downs, A., 144
Duncan, O.D., 37
Durkheim, E., 90

E

Economic inequality, perceived
    sources and consequences

age-group differences, 110–111
distributions, 105–110
prior research on, 104
Economic voting, 264, 273
Education
challenge to dominant ideology of, 26
and distributive justice, 139–140
effects on
explanations for economic position, 92
redistributive attitudes, 169
women's opportunity perceptions, 226–229, 233–234
and socialization, 297–299
and welfare attitudes, 161
Efficiency, cognitive, 14, 15, 29
Egalitarianism, 174
Embourgeoisement, 24
Emotions, 9, 20, 29, 246, 275–286
Equal opportunity
assurance, 293–294
beliefs about, 48–49
Equal pay for comparable work, 239
Equal Rights Amendment. *See* ERA
Equality, 20
of educational opportunity, perceived
and education level, 70
distribution, 45
race and sex differences, 70
of outcomes versus equal opportunity, 239
Equity, 5, 20, 31, 157, 239
individual vs. societal, 112, 114, 149–150
ERA, 215–216, 264
attitudes, determinants of, 229–230
Evans-Pritchard, E.E., 19
Explanations
cognitive processes shaping, 15, 17, 35

for economic outcomes
age-group differences, 82, 92–93
consequences of cognitive processes, 22
determinants, 93
effects on emotions, 284
influence of cognitive processes on, 17
and psychological well-being, 275
race and sex differences, 94–100
status differences, 89, 91–92, 94–100
supporting dominant ideology, 24–25
individual versus structural, 17

F

Fairness of positional inequality, public's evaluations of
defined, 119
distribution, 119–121
Farley, R., 302
Fazio, R., 246
Feagin, J.R., 7, 23, 76, 78, 81, 89, 92, 115, 151
Feather, N., 92
Featherman, D.L., 24, 26, 185, 210, 302
Ferber, M.A., 302
Ferree, M.M., 30, 242
Fiorina, M.P., 259, 272
Fishbein, M., 15, 148, 246
Fitzgerald, F., 298
Folkman, S., 284
Form, W.H., 309
Free, L.A., 15, 88, 292
Freeman, R.B., 45
Frustration, 281–282
Functions of beliefs and attitudes, 20–21

Fundamental attribution error,
    17, 24, 29, 300
Furnham, A., 92

G

Gender gap, 242
Generalization
    of personal experiences, 23–
        24, 27–28, 83, 234
    of personal explanations, 17
General opportunity, beliefs
    about
    distribution, 43–44
    and doubts about education,
        56–57, 60–62
    and equal opportunity, 57–60,
        60–62
    and personal opportunity, 53–
        56, 60–62
    time trend, 44–45
Giddens, A., 289
Gilder, G., 22, 28, 105, 154, 176
Glazer, N., 31
Glenn, N.D., 38
Government, attitudes toward,
    166
Government ownership of indus-
    try, attitudes
    determinants, 166–169
    distribution, 174
Gramsci, A., 23, 34, 295
Greenwald, A.G., 18
Group identification, 25, 100,
    169, 170, 240, 285
Group interests, 19
Group self-interest, 35, 169
Groves, R.M., 310
Guaranteed incomes, attitudes
    toward
    determinants, 162–163
    distribution, 155
Guaranteed jobs, attitudes to-
    ward

determinants, 162–163
distribution, 155
Guilt, 282
Gurin, P., 100, 241, 290, 291

H

Hamilton, D.L., 16
Hamilton, R.F., 247
Happiness, 279
Hastie, R., 13
Heclo, H., 176
Heider, F., 13
Held back, feelings of being, 82–
    83, 84, 234
Heuristics, problem solving, 11
Hochschild, J.L., 88, 104
Huber, J., 5, 11, 15, 22, 23, 25,
    34, 43, 86, 89, 92, 295

I

Inconsistency
    in beliefs, 1–2, 6–8, 11–12, 15,
        21, 29, 152, 165
    in views of the wealthy, 81,
        121, 164–165
Individualism, 31, 75, 89, 100,
    157, 286
Inegalitarianism, 174
Inequality, popular theories of
    classical economic, 105
    conflict perspective, 105
    structural-functionalism, 105
    "trickle-down," 108
Inequality in fact, beliefs about
    age-group differences, 122–124
    vs. justice in principle, 103,
        116, 124
Inglehart, R., 255
Intergroup affect, 6, 19–20, 25,
    30, 32, 34, 35, 146, 149, 162–
    164, 174, 224, 234–235, 240
Iyengar, S., 16

J

Jackman, M.R., 3, 211
Jasso, G., 122
Jencks, C., 45
Johnson-Laird, P.N., 13
Jones, E.E., 17
Just world, 24, 158
  beliefs, 14

K

Katz, D., 20
Kelley, H.H., 13, 140
Kelley, J., 182
Kelman, H., 246
Kinder, D.R., 27, 32, 35, 145, 166,
  182, 211, 233, 234
Kluegel, J.R., 3, 23, 24, 26, 29,
  182, 192, 193, 200, 276
Kohn, M.J., 232
Kornhauser, W., 89
Kriesberg, L., 104
Kuklinski, J.H., 166, 205

L

Ladd, E.C., Jr., 255
Lane, R.E., 15, 24, 28, 34, 87, 104,
  109, 292, 307
Langer, E.J., 14, 284
Lau, R.P., 27, 35, 233
Leahy, R.L., 1, 22, 148, 288
Lefcourt, H.M., 14
Lerner, M.J., 14, 24
Levin, M., 294
Lewis, M., 75, 299
Life satisfaction, 275, 278, 283
Limiting incomes, attitudes to-
  ward
  determinants, 166–169
  distribution, 165
Limiting inheritances, attitudes
  toward

  determinants, 166–169
  distribution, 165
Lipset, S.M., 151, 165, 182, 184,
  201, 255
Lopreato, J., 23, 24, 75, 101, 157,
  163, 289, 299

M

McArthur, L.Z., 15
McConahay, J.B., 19, 161, 182,
  224
Maier, S.F., 14, 275
Mann, M., 15, 34, 88, 292, 295
Marital status, 226
Markus, G.B., 273
Marx, K., 23
Marxist theories, 15, 23, 28, 34
Mason, K.O., 226
Merton, R.K., 20
Miller, D.T., 18
Miller, F.D., 17
Miller, W.E., 6
Miller, W.G., 26
Mills, C.W., 34
Mirowski, J., 275, 284
Mobility experience, 24, 26
Modern racism, 182
Monroe, A.D., 4
Moore, B., Jr., 34, 299
Myrdal, G., 183, 303

N

Nathan, N.P., 247
National Urban League, 100
Negative affect, 283
Neustadt, R.E., 144
Newcomb, T.M., 20
Nilson, L.B., 80, 81, 88, 89, 92,
  93, 100
Nisbett, R.E., 12, 17, 23
Nowak, S., 299
Nunnally, J.C., 126

O

Occupational sex composition,
225, 231–232
Opportunity; *see also* Blacks'
opportunity; Personal op-
portunity; Women's oppor-
tunity
beliefs about
age-group comparisons, 49–
52
race and sex differences, 62–
64, 72–73
status differences, 66–69, 72
declining, 84, 86–87
as major premise in dominant
ideology, 5
Opportunity for women. *See*
Women's opportunity
Overeducation, 45

P

Page, B.I., 4, 154, 267
Parkin, F., 15, 34, 292, 295
Partisanship and stratification beliefs, social liberalism
of Democrats, 260, 261, 262
by race, 262–263
of Independents, 260
of Republicans, 260, 262
Pennebaker, J.W., 14
Perceived amount of income inequality
percentage middle class, 118
percentage poor, 117–118
percentge rich, 118
Personal opportunity, beliefs
about
distribution, 45–48
time trend, 48
Pettigrew, T.F., 17, 185, 211
Piven, F.F., 151, 305
Political beliefs and behaviors,
245–246

Politically important subgroups,
beliefs of
economic elite, 252–255
"new class", 255–256
owners and managers, 247–252
Pollard, P., 15
Positive affect, 282
Poverty, explanations for
age-group differences, 81
determinants of individual, 91
determinants of structural, 91
distribution, 78–81
individual, 86, 101, 162, 164,
170, 276
over-time comparisons, 78–80
relationships among, 87–88
structural, 85, 170, 228
Preferential treatment, for wom-
en and blacks, 239
Presidential election, 1980
beliefs and attitudes by voting
intention, 264–267
determinants of intended vote,
267–272
by party identification, 271–
272
Pride, 279
Psychological control, 13–14, 21,
24–25, 80, 145, 275, 284–286,
300
Psychological well-being, 14

R

Race differences in emotions, 285
Race effects on redistributive attitudes, 170
Race relations, 179
Racial affect, 252, 254, 273, 303;
see also Intergroup affect
Racial beliefs and attitudes, effects of
economic self-interest, 183,
197, 210, 211
racial affect, 197, 201, 209, 211

stratification beliefs, 184–185, 211
Racial prejudice, 26
  traditional, 170–180, 183, 185
Rainwater, L., 104, 118, 122
Ransford, H.E., 146, 183
Reagan, Ronald, 1, 8, 33, 91, 151, 264, 266, 270–273
Redistribution, attitudes toward
  age-group differences, 155, 169
  over-time data, 153–155
  race effects on, 170
  status differences, 170
Reference groups, 20
Regression analyses, specifications, 144–148
Relative deprivation, 20, 26, 27, 32, 146, 158, 162, 164, 174, 183, 240
  egoistic, 19
  fraternal, 19, 169
Religion, 90
  effects on emotions, 285
Reskin, B.F., 302
Robinson, R.V., 92
Rodin, J., 14
Rosenberg, M.J., 18
Ross, L., 17, 23, 24
Routes to economic advancement, perceived, 45
Rumberger, R., 45
Runciman, W., 19, 169
Russell, D., 276
Ryan, W., 80, 297

S

Salience
  and perception, 15, 17, 241
  of explanations, 83–84
Sampson, E.E., 23, 75
Satisfaction. *See* Life satisfaction
Schema, 14–15, 18, 29, 35, 145–146
Schiltz, M.E., 155, 288
Schuman, H., 43, 110, 287

Sears, D.O., 14, 29, 35, 92, 148, 182, 211
Segregation, effects on views of blacks, 238
Self-interest, 18, 20, 25, 30, 32–35, 144, 149, 152, 156, 223, 232–233, 303
Seligman, M.E.P., 14
Sennett, R., 29, 34, 48, 146, 183, 295
Sex-role traditionalism, 26, 215, 219, 224, 240, 252, 254, 273
  determinants, 225–226
  time trends in, 215
Sherman, S.J., 12, 14
Simmons, R.G., 22, 148
Sivacek, J., 246
Skinner, B.F., 13
Smith, A.W., 179
Smith, E.R., 3, 13, 14, 15, 16, 17, 23, 24, 26, 30, 276
Snyder, M.L., 18
Social identity, 19, 24, 25
Socialization, 19, 23, 26–37, 34, 35, 87, 224
Social liberalism, 3, 5–6, 11, 30–31, 33, 84, 92, 100, 146–147, 149, 255, 256, 264, 271, 273, 297, 303
Social policy
  need for sustained commitment, 301–302
  public acceptance of, 305–306
  sources of ambivalence about, 302–303
Stereotypes, 16, 18, 224
Structuralism, 75
Symbolic politics, 27, 35, 157, 166
Symbolic racism, 32, 158, 182, 211, 224, 233

T

Tajfel, H., 19, 25
Taylor, D.C., 179

Taylor, D.G., 6, 26, 30
Taylor, S.E., 7, 11, 14, 15, 16, 17, 241
Thankfulness, 279–280
Thornton, A., 226
Thurow, L., 8
Tufte, E.R., 264

U

Ultimate determinants
  basic social psychological processes, 299–301
  self-interest and experience, 295–297
  socialization, 297–299
Unawareness of inequality, thesis of, 21–22

V

Vanneman, R.D., 19, 34, 183, 285
Verba, S., 3, 294

W

Waksberg, J., 309
Walster, E., 20
Wealth
  explanations for, 76–78, 87
  determinants
    of individual explanations for, 91
    of structural explanations for, 90
  individual explanations for, 165, 238, 275–276
  structural explanations for, 238
Weber, M., 23, 90
Weidner, G., 14
Weiner, B., 276, 280, 282, 283
Welfare, attitudes toward, 151, 152, 158–162, 163–164, 175–177, 271–272
Wellman, D., 183, 211, 212
Wicker, A.W., 245
Wilensky, H.L., 4, 32, 176
Williamson, J.B., 7, 151, 154
Wilson, W.J., 100, 185, 196, 307
Women's opportunity, perceptions of
  age-group differences, 216–218
  comparisons with blacks, 235–239
  determinants, 219–229, 228–229
  self-interest effects, 241
  sex differences, 218–219, 231, 233–234
Worry, 281
Wyer, R.S., 12, 13, 14

XYZ

Zajonc, R.B., 18